RELIGION

Gnostic religion is the expression of a religious worldview which is dominated by the concept of Gnosis, an esoteric knowledge of God and the human being which grants salvation to those who possess it. Roelof van den Broek presents here a fresh approach to the gnostic current of Late Antiquity within its historical and religious context, based on sources in Greek, Latin and Coptic, including discussions of the individual works of preserved gnostic literature. Van den Broek explores the various gnostic interpretations of the Christian faith that were current in the second and third centuries, whilst showing that despite its influence on early Christianity, gnostic religion was not a typically Christian phenomenon. This book will be of interest to theologians, historians of religion, students and scholars of the history of Late Antiquity and early Christianity, as well as specialists in ancient gnostic and hermetic traditions.

ROELOF VAN DEN BROEK is Emeritus Professor of History of Christianity at the University of Utrecht. His books include *Studies in Gnosticism and Alexandrian Christianity* (1996), Dutch translations, with introductions and notes, of ancient hermetic and gnostic texts (2006 and 2010) and *Pseudo-Cyril of Jerusalem, On the Life and the Passion of Christ: A Coptic Apocryphon* (2013). He is co-editor of several books, the most recent being the *Dictionary of Gnosis and Western Esotericism*, 2 vols. (with Wouter J. Hanegraaff, Antoine Faivre and Jean-Pierre Brach, 2005).

GNOSTIC RELIGION IN ANTIQUITY

ROELOF VAN DEN BROEK

CAMBRIDGE
UNIVERSITY PRESS

CAMBRIDGE
UNIVERSITY PRESS

University Printing House, Cambridge CB2 8BS, United Kingdom

Cambridge University Press is part of the University of Cambridge.

It furthers the University's mission by disseminating knowledge in the pursuit of education, learning and research at the highest international levels of excellence.

www.cambridge.org
Information on this title: www.cambridge.org/9781107514799

First published 2013
First paperback edition 2015

A catalogue record for this publication is available from the British Library

Library of Congress Cataloguing in Publication data
Broek, R. van den.
Gnostic religion in antiquity / Roelof van den Broek.
p. cm.
Includes bibliographical references (p.) and indexes.
ISBN 978-1-107-03137-1 (hardback)
1. Gnosticism. I. Title.
BT1390.B735 2013
299′.93–dc23
2012029712

ISBN 978-1-107-03137-1 Hardback
ISBN 978-1-107-51479-9 Paperback

Contents

Preface

This book is a thoroughly revised and expanded version of the introduction to my Dutch translation of five gnostic texts from Nag Hammadi, which was published in 2010. Its primary aim is to provide information about the gnostic movement in Antiquity, with emphasis on its literature and forms of expression.

I have tried to let the sources speak for themselves and to avoid detailed academic discussions as much as possible, though differences of opinion among scholars have been recorded and evaluated. It was unavoidable, however, to make my position clear with respect to two hotly debated issues in gnostic studies, the definition of the gnostic phenomenon and the question of its origin.

The English translations of Latin, Greek and Coptic texts are my own; biblical texts, however, have been quoted after the Anglicized Edition of the New Revised Standard Version.

My thanks are due to Mrs. Rosalie Basten, who made the translation from the Dutch possible, and to Mr. Anthony Runia, who realized it.

Abbreviations

AH	Adversus Haereses
BCNH-É	Bibliothèque Copte de Nag Hammadi. 'Études'
BCNH-T	Bibliothèque Copte de Nag Hammadi. 'Textes'
BG	Berlin Gnostic Papyrus (Papyrus Codex 8502)
EPRO	Études Préliminaires aux Religions Orientales dans l'Empire Romain
FRLANT	Forschungen zur Religion und Literatur des Alten und des Neuen Testaments
GCS	Die Griechischen Christlichen Schriftsteller
JECS	*Journal of Early Christian Studies*
NHC	Nag Hammadi Codex (cited as, for example, NHC I, 4 = Nag Hammadi Codex I, tractate 4; NHC I, 51, 1 = Nag Hammadi Codex I, page 51, line 1)
NHMS	Nag Hammadi and Manichaean Studies (continuation of NHS)
NHS	Nag Hammadi Studies
NRSV	New Revised Standard Version, Anglicized Edition
NTOA	Novum Testamentum et Orbis Antiquus
OBEO	Orbis Biblicus et Orientalis
PGM	*Papyri Graecae Magicae* (Greek Magical Papyri)
RAC	*Reallexicon für Antike und Christentum*
RGRW	Religions in the Graeco-Roman World
SC	Sources Chrétiennes
SHR	Studies in the History of Religions (Supplements to *Numen*)
STAC	Studien und Texte zu Antike und Christentum
TU	Texte und Untersuchungen zur Geschichte der altchristlichen Literatur
VC	*Vigiliae Christianae*

WUNT	Wissenschaftliche Untersuchungen zum Neuen Testament
ZAC	*Zeitschrift für Antikes Christentum*
ZPE	*Zeitschrift für Papyrologie und Epigraphik*

CHAPTER I

Gnosis and gnostic religion

Around 100 CE a Christian who posed as the apostle Paul wrote: 'Timothy, guard what has been entrusted to you. Avoid the profane chatter and contradictions of what is falsely called knowledge; by professing it some have missed the mark as regards the faith' (1 Tim. 6:20–21). It is impossible today to find out what exactly these people taught. Apparently they advocated a view of Christianity centred on the possession of a special kind of knowledge, though the author believes that they have thus strayed from the traditional faith. The word 'knowledge' is represented here by the Greek word *gnōsis*.

Pseudo-Paul's opinion gathered a following, for towards the end of the second century Irenaeus, bishop of Lyons, wrote a work in five parts entitled *On the Detection and Overthrow of What Is Falsely Called Gnosis*. He thus targeted an influential movement in contemporary Christianity which taught that not the faith of the Church but gnosis, spiritual knowledge, was necessary for salvation. Irenaeus saw this as a dangerous heresy requiring refutation. Partly thanks to his influence, the view of the Christian faith which he defended and a corresponding deprecation of gnosis became dominant in the Christian Church.

This book mainly gives a voice to the supporters of gnosis, the gnostics. In 1945 in Egypt a Coptic library of the fourth century was discovered containing a large number of works from their circles. Though a few such books were found in the eighteenth and nineteenth centuries, the great diversity of the Nag Hammadi discovery made it extremely important. It finally ended the situation that our knowledge of ancient gnosis depended almost entirely on its adversaries. But these original sources also revealed something else: the views of the gnostics turned out to be much more varied than the reports of their opponents suggested. It is typical that none of the new writings fits snugly into the gnostic schools and systems described by the gnostics' opponents. This raised a question still paramount in research today: how reliable are the reports of the anti-gnostic authors? This question will be addressed in the fourth chapter of this book. Another question to arise was: given the great diversity of gnostic views, can the phenomenon of gnosis still be clearly defined? Anyone who writes about the Nag Hammadi finds should therefore explain what he means by 'gnosis' and what is usually called 'Gnosticism'.

The Greek word *gnōsis* means 'investigation, knowledge, insight', and the corresponding verb is *gignōskein* or (later form) *ginōskein*, 'to come to know, to know'. Initially, in the Greek world, this concerned only rational knowledge, as a product of mind (*nous*) and reason (*logos*), in combination with sensation and experience, knowledge which leads to truth. But in the centuries around the beginning of the Christian Era the concept of *gnōsis* was considerably broadened. In certain religious circles it took on the meaning of 'knowledge of the divine world and the true nature of things'; this knowledge was no longer seen as the product of correct rational argumentation, but of a divine revelation, an inner enlightenment.[1] It is this knowledge to which the apostle Paul refers when he says that God has shone in our hearts 'to give the light of the knowledge [*gnōsis*] of the glory of God in the face of Jesus Christ' (2 Cor. 4:6). Paul here speaks religious language which was understood by many of his contemporaries, but this does not make him a gnostic. More is needed for that.

The concept of *gnōsis* that pervaded a great deal of the religious experience and reflection in the Graeco-Roman world of the first centuries CE is characterized by some common features. These are:

- the conviction that the essential core of the human being comes from the divine world of light and peace and must return to it, but is held captive in the material world in which it has become entrapped;
- this insight into humankind's origin, present situation and destination means at once the human being's liberation from the stranglehold of material existence and his return to the divine world, in principle now and certainly after death;
- self-knowledge and knowledge of God are therefore two sides of the same coin;

[1] The main difference between classical usage and that of the later period is shown by a comparison of the lemmata *gi(g)nōskō* and *gnōsis* in H. G. Liddell and R. Scott, *A Greek–English Lexicon*, new edn rev. and augmented throughout by H. Stuart Jones and R. McKenzie (Oxford: Clarendon Press, 1940), pp. 350 and 355, with G. W. H. Lampe, *A Patristic Greek Lexicon* (Oxford: Clarendon Press, 1961), pp. 315 and 318–20. Still instructive is R. Bultmann, '*ginōskō*, *gnōsis*, etc.', in G. Kittel *et al.* (eds.), *Theological Dictionary of the New Testament*, vol. 1, trans. G. W. Bromiley (Grand Rapids,MI: W. B. Eerdmans, 1964), pp. 688–719 (= *Theologisches Wörterbuch zum Neuen Testament*, 1, Stuttgart: W. Kohlhammer, 1933, pp. 688–719).

- however, this knowledge does not result from rational argumentation, but from inner enlightenment, which is based on a revelation from the divine world;
- this spiritual insight, gnosis, is not accessible to everyone, but only to those who are worthy, and so its core at least needs to be kept secret.

When the term 'gnosis' is used in this book, it is in an entirely neutral sense, taking it to mean an esoteric, that is partly secret, spiritual knowledge of God and of the divine origin and destination of the essential core of the human being which is based on revelation and inner enlightenment, the possession of which involves a liberation from the material world which holds humans captive. A gnostic is someone whose religious outlook is determined by this understanding of gnosis, which, however, does not necessarily exclude his association with a religious or philosophical group that as such does not share his particular views.

Clearly these definitions apply to many spiritual movements from Antiquity to this very day. The gnosis of these movements almost always has an esoteric and an exoteric side, that is certain aspects are intended only for the initiated and others are also open to outsiders. The form of this gnosis in an elaborated system or a myth may differ vastly case by case, but the central outlook mentioned above is always clearly recognizable.[2]

In the Graeco-Roman world of the first centuries of our era, there were two religious currents in which gnosis in the indicated sense played a predominant role. Scholars are used to calling them 'Hermetism' and 'Gnosticism', though both of these names are problematic, for reasons that will be explained. It is preferable to speak of 'hermetic religion' and 'gnostic religion' (not '*the* hermetic/gnostic religion'). In hermetic religion the Egyptian sage Hermes Trismegistus was the central figure. He is on the one hand a teacher of religious wisdom with a strong philosophical colouring, but on the other hand he also acts as initiator in the hermetic mystery of ascent. According to some scholars these two aspects represent successive stages on the 'Way of Hermes'; others are less certain about this point. In academic research the term 'Hermetism' has become the usual term to indicate the whole complex of hermetic ideas and practices, but like all other 'isms' it suggests a coherence and uniformity which did not exist in reality.[3]

[2] An encyclopedic survey of Western gnostic and esoteric movements can be found in the *Dictionary of Gnosis and Western Esotericism*, ed. W. J. Hanegraaff in collaboration with A. Faivre, R. van den Broek and J.-P. Brach, 2 vols. (Leiden: Brill, 2005; reprinted in one vol. 2006, same pagination).

[3] See G. Fowden, *The Egyptian Hermes. A Historical Approach to the Late Pagan Mind*, rev. paperback edn (Princeton University Press, 1993); R. van den Broek, 'Hermes Trismegistus I: Antiquity',

The other religious current in which gnosis was the dominant factor can best be called 'gnostic religion', for the much-used term 'Gnosticism' has become so problematic that most scholars prefer to avoid it. Although there is a distinct relationship between hermetic and gnostic religion (e.g. with respect to the origin and ascent of the soul), there are also considerable differences (e.g. regarding the origin of the world). The Nag Hammadi library was composed by people of the gnostic persuasion, and that these 'gnostics' were also interested in the writings of the 'hermetists' is shown by the fact that the library has preserved three hermetic works, of which the very important *Discourse on the Eighth and the Ninth* was previously completely unknown.[4] In academic research, it has become customary to deal with hermetic and gnostic religion separately, because of the difference between their respective sources and the skills that are needed for an adequate study of them. This is an understandable, but nevertheless deplorable development, because serious mistakes could have been avoided if students of one of these types of religion had had a more than superficial knowledge of the other type. In this book hermetic religious views and practices will be referred to if necessary, but as a whole the traditional separation between hermetic and gnostic studies will be retained.

Before entering into a discussion of the present state of gnostic studies, attention must be drawn to two other independent gnostic religions in Antiquity, which originated outside the Graeco-Roman world, though one of them became also influential inside it: the Mandaean and Manichaean religions. The Mandaeans were a baptist community which has been able to hold its own in southern Iraq (and nowadays in Europe, the United States and Australia as well) from the beginning of the Christian era to the present. Their name, *mandayi*, derives from the word *manda*, which means 'knowledge, gnosis'; so they referred to themselves as Gnostics.[5]

'Hermetic Literature I: Antiquity' and 'Hermetism', in *Dictionary of Gnosis*, pp. 474–8, 487–99 and 558–70, respectively. Translations of Hermetic literature in B. Copenhaver, *Hermetica. The Greek* Corpus Hermeticum *and the Latin* Asclepius *in a New English Translation with Notes and Introduction* (Cambridge University Press, 1992); *The Way of Hermes*: The Corpus Hermeticum, trans. C. Salaman, D. van Oyen and W. D. Wharton; The Definitions of Hermes Trismegistus to *Asclepius*, trans. J.-P. Mahé (London: Duckworth, 1999).

[4] See p. 35. The gnostic Codex Tchacos also seems to have contained a hermetic text, see p. 24.

[5] Nowadays the term 'Mandaeans' refers to the ordinary believers, the laity, in contrast to the priests; see K. Rudolph, 'Mandaeans', in *Dictionary of Gnosis*, pp. 751–6. In the first half of the twentieth century, before the discovery of the Nag Hammadi library, scholars generally counted hermetists and Mandaeans among the ancient gnostics; modern scholars who hold the same view are, inter alios, W. Barnstone and M. Meyer (eds.), *The Gnostic Bible*, rev. edn (Boston and

The religion of the Manichaeans was founded by Mani (216–77), a charismatic visionary from southern Mesopotamia who developed a gnostic system with a very complicated mythology, characterized by the opposition between the world of Light and the world of Darkness, which had originally existed side by side but had become intermixed. Mani and his disciples undertook many missionary journeys which brought this new gnostic religion as far as China in the East and the Latin Roman world in the West (where Augustine became its most renowned follower and, later, opponent). The study of Manichaeism has become a research area of its own, with several subdisciplines, because of the required knowledge of the many Eastern languagues in which the authentic sources have been transmitted and the syncretistic mixture of all kinds of religious traditions contained in them.[6] Unlike the hermetic and gnostic movements, Mandaeism and Manichaeism were well-organized religions of their own, each with specific doctrines, rituals and a clergy. Their historical sources are later than almost all the authentic hermetic and gnostic documents. For this reason and because of the specific research problems mentioned above, Mandaean and Manichaean traditions will only occasionally be mentioned here.

The study of the gnostic movement of the first centuries has long been dominated by the perspective of Irenaeus and other anti-gnostic writers, who described it as a Christian heresy which undermined the original unity and orthodoxy of the Church. This view seems almost ineradicable among church historians, but it also resonates strongly in the research of the more 'neutral' historians of religion.[7] The modern term 'Gnosticism' itself originated within the context of anti-heretical polemics. It was

London: Shambhala, 2009), pp. 517–85 (texts), and B. A. Pearson, *Ancient Gnosticism. Traditions and Literature* (Minneapolis: Fortress Press, 2007), pp. 273–91, 314–32.

[6] The literature on Manichaeism is abundant, see for example M. Tardieu, *Manichaeism*, trans. M. B. DeBevoise, Introduction by P. Mirecki (Champaign, IL: University of Illinois Press, 2009); J. van Oort, 'Mani' and 'Manichaeism', *Dictionary of Gnosis*, pp. 756–7 and 757–65, respectively; Pearson, *Ancient Gnosticism*, pp. 292–313; selections of texts in, inter alia, I. Gardner and S. N. C. Lieu (eds.), *Manichaean Texts from the Roman Empire* (Cambridge University Press, 2004), and Barnstone and Meyer, *The Gnostic Bible*, pp. 589–674.

[7] Karen L. King, *What is Gnosticism?* (Cambridge, MA and London: The Belknap Press of Harvard University Press, 2003), shows how great this influence was on modern gnosis research, too. The view of gnosis as Christian heresy also explains why the only early Christian author who constantly talks about gnosis and the 'true gnostic', Clement of Alexandria (*c.* 200 CE), is always carefully distinguished from the 'heretical' gnostics. In contrast to most gnostics, Clement in fact considered simple faith to be sufficient for the salvation of a Christian, but he leaves no doubt that the Christian who possesses gnosis (which in Clement, too, implies esoteric knowledge) far surpasses the simple believer; see S. R. C. Lilla, *Clement of Alexandria. A Study in Christian Platonism and Gnosticism* (Oxford University Press, 1971), pp. 142–89.

coined in 1669 by the Cambridge Platonist Henry More, in a commentary on the seven letters to the seven churches in chapters 2 and 3 of the Revelation of John.[8] He employed the term to typify the teaching of a prophetess in Tyatira, who tempted her followers to commit illicit sexual acts and eat sacrificial meat and initiated them into 'what some call "the deep things of Satan"' (Rev. 2:20–25). This negative connotation subsequently remained attached to the word 'Gnosticism' in ecclesiastical circles, in church history too. In recent studies there is a tendency to get rid of the heresiological opposition between Church and heresy by substituting the term 'mainstream Christianity' for 'the Church' and 'sect' or 'cult' or 'splinter group' for 'heresy'. It has been doubted whether this really makes things better,[9] but it should be noted that even strong opponents of Christianity such as the philosopher Celsus (*c.* 180) distinguished between minor Christian groups and 'those of the Great Church', also called 'those of the multitude', that is mainstream Christians.[10]

Before the discovery of the Nag Hammadi library, the academic study of Gnosticism was dominated by the ideas of the German History of Religions school, which laid much emphasis on Hellenistic syncretism as the cradle of gnostic mythology and preferentially traced its basic mythologoumena back to religions that flourished east of the Mediterranean.[11] The apparent inadequacy of this interpretative model and the discovery of many original sources demanded a new approach to the study of Gnosticism and, as a corollary, a widely accepted definition of the terms 'Gnosis' and 'Gnosticism'. The first international colloquium on Gnosticism (Messina, Italy; 1966) produced a 'Final Document', which aimed to provide such a definition.[12] It reserved the term 'Gnosticism' predominantly for 'a certain group of systems of the Second Century A.D., which everyone agrees are to be designated with this term', although 'the

[8] Henry More, *An Exposition of the Seven Epistles to the Seven Churches; Together with a Brief Discourse of Idolatry; with Application to the Church of Rome* (London: James Flesher, 1669), Exposition, p. 99.

[9] See I. Dunderberg, *Beyond Gnosticism: Myth, Lifestyle, and Society in the School of Valentinus* (New York: Columbia University Press, 2008), pp. 19–20: 'the distinction between "mainstream" and "sectarian" forms of early Christianity is none other than the old discourse of orthodoxy and heresy in a new disguise'. He observes, inter alia, that it is not 'easy to say which Christian current was the mainstream in second-century Rome'.

[10] Origen, *Contra Celsum* v, 59 (*apo megalēs ekklēsias*) and 61 (*apo tou plēthous*).

[11] For a devastating criticism of these views, see C. Colpe, *Die religionsgeschichtliche Schule: Darstellung und Kritik ihres Bildes vom gnostischen Erlösermythus*, FRLANT 78 (Göttingen: Vandenhoeck & Ruprecht, 1961).

[12] U. Bianchi (ed.), *Le origini dello gnosticismo / The Origins of Gnosticism. Colloquium of Messina 13–18 April 1966*, SHR 12 (Leiden: Brill, 1967), pp. xxvi–xxix (English version).

question of a *Weltgeschichte* of Gnosticism' is said to seem 'quite legitimate'. The term 'gnosis' is considered the more overarching concept, defined as 'knowledge of the divine mysteries reserved for an élite'. Whereas the Messina description of the characteristics of second-century Gnosticism is still broadly accepted, albeit with qualifications,[13] its definition of 'gnosis' has generally been criticized as much too vague, and its idea of bringing all kinds of movements from various times and places (e.g. the Upanishads, Orphism, Catharism) under the common denominator of 'Gnosticism' has quite rightly not found a following. But there is one aspect of the Messina proposal that deserves to be retained and indeed forms one of the premises of this book: the distinction between the general concept of 'gnosis' and its specific expression in the great mythological systems of the second century CE.

The Messina document failed to impose generally accepted definitions of 'gnosis' and 'Gnosticism'; on the contrary, it triggered endless and fruitless discussions. As the publication and analysis of the Nag Hammadi writings progressed, it became increasingly clear that the differences between the views and writings usually referred to as 'gnostic' are so marked that an adequate definition of 'Gnosticism' is virtually impossible. From this state of affairs the American scholar Michael A. Williams has drawn the radical conclusion that the terms 'gnosis', 'Gnosticism' and 'gnostic' are so vague that they have lost any specific meaning and, therefore, are best not used at all.[14] Though Williams's book is most certainly worth reading and offers a sound antidote to many popular views on Gnosticism, few have followed his radical outlook. This is because avoidance of the terms 'gnosis' and 'gnostic' does not contribute to a better understanding of the spiritual movement usually characterized by these words. Some critics have objected that these terms have become too tainted by association with the 'gnostic heresy' of the first centuries. But the gnostic worldview

[13] *Ibid.*, p. xxv: 'The Gnosticism of the second century sects involves a coherent series of characteristics that can be summarized in the idea of a divine spark in man, deriving from the divine realm, fallen into this world of fate, birth and death, and needing to be awakened by the divine counterpart of the self in order to be finally reintegrated.' See also the definitions of M. Meyer and A. Marjanen quoted in notes 25 and 26 below.

[14] M. A. Williams, *Rethinking "Gnosticism". An Argument for Dismantling a Dubious Category* (Princeton University Press, 1996); also King, *What is Gnosticism?* The title of Dunderberg's book, *Beyond Gnosticism*, reflects the thesis defended by Williams and King. This thesis also dominates the recent book by H. Lundhaug, *Images of Rebirth. Cognitive Poetics and Transformational Soteriology in the* Gospel of Philip *and the* Exegesis on the Soul, NHMS 73 (Brill : Leiden, 2010) in which it is suggested time and again that employing the terms 'gnostic' or 'Valentinian' implies that they are taken in the sense of 'heretical' and 'in opposition to true Christianity'.

is not confined to the first centuries and Christianity, and moreover the term 'heresy' is a religious and not a historical category. The historian does not recognize heresies; he can merely observe that a religious community rejects certain divergent ideas as heresy. He has no opinion on the correctness of this religious belief, because it lies outside his historical competence. So there is no reason to put a negative complexion on the terms 'gnosis' and 'gnostic' or to bring the truth question into discussion, as theologians sometimes do.[15]

Gnostic religion in the first centuries CE was an early representative of the esoteric current in Western culture. What distinguished it from later movements was a specific and highly variegated mythology, which gave expression to the basic gnostic ideas. The gnostic myths are for the greater part artificial, sometimes even carefully constructed.[16] The gnostics of Antiquity were gifted mythmakers, who were able to adapt their myths to various contexts. They were not adherents of a clearly discernible gnostic religion, characterized by a coherent set of ideas and rituals and practised in an identifiable social group, but they were people with a distinct gnostic mentality, a gnostic frame of mind, which could manifest itself in various religious contexts. Gnostic religion, and hermetic religion as well, is characterized by the fact that it can easily attach itself to already existing religious or philosophical systems. Our sources abundantly testify to the existence of a gnostic current in early Christianity.

In recent research, however, there is a strong tendency to consider the gnostic movement of the first centuries an exclusively Christian phenomenon, one of the various competing inner Christian movements that were designed to make Christianity more acceptable to more or less educated people, Christians and non-Christians alike.[17] This idea is often combined with another recent trend in gnostic studies, namely to reserve the term 'gnostics' for a special group of Christians who are supposed to have designated themselves as 'the Gnostics'. This view is based on the observation that Irenaeus most probably indicated the people whose ideas he describes

[15] See below, p. 220n. 31.

[16] See, for instance, pp. 160–2, on the construction of the divine Pleroma in the *Apocryphon of John*.

[17] An influential advocate of this view is the German church historian Christoph Markschies, who sees gnostic mythography as a form of Christian philosophy of religion. See for instance the revised version of a 1999 article, 'Christliche Religionsphilosophie oder vorchristliche antike Religion: Was ist Gnosis?', in his *Gnosis und Christentum* (Berlin University Press, 2009), pp. 23–52, which contains a vehement attack on the almost forgotten Messina definitions, concluded by the wish that nobody should subscribe any longer to the 'both methodically and historically highly problematic' view of Gnosticism as a pre-Christian religion and that finally 'the re-contextualization of this phenomenon within the history and theology of the Christian Church be generally accepted'. See also below, p. 220.

in *Adversus haereses* (hereafter *AH*) I, 29–30, as 'the Gnostics'.[18] Because Irenaeus in *AH* I, 29, shows himself to have been acquainted with at least an early version of the *Apocryphon of John*, this gnostic writing has become the basic source for the ideas and mythology of 'the Gnostics', to which scholars have added an increasing number of other gnostic texts in which similar or related ideas are expressed.[19] Other gnostic groups who used the term 'Gnostic' as a self-designation are taken to belong to 'the Gnostics' of Irenaeus.[20] The result is a neatly arranged picture of early Christianity: among the rival inner Christian movements there were (a) non-gnostic 'mainstream' Christians, (b) 'the Gnostics', (c) the more Church-orientated Valentinians, who, however, should not be called 'gnostics', and (4) other groups which were mostly named after their founder and sometimes were referred to as 'gnostics' by their opponents.

However, with respect to these recent views, some caution seems desirable. To mention only a few dubious points: there is no conclusive evidence that the gnostic current was an exclusively Christian phenomenon; gnostic texts without any trace of Christian influence are unsatisfactorily accounted for; the data used to construct the ideas and practices of 'the Gnostics' are taken from direct and indirect sources that come from entirely different backgrounds; and, finally, there is no satisfactory explanation for the obvious fact that 'the Gnostics' are never indicated by that name in the authentic sources ascribed to them.[21] It should be noted that these recent developments in gnostic studies reflect the perspective and

[18] This attribution is only possible after a correction of the Latin text (elimination of the word 'Barbelo'), for which indeed there are strong arguments; see the edition by Rousseau and Doutreleau, *Irénée de Lyon. Contre les Hérésies, Livre I*, SC 263 (Paris: Les Éditions du Cerf, 1979), vol. I, pp. 296–9. It also implies that the views expressed in *AH* I, 30 were taught by a faction of the same 'Gnostics', even though these views differ almost irreconcilably from those of *AH* I, 29 (later ecclesiastical writers identified them with the Ophites).

[19] B. Layton, 'Prolegomena to the Study of Ancient Gnosticism', in L. M. White and O. L. Yarbrough (eds.), *The Social World of the First Christians. Essays in Honor of Wayne A. Meeks* (Minneapolis: Fortress Press, 1995), pp. 334–50. In his *The Gnostic Scriptures. A New Translation with Annotations and Introductions* (Garden City, NY: Doubleday, 1987), pp. 5–22, Layton had already made a clear distinction between 'the Gnostics', that is the adherents of the 'Gnostic school of thought', or 'Classic Gnosticism' (which other scholars like to call 'Sethianism'; see below, pp. 28–9), and another early Christian group, the 'school of Valentinus'.

[20] In a concentrated and learned argument, A. H. B. Logan, *The Gnostics. Identifying an Early Christian Cult* (London and New York: T&T Clark, 2006), has tried to determine the doctrinal and cultic characteristics of 'the Gnostics' by basing his work on a wide range of authentic and secondary sources, in fact an extension of the material assembled by Layton; see also, following the lead of Layton and Logan, D. Brakke, *The Gnostics. Myth, Ritual, and Diversity in Early Christianity* (Cambridge, MA and London: Harvard University Press, 2010).

[21] Layton, 'Prolegomena', p. 344, has made an unconvincing attempt to explain away this problem: the term '*Gnōstikoi*' was only used as a proper name, indicating to which 'school' these people belonged, meant 'not to say what they were but who they were'.

the interest of church historians, not those of historians of religion in general. Of course, the gnostic interpretation of the Christian faith belongs to the history of early Christianity, but it also belongs to the history of religions of the Graeco-Roman world, as well as to the new and rapidly growing academic discipline of the history of Western esotericism.[22]

Is there, besides the terms 'gnosis' and 'gnostic', any need for the term 'Gnosticism'? Not really. The term is still used in modern scholarship, even after Michael Williams's criticism, but now in a neutral sense and often as an equivalent of 'the Gnostic religion'.[23] Closer scrutiny of what 'Gnosticism' or 'the Gnostic religion' is actually taken to mean shows that it mainly involves the radical form of gnosis expressed in the great gnostic myths of the second century, especially those contained in the texts that many scholars call 'Sethian' and others designate as 'Gnostic', in the restricted sense of 'belonging to the sect of "the Gnostics"'.[24] Characteristic features of this radical form of gnosis are: (1) a distinction is made between the highest, unknown God and the imperfect or plainly evil creator-god, who is often identified with the God of the Bible; (2) this is often connected with an extensive description of the divine world (Pleroma), from which the essential core of human beings derives, and of a disastrous 'fall' of a divine being (Sophia, 'Wisdom') in this upper world; (3) as a result, humankind has become trapped in the earthly condition of oblivion and death, from which it is saved by the revelation of gnosis by one or more heavenly messengers; (4) salvation is often actualized and celebrated in rituals that are performed within the gnostic community.[25]

[22] See W. J. Hanegraaff, *Esotericism and the Academy. Rejected Knowledge in Western Culture* (Cambridge University Press, 2012).

[23] See the discussions in B. A. Pearson, *Gnosticism and Christianity in Roman and Coptic Egypt* (New York and London: T&T Clark, 2004), pp. 201–23 ('Gnosticism as a Religion'); Pearson, *Ancient Gnosticism*, pp. 8–15; and M. Meyer, *The Gnostic Discoveries. The Impact of the Nag Hammadi Library* (San Francisco: HarperSanFrancisco, 2005), pp. 38–43. A quite different, but rather senseless definition of 'Gnosticism' is given by A. Mastrocinque, *From Jewish Magic to Gnosticism*, STAC 24 (Tübingen: Mohr Siebeck, 2005), pp. 4–5: 'In this work, the word *Gnosticism will be used as a synonym for the heresies addressed by Irenaeus* and related heresies of a similar nature' (Mastrocinque's italics); see also Mastrocinque, *From Jewish Magic to Gnosticism*, p. 6: 'We will gladly leave the difficult task of defining more precisely what Gnosticism was or was not to the scholars who are good at discussing nomenclature rather than substance; the accounts of the ancients of sects defined as "gnostic" and the few things they had in common are enough for us to go by.' For Mastrocinque's views, see also below, pp. 13n. 1, 173n. 67, 213n. 13, 218n. 16.

[24] On the 'Sethians', see pp. 28–9.

[25] Cf. the Messina definition of Gnosticism, quoted in note 13 above, and Meyer, *The Gnostic Discoveries*, p. 42: 'Gnostic Religion is a religious tradition that emphasizes the primary place of gnosis, or mystical knowledge, understood through aspects of wisdom, often personified wisdom, presented in creation stories, particularly stories based on the Genesis accounts, and interpreted by means of a variety of religious and philosophical traditions, including Platonism, in

There can be no doubt that this gnostic myth became very well known and influential in diverse variations; it will be a focal point in this book. But it seems advisable, as already noted above, not to speak about this complex of ideas as '*the* gnostic religion', and also to avoid the term 'Gnosticism' completely and instead to speak of 'radical or mythological gnostic religion', because this leaves room for other, less radical forms of gnostic religion. Otherwise, the typical elements of the radical gnostic myth become the criteria for determining whether or not a text is gnostic. A well-known example is the *Gospel of Thomas* (NHC II, 2): anyone who takes the gnostic myth as criterion must declare this gospel to be non-gnostic, because it does not contain the distinction between the two gods, the Pleroma, the fall of Sophia and the like.[26] But this gospel does pivot on an esoteric message brought by Christ: 'the secret words which the living Jesus spoke' (superscription), the same Jesus who says: 'I speak my secrets to those who are worthy of my secrets' (62). What matters is self-knowledge and knowledge of God: 'anyone who knows himself will find it (the Kingdom of God)' (3, Greek text), and elimination of duality and return to the unity before the Fall (11, 22). These are typically gnostic themes. So there is every reason to call the *Gospel of Thomas* gnostic, but it represents a very different form of gnosis from that voiced in the radical gnostic myths. Anyone who reads the gnostic Nag Hammadi texts and the reports of the anti-gnostic writers can only conclude that gnostic religion came in many variations and that it cannot be reduced to one

order to proclaim a radically enlightened way and life of knowledge.' In these definitions, the cultic aspects of gnostic religion are not recognized. Other definitions of Gnosticism and discussions of many aspects of ancient gnostic religion can be found in M. Conner, *Voices of Gnosticism* (Dublin: Bardic Press, 2011), a collection of interviews with thirteen scholars who for the greater part have an intimate knowledge of the original gnostic sources. Unfortunately, Conner does not indicate whether the texts of the interviews have been authorized by his interlocutors. One gets the impression that they were not, otherwise Karin L. King would have noticed that the name of the Canadian scholar she refers to was not Paschaux (pp. 164, 165), but Painchaud. This uncertainty makes the book unfit for use in scholarly discussions.

26 Pearson, *Ancient Gnosticism*, p. 257: 'The Gospel of Thomas is not a Gnostic text, though some scholars argue that it is. But there is no doctrine of pleromatic emanations in it, no Sophia myth, and no ignorant or malevolent Demiurge. What it does share in common with Gnosticism is the emphasis on self-knowledge, but that is not something specific to Gnosticism as we have defined it.' A. Marjanen, '"Gnosticism"', in S. Ashbrook Harvey and D. G. Hunter (eds.), *The Oxford Handbook of Early Christian Studies* (Oxford University Press, 2008), pp. 203–20, a short but excellent introduction to the problems involved in the study of 'Gnosticism', proposes (pp. 210–11) to attach the label 'gnostic' only to texts that combine the idea of an evil or ignorant world creator with that of the human soul or spirit as originating from a transcendental world and having the potential to return to that world after receiving the gnosis of its divine origin. Therefore: 'the Gospel of Thomas cannot be regarded as "gnostic", since it lacks the idea of a distinct creator' (p. 211).

variant. That would be the same as to claim that Roman Catholicism *is* Christianity or Sufism *is* Islam. As the texts show, there was a sliding scale in the gnostic view of reality and the human condition, from extremely radical and one-sided to balanced and open to interpretation. The latter category may sometimes give room for disputes as to whether a certain text can be assigned to the gnostic spiritual movement.

In conclusion, then, the term 'gnostic religion' does not refer to an independent religion in its own right,[27] but to a variety of myths, ideas and practices in which the concept of *gnōsis*, as described above, played a dominant role. It implied a religious worldview which could easily attach itself to existing religious and philosphical traditions, thereby reinterpreting and reshaping them.

[27] As has always been defended by Pearson in particular, see note 23 above.

CHAPTER 2

Gnostic literature I: tradition

THE GREEK TRADITION

Our knowledge of the gnostic movement in Antiquity is almost entirely based on literary sources. There are no archeological finds which inform us with certainty about the way of life and religious customs of the gnostics. Older and again some recent studies talk about 'gnostic' amulets, but in reality these served a magic purpose, whereas their typically gnostic character cannot be proven.[1] We know of only one amulet on which the gnostic names of the evil planets are in fact inscribed, but this, too, points to the close connection between gnostic religion and magic which we also find in a number of gnostic texts.[2] Scholars have also held that the catacomb of the Aurelii on Viale Manzoni in Rome, which contains

[1] A. Mastrocinque (ed.), *Sylloge Gemmarum Gnosticarum*, vols. I and II (Rome: Istituto poligrafico e Zecca dello Stato, 2004, 2008). Mastrocinque calls a magic gem 'gnostic' if it contains names or symbols that derive from Judaism or are thought to be related to it; see, for instance, his *From Jewish Magic to Gnosticism* STAC 24 (Tübingen: Mohr Siebeck, 2005), p. 192: 'If Hippolytus treated heretical astrologists in the same way as the Peratae or Monoimos, and placed them all under the heading of Gnostic heresies, I see no reason why we cannot include in their company the authors of the formulae in magical papyri uttered in the name of Jacob or Adam and addressed to the cosmic pole god, who was perceived as Harpocrates and a winged snake, or the authors of the magical gems linking the figure of Harpocrates to the names of Sabaoth, Iaô and Abraxas.'

[2] C. Bonner, 'An Amulet of the Ophite Gnostics', in *Commemorative Studies in Honor of Theodore Leslie Shear*, Hesperia Supplements 8 (Princeton: American School of Classical Studies at Athens, 1949), pp. 43–6, Plate 8, no. 1; and his *Studies in Magical Amulets, Chiefly Graeco-Egyptian*, University of Michigan Studies, Humanistic Series, 49 (Ann Arbor: University of Michigan Press; London: Oxford University Press, 1950), pp. 135–8, Plate IX, no. 188. On this amulet, see also below p. 174. April D. DeConick, *The Thirteenth Apostle. What the Gospel of Judas Really Says*, rev. edn (London and New York: Continuum, 2009), pp. 181–90, has drawn attention to another magical amulet, in the Bibliothèque Nationale, Paris, which has the name 'Ioudas' on its reverse. Both sides of the gem are interpreted as confirming her thesis that the *Gospel of Judas* does not present Judas as the perfect gnostic, but as a demon who will become closely associated or even identical with Yaldabaoth, the ruler of all demonic powers of the cosmos (see on this p. 59 below). It would seem that a fresh study of the gem, and of its obverse in particular, by an expert on the imagery of magical amulets, is needed before her far-reaching conclusions can be accepted.

a number of mysterious paintings, belonged to a gnostic (Naassene or Valentinian) community, but the evidence for this is weak.[3] So for our knowledge of gnostic religion we rely on texts which derive both from the gnostics themselves and from their opponents. All the gnostic works which are known to us or whose titles have been passed down were originally written in Greek, and the same applies to the great anti-gnostic works by people like Irenaeus, Hippolytus and Epiphanius. Sometimes these quote the writings of their opponents literally and occasionally even in their entirety, but in most cases they confine themselves to summaries, which they then dispute. The fact that, with very few exceptions, the Greek gnostic texts have been lost is partly because they were regarded later on as heretical and no longer copied. But until the mid fourth century there need not even have been a deliberate strategy of detection and destruction of suspect writings. Much of the non-gnostic Christian literature from the second and third centuries has also been lost, for the simple reason that later generations were no longer interested in it because it had been superseded by advancing theological developments. What was no longer considered relevant was not eligible for reproduction. Because texts were almost always written on fragile papyrus, they were rapidly lost if not treated carefully. Virtually the only country in the Graeco-Roman world where papyrus had any chance of survival was Egypt. In the modern age thousands of Greek papyri have been found in the dry desert sand, both commercial and personal documents and (fragments of) literary texts, including some gnostic ones. These finds also teach us that there was great interest in gnostic writings in Egypt until far into the fourth century, and not just among Greek speakers, but also for people whose mother tongue was Coptic. In fact it is a curious phenomenon that almost all authentic gnostic texts have been passed down in Coptic translation. The Coptic tradition will be discussed below, but first the few Greek remnants of gnostic literature will be dealt with.

[3] For a meticulous description of the paintings, accompanied by some rather vague photographs, and their attribution to a gnostic community of the Naassene type, see A. H. B. Logan, *The Gnostics. Identifying an Early Christian Cult* (London and New York: T&T Clark, 2006), pp. 89–123, who largely follows J. Carcopino, *De Pythagore aux Apôtres. Études sur la conversion du monde romain* (Paris: Flammarion, 1956), pp. 83–221. The gnostic interpretation is more a question of belief than of established facts. It was strongly rejected by N. Himmelmann, *Das Hypogäum der Aurelii am Viale Manzoni: Ikonographische Beobachtungen*, Akademie der Wissenschaften und der Literatur. Mainz, Abhandlungen der geistes- und sozialwissenschaftlichen Klasse 7 (Wiesbaden: Steiner, 1975). On the basis of the literary evidence, the paintings *can* be interpreted in a gnostic sense (e.g. that the three figures in the central medallion of the vault of Chamber B represent the gnostic trinity of Father, Mother and Son; Logan, *The Gnostics*, p. 101), but the paintings themselves offer not a single indubitable reference to any characteristic idea of the Naassenes or other gnostics.

Greek fragments of some Coptic gnostic writings from Nag Hammadi are now also known. These are always contained in Greek papyri found much earlier, though scholars did not know from which work they derived. Thus we now possess a limited number of Greek fragments of the *Gospel of Thomas*, the *Gospel of Mary* and the *Wisdom of Jesus Christ*. Clearly this is important, because it allows a limited comparison of the Coptic text with the Greek. This can contribute to a better understanding of the Coptic text, but it also tends to create new problems. If the translation differs in content from the Greek text, this may mean that the translator or a later copyist changed the original text, but it may equally be that the translator used a Greek text that diverged from the rediscovered papyrus fragment. In many cases it is difficult to ascertain which of the two possibilities applies. One example may serve to clarify this. According to the Coptic text of the *Gospel of Thomas*, 5, Jesus says: 'For nothing is hidden that will not come to light', a statement that occurs with variants in Mark 4:22, Matthew 10:26 and Luke 8:17 and 12:2. But the Greek text of the *Gospel of Thomas* is longer here: '[For nothing is] hidden that [will] not [come] to light *and nothing is buried that* [*will not be raised*].' The correctness of the last addition to the text is shown by the fragment of a shroud found in a grave in Oxyrhynchus, with the text: 'Jesus says: Nothing is buried that will not be raised.'[4] So these words of Jesus circulated separately too, but the exordium ('Jesus says') makes it likely that the *Gospel of Thomas* is also the ultimate source here and that in any case Jesus' statement formed part of the Greek tradition of this gospel. This clear reference to physical resurrection was probably erased by a gnostic, for gnostics preferred to interpret resurrection spiritually. But it is no longer possible to determine whether this was already the case in the Greek text on which the Coptic translation is based or goes back to the translator or a later gnostic copyist.

Besides the Greek fragments mentioned, there is a Greek papyrus which has been declared gnostic. It is the *Prayer of Seth*, fragments of which have been preserved in the lower part of a Berlin papyrus leaf.[5] The title is easily legible, but the content has largely been lost. We do know that a few heavenly powers are invoked, whose names are also mentioned in some Nag Hammadi codices (NHC) in prayers which are interrelated, most clearly in *Allogenes* (NHC XI, 54, 28–31) and the *Three Steles of Seth*

[4] See H.-C. Puech, 'Un logion de Jésus sur bandelette funéraire', in *En quête de la Gnose*, vol. II, *Sur l'Évangile selon Thomas. Esquisse d'une interprétation systématique* (Paris: Gallimard, 1978), pp. 59–62, frontispiece (first published in *Revue de l'Histoire des Religions*, 147 (1955), 126–9).

[5] W. Brashear, 'Seth-Gebet', *Archiv für Papyrusforschung und verwandte Gebiete* 42 (1996), 26–34.

(NHC VII, 126, 6–8). These are strangely formed names such as often occur in magic papyri, too, but the order is different in each text.[6] So it is not in fact at all certain whether the *Prayer of Seth* is gnostic, it may just as easily be a magic prayer. The connection between gnostic religion and magic conceptions will be frequently discussed in what follows. But the *Prayer of Seth* is too fragmentary and its gnostic content too uncertain to be designated as a source for our knowledge of gnostic ideas.

More extensive remnants of Greek gnostic works have been found in some Church Fathers. The best-known example is the famous *Letter to Flora* by the gnostic teacher Ptolemy (*c.* 160–80), which has been passed down integrally in Epiphanius (*c.* 380), *Panarion* 33, 3–7. In this work Ptolemaeus gives his view of the Old Testament. The ecclesiastical opponents of the gnostics preferred to target the Valentinians, because they were consciously Christian and saw themselves as belonging to the Church. This explains why so many literal quotations of Valentinian gnostics have been preserved. Thus in his *Panarion* 31, 5–6, Epiphanius incorporated a long passage from a Valentinian doctrinal epistle, the so-called *Letter of Instruction*, in which the author sets out an important part of the Valentinian system in his own way. The gnostics Theodotus and Heracleon, who both lived in the second half of the second century, are the best-known Valentinians fragments of whose writings have survived. Clement of Alexandria (*c.* 200) compiled a collection of statements by Theodotus and other Valentinian theologians which has become known as the *Excerpta ex Theodoto*. The same Clement, in his principal work *Stromateis* ('Patchwork', i.e. 'Miscellanies'), also passed down six literal quotations of Valentinus himself. As far as we know, the Valentinian Heracleon was the first to write a commentary on the Gospel of John. Fragments of it have been preserved in the great commentary which Origen (185–254) devoted to the same gospel. Finally, we should draw attention to two Greek inscriptions found in Rome, the 'bridal chamber inscription' and the epitaph for a certain Flavia Sophe, which are both usually regarded as Valentinian. The next chapter will look more closely at most of the texts mentioned here.

THE COPTIC TRADITION

Coptic is the last stage of Egyptian, which was spoken by the Christians in Egypt from *c.* 200 to 1000. Coptic script uses the Greek alphabet, to

[6] See p. 141 below.

which in the most common, Sahidic, dialect six letters have been added which derive from the penultimate stage of Egyptian, demotic. The earliest texts in standardized Coptic are Bible manuscripts from *c.* 300 CE.[7]

The Codex Askewianus in London[8]

The first gnostic text to become known in the West was the *Pistis Sophia.* Only one manuscript has survived, which was probably purchased around 1770 by the physician and book collector Anthony Askew in an antiquarian bookshop in London.[9] In 1785 this manuscript on parchment came into the possession of the British Museum (now in the British Library) and since then is referred to as the Codex Askewianus or Askew Codex. A codex is a manuscript in the form of a book, so not a scroll. The first edition, prepared by M. G. Schwarze, was published after his death by J. H. Petermann (Berlin, 1851); the best scholarly edition is that by Carl Schmidt (Copenhagen, 1925), who also published a much-used German translation (Leipzig, 1905; fourth edn 1981). The extensive Coptic manuscript (385 pages) is generally dated to the mid fourth century. It is hard to determine when the Greek original was written, but there are indications that it should be dated to around the mid third century, as we will see below.

The Codex Brucianus in Oxford

In the eighteenth century two other gnostic texts came to light. Around 1770 in Upper Egypt the Scottish explorer James Bruce bought a Coptic papyrus codex, which has reposed in the Bodleian Library in Oxford since 1848.[10] The manuscript, which is known as the Codex Brucianus or Bruce Codex, contains two texts usually referred to as the *Books of Jeu* and the *Untitled Gnostic Treatise.* The first part of the manuscript, containing

7 B. Layton, *A Coptic Grammar, with Chrestomathy and Glossary. Sahidic Dialect*, Porta Linguarum Orientalium 20 (Wiesbaden: Harrassowitz, 2000), pp. 1–4.

8 Much information on the manuscripts in London, Oxford and Berlin can be found in M. Tardieu and J.-D. Dubois, *Introduction à la littérature gnostique*, vol. 1, *Histoire du mot 'gnostique'; Instruments de travail; Collections retrouvées avant 1945* (Paris: Éditions du CERF/Éditions du CNRS, 1986).

9 On Askew (1722–74): M. J. Mercer, 'Askew, Anthony', in *Oxford Dictionary of National Biography*, vol. 11 (Oxford University Press, 2004), p. 712.

10 On Bruce (1730–94): N. Leask, 'Bruce, James, of Kinnaird', in *Oxford Dictionary of National Biography*, vol. VIII (Oxford University Press, 2004), pp. 303–6. Bruce bought the manuscript during his celebrated journey to Ethiopia, but it is unclear whether he did this on the outward journey (1768/9) or on the return trip (1773).

the *Books of Jeu*, dates from the mid fourth century, the second part from its second half. The texts of the Codex Brucianus were first published, unsatisfactorily, by E. Amélineau (Paris, 1891), soon followed by an excellent edition prepared by Carl Schmidt (Leipzig, 1892). Charlotte Baynes published a commentary on the *Untitled Gnostic Treatise* which is still most useful (Cambridge, 1933). The first work is also mentioned in the *Pistis Sophia* II, 99, where Jesus says that his disciples can find a description of the heavenly mysteries 'in the two Books of Jeu, which Enoch wrote when I spoke with him from the Tree of Knowledge and from the Tree of Life in Adam's Paradise'. The same is said in *Pistis Sophia* III, 134, with the addition: 'And I had him place them on the rock of Ararat and I appointed the ruler (*archōn*) Kalapatauroth ... to guard the Books of Jeu on account of the Flood and to prevent any of the rulers from being jealous of them and from wanting to destroy them.' The current title derives from this reference; the title *Books of Jeu* does not occur in the two books themselves. The (or an) original title is mentioned at the end of the first book: the *Book of the Great Mystery Treatise*.

Papyrus Codex 8502 in Berlin

At the end of the nineteenth century a third Coptic codex with gnostic texts was discovered in Upper Egypt, in Akhmim. In 1896 it came into the possession of the Egyptian Department of the State Museums in Berlin. The manuscript was given the accession number Papyrus Berolinensis 8502 (P. Berol. 8502), but in Coptic and gnostic studies it is always referred to by the abbreviation BG ('Berlin Gnostic Papyrus'), introduced by W. E. Crum in his *Coptic Dictionary* (Oxford, 1939). On paleographical and linguistic grounds the codex is dated to the late fourth or early fifth century. However, BG is not an exclusively gnostic manuscript, since the last of the four writings which it contains, the *Act of Peter*, is not gnostic; it belongs to the genre of the apocryphal Acts of the Apostles. The gnostic writings are: the *Gospel of Mary*, the *Apocryphon of John* and the *Wisdom of Jesus Christ*. Its publication was beset by misfortune. Carl Schmidt had prepared an edition which was entirely lost in 1912, owing to a leaking water pipe at the printing works. During the First World War and the years following it proved impossible to resume the work. Schmidt did work on it shortly before his death (1938), but it took until 1943 before the eventual publisher, Walter C. Till, had the manuscript ready for printing. As a result of the Second World War and the difficult conditions afterwards, it was not until 1955 that Till's edition was published, and then it was actually too early. For meanwhile the Nag Hammadi library had been discovered, and it was found to contain one other version of the *Wisdom of Jesus Christ* and three of the *Apocryphon of John*. Till was able to incorporate a number of divergent readings of NHC III in his edition, but his work mainly has significance as the (excellent) edition of the Berlin codex.

The Nag Hammadi manuscripts in Cairo

In December 1945 an unlettered farm worker, Muḥammed 'Ali al-Sammān, accidentally dug up an earthenware jar containing a number of Coptic codices. Some of these codices were wrapped in leather covers. It is not known how many codices there originally were. Eventually thirteen ended up in the Coptic Museum in Cairo, where they were conserved and are still kept. In actual fact there are twelve codices and part of a thirteenth, which had already been torn from its original context in Antiquity and tucked into the cover of what would later be called Codex VI. One codex was smuggled out of Egypt and after some wanderings ended up in Brussels, where it was purchased in 1952 by Professor Gilles Quispel from Utrecht on behalf of the Carl Gustav Jung Institute in Zurich. This codex was – and sometimes still is – referred to as the Jung Codex or Codex Jung. After initially using various classifications of the codices, scholars finally arrived at an internationally accepted numbering, in which Codex Jung is designated as Codex I and the torn-out codex section as Codex XIII.[11]

The thirteen codices of Nag Hammadi contain fifty one writings, with in Codex XII some fragments of one or more others. Some of these writings are present in more than one copy, but never in one and the same codex, which points to an earlier history of the constituent parts of the collection.[12] Four texts occur twice: the *Gospel of Truth* (I, 3 and XII, 2),

[11] The history of the discovery and the fortunes of the find have been described several times by J. M. Robinson, most extensively in 'From the Cliff to Cairo. The Story of the Discoverers and the Middlemen of the Nag Hammadi Codices', in B. Barc (ed.), *Colloque international sur les textes de Nag Hammadi (Québec, 22–25 août 1978)*, BCNH-É 1 (Quebec: Presses de l'Université Laval; Louvain: Éditions Peeters, 1981), pp. 21–58, and 'Nag Hammadi: The First Fifty Years', in J. D. Turner and A. McGuire (eds.), *The Nag Hammadi Library after Fifty Years. Proceedings of the 1995 Society of Biblical Literature Commemoration*, NHMS 44 (Leiden: Brill, 1997), pp. 3–33.

[12] For an excellent survey of the scholarly research on the provenance and character of the Nag Hammadi library and its components, see Logan, *The Gnostics*, pp. 12–23, who himself sees the codices 'as the library of an ascetic Sethian gnostic community, assembled from several smaller collections, either exchanged with other related groups from elsewhere in Egypt or acquired because of their content' (p. 29).

the *Holy Book of the Great Invisible Spirit* (II, 2 and IV, 2), *Eugnostus* (III, 3 and V, 1) and the *Origin of the World* (II, 5 and XIII, 2). The *Apocryphon of John* is even present in three copies (II, 1; III, 1 and IV, 1). This implies that the Nag Hammadi discovery has given us forty-five different works. Forty of these were completely unknown before, though in retrospect some brief papyrus fragments of these texts had been discovered earlier. Moreover, copies of four writings have also been found in other codices: in the Berlin Codex (BG) a version of the *Apocryphon of John* (which brings the total to four manuscripts) and one of the *Wisdom of Jesus Christ* (of which two versions are thus known) and in the Codex Tchacos (see below) a copy of the *Letter of Peter to Philip* (= NHC VIII, 2) and of the *(First) Apocalypse of James* (= NHC V, 3). The codices of Nag Hammadi contain the following works:

Codex I

1 *Prayer of the Apostle Paul*
2 *Secret Book* (or *Apocryphon*) *of James*
3 *Gospel of Truth*
4 *Treatise on Resurrection*
5 *Tripartite Tractate* (or *Tractatus Tripartitus*)

Codex II

1 *Secret Book* (or *Apocryphon*) *of John*
2 *Gospel of Thomas*
3 *Gospel of Philip*
4 *Nature* (or *Hypostasis*) *of the Rulers*
5 *On the Origin of the World*
6 *Treatise* (or *Exegesis*) *on the Soul*
7 *Book of Thomas*

Codex III

1 *Secret Book* (or *Apocryphon*) *of John*
2 *Holy Book of the Great Invisible Spirit*
3 *Eugnostus the Blessed*
4 *Wisdom of Jesus Christ*
5 *Dialogue of the Saviour*

Codex IV

1 *Secret Book* (or *Apocryphon*) *of John*
2 *Holy Book of the Great Invisible Spirit*

Codex V

1 *Eugnostus*
2 *Revelation of Paul*
3 (*First*) *Revelation of James*
4 (*Second*) *Revelation of James*
5 *Revelation of Adam*

Codex VI

1 *Acts of Peter and the Twelve Apostles*
2 *The Thunder – Perfect Mind*
3 *Authoritative Teaching* (or *Authentikos Logos*)
4 *Concept of Our Great Power*
5 *Excerpt from Plato's Republic* (588a–589b)
6 *Discourse on the Eighth and Ninth* (or *On the Odoad and the Ennead*)
7 *Prayer of Thanksgiving*
8 *Excerpt from the Perfect Discourse* (= *Asclepius* 21–9)

Codex VII

1 *Paraphrase of Seëm*
2 *Second Treatise of the Great Seth*
3 *Revelation of Peter*
4 *Teachings of Silvanus*
5 *Three Steles of Seth*

Codex VIII

1 *Zostrianus*
2 *Letter of Peter to Philip*

Codex IX

1 *Melchizedek*
2 *Thought of Norea*
3 *True Testimony*

Codex X

1 *Marsanes*

Codex XI

1 *Interpretation of Knowledge*

2 *A Valentinian Exposition*, with Valentinian liturgical readings
 2a *On the Anointing*
 2b *On Baptism* A
 2c *On Baptism* B
 2d *On the Eucharist* A
 2e *On the Eucharist* B
3 *Allogenes*
4 *Hypsiphrone*

Codex XII

1 *Sentences of Sextus*
2 *Gospel of Truth*
3 Fragments

Codex XIII

1 *Three Forms of First Thought* (or *Trimorphic Protonoia*)
2 *On the Origin of the World.*

Though many of these texts have also been published in separate editions and translations, two large international academic projects have made it their aim to publish and translate the complete collection. This has led to two extensive series, one in English and the other in French, entitled The Coptic Gnostic Library and Bibliothèque Copte de Nag Hammadi respectively. The first was published between 1975 and 1996 under the auspices of the Institute for Antiquity and Christianity (Claremont, CA); the second, which is not yet wholly complete, has been published since 1977 by a group of researchers at the Université Laval (Quebec, Canada). A complete French translation of the Nag Hammadi codices, *Écrits gnostiques*, by the same group of researchers, with excellent introductions and commentaries, was published in Paris in 2007. The American group had already released a complete English translation in 1977, *The Nag Hammadi Library in English*, of which a wholly revised edition appeared in 1988. The two groups cooperated in the latest English translation of all the Nag Hammadi codices, *The Nag Hammadi Scriptures*, which was published by Marvin Meyer in 2007. In the German-speaking world two complete scholarly translations have appeared, one by Gerd Lüdemann and Martina Janssen, *Bibel der Häretiker* (1997), and the (excellent) other one by members of the Berliner Arbeitskreis für Koptisch-Gnostische Schriften, *Nag Hammadi Deutsch* (two volumes, 2001–3). Detailed information can be found in the Bibliography.

Codex Tchacos in Basle/Cairo

Around 1978 another Coptic codex with gnostic texts was discovered in Upper Egypt, reportedly at the clandestine excavation of a grave some sixty kilometres north of the town of Al Minya.[13] From 1982 the codex was offered for sale in Europe and the United States, allowing expert Coptologists access to at least superficial information about the manuscript. But the most important text of the codex, the *Gospel of Judas*, remained unnoticed. From 1983 to 2000 the manuscript was stored in a safe in New York, without a buyer coming forward. In 2000 it was bought by Mrs Frieda Nussberger-Tchacos, who sold it on in 2001 to the Maecenas Foundation for Ancient Art in Basle. Earlier a potential American buyer, an antiquarian dealer in Ohio, had worsened the already poor state of the codex in a totally incompetent attempt at restoration. Moreover, in returning the manuscript to Mrs Nussberger-Tchacos, he kept parts of it back, as he admitted in court in 2008. Since 2004 the manuscript, which is probably to be dated to the first half of the fourth century, has been known as the Codex Tchacos. In spring 2006 the text and an English translation of the *Gospel of Judas* finally became available, which was announced with much ado via the National Geographic Society. The year 2007 saw the publication of a critical edition of the entire codex by Rodolphe Kasser and Gregor Wurst. The fragments which the American antiquarian dealer had held back were photographed in 2008 and sent to the German scholar Gregor Wurst for identification. He found that they contained, inter alia, important fragments of the *Gospel of Judas*, which were published in 2010. In the same year the fragments were handed over to the Egyptian authorities, who had sought the immediate return of both the fragments and the Codex Tchacos as a whole. The fragments are now in the Coptic Museum in Cairo, where the Nag Hammadi codices also reside, but for the time being the main part of the Codex Tchacos remains in Switzerland, in the possession of the Maecenas Foundation.

Of the Codex Tchacos sixty-six pages have now been identified, almost all of which are seriously damaged. The original length of the codex is unknown, but a fragment with the page number 108 shows that it must

[13] For the vicissitudes of the codex, see H. Krosney, *The Lost Gospel: The Quest for the Gospel of Judas Iscariot* (Washington, DC: National Geographic, 2006), and H. Krosney, 'The Tchacos Fragments in Court', in H. Krosney, M. Meyer and G. Wurst, 'Preliminary Report on New Fragments of Codex Tchacos', *Early Christianity* 1 (2010), 282–5.

have had many more pages. The extant part of the manuscript contains four texts:

- the *Letter of Peter to Philip* (pp. 1–9), which also occurs, with small differences, in the Nag Hammadi library (NHC VIII, 2);
- *James* (pp. 10–30), also known from Nag Hammadi as the *(First) Revelation of James* (NHC V, 3);
- the *Gospel of Judas* (pp. 33–58);
- the *Book of Allogenes* (pp. 59–66), a modern title devised by the first editors on the basis of the contents (no connection with the work *Allogenes* in NHC XI, 3). The original title has been lost.

In 2006 the editors of the Codex Tchacos gained access to photographs of about fifty fragments that had been made when they still were in the possession of the Ohio antiquarian dealer. Two of these fragments have been identified as belonging to Corpus Hermeticum XIII, 1 (Ohio 4579) and 2 (Ohio 4578),[14] which implies that the Codex Tchacos contained a Coptic translation of one of the most famous hermetic treatises, on rebirth and initiation into the hermetic mystery.

[14] See G. Wurst, 'Preliminary Codicological Analysis of Codex Tchacos', in *The Gospel of Judas together with The Letter of Peter to Philip, James, and a Book of Allogenes from Codex Tchacos. Critical Edition*, Coptic text ed. R. Kasser and G. Wurst, introductions, translations and notes R. Kasser, M. Meyer, G. Wurst and F. Gaudard (Washington, DC: National Geographic, 2007), pp. 29–30.

CHAPTER 3

Gnostic literature II: texts

CLASSIFICATION

For various reasons it is impossible to write a 'History of Gnostic Literature in Antiquity'. The main reason is that it is extremely hard to indicate a chronological development in this literature, both in terms of literary genres which succeed and influence each other and in terms of content. This has to do with the great diversity of the gnostic experience, which from the outset was expressed in all kinds of forms. Moreover, almost all the works mentioned above were written in a short period of 125 years, between 125 and 250 CE, which makes it difficult to date the works individually. Nevertheless, an attempt will be made below to give a survey, not a history, of gnostic literature.[1] The procedure will be to classify the texts according to their content, regardless of the title given to a work. In many cases the titles do not cover the content at all. Thus there are several works which have the word 'Gospel' in their title, but actually belong to entirely different literary genres. A clear example is the *Gospel of Truth* (NHC I, 3): it does not resemble the well-known gospels in any way, but is a profound Valentinian meditation on the significance of Christ. The *Gospel of Mary* (BG I) is not a gospel in the standard sense either, containing a revelation to Mary, with strong mythological accents, and having a clear polemic thrust. This example shows that a content-based approach poses problems, too: it is possible to distinguish between 'revelations to individuals', 'mythological texts' and 'polemical texts', but in practice the

[1] Complete surveys of the authentic gnostic literature are rare. Pearson, *Ancient Gnosticism*, gives an excellent overview in which the authentic works and the reports of anti-gnostic authors are mostly discussed in connection with the ideas of the various gnostic groups; it is meant for the general reader (no footnotes). Meyer, *The Gnostic Discoveries*, deals with a number of gnostic texts and traditions, with an appendix (pp. 172–209) in which all the texts of the Nag Hammadi library and the Berlin Codex are too briefly surveyed. A concise survey is R. van den Broek, 'Gnosticism II: Gnostic Literature', in *Dictionary of Gnosis*, pp. 417–32 (with a different classification from that put forward in this book).

characteristic elements of these categories often occur in one and the same text. In the following survey the main emphasis on the content of a work will determine the classification into a certain group, though the question of the main accent in a certain work is always open to discussion.

Not all the writings in the Coptic codices can be regarded as gnostic. The gnostic content of some works is disputable, others are clearly not gnostic. But even these works were attractive for the most radical gnostic, because of their strongly ascetic character. For the sake of completeness we will also briefly discuss these texts which are hardly gnostic, if at all.

Some 'gnostic gospels' among the Nag Hammadi finds have attracted wide interest. Of these, only the *Gospel of Thomas* can be called a gospel in the proper sense, and even then only to a certain extent, because it only contains sayings by Jesus without any narrative. Because of the importance of this gospel, it will be discussed separately, together with some other texts which seem to come from the same milieu and also contain words of Jesus.

Almost all gnostic writings start from a mythical view of reality, characterized by a sharp distinction between the invisible divine world and the earthly conditions in which we live. Various gnostic myths circulated, which are described in detail in some writings, and are casually touched upon in others. In the latter case it is often difficult to determine which myth the author of a text exactly had in mind. The various myths have a common presupposition: the human inner self originates from the divine world, but has become alienated from it. In their complete form they therefore have an unvarying pattern containing the following parts: a description of the perfect divine world, an explanation of the origin of evil and of the material world in which people are imprisoned and the activity of one or more saviour figures who enlighten the clouded understanding of the human being through gnosis and thus save him or her from the powers of darkness.

In the surviving gnostic literature we can distinguish at least one group of writings which are based on a clearly defined myth, which, however, could be elaborated in various ways. These are the so-called Valentinian writings, that is works which come from the school of Valentinus (*c.* 140) and were largely written in the second half of the second century. It is disputed how far the myth of the Valentinians goes back to Valentinus himself, but we do know for certain that this gnostic myth, clearly inspired by Christian elements, was not the oldest.

An elaborate mythological system, evidently not Valentinian, can be found in the *Secret Book of John* (NHC II, 1; III, 1; IV, 1; BG 2). It describes at length the structure of the divine world, the origin of evil through the 'fall' of Sophia, the creation of the cosmos, the material world and mankind by the ignorant Demiurge, a gnostic view of the primeval biblical history from Adam to Noah and the activity of the divine Enlighteners, including Christ. Thanks to this complete description of 'salvation history', the *Secret Book of John* is the best-known text of mythological gnosis. However, in modern scholarship this has led to a certain narrowing of vision, so that the *Secret Book* is often presented as offering *the* gnostic myth. There were also very different myths, as Chapter 5 below will show. Moreover, it is certain that the *Apocryphon* in its present form is younger than the description of the Valentinian myth in Irenaeus, *AH* I, 1–8. In the present book it will be argued that the *Secret Book of John* is composed of two main parts which were originally separate: a gnostic version of an older, non-Christian, magic cosmological system, in which the demonic and divine powers were referred to by strange, magic names, and a gnostic exegesis of the primeval biblical history. In the magic system the supreme divine power was referred to as 'the invisible [or virginal] Spirit' and his female opposite as 'Barbelo'. It seems that various gnostic authors, including the author of the *Secret Book*, took this mythical system of the demonic and divine world and adapted and developed it in a gnostic sense, without the magic background being entirely lost. This explains why, despite the obvious intermesh, there are such marked differences between texts like the *Secret Book* and, for instance, the *Holy Book of the Great Invisible Spirit* (NHC III, 2; IV, 2) and *Zostrianus* (NHC VIII, 1). Because Barbelo is the highest divine figure with a strange, magic name in this system, the myth which describes it can be indicated as the 'Barbelo myth'. Initially this myth seems to have centred solely on magic knowledge of the divine world and the path of ascent towards it, past the demonic powers that rule the spheres of the earth and the planets. In gnostic circles the Barbelo myth evolved in two directions. On the one hand it was elaborated into an extensive system of spiritual levels past which the gnostic ascends to the supreme deity. Books like *Zostrianus* testify to this system on which Christianity seems to have had no influence at all. On the other hand the Barbelo myth was connected with Jewish and Christian traditions, including a specific gnostic exegesis of Genesis, the emphasis thus shifting to the way humans were enthralled by the demonic powers and how they can be liberated. The *Secret Book of John* is the most complete testimony to this, but writings like the *Hypostasis of the Archons* (NHC II, 4) and the *Origin of the World* (NHC II, 5) also belong to this category, though they are sketchy on the structure of the divine world. There is a fairly large number of writings that contain elements of the Barbelo myth and of the exegesis of Genesis and that will therefore be discussed in this category.

The works that belong to the two groups of texts with the Barbelo myth are often called 'Sethian', because they supposedly originated from a gnostic movement in which Seth was regarded as the principal saviour. However, it is highly questionable whether 'Sethianism' ever existed as a clearly recognizable movement. It is a modern construction based on the observation that the same mythical elements occur in a number of texts.[2] In Antiquity there were gnostics who were called 'Sethians', but the elaborate system which they supported according to Hippolytus, *Refutatio* v, 19–22, in no way resembles the 'Sethianism' of modern research. Entirely different views are attributed to the Sethians by Pseudo-Tertullian, *Adversus omnes haereses* 2, 7–9, but these, too, have only a few points in common with what is nowadays called 'Sethianism'. However, it cannot be denied that specific elements of the Barbelo myth are present in a number of texts, and that a certain relationship thus exists between them. From the outset there were scholars who rejected the concept of 'Sethianism' as a modern construction that failed to do justice to the texts.[3] Other scholars prefer to speak of 'Classic Gnostic' instead of 'Sethian' texts or to replace the term 'Sethian' by 'Gnostic', in the narrow sense of 'belonging to the cult movement of "the Gnostics"', or argue that most of the 'Sethian' views in fact derive from the earlier sect of the Ophites.[4] Unfortunately, the attempts to construct a coherent 'Sethian' or

[2] The principal studies by the two main defenders of Sethianism are: H.-M. Schenke, 'The Phenomenon and Significance of Gnostic Sethianism', in B. Layton (ed.), *The Rediscovery of Gnosticism. Proceedings of the International Conference on Gnosticism at Yale, New Haven, Connecticut, March 28–31, 1978*, vol. II, *Sethian Gnosticism*, SHR 41 (Leiden: Brill, 1981), pp. 588–616, and J. D. Turner, 'Sethian Gnosticism: A Literary History', in C. W. Hedrick and R. Hodgson, Jr (eds.), *Nag Hammadi, Gnosticism, and Early Christianity* (Peabody, MA: Hendrickson, 1986), pp. 55–86; *Sethian Gnosticism and the Platonic Tradition*, BCNH-É 6 (Quebec: Presses de l'Université Laval; Paris and Louvain: Éditions Peeters, 2001); and 'Sethian Gnosticism: A Revised Literary History', in N. Bousson and A. Boud'hors (eds.), *Actes du huitième congrès international d'études coptes. Paris, 28 juin–3 juillet 2004*, vol. II, Orientalia Lovaniensia Analecta 163 (Louvain: Éditions Peeters, 2007), pp. 899–908.

[3] Thus F. Wisse, 'Stalking Those Elusive Sethians', in Layton (ed.), *The Rediscovery of Gnosticism*, vol. II, pp. 563–78; see also W. A. Löhr, 'Sethians', in *Dictionary of Gnosis*, pp. 1066–8 (very reserved) and G. P. Luttikhuizen, 'Sethianer?', *ZAC* 13 (2009), 76–86 (dismissive).

[4] The term 'Classic Gnostic' was introduced by Layton, *The Gnostic Scriptures*, p. 5; Pearson, *Ancient Gnosticism*, pp. 98–100, believes on the one hand that 'there were no groups of people who referred to themselves as "Sethians"', but on the other hand does not object to the modern term 'Sethianism' to denote a body of views which occurs in a number of texts. In that case he speaks of 'Sethian or Classic Gnostic traditions'. For the Christian group of 'the Gnostics', see above pp. 8–9. For his reconstruction of their system, Logan, *The Gnostics*, not only made use of the texts of the traditional 'Sethian' corpus, but also of other texts and information gathered

'Gnostic' system differ considerably from one scholar to another. Hence the terms 'Sethianism' and 'Sethian', as used by modern scholarly jargon, will only be used in this book if they are unavoidable in a certain context, and always between inverted commas.

Besides the works which presuppose a form of the Barbelo myth or the Valentinian myth, we can distinguish some other groups of texts. These are writings where the type of gnosis is less clear, but which strike a sharp polemic note and, finally, three works each describing a mythological system that deviates strongly from the gnostic mythologies mentioned above. All these considerations lead to the following division of gnostic literature and of the rest of this chapter:

- non-gnostic or hardly gnostic writings in gnostic collections
- the *Gospel of Thomas* and related texts
- the Barbelo myth and the gnostic exegesis of Genesis
- the Barbelo myth and heavenly journeys
- Valentinian texts
- Polemical texts
- other mythological traditions.

The most important editions and translations (often with commentaries) of the works to be discussed below are briefly indicated in the notes to the individual writings, by mentioning the editor(s), series and publication date. There are countless studies, of which only the most important are mentioned here; a full survey can be found in the bibliographies by David M. Scholer.[5]

NON-GNOSTIC OR HARDLY GNOSTIC WRITINGS IN GNOSTIC COLLECTIONS

Though the entire library of Nag Hammadi and the whole Berlin Codex must have been attractive literature for all kinds of gnostics, they contain some writings which are not gnostic by origin. The most famous example is a fragment from Plato's *Republic* (NHC VI, 5), but in the *Acts of Peter and the Twelve Apostles* (NHC VI, 1), too, there is nothing

from anti-Gnostic writers. The Ophites were brought in by T. Rasimus, *Paradise Reconsidered in Gnostic Mythmaking: Rethinking Sethianism in Light of the Ophite Evidence*, NHMS 68 (Leiden: Brill, 2009), pp. 9–62, and *passim*.

[5] D. M. Scholer, *Nag Hammadi Bibliography, 1948–1969*, NHS 1 (Leiden: Brill, 1971); *Nag Hammadi Bibliography, 1970–1994*, NHMS 32 (Leiden: Brill, 1997); *Nag Hammadi Bibliography, 1995–2006*, NHMS 65 (Leiden: Brill, 2009).

specifically gnostic, and the same holds for the *Act of Peter* (BG 4). The *Sentences of Sextus* (NHC XII, 1) and the *Teachings of Silvanus* (NHC VII, 4) certainly do not have gnostic roots, either. This also seems to apply to the work *Hypsiphrone* (NHC XI, 4), so far as this can be gauged from the very fragmentary contents. A more controversial question relates to the (non-)gnostic character of the *Treatise on the Soul* (NHC II, 6), the *Authoritative Teaching* (NHC VI, 3) and, more strongly, the *Apocryphon of James* (NHC I, 2). The gnostic character of the *Dialogue of the Saviour* (NHC III, 5) is also far from certain. Since it contains a tradition of sayings of Jesus, it will be discussed in connection with the *Gospel of Thomas*. Finally, Nag Hammadi also yielded three hermetic writings, which obviously do belong to the broad movement of gnostic religiosity, but fall outside the forms of gnosis discussed in this book. They are the *Discourse on the Eighth and Ninth* (NHC VI, 6), the *Prayer of Thanksgiving* (NHC VI, 7) and an *Excerpt from the Perfect Discourse* (= *Asclepius* 21–9; NHC VI, 8).

Excerpt from Plato's Republic We know for certain that the fragment from Plato's *Republic* 588b–589b (NHC VI, 5)[6] was not translated directly from Plato's work, but derived from a doxographical handbook, that is a collection of statements by famous philosophers. For virtually the same quotation was included by Eusebius of Caesarea in his *Praeparatio evangelica* XII, 46, 2–6, while Neoplatonic philosophers also mention it. In Plato the passage forms part of a discussion on just and unjust action and obviously has nothing to do with gnostic speculations. The most striking feature of NHC VI, 5 is that it has been translated so badly into Coptic that the original text has become all but unrecognizable. Scholars generally agree that the 'translator' had insufficient knowledge of Greek and could not follow Plato's train of thought. He is thus an exception among the translators of the library of Nag Hammadi, since most of them were quite equal to their task.

Acts of Peter and the Twelve Apostles The work *Acts of Peter and the Twelve Apostles* (NHC VI, 1)[7] has nothing to do with the gnostic current, either. It belongs to the genre of the apocryphal Acts of the Apostles and is highly interesting in itself, both because of its content and on account of its complicated structure, which indicates a long historical development. In the story a certain Lithargoel plays an important role. He figures as a pearl merchant and physician and is effectively a manifestation of Jesus. The narrative almost certainly dates back to the second century, but from

[6] Ed. J. Brashler, NHS 11 (1979), pp. 328–39; L. Painchaud, BCNH-T 11 (1983), pp. 109–54.
[7] Ed. R. McL. Wilson and D. M. Parrot, NHS 11 (1979), pp. 197–229.

the many and sometimes contradictory additions we can infer that the final redaction should be dated to the first decade of the fourth century.

Act of Peter The *Act of Peter* (BG 4) also belongs to the genre of the apocryphal Acts of the Apostles.[8] It shows no relationship with the *Acts of Peter and the Twelve Apostles*, but originally it might have been part of the well-known *Acts of Peter* (Actus Vercellenses). It contains a story about Peter's daughter, who was abducted by a certain Ptolemy, but whose virginity was preserved because she became paralyzed before Ptolemy could have intercourse with her. The work clearly aims to promote sexual restraint and virginity, which will have made it attractive to gnostics, but it does not contain typically gnostic ideas.

Sentences of Sextus The *Sentences of Sextus* (NHC XII, 1)[9] and the *Teachings of Silvanus* (NHC VII, 4)[10] certainly do not have a gnostic origin, either, though they, too, will have been appreciated by the compilers of the Nag Hammadi codices for their ascetic attitude. Both writings belong to the rather rare genre of early Christian wisdom literature. The *Sentences of Sextus* had long been known in their original Greek form and via translations in Latin, Syriac, Armenian, Georgian and (at least partly) Ethiopian. The work contains 451 sayings, to which more maxims have been added in some manuscripts. The sentences rely strongly on earlier, non-Christian collections of sayings, but various small changes and the addition of new sayings show that the author was a Christian who wanted to give his fellow believers guidelines for a proper way of life. The work must have originated around the year 200.[11] The poor condition of the Coptic manuscript means that only sentences 157–80 and 307–97 have been preserved.

Teachings of Silvanus The *Teachings of Silvanus* are much more overtly Christian than the *Sentences of Sextus*. Moreover, the *Teachings* are not so much short wisdom maxims as an ongoing discourse in which biblical and non-biblical wisdom sayings have been incorporated. In particular the second part talks about Christ in a way that not only betrays the influence of the great theologian Origen (185–254), but also fits perfectly into the Christological discussions of the first decades of the fourth century. This means that the work was probably written around 320, though

[8] Ed. W. C. Till and H.-M. Schenke, TU 60 (2nd edn, 1972), pp. 296–319; J. Brashler and D. M. Parrott, NHS 11 (1979), pp. 474–93; L. Roy, BCNH-T 18 (1987), pp. 165–233.

[9] Ed. P.-H. Painchaud, BCNH-T 11 (1983), pp. 1–82; F. Wisse, NHS 28 (1990), pp. 295–327.

[10] Ed. Y. Janssens, BCNH-T 13 (1983); M. Peel and J. Zandee, NHMS 30 (1996), pp. 249–369.

[11] H. Chadwick, *The Sentences of Sextus. A Contribution to the History of Early Christian Ethics* (Cambridge University Press, 1959).

it has certainly assimilated much older material, from wisdom literature for instance.[12]

Hypsiphrone The work *Hypsiphrone* (NHC XI, 4)[13] covered over three or five pages in the manuscript; the title heads the text. It has been preserved so fragmentarily that it is almost impossible to say anything about the contents, but it does not contain any typically gnostic terms or conceptions. The text starts with the words: 'The book [about the things] that were seen by [Hypsi]phrone, being [revealed] in the place of [her] virginity' (69, 22–5). Apparently it is an account by Hypsiphrone of what happened to her. There is talk about her brothers, of whom a certain Phainops seems to be one. The name Hypsiphrone means 'she of high mind' or 'she who is proud', but is otherwise unknown as a proper name. Phainops means 'he with the bright eyes (or face)'. From the text we can also infer that Hypsiphrone went from the place of her virginity, probably into the world, and that something was done to her there by Phainops. In this context we read about blood and fire, but there is no way of knowing what exactly this means. It is often assumed that the text deals with sexuality and reproduction, whether or not in connection with astrological predictions. It could also be about an allegory of the soul, as in the two writings discussed next. But the text has been passed down too fragmentarily to allow positive statements on this point. In the same way we cannot say anything with certainty about its time and place of origin.

Treatise on the Soul Two texts, the *Treatise on the Soul* (NHC II, 6)[14] and the *Authoritative Teaching* (NHC VI, 3), discuss the vicissitudes of the soul, from her fall into matter to the return to her celestial origin. Though these texts are often explained in a gnostic vein, there is actually little reason to do so, since the conceptions they put forward were far from exceptional in second- and third-century Platonism. The *Treatise on the Soul* is also called the *Exegesis on* (or *of*) *the Soul*, after the original Greek title, which is clearly recognizable in Coptic: *texēgēsis etbe tpsychē* (= *hē exēgēsis peri tēs psychēs*). However, the word 'exegesis' does not mean explanation here, but exposition, treatise or narrative. According to this text, the soul was with 'the Father' in an androgynous and virginal state, but in falling she became the victim of robbers (the passions), who prostituted her. She also prostituted herself by regarding everyone who forced himself on her

[12] For this date and the influence of older Greek wisdom literature, see R. van den Broek, *Studies in Gnosticism and Alexandrian Christianity*, NHMS 39 (Leiden: Brill, 1996), pp. 235–83.

[13] Ed. J. D. Turner, NHS 28 (1990), pp. 269–79.

[14] Ed. J.-M. Sevrin, BCNH-T 9 (1983); W. C. Robinson, Jr and B. Layton, NHS 21 (1989), pp. 135–69; C. Kulawik, TU 155 (2006); H. Lundhaug, NHMS 73 (2010), pp. 446–67.

as her husband. All her seducers abandoned her, her children proved deaf, blind and sickly, and she was left behind, lonely and poor. But when she begs the Father for help in this situation, he takes pity on her. She purifies herself, and her bridegroom, her male counterpart in heaven, descends to her in the bridal chamber, where they unite and regain their original wholeness.[15] This myth of the soul is clarified and confirmed by a large number of quotations from the Old and the New Testament and Homer's *Odyssey*. A striking feature here is the equal authority assigned to all these texts. The same style of quotation is found around 200 in Clement of Alexandria, and it is therefore not unlikely that the author wrote his work in the same period, perhaps in Alexandria, too. Like Clement, the author was a Christian with a strong inclination towards ascesis and a negative view of sexuality.

Authoritative Teaching The *Authoritative Teaching* (or *Authentikos logos*; NHC VI, 3)[16] strongly resembles the *Treatise on the Soul* in its view of the soul. Though the work shows strong Platonic influence and in particular displays similarities to the ideas of Porphyry (second half of the third century), it presents its doctrine in the form of a myth. The soul comes from the divine world and abandons herself to all kinds of passions in her earthly existence and behaves like a prostitute in a brothel. But the heavenly Father does not lose sight of her and her bridegroom nourishes her with the Logos and applies it as a medicine to her blinded eyes, so that she can see with her mind (*nous*) and can recognize her spiritual kin. Ultimately she finds the way back to God, achieves rest in Him who rests, lies down in the bridal chamber and enjoys eternal nourishment. This myth is peppered with ethical opinions and admonitions, which have a strongly ascetic character. The body is held in very low esteem. There are some veiled allusions to passages in the gospels, but the historical Jesus is absent, there is only a divine, healing power operative in the soul. In view of the close parallels with Porphyry, the work was probably written in the mid third century.[17] Like the *Treatise on the Soul*, the *Authoritative Teaching* does not have typically gnostic features, though gnostics may certainly have seen it as a description of the fate of their own soul or inner self.

Secret Book of James The gnostic or non-gnostic character of some Nag Hammadi writings is far from evident. A clear instance of this is the

[15] For a study of the female images in this tractate, see Lundhaug, *Images of Rebirth*, pp. 65–152, who, however, does not refer to the related views of the *Authoritative Teaching*.

[16] Ed. J. É. Ménard, BCNH-T 2 (1977); G. W. MacRae, NHS 11 (1979), pp. 257–89.

[17] See van den Broek, *Studies in Gnosticism*, pp. 206–34; the date mentioned there ('the last decades of the second century A.D.') seems too early.

Secret Book (or *Apocryphon*) *of James* (NHC I, 2), which has been seen both as a product of Valentinian gnosis and as non-gnostic.[18] In the manuscript the work has no title; the modern name is based on the contents. The work presents itself as a letter by James to an addressee whose name has been lost (only the last syllable, *-thos*, is preserved). Presumably 'James' refers to the leader of the Jewish-Christian congregation in Jerusalem, 'James, the Lord's brother' (Gal. 1:19; Acts 15:13; 21:18). James sends his correspondent a book with a secret revelation (*apokryphon*) which he had received with Peter from the risen Christ, and he refers to another secret revelation to which only he had been made privy and of which he had sent an account ten months earlier. The rest of the *Apocryphon* describes the revelation to James and Peter, which is said to have taken place 550 days after the resurrection. Much emphasis is put on being filled with the Spirit, which finds its highest expression in the acceptance of martyrdom. Strikingly, despite the emphasis on the operation of the Spirit, prophecy is sharply rejected. The author stresses the possession of gnosis: those who lack it will be unable to find the Kingdom of Heaven (8, 23–7), but at the same time he underlines the necessity of faith: 'But through faith and knowledge you have received life' (14, 8–10). This means that, like Clement of Alexandria, he considers gnosis important, but does not see faith as superfluous. The author was acquainted with the exegetical discussions about John the Baptist as the end of prophecy, as we know them from the gnostic Heracleon (second half of the second century) and the non-gnostic Origen (first half of the third century).[19] Sometimes he seems to reflect Valentinian views, but these were probably more widespread than the anti-gnostic authors would have us believe. Most likely this work attests to the type of Christianity prevalent in Alexandria in the late second and early third century, before the reins of doctrine and church order were tightened under Bishop Demetrius.

Hermetic texts Finally, we need to look more closely here at the three hermetic texts discovered in Nag Hammadi in Coptic translation (NHC VI, 6, 7 and 8). As we noted earlier, the hermetic and gnostic currents are closely related, but diverge from each other on some essential points.[20] Of the texts recovered, one was previously entirely unknown, the original title

[18] Ed. F. E. Williams, NHS 22 (1985), pp. 13–53, notes in NHS 23 (1985), pp. 7–37; D. Rouleau, BCNH-T 18 (1987).

[19] See J. van der Vliet, 'Spirit and Prophecy in the Epistula Iacobi Apocrypha (NHC I, 2)', *VC* 44 (1990), 25–53.

[20] See p. 4. The main differences and similarities between the gnostic and hermetic views are discussed in van den Broek, *Studies in Gnosticism*, pp. 3–21.

lost. On the basis of its content it is usually denoted as the *Discourse on the Eighth and Ninth (Spheres)* or *On the Ogdoad and the Ennead* (VI, 52, 1–63, 32). The other two were already known: the *Prayer of Thanksgiving* (VI, 63, 33–65, 7) and an *Excerpt from the Perfect Discourse* (VI, 65, 15–78, 43). Between the last two we find a note by the copyist, moreover, in which he reports that he possesses many more hermetic texts (VI, 65, 8–14).

Discourse on the Eighth and Ninth The *Discourse on the Eighth and Ninth* (NHC VI, 6)[21] is the most important hermetic text discovered in the twentieth century. A better title would be the *Initiation into the Eighth and Ninth Spheres*, since it describes, in the form of a conversation between Hermes Trismegistus and an unnamed pupil, the initiation into the hermetic mystery: the inner experience of the divine world of the eighth and ninth heavenly spheres. The work sheds new light on questions which in the past led to heated debate among students of Hermetism. One of these questions is whether real hermetic communities existed, with instruction, rituals and even initiations, or whether allusions to this are no more than literary fiction. The *Discourse* talks about the pupil as a spiritual child of Hermes who is brought into a community of brothers (52, 27–53, 15), who are present at the initiation (53, 27–31; 54, 18–22). There is mention of books studied by the pupil, which points to regular instruction (54, 16, 25 and 32). It also describes collective mystical experiences, in the halting tongue of rapture, which make an impression of complete authenticity (57, 26–60, 10). The wealth of information we now have from these and other texts inevitably suggests that hermetic teachers were in fact surrounded by small hermetic groups, in which not only spiritual instruction but also prayers, hymns, rituals and initiations were practised.[22] As in many of the gnostic texts to be discussed below, a strong influence of magic (and astrology) can be demonstrated in this hermetic work, too. For instance, as in the magic papyri, the holy name of the unknown God is invoked through a series of vowels: 'Zōxathazō, a ōō ee ōōō ēēē ōōōō iiii ōōōōō ooooo ōōōōōō uuuuuu ōōōōōōō ōōōōōōōō <ōōōōōōōōō>, Zōzazōth' (56, 17–22; also 61, 10–15).

[21] Ed. J.-P. Mahé, BCNH-T 3 (1978), pp. 29–134; A. Dirkse, J. Brashler and D. M. Parrott, NHS 11 (1979), pp. 341–73.

[22] Cf. R. van den Broek, 'Religious Practices in the Hermetic "Lodge": New Light from Nag Hammadi', in R. van den Broek and C. van Heertum (eds.), *From Poimandres to Jacob Böhme: Gnosis, Hermetism and the Christian Tradition* (Amsterdam: In de Pelikaan, 2000), pp.77–95; J.-P. Mahé, 'L'Hymne hermétique: une propédeutique du silence', in Y. Lehman (ed.), *L'Hymne antique et son public* (Turnhout: Brepols, 2007), pp. 275–89; A. van den Kerchove, *La voie d'Hermès. Pratiques rituelles et traités hermétiques*, NHMS 77 (Leiden: Brill, 2012).

Prayer of Thanksgiving The *Prayer of Thanksgiving* (NHC VI, 7)[23] is now known in three versions: besides the Coptic there is a Greek version, preserved as part of a prayer in the magic Papyrus Mimaut (Louvre, Papyrus 2391), and a Latin one, which forms the conclusion to the *Asclepius* (41b). Though it is conceivable that from the outset the *Prayer* formed part of the *Logos Teleios*, the Greek original of the Latin *Asclepius*, it seems more likely that it was originally an independent composition. The *Prayer* praises the Father of the All for the gift of gnosis, in terms strongly reminiscent of the eulogies found in various Nag Hammadi texts, for instance: 'We rejoice, enlightened by your knowledge [*gnōsis*]. We rejoice, because you have shown yourself to us. We rejoice, because in our bodily existence you have made us divine through your knowledge [*gnōsis*], while we still were in the body' (64, 16–19).

Excerpt from the Perfect Discourse The *Excerpt from the Perfect Discourse* (NHC VI, 8)[24] runs parallel to chapters 21 to 29 of the Latin *Asclepius*. The text contains the so-called 'Hermetic Apocalypse', a description of the disasters which will strike Egypt before a new period of happiness dawns.[25] Since only a few original fragments of the *Perfect Discourse*, in Greek *Logos Teleios*, have been preserved, the Coptic excerpt is of great importance because a comparison with the Latin translation in the *Asclepius* now allows us to gain an impression of the original Greek text. This comparison shows that the Latin translator permitted himself all kinds of liberties in relation to the Greek original: he sometimes abridged, extended or changed the text. A good example of abridgement of the original is found in the description of Egypt's desolate state after the gods have withdrawn to the heavens:

Latin (*Asclepius* 24)	Coptic (NHC VI, 70, 30–6)
Then this most holy land,	On that day, the land that is more pious than all [other] lands will become impious,
seat of shrines and temples,	no longer will it be full of temples
will be completely full of tombs	but it will be full of tombs, neither will it be full of gods
and corpses.	but [it will be full] of corpses.

[23] Ed. J.-P. Mahé, BCNH-T 3 (1978), pp. 134–67; P. A. Dirkse and J. Brashler, NHS 11 (1979), pp. 375–87.

[24] Ed. P. A. Dirkse and D. M. Parrott, NHS 11 (1979), pp. 395–451; J.-P. Mahé, BCNH-T 7 (1982), pp. 45–272.

[25] In his excellent edition, pp. 172–3, Mahé has juxtaposed the Coptic and Latin texts, thus clearly bringing out the similarities and differences. For the late classical interpretation of these and other apocalyptic predictions, see R. van den Broek, 'The Hermetic Apocalypse and other Greek Predictions of the End of Religion', in van den Broek and van Heertum (eds.), *From Poimandres to Jacob Böhme*, pp. 97–113.

A single glance makes it clear that the Coptic translation is to be preferred here. The fine antithetical parallelism (pious/impious, temples/tombs, gods/corpses), which the Coptic translator doubtless found in the original, has been completely lost in the Latin translation. This may suffice to show that the long-known hermetic texts from Nag Hammadi are also crucial to the study of hermetic literature.

THE *GOSPEL OF THOMAS* AND RELATED TEXTS

Six gnostic texts present themselves as gospels. After the *Gospel of Mary* in the Berlin Codex, the Nag Hammadi library yielded three writings which pass themselves off as gospels: the *Gospel of Truth* (NHC I, 3 and XII, 2), the *Gospel of Thomas* (NHC II, 2) and the *Gospel of Philip* (NHC II, 3), while the *Holy Book of the Great Invisible Spirit* (NHC II, 2 and IV, 2) is referred to in the colophon as the *Egyptian Gospel*. Moreover, the Codex Tchacos has given us the *Gospel of Judas*. Of these texts, however, only the *Gospel of Thomas* is a gospel in the proper sense of the word. And even this only partly, because it does contain sayings by Jesus, but no references to his life, acts, death and resurrection. In fact, many gnostic writings contain statements by Jesus, usually in conversations with his disciples, but these almost always involve typically gnostic views which are put into Jesus' mouth and teach us nothing about the views of the historical Jesus. The *Gospel of Truth* and the *Gospel of Philip* are Valentinian writings. They will therefore be discussed after this, together with other works from the school of Valentinus. But the *Gospel of Philip* does contain a number of statements by Jesus, to which attention will be paid in this section. The *Egyptian Gospel* is a representative of the Barbelo myth and will therefore be discussed together with the other writings from the same category. The *Gospel of Judas* was strongly influenced by the same mythological tradition; it does not teach us anything about the historical Jesus or Judas. So this section will deal at length only with the *Gospel of Thomas*. Furthermore, the *Book of Thomas* (NHC II, 7) will also be mentioned here, because it comes from the same milieu as the *Gospel of Thomas*. The *Dialogue of the Saviour* (NHC III, 5) also deserves to be discussed here, because it preserves a tradition concerning the words of Jesus.[26]

[26] Layton ascribed the *Gospel of Thomas* and the *Book of Thomas*, together with the *Acts of Thomas*, to what he called 'The School of St. Thomas'; see his *Gnostic Scriptures*, pp. 359–409; Pearson, *Ancient Gnosticism*, pp. 256–72, discusses the same texts under the heading 'Thomas Christianity'; Meyer, *Gnostic Discoveries*, p. 48, suggests that the *Dialogue of the Saviour* may also belong to this group.

Gospel of Thomas The *Gospel of Thomas* (NHC II, 2)[27] consists of 114 sayings by Jesus, which are usually referred to as *logia* or *logoi* ('words') in the modern literature. Around half of these also occur in the synoptic gospels, those of Matthew, Mark and Luke, though there are always small, usually insignificant divergences. Of the other logia some were already known from early Christian literature, but most were completely new when the Nag Hammadi library was found. Some words of Jesus form clear doubles or contradict each other, indicating that the *Gospel of Thomas* drew on various sources and reflects a historical development.[28] It must have been quite widely known in Egypt, since besides the complete Coptic translation (from *c.* 300 CE), papyrus fragments of three different Greek manuscripts were found in Oxyrhynchus, which on paleographical grounds are dated to between the late second and late third century: P. Oxy. 1 (shortly after 200), P. Oxy. 654 (late second to late third century) and P. Oxy. 655 (between 200 and 250). These papyri had already been published in 1897 and 1904, but only after the Nag Hammadi discovery were they found to be fragments of the Greek *Gospel of Thomas*. It is quite generally assumed that this gospel in its present form should be dated to the mid second century.

The discovery immediately raised two main questions. The first related to the gnostic or non-gnostic character of the work. We have already considered this subject when defining the terms 'gnosis', 'gnostic' and 'gnostic religion'.[29] Scholars are now quite generally agreed that the *Gospel of Thomas* does not belong to the radical, mythological form of gnostic religion, because it does not presuppose anywhere the fall of Sophia and the evil creator-god. However, as already noted, this does not prevent its characterization as gnostic in a broader sense. The heading already indicates its esoteric character: 'These are the secret words which the Living Jesus spoke and which Didymus Judas Thomas wrote down.' And the first logion, of which it is uncertain whether this is a saying of Jesus or a statement by Thomas, reads: 'Whoever finds the interpretation of these words will not taste death.' So the words of Jesus, including the statements known from the biblical gospels, have a deeper meaning which must be found. The second question which has exercised

[27] Ed. B. Layton, O. Lambdin and H. Koester, NHS 20 (1989), pp. 38–93; Greek fragments: ed. H. W. Attridge, NHS 20 (1989), pp. 95–128.

[28] A. D. DeConick, *Recovering the Original Gospel of Thomas: A History of the Gospel and its Growth*, Library of New Testament Studies 286 (London and New York: T&T Clark, 2005); also J. M. Asgeirsson, A. D. DeConick and R. Uro (eds.), *Thomasine Traditions in Antiquity: The Social and Cultural World of Thomas*, NHMS 59 (Leiden: Brill, 2006).

[29] See p. 11.

many scholars is this: does the *Gospel of Thomas* contain a tradition concerning Jesus' words which is independent of the now canonical gospels? This, then, relates mainly to the logia which also occur in the biblical gospels. On this matter serious scholars have not yet reached a consensus. In theory a collection of statements by Jesus deriving from the oral tradition and independent of the well-known gospels is perfectly possible. It is generally believed that Matthew and Luke already used such an existing collection of words of Jesus (the famous source Q, from German *Quelle*, 'source'). Although the question is still a subject of much debate, more and more researchers assume that in any case a number of logia represent an independent tradition.[30] Naturally the question then is whether this also applies to the statements which have no parallel in the biblical gospels. In theory this is perfectly possible, but it is going much too far to claim – as many popular books do – that the true Jesus is speaking in the *Gospel of Thomas* and that the canonical gospels were revised to fit in with later ecclesiastical views. This is just as incorrect and unhistorical as the opinion that the statements by Jesus in the biblical gospels are all authentic and those in the extra-biblical tradition are all fabrications by people with their own (heretical) agenda. All the gospels, including the biblical ones, have their own agenda, and never offer purely historical information. We actually know very little about the 'historical Jesus'. All the gospels interpret the tradition regarding Jesus in the light of the time in which they originated; they give answers to questions which were topical in the Christian communities in which they were written. This means that in the biblical gospels, too, it is very difficult to determine whether a particular logion is original, adapted or simply fabricated.

One example may suffice to show what is meant here. In Matthew 16:18 Jesus says to Peter, who was actually called Simon Bar-Jona: 'And I tell you, you are Peter [*Petros*], and on this rock [*petra*] I will build my church [*ekklēsia*].' The pun *Petros-petra* – both Greek words mean rock or stone – goes back to Aramaic, in which the word for rock is *kēfa'*. Peter was therefore referred to by the first Christians in Aramaic as *Kēfa'* and in Greek as *Kēphas* (e.g. 1 Cor. 1:12; 3:22; 9:5; 15:5). So Matthew depicts Peter as fundamental for the building of the church, and this has had far-reaching consequences, for it still forms the basis for the authority of

[30] See for example T. Zöckler, *Jesu Lehren im Thomasevangelium*, NHMS 47 (Leiden: Brill, 1999). On early gospel traditions in general, H. Koester, *Ancient Christian Gospels: Their History and Development* (London: SCM Press; Philadelphia: Trinity Press International, 1990).

the pope. But in the *Gospel of Thomas* Jesus does not pronounce Peter but James the Just, 'the Brother of the Lord', to be the head of the church. In logion 12 the disciples ask: 'We know that you will leave us. Who will then be our leader?' Jesus answers: 'Wherever you are, go to James the Just, for whose sake heaven and earth came into being.' This statement, too, must have a Jewish-Christian background. James the Just was the leader of the original congregation in Jerusalem. And the expression 'for whose sake heaven and earth came into being' is a characteristic Jewish hyperbolic expression to indicate that something or somebody is of exceptional importance. In the rabbinic midrash on Genesis, *Bereshit rabba* 1, 4, the same is said about both the Torah and Moses. Peter and James both played a crucial role in the Jerusalem congregation: Paul reports that on first visiting the city after his conversion he had met only the apostles 'Kephas' and 'James, the Brother of the Lord' (Gal. 1:18–19). So in Matthew and Thomas we are dealing with two ancient traditions about the leadership of the Church, which both base themselves on a statement by Jesus. But what exactly did Jesus say about this? Or did he say anything about it at all? The answer to this last question should probably be negative. The most obvious explanation is that both statements were put into Jesus' mouth to legitimize rival claims to the Church's leadership. The Jewish-Christian part of the earliest Church (Jerusalem) thus claimed the primacy of James, the more pagan-Christian part (Antioch, where Matthew was probably written) saw Peter as the foundation of the Church. Even apart from this matter the text in Matthew is suspect, because it uses the word *ekklēsia* to refer to the Christian congregation. In the gospels this occurs elsewhere only in Matthew 18:16, where it is said that if persistent sinners refuse to listen to the *ekklēsia*, they should be treated as a heathen or a publican – a situation which clearly presupposes the existence of an ordered Christian congregation. But there is no evidence in the gospels that Jesus ever intended to found a church. As the French theologian Alfred Loisy observed more than a century ago: 'Jesus announced the Kingdom, and what came was the Church.'[31]

Matthew, Mark and Luke were probably written in the seventh and eighth decades of the first century and reflect the situation of the Christians of that time. In these gospels Jesus manifests himself as an eschatological prophet who expected the Kingdom of God to come very soon and partly saw this realized in his own person (Matt. 10:23 and

[31] A. Loisy, *L'Évangile et l'Église* (Paris: Picard, 1902), p. 111: 'Jésus annonçait le royaume, et c'est l'Église qui est venue.'

11:2–5). This may well be historically correct, but in any case he was mistaken, since the end of the world did not come. It was therefore necessary to assume that the Kingdom would come later or to interpret it differently. In fact the Gospel of John (late first century) offers an entirely different interpretation of Jesus' message, and this also applies to the *Gospel of Thomas*. In both these gospels the expectation of an imminent end has disappeared, and the Kingdom of God has primarily become an inner matter. In *Thomas* this means finding the original paradisal unity of the human being. It is becoming one with Jesus: 'Whoever drinks from my mouth will become like me and I myself will become him, and the mysteries will be revealed to him' (logion 108). And it is rediscovering the lost unity of oneself: 'If you make the two one … and if you make the male and the female one and the same, so that the male will not be male nor the female be female … then you will enter the Kingdom' (logion 22). In his turn Paul put an entirely different interpretation on the significance of Jesus. The conclusion must therefore be that from the beginning different interpretations of the person of Jesus circulated. It can no longer be determined which was the only correct one. The choices made in this matter depend more on intuitive faith, whether or not determined by the tradition, than on scholarly analyses.

Book of Thomas The fact that the *Gospel of Thomas* did not take shape in a vacuum is shown by some other texts in which the apostle Thomas plays a role. Nag Hammadi also brought to light the previously unknown *Book of Thomas* (NHC II, 7).[32] Its opening words are strongly reminiscent of those of the *Gospel of Thomas*: 'The secret words which the Saviour spoke to Judas Thomas, which I, Mathaias, wrote down.' The name Judas Thomas points to Syria, for only there was it taught that Thomas (Aramaic *t'ōma'* = Greek *didymos*, twin) was Jesus' twin brother and in reality was called Judas. The same idea and the view that Thomas is the receiver of secret revelations is also found in the third work belonging to the Thomas cycle, the *Acts of Thomas*. In this work an ass's foal addresses the apostle as follows: 'Twin brother of Christ, apostle of the Highest One and initiate into the secret word of Christ, who receives his hidden pronouncements' (39). In Syrian Christianity the apostle Thomas was regarded as the one who initiated the Christianization of Syria; he was supposedly also buried in its centre, the town of Edessa, present-day Urfa in Turkey. The three Thomas writings are strictly ascetic; in particular the *Book of Thomas* and the *Acts of Thomas* see the meaning of Christianity almost exclusively in

[32] Ed. R. Kunzmann, BCNH-T 16 (1986); J. D. Turner, NHS 21 (1989), pp. 171–205.

the rejection of sexuality. They are usually dated to the first decades of the third century. The *Book of Thomas* consists of two parts, which may originally have circulated independently. The first part consists of a revelatory conversation between Jesus and Thomas, in which the Saviour presents himself as the one who reveals the true light and the hidden truth in a world which knows only the fire and folly of the passions. In the second part Thomas is no longer mentioned; it is a long monologue by the Saviour, including a series of lamentations about the people who are guided by the fire of their passions and a few beatifications of the people who refrain from this and must suffer greatly.

Dialogue of the Saviour Of the Thomas writings the *Gospel of Thomas* is the only one that may contain unknown but authentic sayings of Jesus. This also applies to the *Dialogue of the Saviour* (NHC III, 5),[33] which in any case shows clear similarities in content to the *Gospel of Thomas* and the *Book of Thomas* and may come partly from the same milieu. It puts great emphasis on the salvational necessity of knowledge, both of oneself and of the mysteries of the Pleroma. The difference between the world of light from which the disciples come and to which they will return and the material world in which they are fettered to the body is set out at length and leads to a call for ascesis. Yet there is no question of an evil creator-god; the creation is effected by the Father via the Logos. The author makes use of gnostic terminology known from other sources, but there are no signs that he adhered to some radical form of gnostic religion. Salvation is depicted as an entry into the bridal chamber. This could point to Valentinian influence, but the conception was also known in wider circles. The work must have had a complicated genesis. One of its sources is a dialogue between Jesus and his disciples Judas (probably the Syrian Judas Thomas), Mary Magdalen and Matthew. Regrettably, the state of the manuscript is so poor that much of the text remains unclear. Jesus' statements have parallels in the gospels of Matthew and Luke and especially in those of John and Thomas, but one still gets the impression that the conversation drew on an independent gospel tradition. In any case the author knew a text which according to Clement of Alexandria was also contained in the *Gospel of the Egyptians*, a second-century work which offers strongly ascetic interpretations of possibly authentic words of Jesus. There Salome, on asking 'How long will death have power?', is told by Jesus: 'As long as you women bear children!' He also says: 'I have

[33] Ed. S. Emmel, NHS 26 (1984); P. Létourneau, BCNH-T 29 (2003).

come to abolish the works of the female!'[34] The *Dialogue of the Saviour* clearly alludes to this scene in the *Gospel of the Egyptians* in an ascetic and anti-female passage. Judas asks: 'How should we pray?' Jesus answers: 'Pray where there is no woman!', to which Matthew responds with the words: 'He says to us "Pray where there is no woman!", which means: "Abolish the works of the female!", not because there is another manner of birth, but because they will stop giving birth' (144, 12–21 (sections 90–2)). This involves a strongly ascetic interpretation and transformation of a word of Jesus, which according to Epiphanius, *Panarion* 30, 16, 5, could be found in the Jewish-Christian *Gospel of the Ebionites*: 'I have come to abolish the sacrifices, and if you do not stop sacrificing, wrath will not stay away from you.' The *Gospel of the Egyptians* was written in the first half of the second century in Egypt and was very popular there among the so-called Encratites, an extremely ascetic Christian group. The fact that this gospel is used in the *Dialogue of the Saviour* indicates that the source with sayings of Jesus should not be dated too early (scholars have even suggested the last decades of the first century). A genesis for the entire work around the mid second century is certainly possible.

Gospel of Philip The *Gospel of Philip* (NHC II, 3), which will be explored in more depth below with the Valentinian texts, contains fifteen sayings of Jesus, of which seven occur in the canonical gospels and two in similar form in the *Gospel of Thomas*. The six others are otherwise unknown, but often have a rather gnostic, sometimes clearly Valentinian colouring, for instance in a prayer of thanks by Jesus, 58, 11–15 (section 26b): 'You who have united the perfect Light with the Holy Spirit, unite the angels with us too, as their images.' But we also find a short story and a saying of Jesus which would not be out of place in a biblical gospel: 'The Lord went into Levi's dye works. He took seventy-two coloured cloths and threw them into the cauldron. He took them out all white and said: "Thus the Son of Man has come: as a dyer!"' (63, 25–30 (section 54)).[35] Such stories about the historical Jesus are relatively rare in gnostic literature. Only his crucifixion receives attention, almost always in order to argue that the divine Christ in Jesus did not suffer, could not suffer.[36] The *Pistis Sophia* I, 61, does narrate a curious event

[34] Clement of Alexandria, *Stromateis* III, 45, 3; 63, 1–2; 64, 1; 66, 1–2; *Excerpta ex Theodoto* 67, 2. On this, see van den Broek, *Studies in Gnosticism*, pp. 184–7, and the more gnostic explanation by P. Létourneau, *Le Dialogue du Sauveur (NH III, 5)*, BCNH-T 28 (Quebec: Presses de l'Université Laval; Louvain: Éditions Peeters, 2003), pp. 296–9.

[35] As a rule, this book uses inclusive language, an exception being made for the term 'Son of Man' (as in the NRSV) and some related expressions, such as 'Heavenly Man'.

[36] See pp. 198–202.

from Jesus' youth. His mother Mary relates that Jesus was once in the vineyard with Joseph, when the Spirit entered the house in the form of Jesus and asked after his brother Jesus. Thinking it was an apparition, she tied the *doppelgänger* to a bed-leg and went to get Joseph and Jesus. When the two Jesuses saw each other, they embraced and became one. Obviously the point of the story is to underline that the divine Spirit was connected with the man Jesus, which is not in itself a typically gnostic idea.

THE BARBELO MYTH AND THE GNOSTIC EXEGESIS OF GENESIS

The *Secret Book of John* (NHC II, 1; III, 1; IV, 1; and BG 2) and the *Holy Book of the Great Invisible Spirit* (NHC III, 2 and IV, 2) are two important witnesses to the Barbelo myth. Both describe the same structure of the divine world, the apex being formed by the Great Invisible Spirit, Barbelo, and the Self-Begotten One (Father, Mother and Son), but at the same time the differences between them are so great that no direct dependence, in whatever sense, can be assumed. The *Holy Book* does mention some stories from Genesis, but it does not contain the gnostic exegesis of the first chapters of Genesis found in the *Secret Book of John*. The opposite relationship is found in the *Hypostasis of the Archons* (NHC II, 4) and the *Origin of the World* (NHC II, 5 and XIII, 2), which show a clear affinity. They pay little attention to the structure of the divine world, but do talk at length about the creation and primeval biblical history, though they stress different points. Not the entire myth of the *Secret Book* but important aspects of it return in the *Letter of Peter to Philip* (NHC VIII, 2 and Codex Tchacos 1), the *Gospel of Judas* (Codex Tchacos 3), the *Three Forms of First Thought* (NHC XIII, 1), the *Thought of Norea* (NHC IX, 2), the *Revelation of Adam* (NHC V, 5), the *Wisdom of Jesus Christ* (NHC III, 4 and BG 3), the *(Second) Apocalypse of James* (NHC V, 4) and in a large part of the *Pistis Sophia* (Codex Askewianus), which will therefore also be treated in this section. Finally, there is the mysterious work *The Thunder – Perfect Mind* (NHC VI, 2), in which the female figure who utters her revelations has sometimes been identified with Sophia.

Secret Book of John The *Secret Book* (or *Apocryphon* or *Secret Revelation*) *of John* (NHC II, 1; III, 1; IV, 1; and BG 2) is the most complete document of mythological gnostic religion.[37] It describes the divine world, the birth

[37] Ed. M. Waldstein and F. Wisse, NHMS 33 (1995). Unfortunately, the editors of this standard edition have neglected to introduce a division of the text into sections that applies to all the manuscripts. The translations by Tardieu (*Codex de Berlin*, 1984), Waldstein (*Nag Hammadi Deutsch*,

of evil through the fall of Sophia, the creation by the evil Demiurge, primeval biblical history from a gnostic perspective and salvation through gnosis. The *Secret Book* has been a keen focus of scholarly attention, often leading to the impression that it offers the gnostic myth par excellence. However, it is one of the many forms of this myth which circulated from the second century onwards. As is shown by his *AH* I, 29, Irenaeus knew a text which closely resembled that of the first part of the *Secret Book of John*, while the *Holy Book of the Great Invisible Spirit* provides a very different elaboration of the same material. Two versions of the *Apocryphon* have survived in four manuscripts. BG 2 and NHC III, 1 contain the so-called 'short recension' and NHC II, 1 and IV, 1 the 'long recension'. The most salient difference between the two redactions is that the long one has two passages lacking in the short one: in the creation of Adam a long enumeration of demons or angels who rule over the various bodily parts and psychic aspects of the human being (II, 15, 29–19, 10) and at the end a hymn on the threefold descent of Pronoia, 'Providence', from the world of light to that of darkness (II, 30, 11–31, 26). Regardless of whether these are additions or deliberate omissions, scholars generally hold that the short recension reflects an earlier stage of the text.

The *Secret Book* presents itself as a revelation of the glorified Christ to John, with a prologue and epilogue that function as a frame story. The prologue describes how John wonders in sorrow and despair how he should understand Christ and the purpose of his coming to the world. Then Christ appears to him in various forms and shows himself to be the revelation of the highest God (BG 19, 6–22, 16; NHC II, 1, 5–2, 25). In the epilogue John is ordered to write down the revelation and keep it safe (BG 75, 15–77, 5; NHC II, 31, 28–32, 6). The manifestation of Christ is followed by the first main part: a lengthy description of the structure of the divine world or 'the Pleroma', as it is termed in many gnostic writings (BG 22, 16–36, 12; NHC II, 2, 25–9, 24). The Father is described in the language of negative theology: he is so absolutely transcendent that he can only be defined in negative terms. This is not gnostic in itself, since the terminology used here was developed in Greek philosophy to describe the highest divine being and it was often employed by non-gnostic

vol. I, 2001), King (*The Secret Revelation of John*, 2006) and Barc (*Écrits gnostiques*, 2007) do offer such divisions, but they are all different (for the bibliographical data for these translations, see the Bibliography at the end of this book). The best way of referring to the *Apocryphon* is to mention the pages and lines of the Synopsis by Waldstein and Wisse. Because most readers will not have this edition at their disposal, reference will be made to BG for passages in the short recension and to NHC II for those in the long recension.

theologians, too.[38] But the genesis of the Mother, Barbelo, is cast in a mythological image: the Father sees himself reflected in the light-water surrounding him and realizes that he is seeing himself. Barbelo is therefore the First Thought of the Father, by which he becomes aware of himself.[39] Barbelo receives a spark of light from the Father and produces a Light, the Son, who is anointed by the Father with his goodness, and is therefore called the Anointed or Christ. Both Barbelo and the Son receive from the Father three helpers (aeons, divine powers). These then unite into pairs, which in their turn produce new aeons. The second of these pairs, Christ and Incorruption (*Aphtharsia*), generate the four great servants of Christ, called the Luminaries or Lights (*Phōstēres*): Harmozel, Oroiael, Daveithe and Eleleth.

The last aeon to be born, Sophia ('Wisdom'), disturbs the perfect peace and calm of the Pleroma and thus instigates the creation of the world. This forms the beginning of the second main part of the *Secret Book*, comprising the origin of the creator, the creation of the cosmos and the origin and earliest history of mankind (BG 36, 16–64, 13; NHC II, 9, 25–25, 16). The reason for the 'fall' of Sophia is said to be that, like the Father, she wanted to create something from herself, which resulted in a monstrum that she expelled from the Pleroma, where he developed into the evil creator of the world, the Demiurge, called Yaldabaoth.[40] Yaldabaoth inherited from his Mother a divine power and a vague memory of the Pleroma and on this basis he creates his own world, with his own servants: the twelve signs of the zodiac, the seven planets and countless aeons. This worldview has a clearly magical background, as is shown by the many strange, 'magic', names and the occurrence of the planetary names on a magic stone and in magic papyri. These names were not invented by the author of the *Secret Book of John* himself, because they also occur in other gnostic texts which presuppose an entirely different

[38] See further below, pp. 151–2.

[39] The etymology of the name Barbelo has been much discussed, but no consensus has been reached; for seven different opinions, see A. H. B. Logan, *Gnostic Truth and Christian Heresy. A Study in the History of Gnosticism* (Edinburgh: T&T Clark, 1996), pp. 98–100. Logan assumes that the meaning of the mythical names in the *Secret Book* must be determined from their context, but that is by no means certain. H. M. Jackson, 'The Origin in Ancient Incantory *Voces Magicae* of some Names in the Sethian Gnostic System', *VC* 43 (1989), 74–5, argued for a derivation of the name from the magic tradition.

[40] The etymology of the name Yaldabaoth is an unresolved problem, though various solutions have been proposed; see Logan, *Gnostic Truth and Christian Heresy*, pp. 126–7. Jackson, 'The Origin', pp. 71–4, assumes that the name Yaldabaoth was first used in magical incantations; Mastrocinque, *From Jewish Magic to Gnosticism*, pp. 70–9, however, thinks that the name originated in a gnostic environment and was taken over by magicians.

Pleroma.[41] The creation of the cosmos also marks the beginning of the gnostic exegesis of primeval biblical history. This exegesis comes in different variants, and if we compare these, we find that the author of the *Secret Book* has introduced some highly individual emphases.

The Demiurge thinks that he stands supreme and he proudly calls out after creating the cosmos: 'I am a jealous God and there is no other God besides me' (cf. Exod. 20:5 and Isa. 45:5). He is immediately corrected by a voice from the higher world, which cries: 'Man exists and the Son of Man.' Here in the *Secret Book* we find different traditions running together, which we will look at in another context.[42] Together with the voice from the divine world, the reflection of heavenly Man appears on the waters of the primordial chaos. Following this, Yaldabaoth urges the planetary powers to create a human being 'in God's image and after our likeness' (cf. Gen. 1:26). Typically for the *Secret Book*, the planetary powers and their 365 angels and demons make a *psychic* body.[43] But they are not capable of making their product stand up. A ruse by the 'Mother-Father of the All' induces Yaldabaoth to blow something of his Spirit, that is the power which he had inherited from Sophia, into Adam's face (cf. Gen. 2:7). As a result, Adam became a living being and was able to stand up, but more importantly the inspiration of Sophia's divine power also gave him a divine spark. Understanding that Adam was stronger and had more insight than they, the powers threw him down, to the bottom of matter. But then, even before the material Adam has been created, the salvation of his divine component starts. The highest God sends a helper to Adam, who is called Enlightening Insight ('luminous *Epinoia*')[44] (cf. Gen. 2:18–24). She

[41] See below, pp. 58, 174 and 217.

[42] See p. 175.

[43] The long list of demonical powers that create and dominate the various parts of the body according to the long recension (NHC II, 15, 29–19, 1) clearly derives from a magic background; see Jackson, 'The Origin', pp. 75–7, and J. F. Quack, 'Dekane und Gliedervergöttung. Altägyptische Traditionen im Apokryphon des Johanne's, *Jahrbuch für Antike und Christentum* 38 (1995), 97–124.

[44] Lit. 'Epinoia of (the) light'. The exact meaning of Epinoia is disputed; other translations are 'Intelligence-lumière' (Tardieu, *Codex de Berlin*, pp. 134–5), 'luminous afterthought' or 'afterthought of the light' (Layton, *Gnostic Scriptures*, p. 44), 'Reflection of the Light' and 'luminous reflection' (Waldstein and Wisse, pp. 118–19), 'Nachsehung (Epinoia) von Licht' (Walstein, in *Nag Hammadi Deutsch*, I, pp. 132–3), 'enlightened Insight' (Meyer, *Nag Hammadi Scriptures*, p. 125). The Greek word *epinoia* means 'thought, notion, conception, idea, inventiveness, invention, devise, purpose, design, afterthought, second thoughts, intelligence, reflection, retrospection' (Liddell and Scott, *Lexicon*, p. 648). The meaning 'afterthought', introduced by Layton (in his terminology 'Pronoia' is 'Forethought' and 'Epinoia' 'Afterthought') and followed by several scholars, is very unlikely here, because it is typically Sophoclean idiom; see M. Griffith, *Sophocles: Antigone* (Cambridge University Press, 1999), p. 193.

is a spiritual Eve, who is called Life and brings gnosis to Adam even before his material body is created.

Adam's earthly body is created by Yaldabaoth's powers to tighten their hold over him. They put him in paradise so that its pleasures will enslave him even more to matter. The creation of Eve is actually an attempt by Yaldabaoth to take possession of Enlightening Insight, who resides in Adam. But she withdrew and Yaldabaoth formed a woman in the image of Enlightening Insight and placed in her, too, some of the divine power which he had received from his mother. This is the 'rib' mentioned in Genesis 2:21–22. Because Adam and Eve disobey the commandment of the Demiurge and eat of the Tree of Knowledge, they receive knowledge of their origin and destiny, but are punished by being expelled from paradise. Yaldabaoth then begets two children with Eve, Eloim and Yave, that is Cain and Abel. They are demonic powers who are placed over the four elements making up the human body. But Seth is begotten by Adam, as an image of the Son of Man and the spiritual father of the gnostics, the Sethian race.

The mention of Seth's children leads the author to interrupt his account of primeval history for a discussion of the fate that awaits humankind after death (BG 65, 13–71, 2; NHC II, 25, 16–27, 30). He does this in the form of seven questions asked by John and the answers given by Christ. Thus begins the third main part of the *Secret Book of John*. The author is found to support a broad, almost non-gnostic doctrine of salvation. What it amounts to is that only those who have received gnosis, but later reject it, are lost for ever. All others, including non-gnostics, will be saved.

When Yaldabaoth sees that he is in danger of losing his hold over humanity, he takes several countermeasures (BG 71, 3–75, 10; NHC II, 27, 31–30, 11). First he produces, together with his powers, the bitter Fate that inexorably visits all kinds of evils on people and keeps them enthralled to oblivion. Next he decides to destroy all mankind in an enormous flood, but this is prevented by Enlightening Insight, who informed Noah. Finally, the Demiurge devises a new plan to subjugate the people: he has his angels beget offspring with human females (cf. Gen. 6:1–14), which is therefore placed after the Flood here. This is immediately followed in the longer redaction, without any transition, by the Song of Pronoia (NHC II, 30, 11–31, 26).

It is a controversial question whether the Song of Pronoia, also called the Providence Monologue, was later added in the longer redaction or omitted from the shorter. However that may be, it is certain that the concluding hymn was not written by the author of the *Apocryphon*, but is older and originally circulated as an independent piece. In the hymn 'the Perfect Providence [*Pronoia*] of the All' tells about her three descents from the world of Light into the darkness of chaos, that is to say our world, which is presented as a prison and as the underworld. Twice her mission failed, because the 'foundations of chaos', meaning the evil powers, threatened to destroy her and the imprisoned. But the third time her mission was successful: she arrived at the centre of the prison and cried out: 'Let whoever hears arise from his deep sleep.' She awakens the human being from his sleep of ignorance and brings him gnosis. At the end she says: 'I raised and sealed him in the light of the water, with five seals, so that death might not have power over him from that moment on.' This is an allusion to a baptismal ritual, the 'sacrament of the five seals', which was practised by the gnostics of the Barbelo myth and which we will encounter several times again.

The dating of the *Secret Book of John* is disputed. All signs indicate that both redactions had a long genesis, it being clear that the long recension underwent more revision and in this sense is 'younger' than the short one. It is therefore likely that both versions took on their present form only in the course of the third century.[45] Irenaeus, *AH* I, 29, apparently knew a form of the *Apocryphon* agreeing most closely with the short recension, though the latter is more strongly revised. It follows that in any case the original Greek version must have been written before 170.

Holy Book of the Great Invisible Spirit In the manuscript colophon the *Holy Book of the Great Invisible Spirit* (NHC III, 2; IV, 2)[46] is also called the *Egyptian Gospel* by the copyist. It was long known as the *Gospel of the Egyptians*, but this was based on a completely unnecessary textual correction by the first editors of the text, which also led to confusion with the second-century apocryphal gospel of that name, fragments of which are preserved in Clement of Alexandria.[47] The *Holy Book* must have been quite popular, since the two Coptic translations were made independently of each other and moreover go back to two different versions of the Greek text. Unfortunately, owing to the poor condition of the manuscript, the text of NHC IV, 2 in particular has been passed down in a very fragmentary state, but the text of NHC III, 2 also contains quite a few lacunae, and pages 45–8 have been lost altogether. But we are dealing here with an important text,

45 There are extensive discussions of the dating of the *Apocryphon*'s stages of development in M. Tardieu, *Écrits gnostiques. Codex de Berlin* (Paris: Les Éditions du Cerf, 1984), pp. 40–6, and Logan, *Gnostic Truth and Christian Heresy*, pp. 42–56.

46 Ed. A. Böhlig and F. Wisse, NHS 4 (1975).

47 See pp. 42–3.

which falls into two parts after a eulogy to the Great Invisible Spirit. The first part provides a lengthy description of the Pleroma and the origin of the evil powers. On the one hand this description is clearly connected with the views in the *Secret Book of John*, but on the other it gives an entirely distinctive, rather confusing, representation, because a large number of new celestial figures are introduced. It is therefore quite clear that the *Holy Book* does not depend directly on the *Apocryphon*. A striking feature is the use of magic formulas, like the seven vowels, which are each repeated twenty-two times in the order *i ē o u e a ō*, to describe the secret divine name (NHC III, 44, 3–9) or the designation of the heavenly Adamas as a threefold *ien ien ea ea ea* (NHC III, 49, 6–7). The second part treats of the Great Seth, a heavenly figure who appears several times as a saviour and as such has 'put on' the physical shape of the 'living Jesus' (NHC III, 64, 1–2). However, the Christian influence in this work is minimal.[48] It is all the more interesting that particularly the second part puts great emphasis on baptism as the moment when salvation is brought about, in connection with which various hymnic texts are quoted (NHC III, 66, 8–68, 1). The *Holy Book* has preserved here some liturgical documents which were probably used in the baptismal practice of the gnostic, barely Christian, community in which this text originated. To give an impression of the nature of these hymns, I quote the first here, after NHC III, 66, 8–22:[49]

Iē Ieus ēō ou ēō ōua!
Truly, truly!
Yesseus Mazareus Yessedekeus, Living water!
Child of the child, glorious name!
Truly, truly! aeon-that-is!
iiii ēēēē eeee oooo uuuu ōōōō aaaa!
Truly, truly!
Ēi aaaa ōōōō, He-Who-Is, who sees the aeons!
Truly, truly!
Aee ēēē iiii uuuuuu ōōōōōōōō, who exists eternally!
Truly, truly!
Iēa aiō, in the heart He-Who-Is.
Uaei eisaei eioei eiosei!

The magic character of these hymns is obvious. Hence they could also relate to a baptism in the celestial regions, which is particularly mentioned in texts of the 'heavenly journeys' type read in the school of Plotinus and to be discussed below. But even then it remains likely that a baptismal

48 On this, see pp. 185–8.
49 For another example, see p. 187

ritual was practised in the gnostic community where these liturgical texts had their origin. Also, the names of divine powers mentioned in the *Holy Book* return in various later texts, including Yesseus Mazareus Yessedekeus (NHC III, 64, 10–11, 66, 10; IV, 75, 25–6, 78, 12–13) and the three angelic powers Micheus, Michar and Mnesinous, 'who have control over the source of truth' (NHC III, 64, 14–16 (see also 20); IV, 76, 2–4 (see also 9–10)).[50] It seems probable that these later works drew on the same tradition as the *Holy Book* or were directly influenced by it. Because we do not know the background and age of these baptismal conceptions and cannot properly determine the relationship between the *Holy Book* and the *Secret Book of John*, the work is hard to date. It may well have been written in the second half of the second century.

Nature of the Rulers The *Nature of the Rulers* (or *Hypostasis of the Archons*; NHC II, 4)[51] consists of two parts, preceded by a short introduction. The first part contains a version of the gnostic exegesis of primeval biblical history (NHC II, 86, 27–92, 18 (sections 2–14)),[52] the second part a revelation of the angel Eleleth regarding the origin, the history and the eventual destruction of the rulers or archons, the evil powers that rule the world (NHC II, 93, 18–97, 21 (sections 19–39)). The two parts go back to originally separate sources which have been connected in this text in a not entirely successful way. In the short introduction the author refers to Paul's remark that our struggle is not against flesh and blood, but against the evil powers of the cosmos (Eph. 6:12).

The first part deals with the wicked activity of the rulers, but also makes it clear that liberating gnosis was revealed to people from the start. Here, too, there is the proud cry of the Prince of the rulers: 'I am God, there is no one besides me', which is answered by a voice from Incorruptibility that says: 'You are mistaken, Samael' – a name which is explained as 'God of the blind'; the name Yaldabaoth only occurs in the second part. The Pleroma is not described, but simply referred to as Incorruptibility. The powers cannot gain control over the reflection of Incorruptibility that appears on the waters of the primeval chaos, and they therefore decide to fashion a man from the dust of the earth 'after their body and after

[50] See pp. 60–1. An important discussion of these texts can be found in J.-M. Sevrin, *Le dossier baptismal séthien. Études sur la sacramentaire gnostique*, BCNH-É 2 (Quebec: Presses de l'Université Laval, 1986).

[51] Ed. B. Barc, BCNH-T 5 (1980), pp. 1–147; R. A. Bullard and B. Layton, NHS 20 (1989), pp. 219–59; U. U. Kaiser, TU 156 (2006).

[52] The sections refer to the division of the text in Layton's edition. Unfortunately, this division was not taken over in later English, French and German translations.

the image of God that had appeared to them in the water.' The rest of the story follows the same pattern as the *Secret Book of John*, but with all kinds of differences. When the first people see their nakedness after eating from the Tree of Knowledge, they realize 'that they were naked of the spiritual'. Adam and Eve not only have sons, but also a daughter, Norea (here also Orea), whom other texts sometimes present as Seth's wife and sometimes as Noah's.[53] In this text she is in any case associated with Noah, since he refuses to let her come on board of the ark, after which she sets fire to the ark! When the archons want to rape her, the great angel Eleleth descends to save her and instruct her about her origin (NHC II, 92, 18–93, 13 (sections 15–18)). This is followed by Eleleth's revelation concerning the powers, which is related by Norea.

The *Nature of the Rulers* has the same motif of Sophia's fall as the *Apocryphon of John* (NHC II, 94, 5–8 (section 22)). Her product, in the form of a lion, is called Samael, Saklas ('Fool') and Yaldabaoth. There are similarities to the report in the *Apocryphon of John*, but with one huge difference. When for the second time Yaldabaoth calls out to his children: 'I am the God of the All', Zoe ('Life'), the daughter of Pistis Sophia, cries: 'You are mistaken, Saklas!', and has him bound and cast down into the underworld. His son Sabaoth then repents and is placed by Sophia and Zoe in the seventh heaven. Sophia seats her daughter Zoe on his right and the 'Angel of Wrath' on his left. Through Envy and Death Yaldabaoth then begets the rulers of the 'heavens of chaos' (NHC II, 95, 4–96, 17 (sections 26–3)).

The work ends by predicting the destruction of the evil powers and the salvation of Norea and her children (NHC II, 96, 17–97, 22 (sections 32–39)). This will come to pass when 'the true Man in a human body reveals [the Spirit?] of Truth sent by the Father'. This is an unmistakable allusion to Christ. He brings gnosis, he will 'instruct them about everything ... Then they will cast off blind thought and trample underfoot death, which belongs to the powers. And they will ascend into the limitless light, where this race belongs.'

The most striking aspect of the *Nature of the Rulers* is that Yaldabaoth is relegated to the level of the devil and so is no longer identified with the God of the Old Testament. This role is now taken over by his son Sabaoth, who is judged much more positively, though he preserves the strictness and the injustice of his father the archon via the Angel of wrath. Most

[53] See B. A. Pearson, 'The Figure of Norea in Gnostic Literature', in *Gnosticism, Judaism, and Egyptian Christianity* (Minneapolis: Fortress Press, 1990), 84–94.

scholars see this elevation of Sabaoth above Yaldabaoth as an attempt to make the gnostic interpretation of the Jewish Bible more acceptable for Jews. The same motif occurs in the *Origin of the World*, which will be discussed below.

There are conjectures but no hard facts regarding the work's place of origin and date. Most scholars assume on rather shaky grounds that the text originated in Alexandria in the first half of the third century. But in fact there is no reason why the work could not have been written in the second century. The assimilated sources could well derive from the first half of that century.

Origin of the World The *Origin of the World* (NHC II, 5)[54] does not have a title in the manuscript, and was therefore called the *Treatise without Title* by the first editors. This name is sometimes still used, but because it is meaningless and the second text of the Bruce Codex bears a similar name, the more indicative title now prevails. The work must have been popular in the fourth century, since three Coptic manuscripts are known. Besides the well-preserved manuscript of NHC II, 5, the first ten lines of the text also survive in NHC XIII, 2.[55] Though there is little reference material, it is quite clear that the texts of NHC II, 5 and XIII, 2 are copies of the same translation from Greek. Of the third manuscript there are no more than a few shreds of papyrus, stored in the British Library (BL Or. 4926–1).[56] It is certain that this Coptic text harks back to a translation from Greek that was independent of the other texts. It is always surprising that gnostic texts were so popular among the Coptic-speaking population of fourth-century Egypt that some of them were translated more than once.

The *Origin of the World* is confusingly complex, but the basic structure is perfectly clear. It is determined by the combination of the same two sources underlying the *Nature of the Rulers*, but in reverse order. The first part deals with the origin of the powers of chaos and the creation of heaven and earth (NHC II, 97, 24–112, 25 (sections 1–65)),[57] the second part discusses the creation of Adam and Eve until their life outside of paradise (II, 112, 25–123, 31 (sections 66–127)) and a short concluding part talks about salvation and the end of time (II, 123, 31–127, 17 (sections 128–50)). A comparison with the *Nature of the Rulers* shows that the author

54 Ed. H.-G. Bethge, B. Layton *et al.*, NHS 21 (1989), pp. 12–93; L. Painchaud, BCNH 21 (1995).

55 Ed. B. Layton, NHS 21 (1989), p. 94, and J. D. Turner, NHS 28 (1990), pp. 455–7; L. Painchaud, BCNH-T 21 (1995), p. 527.

56 Ed. B. Layton, NHS 21 (1989), pp. 95–134; L. Painchaud, BCNH-T 21 (1995), pp. 529–70.

57 The sections refer to the division of the text in Layton's edition. In this case, too, this division was not taken over in later English, French and German translations.

has revised and supplemented his sources in various particulars. But it is unthinkable that he is also responsible for passages which flatly contradict what he had just claimed. These are apparently additions by later redactors who wanted to correct the views of the original author. The corrective additions have often been introduced into the text in a rather unfortunate manner, so that the work is full of abrupt transitions and internal contradictions. Given the nature of the additions, it is clear that in any case a Valentinian gnostic thoroughly revised the text, but certainly more hands were involved. This emerges for instance from the description of the elevation of Sabaoth, who occupies an important place in this text, too. Here various contradictory conceptions have been jumbled together, making it difficult to determine what is original and what has been added later and in what order.

The creation of the world is introduced by a passage about the birth of Eros, an androgynous figure, presented here as the inspiration of sexuality and the reproductive urge, which are strongly rejected. It is to him that not only people but also plants and animals owe their existence (NHC II, 109, 1–110, 1; 111, 8–28 (sections 49–53, 58–60)). Paradise is relatively good, it is located above the spheres of the moon and sun and attributed to 'Justice', by which Sabaoth is meant (II, 110, 2–111, 8 (sections 54–7)).

The creation of Adam and Eve broadly proceeds along the usual lines of the gnostic exegesis of Genesis. Except that here the spiritual Eve, an androgynous creature, is created first: she is given the task of teaching the coming Adam about his divine origin and thus liberate him from the evil powers. So there is already an Enlightener before the humans are created! But the history of Adam and Eve is also punctuated with various additions that render it incoherent. One of these is the remark that there are three Adams: a spiritual, a psychic and a material Adam (NHC II, 117, 28–118, 2 (section 98)).[58] Later this is developed so that there are three kinds of people in the same sense. This tripartition clearly reveals the hand of the Valentinian reviser, but the passage is immediately followed by a difficult argument about three phoenixes, the irrigation works of Egypt[59] and two Egyptian bulls, of which the first refers to 'the angels', the second to baptism and the bulls to Sabaoth and Yaldabaoth (II, 122,

[58] See p. 216.

[59] The Coptic words *nhydria mmoou* have provoked much debate; these 'water hydria' are mostly interpreted as 'water serpents' (crocodiles or otters) or 'water pots'. I take the Greek word *hydria* as a Graeco-Egyptian spelling of *hydreia*, 'drawing or distribution of water, watering, irrigation' (Liddell and Scott, *Lexicon*, 1844b). The word is attested in the Greek documentary papyri, with respect to the irrigation tax (*phoros hydreias*), in P. Panop. 8.9 [papyrus: *hydrias* (!)] and 10.6, edited by L. C. Youtie, D. Hagedorn and H. C. Youtie, 'Urkunden aus Panopolis I', *ZPE*

6–123, 2 (sections 116–22)). Again it is hard here to establish what is original and what was added later.

In this text, too, salvation means the gift of gnosis, by which gnostics gain knowledge of their origin, present situation and destiny. Again salvation starts here immediately after the schism in the Pleroma, with the creation of the spiritual Eve, the 'teacher of Life' (NHC II, 113, 17–34 (sections 70–2)). She is identical with Sophia Zoe, whose breath gives Adam life and with Zoe herself, who causes Adam to stand up and later goes in to the Tree of the Knowledge of Good and Evil, whence she teaches the principle of gnosis to Adam and Eve, which is 'that they were naked of knowledge' (II, 119, 13–15 (section 104)). In the time of the Flood the fourth great Light, Eleleth, brings gnosis to Norea, who on the one hand is also a saviour figure and on the other the prototype of the saved gnostic. Towards the end a picture of salvation is drawn in which various, sometimes contradictory traditions have been incorporated. The dominant, Valentinian conception here is that of the heavenly counterparts of the gnostics, their 'angels'. According to the text, these angels appear in our world to reveal the imperishable world and expose the true nature of the powers that rule us (II, 124, 4–32 (sections 130–4)). Christ has only relative importance in the work of salvation. His function is nothing but that of the 'angels', the heavenly likenesses of the gnostics: to reveal what was previously hidden (II, 125, 15–19 (section 139)). These Valentinian deliberations are suddenly interrupted by a conflicting view: it is said that the Saviour instituted a fourth race, elevated above the other three (II, 124, 32–125, 7 (sections 135–6)). A later reader/redactor apparently found too much subtlety in the Valentinian distinction between three categories. He calls this fourth kind the 'race-without-king', a term used in some non-Valentinian circles to denote the gnostics, as a group which differed totally from the rest of mankind.

The fact that the Valentinian view of salvation is not original, but was added by a later reviser, is not only shown by its abrupt appearance, but also because earlier the text talks about another Saviour: Immortal Man or True Man. He is the manifestation of the Unknown God, whose reflection became visible on the waters of the primeval chaos and who will appear in the last days. The gnostics 'are produced by the True Man at the consummation through the Word' (NHC II, 117, 10–12 (section 93)), they belong with the Immortal Man (II, 123, 32–34 (section 128)).

7 (1971), pp. 23–5 and 27–9 respectively; also in *Sammelbuch griechischer Urkunden aus Ägypten*, vol. XII (Wiesbaden: Harrassowitz, 1976–7), nos. 10975 and 10977.

The *Origin of the World* was almost certainly composed in Egypt: this is suggested not only by the mention of some typically Egyptian matters (phoenix, irrigation, bulls) and the remark that only Egypt resembles the paradise of God (NHC II, 122, 33–123, 2 (section 122)), but also by various conceptions which in combination can only really have their background in Alexandria. The final redaction of the work should perhaps be dated as late as the first decades of the fourth century, if it is in fact true that a clearly Manichaean influence can be detected, since the view that plants grew from blood poured onto the earth by the evil powers (II, 109, 25–28; III, 8–28 (sections 53, 58–60)) strongly recalls a similar conception in Manichaeism, though there the body fluid is semen not blood. But even if this is discounted, the complex redactional history of the text suggests that its present form was not reached until the third century. The Valentinian redactor could have carried out his revision at the end of the second century, which implies that the original version was written earlier. As we noted for the *Nature of the Rulers*, the sources may go back to the first half of the second century. The situation for the dating of most gnostic writings applies here, too: there are more uncertainties than conclusive proofs.

Letter of Peter to Philip The *Letter of Peter to Philip* survives in two manuscripts (NHC VIII, 2 and Codex Tchacos I).[60] These contain two independent translations from Greek, though in content the two versions are not very different. The title derives from a short letter of Peter to Philip which opens the work. Peter, 'the apostle of Jesus Christ', reports there that Christ enjoined the disciples to come together to be instructed in the proclamation of the gospel. But apparently Philip had left the other apostles and avoided a meeting with them. Perhaps the implication is that he went to proclaim the gospel on his own authority, without having received the Holy Spirit (cf. Acts 8, esp. verses 14–17).[61] Peter asks him to come after all, 'as our God Jesus commanded'. Philip agrees and Peter convenes the entire group of apostles on the Mount of Olives. What follows is largely based on the account in Acts 1 and 2. A eulogy to the Father and a prayer to Christ for help is followed by the appearance of a great light, from which Christ assures them that he is always with

[60] NHC VIII, 2: Ed. J-É. Ménard, BCNH-T 1 (1977); M. W. Meyer and F. Wisse, NHS 31 (1991), pp. 227–51; H.-G. Bethge, TU 141 (1997). Codex Tchacos: Kasser, Wurst *et al.*, *The Gospel of Judas … Critical Edition*, pp. 79–114; J. Brankaer and H.-G. Bethge, TU 161 (2007), pp. 5–80; G. Wurst and M. Meyer, in Krosney, Meyer and Wurst, 'Preliminary Report', pp. 289–94.

[61] M. Kaler, 'The Letter of Peter to Philip and its Messages of Gnostic Revelation and Christian Unity', *VC* 63 (2009), 264–95, rightly points to a strong intertextual relationship with Acts 7–9; in Philip's return he sees an appeal for Christian unity, which seems less probable.

them. They then ask him some questions which are vitally important for gnostics and are in fact formulated in various gnostic texts: what caused the shortcomings in the aeons and the Pleroma, how are we detained in this world, how did we come here and how shall we depart, how do we gain the power to speak out freely and why do the powers fight against us? Christ answers by briefly summarizing the gnostic myth (the fall of Sophia, the Mother and the origin of the rulers), a remarkable feature being some close similarities to the *Nature of the Rulers*. The author's brief and unparticularized allusions indicate that he assumes his readers to be familiar with the myth. The apostles are told that they are detained in the world because they belong to Christ: they are to become bringers of light amidst dead people. Their main task is to fight against the demonic rulers of this world. The purpose of the summary was clearly therefore to instruct the disciples about the archons. Back in Jerusalem the disciples return to the temple, where Peter, as in Acts 2, delivers a speech, if only to the disciples and before the descent of the Holy Spirit. It is interesting that he utters a hymn-like confession of Christ to which few Christians could have objected. It was probably an existing liturgical text, but one to which the author added a denial of Christ's suffering, so that the tone of the whole piece becomes polemical. The passage reads:

> Our Enlightener, Jesus, came down
> and was crucified,
> and he wore a crown of thorns
> and he put on a purple garment,
> and he was nailed to a tree
> and he was buried in a tomb
> and he rose from the dead.
> My brothers, Jesus is a stranger to this suffering, but it is we who have suffered through the Mother's transgression. (139, 15–23)

The work ends with two appearances by Jesus and the gift of the Holy Spirit, after which the apostles dispersed to 'proclaim the Lord Jesus'. Again it is impossible to date this work accurately, but the incorporation of New Testament elements and the similarities to apocryphal literature on the apostles suggest that the work may have taken shape around 200.

Gospel of Judas Until recently the *Gospel of Judas* (Codex Tchacos 3)[62] was only known from a brief mention in Irenaeus of Lyons, *AH* I, 31, I. Irenaeus wrote around 180 CE and there is no reason to assume that he was

62 Ed. Kasser, Wurst *et al.*, *The Gospel of Judas … Critical Edition*, pp. 183–252; G. Wurst and M. Meyer, in Krosney, Meyer and Wurst, 'Preliminary Report', pp. 289–94; J. Brankaer and H.-G. Bethge, TU 161 (2007), pp. 255–372.

not referring to the lately rediscovered gospel. It was probably written in the mid second century. On the one hand the text offers a sharp rejection of the ecclesiastical institutions and Christology of non-gnostic Christianity. One the other it provides an exposition of gnostic views on the divine world of light, the demonic rulers and their destruction, humankind and the salvation of the elect (47, 1–57, 15).[63] The summary of the gnostic myth is longer than in the *Letter of Peter to Philip*, though here, too, the author assumes much to be known. In a large, unlimited world lives the Great Invisible Spirit, who is totally unknowable. From a great cloud of light he brings into being a great angel, 'the Self-Begotten, the God of light', from another cloud he brings into being four angels to serve him. In the *Apocryphon of John* and other texts we also encounter the 'Self-Begotten' (*Autogenēs*) Son with his four servants, the great Lights. The Mother, Barbelo, is not mentioned in this context, but her presence in this myth is affirmed earlier in the gospel, when Judas professes of Christ: 'You have come from the immortal world [aeon] of Barbelo' (35, 17–18). Next, 360 lights and for them 360 firmaments or celestial spheres come into being, a conception which also occurs with the same calculation in *Eugnostus*, NHC III, 84, 12–85, 7 (and with regard to the demonic powers in the short redaction of the *Apocryphon of John*, BG 39, 10–15, via a slightly different calculation). The rulers of the world of chaos, led by two creative demonic powers, Nebro and Saklas, come into being on the initiative of the fourth great Light, Eleleth – an account which strongly resembles that in the *Holy Book of the Great Invisible Spirit* (NHC III, 56, 22–58, 22) and the *Three Forms of First Thought* (NHC XIII, 39, 13–28). The (magic) names of the twelve signs of the zodiac, of which only five are mentioned here, also occur with variants in the *Apocryphon of John* (BG 40, 5–18; NHC II, 10, 28–11, 4) and the *Holy Book* (NHC III, 58, 8–22; IV, 70, 1–5).[64] But Jesus laughs at all these powers: 'they will all be destroyed, together with their creatures' (Codex Tchacos 55, 19–20). It is hard to imagine that the author has picked up his material here from the related works mentioned; it is more likely that he and the other gnostic authors drew on a magic-astrological work, now lost, that was revised along gnostic lines.

[63] Since its discovery scholars have paid a great deal of attention to the *Gospel of Judas*. Here only two conference volumes may be mentioned: M. Scopello (ed.), *The Gospel of Judas in Context. Proceedings of the First International Conference on the Gospel of Judas, Paris, Sorbonne, October 27th–28th, 2006*, NHMS 62 (Leiden: Brill, 2008), and A. D. DeConick (ed.), *The Codex Judas Papers. Proceedings of the International Congress on the Tchacos Codex held at Rice University, Houston, Texas, March 13–16, 2008*, NHMS 71 (Leiden: Brill, 2009).

[64] See the penetrating analysis by J. D. Turner, 'The Place of the *Gospel of Judas* in Sethian Tradition', in Scopello (ed.), *The Gospel of Judas in Context*, pp. 187–237.

The role Judas plays in the gospel that bears his name has become a subject of much debate. The first editors interpreted the figure of Judas as the perfect gnostic, who was the only disciple who recognized Jesus' true nature and was initiated by him into the mysteries of the divine world and was promised that he finally would enter that world. He was not the traitor, as tradition depicted him, but the friend of Jesus, who realized the deliverance of Jesus' divine inner being from his carnal body by handing him over to the Jews, in order to be crucified by the evil powers of the cosmos. This view of the 'good Judas' became generally known to the public at large, but it was disputed by scholars almost immediately after the publication of the Coptic text. They convincingly argued that the first editors had misread and even occasionally mistranslated the text, and that Judas also in his *Gospel* is the traitor he always was, though his real function remains a matter of dispute. According to some scholars, his privileged position points to some kind of salvation, according to others he is a demonic figure, doomed by fate to betray Jesus and to end up in the realm of Saklas or Yaldabaoth.[65] This debate will certainly continue, but it seems certain that the function of Judas in his *Gospel* is more complicated than the dilemma: 'hero or villain?' suggests.

Revelation of Adam The *Revelation* (or *Apocalypse*) *of Adam* (NHC V, 5)[66] is a gnostic representative of the Adamic literature popular among Jews and Christians in the first centuries CE. Epiphanius, *Panarion* 26, 8, 1, reports that 'the gnostics' used various 'Apocalypses of Adam', such as 'books under the name of Seth', but the contents of these are unknown. The Manichaeans also knew an 'Apocalypse of Adam'. The Cologne Mani-Codex, 48, 16–50, 7, quotes its beginning, which shows that it was a different work from the Nag Hammadi text. In it Adam, in the seven-hundredth year of his life, relates to his son Seth what happened to him and Eve in paradise and foretells what the future of the chosen race of Seth will be. Initially Adam and Eve were one and they possessed the gnosis of the eternal God. But the creator-god, who is called 'the All-Sovereign' (*pantokratōr*) and Sakla, 'Fool', divided them into two, so that with their

65 The positive view of Judas was already severely criticized at the first international conference on the *Gospel of Judas* (Paris, 2006) by E. Thomassen, L. Painchaud, J. D. Turner and A. D. DeConick; see their contributions in Scopello (ed.), *The Gospel of Judas in Context*, under the heading 'Judas: Hero or Villain?', pp. 157–264. See also DeConick, *The Thirteenth Apostle*, who argues that Judas finally became identical with Yaldabaoth. B. A. Pearson was another leading scholar who rejected the view of the 'good Judas'; see DeConick, *Thirteenth Apostle*, p. xxiv. E. Pagels and K. L. King, *Reading Judas. The Gospel of Judas and the Shaping of Christianity* (New York: Viking Penguin, 2007), read the *Gospel of Judas* primarily as a vehement protest against the idea of other Christians that God desired the bloody sacrifice of Christ for the atonement of mankind and that Christians ought to glorify themselves through martyrdom.

66 Ed. G. W. MacRae, NHS 11 (1979), pp. 151–95; F. Morard, BCNH-T 15 (1985).

unity they also lost their gnosis (64, 6–28). The text suggests that this loss was caused by the sexual desire aroused in Adam, so that he fell into the power of death (67, 2–14). Three heavenly figures reveal to Adam in a vision how the creator-god will vainly try three times to destroy the Sethian race: by water (the Flood), by fire (Sodom and Gomorrah?) and with the arrival of the 'Enlightener with gnosis', at the end of days. This Enlightener is an incarnation of the heavenly Seth, after whom the earthly Seth was named (65, 5–8). The powers of the creator-god wonder who he is. What follows is a long list with statements by the thirteen 'kingdoms' of these powers about the nature of the Enlightener, all ending with the curious sentence: 'And thus he came to the water.' All thirteen statements are false, only the 'race-without-king', the Sethian race, knows the right answer. At the end of time those who persecuted the Enlightener and the elect will realize their mistake and beg for mercy, but 'Micheus, Michar and Mnesinous, who oversee the holy baptism and the living water' (84, 5–8), will reject them. They say that the words of the 'God of aeons' have not been put to paper, but will be written 'on a tall mountain, on a rock of truth'. This reflects the well-known tradition that the descendants of Seth wrote the wisdom from before the Flood on two steles (Flavius Josephus, *Jewish Antiquities* I, 70–1). The text ends with these words: 'This is the hidden gnosis of Adam, which he gave to Seth, that is to say, the holy baptism of those who know the eternal gnosis by those born from the Logos and the immortal Enlighteners, who came forth from the holy seed: Yesseus, Mazareus, Yessedekeus, [the living] water' (85, 22–31). The mention of baptism and the names of the angelic powers who play a role in it show that the gnostic community in which this text originated followed probably the same baptismal rituals as those mentioned in the *Holy Book of the Great Invisible Spirit*. Strikingly, the text shows no sign of any Christian influence. Perhaps it derives from an (originally) Jewish and gnostic baptist group. It need not depend directly on the *Holy Book*; both probably originated in the same milieu. The *Apocalypse of Adam* could well be the older of the two; a date in the second century is certainly a possibility.

Three Forms of First Thought The *Three Forms of First Thought* (NHC XIII, 1)[67] is a self-revelation of the universal First Thought (*Protennoia*) of the great unknowable Spirit, who declares herself to be identical with the divine mother Barbelo. The work starts with a long presentation of Protennoia herself, in short sentences all of which start with 'I', for instance in XIII, 35, 24–33:

[67] Ed. Y. Janssens, BCNH-T 4 (1978); J. D. Turner, NHS 28 (1990), pp. 371–454; P.-H. Poirier, BCNH-T 32 (2006).

I am the Invisible One in the All.
I consider what is hidden,
for I know everything found in it.
I am uncountable, more than anyone else.
I am immeasurable, ineffable.
But I will reveal myself if I want to.
I am [the movement] of the All,
because I precede the All.
I am the All, because I am in everybody.
I am a sound [resounding sof]tly.

Such a self-presentation in the 'I am' form is found more often, most impressively in *The Thunder – Perfect Spirit* (NHC VI, 2).[68] Protennoia reports that she descended three times into the world of chaos in which people live, first manifesting herself as a vague sound, then as a voice and finally as articulated speech, the word, which is identified with *the* Word, the Logos. These manifestations are at the same time expressions of the gnostic trinity of Father, Mother and Son. The description of the three self-revelations, which are often also characterized by series of statements in the first person, is regularly interrupted by reflections on the gnostic myth and the salvation acquired via gnosis. Here, too, the Son is called the Self-Begotten (*Autogenēs*); his four servants, the great Lights, are mentioned by name, but here they have more extended names than in the *Secret Book of John* and other related texts (38, 33–39, 7). As we noted before, the description of the genesis of the powers of chaos shows a close resemblance to the *Gospel of Judas* and the *Holy Book of the Great Invisible Spirit*. In accordance with the standard gnostic myth, the evil world creator is called Saklas, Samael and Yaltabaoth, with the usual mention of his boast that he is the only God. As regards salvation, there are also similarities to the *Holy Book of the Great Invisible Spirit* and to later works like *Zostrianus*, such as the emphasis on a baptism of the gnostic in the heavenly regions and the mention of the three angels who play a part in this: 'And I gave him to the baptizers, Micheus, Michar and Mnesinous, and they baptized him and washed him in the spring of the water of life' (48, 18–21).

The *Three Forms of First Thought* has come to play an important role in debates over the origin of the Prologue to the Gospel of John (1:1–18), because various scholars believe that the conceptions in the *Three Forms* are more coherent and older than those of the Prologue. It seems more likely, however, that there is no interdependence, in whatever sense, but

[68] See p. 70.

that both texts are dependent on early Jewish speculations about the divine Wisdom.[69] Everything shows that the *Three Forms of First Thought* had a complicated genesis. The relationship with the *Holy Book of the Great Invisible Spirit* and fairly late writings like *Zostrianus* suggests that it did not assume its final form until the first half of the third century.

Melchizedek The work *Melchizedek* (NHC IX, 1)[70] has been passed down only fragmentarily owing to the poor state of the manuscript: more than half has been lost and of the roughly 750 lines only 19 have been preserved without lacunae. Not surprisingly, therefore, the work has been given rather differing interpretations. According to some researchers, it is an originally non-gnostic Judaeo-Christian work to which a light gnostic touch has been added,[71] others see it as a 'Sethian' work, though one in which the author has moved so far towards orthodoxy that his work can no longer really be called gnostic,[72] and still others seem to see no problem in the poor transmission and believe that the text offers a clear, purely gnostic ('Sethian') system.[73] Some caution in judging the text is therefore required. In any case the work fits in with the speculations about Melchizedek that were popular among Jews and Christians in the first centuries CE. Genesis 14:18 says of this mysterious priest of Salem, who brought bread and wine to Abraham: 'He was the priest of God Most High.' The kings of Israel saw themselves as priests in Jerusalem, in the style of Melchizedek (Ps. 110:4). In earliest Christianity the traditions about Melchizedek were used to interpret the figure of Christ. This is already the case in the New Testament Letter to the Hebrews (5:6 and 10; 6:20; 7), and it seems to be mainly this interpretation which forms the background to *Melchizedek*.

Despite the many lacunae, it seems certain that *Melchizedek* consists of two revelations that came to Melchizedek (NHC IX, 1, 1–14, 15 and 18 end–27, 10) with in between a liturgical passage (14, 15 up to 18 end). Without

69 See M. Waldstein, 'The *Providence Monologue* in the Apocryphon of John and the *Johannine Prologue*', *JECS* 3 (1995), 369–402, and van den Broek, *Studies in Gnosticism*, pp. 86–116; for another view (influence of the first chapters of Genesis), see N. Denzey, 'Genesis Traditions in Conflict? The Use of some Exegetical Traditions in the *Trimorphic Protennoia* and the Johannine Prologue', *VC* 55 (2001), 20–44, and G. P. Luttikhuizen, *Gnostic Revisions of Genesis Stories and Early Jesus Traditions*, NHMS 58 (Brill: Leiden, 2006), pp. 157–61.

70 Ed. B. A. Pearson and S. Giversen, NHS 15 (1981), pp. 19–85; W.-P. Funk, J.-P. Mahé and C. Gianotto, BCNH-T 28 (2001).

71 Pearson, in NHS 15 (1981), pp. 34–38, and 'The Figure of Melchizedek in Gnostic Literature', in *Gnosticism, Judaism, and Egyptian Christianity*, pp. 110–16.

72 H.-M. Schenke, in *Nag Hammadi Deutsch*, vol. II, p. 680.

73 Mahé in his introduction to the edition by Funk, Mahé and Gianotto, pp. 1–61; also Mahé, in *Écrits gnostiques*, pp. 1347–56.

any introduction the work starts immediately with a revelation about the coming of Jesus Christ and his crucifixion and resurrection. This revelation is almost certainly given by Gamaliel, who in the *Holy Book of the Great Invisible Spirit* is the servant of the first Great Light, Armozel, who in turn is the first servant of Christ. It is his task to wrest 'the assembly [*ekklēsia*] of the children of Seth' from the powers of darkness (5, 17–22); Gamaliel has the same task in the *Three Forms of First Thought* (48, 27–8). The most striking aspect of this first revelation, which happens to occur in the best-preserved passage of the entire work, is the sharp rejection of the notion that Jesus had a phantom body. Though this is not entirely exceptional in a gnostic text, it is surprising to find the following prophecy:

They will also say of him:
'He was not born,' though he was born;
'He does not eat,' though he eats;
'He does not drink,' though he drinks;
'He is not circumcised,' though he was circumcised;
'He is without flesh,' though he came in the flesh;
'He did not suffer,' though he suffered;
'He did not rise from the dead,' though he rose from the dead. (5, 1–11)

This is almost directly followed by a typically gnostic invocation of the upper echelon of the divine world, also known from other witnesses of the Barbelo myth: the unnameable God (the Father), the Self-Begotten (the Son), Barbelo (the Mother), Doxomedon Domedon (otherwise only mentioned in the *Holy Book of the Great Invisible Spirit*), Jesus Christ, the great Lights: Armozel, Oroiael, Daveithe and Eleleth, Pigeradamas and Mirocheirothetou (who is otherwise unknown). The same persons are addressed with a thrice 'holy' in a eulogy by Melchizedek (16, 17–18, 7) which forms part of the central section between the two revelations. In this section Melchizedek also talks about his calling: he calls himself 'the high priest of God Most High', who is the image of 'the true high priest of God Most High' (15, 8–13). Doubtless we find influence here of Hebrews 7:3, where it is said of Melchizedek that he 'resembles the Son of God'.

Melchizedek receives the second revelation from some unnamed heavenly messengers, referred to at the end as 'the brothers who belong to the generations of life'. Though the text is severely damaged, it is clear that they sharply reject animal sacrifices. Also, Christ speaks in the first person about his suffering, crucifixion and resurrection, but it is unclear exactly how this fits into the revelation to Melchizedek. Some scholars assume that Melchizedek and Christ are somehow identified here, but for others this is based on a misinterpretation of the (very fragmentary) text, which is probably right. Finally, the seer is given a warning: 'Do not disclose these revelations to anyone who is in the flesh – for it is something non-fleshly – unless you receive a revelation to do so' (NHC IX, 27, 3–6; likewise after the first revelation, 14, 9–15).

Melchizedek is undoubtedly a gnostic text, which draws on the tradition of the Barbelo myth as it comes to the fore particularly in the *Holy Book of the Great Invisible Spirit*. There are no reasons for seeing these gnostic elements as secondary. Nor does the repeated mention of Jesus' real suffering and death argue against the text's gnostic character, since gnostics, too, could give a meaningful interpretation of Jesus' physical death.[74] But all this gives us little to go on as regards a reliable dating and location of the work. Scholars usually date it to around 200 or the early third century, which may well be right. Its place of origin is often said to be Egypt, on the dubious grounds that Melchizedek was revered there as a heavenly figure (which he is not in *Melchizedek*) among certain groups of Christians in the fourth century. There are no convincing arguments in favour of an Egyptian origin.

Wisdom of Jesus Christ The *Wisdom (Sophia) of Jesus Christ* survives in a Greek papyrus fragment (P. Oxy. 1081; early fourth century) and two Coptic translations (BG 3 and NHC III, 4).[75] The Coptic translations were made independently of each other after a Greek text which diverged from that of the papyrus. The BG text has been excellently preserved, that of NHC III, 4 lacks four pages and also has quite a few lacunae. The Greek papyrus, which runs parallel with BG 87, 15–91, 17 and NHC III, 96, 21–99, 13, is in very poor condition. In any case the extant texts show that this work was popular among Greek- and Coptic-speaking readers in the fourth century. The Greek word *Sophia* in the title could refer to the divine figure of Sophia, who according to the myth brought about the genesis of the world and human beings. But this is improbable, because she plays only a subordinate role in the work. The title doubtless alludes to the wisdom (*sophia*) of Jesus Christ, the Saviour, as teacher of the gnosis brought to light in this work. So the title is comparable with those of well-known books like the *Wisdom of Jesus Sirach* or the *Wisdom of Solomon*.

The most remarkable aspect of the *Wisdom of Jesus Christ* is that it is a Christian-gnostic revision of *Eugnostus* (NHC III, 2 and V, 1),[76] in the

[74] See the discussion of gnostic Christology on pp. 195–202.

[75] Ed. W. Till and H.-M. Schenke, TU 69^2 (1972), pp. 52–61, 194–295; D. M. Parrott, NHS 27 (1991); C. Barry, BCNH-T 20 (1993).

[76] See pp. 116–19 below.

sense that the latter work is almost entirely incorporated into it. The text of *Eugnostus* used by the author accords most with that of NHC III, 2. The author has repeatedly interrupted the discourse of *Eugnostus* to introduce questions asked by the disciples, which are then answered by Jesus in the literal wording of *Eugnostus*. The result is that the answers often barely address the question. The epistolary character of *Eugnostus* has been replaced in the *Wisdom* by a frame narrative, which starts with an appearance of the risen Christ to twelve male and seven female disciples on a mountain in Galilee and ends with the disappearance of Christ and the beginning of the disciples' proclamation of 'the Gospel of God, the eternal, immortal Spirit'.

The strong dependence on *Eugnostus* means that researchers have paid little attention to the views of the reviser.[77] To get some idea of these views, we need to be alert to what has been omitted from *Eugnostus* and what has been added in the *Wisdom*. Thus the reviser has left out a long passage on the six androgynous children of the Saviour and Pistis Sophia (III, 82, 7–85, 7), because he identified the Saviour with Christ and therefore had no use for such a passage. More interesting is what the reviser has substituted for it. Everybody who comes into the world has been sent by the Saviour, 'as a drop of Light', to be shackled by the chains of oblivion in the kingdom of the creator, 'the All-Sovereign [*pantokratōr*]', albeit by virtue of Sophia's will. The purpose of this is to demonstrate to the whole world living in poverty the arrogance and blindness of the creator. This is effected by the coming of the Saviour: 'But I came from the places above, by the will of the Great Light. I unloosed that fetter, I broke up the work of the tomb of the robbers, I awakened that drop sent by Sophia, to bear much fruit through me and become perfect' (BG 103, 10–104, 16; III, 106, 24–107, 20). Finally, after assimilating the *Eugnostus* material, the author of the *Wisdom of Jesus Christ* puts a summary of his views into the Saviour's mouth. Sophia wanted people to come into being, separately from her male fellow, but this did not take place without the will of the Father of the All. He created a spiritual curtain between the Immortals and the later creatures. Again the author mentions the 'drop of Light and Spirit', which represents the divine in the regions of chaos, where the primeval Father, Yaldabaoth, rules. The drop is connected with the breath of life breathed into Adam according to Genesis 2:7 – a well-known motif

[77] See, however, Barry's edition and A. Pasquier, *Eugnoste. Lettre sur le Dieu transcendant (NH III, 3 et V, 1). Commentaire*, BCNH-T 33 (Quebec: Presses de l'Université Laval; Louvain, Paris and Walpole, MA: Éditions Peeters, 2010), 237–87.

in the gnostic exegesis of Genesis. Christ, the Saviour who appeared on earth, is the messenger of the heavenly Immortal Man. He returns original unity to people through his gift of Spirit and Breath of Life, 'so that they might become one out of two, as it was from the beginning' (BG 122, 5–11; III, 117, 1–3). Sexual union and procreation are rejected. Interestingly, this final passage distinguishes between people who have the pure gnosis of the Father and those who know it only partly: the first category will ascend to the Father and 'rest in the Unbegotten Father', the second will retain its shortcomings and find rest in the eighth celestial sphere, the Ogdoad. The second category probably refers to the non-gnostic Christians, for whom therefore partial salvation is considered possible. In a further qualification they are designated as people who 'know the Son of Man in gnosis and love'.

Rather varying dates have been proposed for the *Wisdom of Jesus Christ*, from the late first/early second to mid third century. Because the work presupposes the gnostic myth (Sophia's fall, Yaldabaoth as the creator-god who declares himself God, the Saviour from the world of light who brings saving gnosis), a genesis before the mid second century seems unlikely. A date in the second half of that century is certainly possible, but the early third century cannot be ruled out.

Second Revelation of James The *(Second) Revelation* (or *Apocalypse*) *of James* (NHC v, 4)[78] is one of the few gnostic writings to have a Jewish-Christian background. It does not show the typical features of the Barbelo myth. NHC v contains two works bearing the title *Apocalypse of James*. In order to distinguish them, it has become common practice to refer to NHC v, 3 as the *(First) Revelation of James*[79] and NHC v, 4 as the *(Second) Revelation of James* (the parentheses are sometimes left out). The James who plays the principal role in both works is James 'the Just', also called 'the Brother of the Lord', the leader of the Jewish Christians in Jerusalem (cf. Gal. 1:19; 1 Cor. 15:7; Acts 12:17 and 21:18). After a short introduction, the *Second Apocalypse* contains an address held by James (46, 1(?)–60, 23), which was supposedly written down by a certain Mareim. The report pretends to go back ultimately to an unnamed priest, who in turn conveyed it to Theudas, the father of James. At least, that is the impression one gets from the not entirely clear beginning of the text. Why the father of James is called Theudas here, and not Joseph, as one would expect, is an unsolved mystery. Mary is here the wife of Theudas (44, 22). The author

[78] Ed. C. W. Hedrick, NHS 11 (1979), pp. 105–49; A. Veilleux, BCNH-T 17 (1986), pp. 115–98.
[79] See p. 75.

rejected the view that James was a physical brother of Jesus. This emerges from the description of a manifestation of Jesus to James, at which Mary was also present, in 50, 5–21:

He said to me: 'Greetings, my brother. My brother, greetings!' When I raised my face to look at him, my mother said: 'Don't be afraid, my son, because he addressed you as "my brother". For you were nourished with the same milk. That is why he calls me "my mother". For he is no stranger to us. He is your stepbrother.'

But they do have the same heavenly Father: 'Your father is not my Father, but my Father has become a father to you,' says Jesus (51, 19–22). The *First Apocalypse of James* also denies that Jesus and James were brothers in a literal sense. The report of James's speech is followed, without any transition, by an account of his martyrdom (60, 23–63, 32).

James's speech draws a gnostic picture of Jesus, as the one who first revealed the unknown God. He penetrated the kingdom of the Demiurge and his henchmen, in which 'those who are from the Father' (54, 10–12) are imprisoned. James must continue Jesus' work: exposure of the evil powers and proclamation of the unknown God. Jesus says to him: 'For you are not a saviour or helper of strangers. You are an enlightener and saviour of those who are mine but now are also yours. You shall give them revelation and bring good among them all' (55, 15–22). Incidentally, Jesus is not described as an ordinary man of flesh and blood: he embraces and kisses James, but James does not feel a normal human body (56, 14–57, 19). At the end of his discourse James calls on his listeners to repent and accept Jesus and his message. A hymnic passage sings of the Saviour as a heavenly figure, who was equal with God and was not recognized by the creator of heaven and earth, 58, 2–23:

He was life. He was light. He was the one who will come to be. And he will also provide an end to what has begun and a beginning to what will be ended. He was the Holy Spirit and the Invisible One, who did not descend upon the earth. He was the Virgin, and what he wills, happens to him. I have seen him: he was naked and wore no garment.

James calls to his listeners, 59, 1–6: 'Leave this difficult road, which is so variable, and walk in accordance with him who wants you to become free people with me, when you have overcome every dominion.'

James's martyrdom takes place after he has made some other speeches, the content of which is not reported. He is thrown from the roof of the temple and finally stoned. Before his death he utters a dying prayer, which is undoubtedly older than the *Second Apocalypse* itself. It belongs to the same genre which includes the *Prayer of the Apostle Paul* (NHC I, 1), a number of Manichaean prayers and the prayer of the dying Virgin Mary according to the oldest version of Mary's death and assumption.[80]

The *Second Revelation of James* must have originated in a gnostic milieu in which Jewish-Christian traditions played an important role. Other sources show that such traditions long survived, particularly in Syrian Christianity, with Edessa as capital. The *Second Apocalypse* is therefore usually situated in this area, though the work itself contains no indications in that direction. The type of gnosis it teaches is not typically Jewish-Christian nor does it provide any geographical clues. This last also applies to the time of its origin. Knowledge of the gnostic myth is taken for granted, for example the Demiurge's boast that only he is God (56, 25–57, 1). This makes it unlikely that the work can be dated before the mid second century. Both the second half of the second century and the third century are possible.

Thought of Norea The *Thought of Norea* (NHC IX, 2)[81] does not have a title in the manuscript, and the modern name derives from the end of this short text, in which Adamas, here 'the Father of the All', is said 'to have the thought of Norea'. It would be better to call the piece 'The Salvation of Norea'; 'The Ode on Norea' has also been proposed. Norea is known as the daughter of Eve and the wife of Seth or as the wife of Noah, but she assumes the features here of the fallen Sophia.[82] She has the same function in the *Nature of the Rulers* and the *Origin of the World*.[83] She invokes the powers of the Pleroma for assistance, and this is given to her by 'the four helpers', which refers to the four great Lights, the servants of the Son. She is taken up into the tranquillity of the Pleroma and as such is also an image of the saved gnostic. The date and place of origin are unknown.

Pistis Sophia The *Pistis Sophia*,[84] the only text in the Codex Askewianus, also talks at length about the salvation of Sophia. This extensive work contains conversations which Jesus supposedly held with his disciples, including Mary Magdalen, over a period of eleven years after

[80] See p. 107, and R. van den Broek, 'Manichaean Elements in an Early Version of the Virgin Mary's Assumption', in A. Houtman, A. de Jong and M. Misset-van de Weg (eds.), *Empsychoi Logoi: Religious Innovations in Antiquity. Studies in Honour of Pieter Willem van der Horst*, Ancient Judaism and Early Christianity 73 (Leiden: Brill, 2008), pp. 293–316.

[81] Ed. M. Roberge, BCNH-T 5 (1980), pp. 149–71; B. A. Pearson and S. Giversen, NHS 15 (1981), pp. 87–99.

[82] See p. 52, note 53 above. [83] See pp. 52 and 55.

[84] C. Schmidt (ed.), *Pistis Sophia, neu herausgegeben mit Einleitung nebst griechischem Wort- und Namenregister*, Coptica 2 (Copenhagen: Gyldendalske Boghandel-Nordisk Forlag, 1925); V. MacDermot (ed.), *Pistis Sophia*, NHS 9 (Leiden: Brill, 1978), reprint of Schmidt's 1925 edition, translation and notes by MacDermot.

his resurrection. The book consists of four parts, clearly indicated in the manuscript. The first three parts belonged together from the beginning, the fourth was originally probably an independent treatise and is generally assumed to be older than the first three books. Above the second book we find in a later hand: 'The second book of the Pistis Sophia'. The person who wrote this presumably regarded the preceding book as 'The first book of the Pistis Sophia'. But at the end of books II and III we find: 'A part of the Books of the Saviour'. The first three books probably had as their original title *The Books of the Saviour*. The name *Pistis Sophia* is based on the important role which this heavenly figure plays in the first two books; in the modern literature this title is now commonly used for all four books. The first book starts with a rather complicated description of the divine world, which contains twenty-four worlds, called 'mysteries', with numerous subdivisions. The Barbelo myth has been almost totally supplanted here by later speculations. Barbelo is mentioned several times, but she no longer has the clear position which she occupied in the original myth. Sophia, who is consistently called Pistis Sophia here, belongs in the thirteenth aeon, together with twenty-three other 'emanations', but because of her 'fall', she has ended up below, in the world of chaos. The reason for her fall was that she addressed her praises to the 'Treasure of the Light' and neglected the praises of the thirteenth aeon. The largest part of the first two books deals with the fate, supplications and salvation of Pistis Sophia (I, 29–II, 82). Characteristic here are the many exegetical discussions of a number of religious songs: biblical Psalms, five *Odes of Solomon* and a few *Psalms of Solomon*, which are explained with a view to the vicissitudes of Pistis Sophia and their meaning for the individual gnostic. The rest of the second and third books contains questions of the disciples and answers of Jesus regarding the heavenly mysteries and the fate that awaits various kinds of souls after death. The fourth part is a revelation about the powers that rule the cosmos and what punishments are imposed in the hereafter for all kinds of sins.

The *Pistis Sophia* is a long-winded work and confusingly complex as a whole. Striking, too, is the close relationship with the world of late classical magic. The work contains magic formulas, with to us meaningless words and strangely formed names with Greek, Egyptian and Hebrew elements (*voces magicae*, *nomina barbara*) so characteristic of Greek magic papyri (I, 10; IV, 136, 137, 142). The magic influence is also shown by the identification of Jesus with Aberamentho ('Jesus, who is Aberamentho', in IV, 136, 139, 141). The word *aberamenthō* derives from a palindrome which occurs in numerous magic papyri (*aberamenthōoulertheanaxethreluoōthne mareba*) and Michel Tardieu has argued that the formula is a paraphrase of the god Thot-Hermes (the syllable *-tho* in Aberamentho is supposedly an abbreviated form of the Greek and Coptic form *Thōouth*). So in that case Jesus is identified with Thot-Hermes here.[85] As will be indicated below, the *Pistis Sophia* exhibits the same spiritual climate which produced the works of the Codex Brucianus.

The Thunder – Perfect Mind *The Thunder – Perfect Mind* (NHC VI, 2)[86] is a long monologue by a female divine figure, who presents herself as an ambassador of the highest God and calls on her listeners to return from the world of death to true life. It is a fascinating work, in which the speaker comments on herself and her listeners in countless paradoxical and antithetical images, of which one example may suffice:

I am the first and the last,
I am the honoured and the scorned,
I am the whore and the chaste,
I am the wife and the virgin,
I am the mother and the daughter,
I am the limbs of my mother,
I am the barren one who has many children,
I often married and I have no husband,
I am the midwife and she who gives birth,
I am the solace of my birth pains,
I am the bride and the groom
and my husband begot me,
I am the mother of my father
and the sister of my husband
and he is my child. (13, 16–32)

The whole work is mysterious, starting with the double title, which consists of three Greek words. It is unclear whether 'Perfect Mind' (*Nous teleios*) is a specification of 'The Thunder' (*Brontē*), and also what is meant by the thunder. Because thunder was seen in Jewish and Greek tradition as a manifestation of the divine (the 'voice of God'), scholars have surmised that the divine perfect mind is speaking in this work as the voice of God. But the word *nous* (mind/consciousness) is masculine, whereas the speaker is a woman. Moreover, the word 'thunder' does not occur anywhere in the text, and this also applies to 'perfect Mind', unless one

85 M. Tardieu, 'Aberamenthō', in R. van den Broek and M. J. Vermaseren (eds.), *Studies in Gnosticism and Hellenistic Religions Presented to Gilles Quispel on the Occasion of his 65th Birthday*, EPRO 91 (Leiden: Brill, 1981), pp. 412–18; see also Mastrocinque, *From Jewish Magic to Gnosticism*, pp. 184–91.

86 Ed. G. W. MacRae, NHS 11 (1979), pp. 231–55; P.-H. Poirier, BCNH-T 22 (1995).

fills in the word 'perfect' in the lacuna in 18, 9. So there is no convincing explanation of the title nor a demonstrable connection between title and content.

But the greatest mystery of the text is the identity of the speaker. On the one hand she says of herself 'I have been sent out by the Power', 'I am the first and the last' (13, 1 and 16), but on the other hand she is in a state of humiliation (15, 2–14). She calls on people to let go of everything which prevents them from returning to God (21, 20–32).

Who is this Envoy? Scholars have identified her with the Simonian Helen, who as incarnated First Thought of God was supposedly found by Simon Magus in a brothel in Tyre. A more likely identification is with Wisdom, which could be both Jewish Wisdom and gnostic Sophia. What is certain is that the speaker of the *Thunder* played a role in gnostic traditions, for both in the *Nature of the Rulers*, NHC II, 89, 16–17 (section 8), and in the *Origin of the World*, NHC II, 114, 5–15 (sections 74–5), the nature of the spiritual Eve is characterized by means of quotations from the *Thunder* (or, less probably, from a common source). This spiritual Eve is a divine figure who is the first to bring gnosis to Adam and Eve and is best understood as a manifestation of Sophia. But there is no indication that the author of the *Thunder* also interpreted the Sent One as the spiritual Eve. All things considered, the best solution seems to interpret her as the first manifestation of the highest God, who had her origin in Jewish Wisdom and assumed her mature form in gnostic Sophia, who occurred under various names and figures. But it is impossible to connect her with one of the well-known gnostic systems.

It is unknown where the work originated. The entire gist of the work suggests that it came from a Jewish-Hellenistic, gnostically orientated milieu, such as existed in Alexandria at the beginning of the Christian era. A date is also hard to give. The fact that the *Thunder*, or an earlier version of it, is quoted in the joint source of the *Nature of the Rulers* and in the *Origin of the World* implies that it may already have circulated in the second century. An origin in that century seems the most probable, though the first century cannot be ruled out.

THE BARBELO MYTH AND HEAVENLY JOURNEYS

The basic gnostic myth obviously presupposes that the human soul, or at least its core, returns after death to the divine world from which it hails. From the beginning the fate of the various kinds of souls was therefore an important theme for the gnostics. The views on this which were already put into Jesus' mouth in the *Secret Book of John* (BG 64, 13–71, 2; NHC II, 25, 16–27, 30) are set out at length in the *Pistis Sophia* III, 111–19.[87] It is crucial that the soul knows the right passwords or possesses 'seals' to be able to pass the stern planet guards and the angels in the higher worlds. Such passwords, which often have the form of an answer to a question, occur in various texts. A well-known example is the *Gospel of Thomas*, logion 50: 'If they say to you: "Where have you come from?", say to them: "We have come from the light, from the place where the light came into being by itself."' Here the motif of the ascent through the hostile spheres is mentioned only in passing, but in other texts, like the *Gospel of Mary* (BG 1) and the *(First) Revelation of James* (NHC V, 3 and Codex Tchacos, 2) and partly also in the *Revelation of Paul* (NHC V, 2), it occupies a more central position, though other subjects are also discussed. But above the spheres of the planets, in the super-celestial world, there are also guards who allow the soul to pass only if it can identify itself with a password or sign. This is the case in the *Books of Jeu* (Codex Brucianus 1), in which the description of the supra-celestial spheres testifies to an unbridled urge to speculate and fantasize. This is even stronger in a series of related texts which describe the structure of the Pleroma with its many articulations and the heavenly powers that reside there: *Zostrianus* (NHC VIII, 1), *Marsanes* (NHC X), *Allogenes* (NHC XI, 3), the *Untitled Gnostic Treatise* (Codex Brucianus 2) and the *Three Steles of Seth* (NHC VII, 5). This last group is characterized by a strong influence of later Platonism. People who referred to these writings attended the school of Plotinus in Rome in the mid third century, but their views met with determined opposition. Plotinus himself wrote his *Against the Gnostics* (*Enneads* II, 9) against them and urged his pupils to do the same.[88] Because the *Gospel of Mary*, the *(First) Apocalypse of James* and the *Revelation of Paul* do not presuppose the Barbelo myth and are entirely unconnected with the Platonizing works mentioned, they will be discussed first, followed by the *Books of Jeu*, which has nothing to do with the Platonizing works, either. In connection with *Allogenes* we will also pay attention to the *Book of Allogenes*, of which fragments have been recovered in the Codex Tchacos.

Gospel of Mary Unfortunately, the *Gospel of Mary* (BG, 1)[89] has not been preserved in its entirety: of the original nineteen pages, ten have been lost (pages 1–6 and 11–14). But some Greek papyrus fragments have

[87] See van den Broek, 'Manichaean Elements', pp. 311–13.
[88] See pp. 133–5.
[89] Ed. W. C. Till and H.-M. Schenke, TU 60² (1972), pp. 24–32, 62–78; R. McL. Wilson and G. W. MacRae, NHS 11 (1979), pp. 454–71; A. Pasquier, BCNH-T 10 (1983).

been recovered: Oxyrhynchus Papyrus 3525 (in London; = BG 9, 1–10, 14) and Rylands Papyrus 463 (in Manchester; = BG 17, 4–19, 2). These Greek witnesses come from various manuscripts and date to the early third century. They show considerable differences from the Coptic version, which indicates that changes were introduced in the text of this gospel at an early stage. The original Greek version was written in the second century. The Mary after whom the gospel is named and who plays the principal role in it is not the mother of Jesus but Mary Magdalen. According to the biblical gospels, this Mary of Magdala was present at Jesus' crucifixion and, together with some other women, was the first witness of his resurrection (e.g. Mark 15:40 and 16:1–8). Although in somewhat veiled terms, she is said to have been a disciple of Jesus from the outset (Mark 15:41). This role has been strongly magnified in gnostic literature. In the *Pistis Sophia* she is one of Jesus' most important interlocutors, so much so that Peter once cries out: 'My Lord, let the women stop asking questions. Then we can ask some questions too.' Jesus then says to Mary and the other women: 'Make way for your brothers, the men, and let them ask questions too' (*Pistis Sophia* IV, 146). The same animosity of Peter towards Mary is expressed in Peter's notorious exclamation in the *Gospel of Thomas*, 114: 'Let Mary leave us, for women are not worthy of life!' In the *Gospel of Mary* Peter also turns against Mary. The main theme of this gospel is the question whether women can act as teachers in a Christian community and so play a leading role in it. We cannot recover what was contained in the first six pages of the work. When the text starts on p. 7 of the manuscript we are in the middle of a conversation between the disciples and Jesus about the nature of matter and sin in the world. Jesus, who is consistently called 'the Saviour', says about this last: 'Sin does not exist, but it is you who make sin' (7, 13–14). The conversation ends with the charge to proclaim the gospel and not impose any other regulations on people than those instructed by Jesus. Then the Saviour disappears and the disciples are left behind downhearted and frightened: 'If he was not spared, how shall we be spared?' (9, 10–12). At that point Mary comes forward and inspires them with courage, after which Peter asks Mary to tell the others what the Saviour said only to her. This is followed by a report of a conversation between Jesus and Mary in connection with a vision received by Mary, but because another four pages are lost here we do not know how this conversation continued. But its conclusion has been preserved from page 15 onwards. The subject there is the soul's ascent through the territory of four cosmic powers. We are told what the soul must answer to the questions of the evil powers in order to pass them undisturbed. The passage about the first power has been lost; the other three are called Desire, Ignorance and Wrath, of which the last has seven forms, which again suggests the seven planetary powers. To give an impression of the questions and answers, it may suffice to quote the conclusion of Jesus' revelation to Mary, with some clarifications in italic within square brackets:

> These are the seven powers of Wrath. They asked the soul: 'Where do you come from, murderess?' and 'Where are you going, you who destroys your place of abode?' The soul answered: 'What binds me has been killed, and what surrounds me has been destroyed [*i.e. the material body*]. My desire has ended and ignorance has died [*cf. the two preceding powers*]. I have been freed in a world by [another] world and in an image [*the body as image of the world-creator*] by an Image from above [*the Saviour as image of God*]. The shackle of oblivion is but temporary. From this moment I will receive rest, [apart from] the world's further course of time [*partly based on Rylands Papyrus 463; the sentence is hard to translate*], in silence.' When Mary had said this, she was silent, because that was how far the Saviour had spoken to her. (16, 13–17, 9)

The rest of the gospel has a clearly polemical thrust, targeted at the conception of ecclesiastical office endorsed by incipient orthodoxy. To that extent it could be treated together with the polemical texts, but for the sake of cohesion it seems better to discuss the end of the gospel here as well. When Mary has given her account, Andrew doubts whether the Saviour really said this: 'for what is taught here are clearly deviant ideas' (17, 14–15). Peter goes one step further and cries out: 'Did he then talk to a woman in secret without our knowing it? Should we then turn around and all listen to her? Did he prefer her over us?' (17, 18–22). Peter's reaction here is rather curious, because it was he who had asked Mary to tell what Jesus had said only to her. This may point to the use of various sources. However this may be, Mary bursts into tears on hearing Peter's words: 'My brother Peter, what do you think? Do you think I devised this myself in my heart or that I am lying about the Saviour?' The apostle Levi then sides with Mary and blames 'hot-tempered' Peter for talking to her like 'the opponents': 'If the Saviour judged her worthy, who are you then to reject her? It is certain that the Saviour knew her very well and therefore loved her more than us' (18, 10–15).[90] This passage reflects the discussions in second-century Christian communities about the position of women. Peter expresses the view which started to become dominant in incipient

[90] Cf. the *Gospel of Philip*, 55 (NHC II, 63, 34–64, 5): 'And the companion of the S[aviour is Ma] ry Magdalen. The [Saviour] loved her more than all the disciples and often kissed her on her [mouth]. The other [disciples …]. They said to him: "Why do you love her more than all of us?" The Saviour answered them: "Why don't I love you as I love her?".'

orthodoxy: Jesus revealed his complete doctrine to his male disciples, but he did not give secret revelations and certainly not to female followers. The leadership of the Church therefore rests with the male disciples and their male successors – a view already taught by Pseudo-Paul about the year 100: 'Let a woman learn in silence with full submission. I permit no woman to teach or to have authority over a man; she is to keep silent' (1 Tim. 2:11–12).

First Revelation of James The *(First) Revelation* (or *Apocalypse*) *of James* (NHC v, 3)[91] has also been preserved as the second text in the Codex Tchacos under the simple title of *James*. In discussing the *(Second) Apocalypse of James* we noted that both NHC v, 3 and 4 bear the title *Apocalypse of James* in the manuscript, and that it has therefore become usual to distinguish the texts by means of the additions 'First' and 'Second'. However, the two texts are not related to each other, nor do they follow on from each other. The availability of a second copy of the *First Apocalypse* is crucial, because both texts have considerable lacunae and often supplement each other. In many places the version of the Codex Tchacos has been better preserved than that in NHC v, 3, but in terms of content there are sometimes striking differences.[92]

The *First Revelation of James* consists of two conversations between Jesus and James, the first of which is situated before Christ's suffering and the second after his resurrection. The theme of both conversations is suffering as the way by which liberation from the demonic powers, the archons, is brought about. The main emphasis is on the suffering of James, in imitation of that of Jesus. Here, too, 'James' refers to the leader of the Jewish-Christian congregation of Jerusalem, who is known as 'James the Just' and as 'Brother of the Lord' (though, just as in the *Second Revelation*, the usual physical interpretation of this term is rejected here, too: v, 24, 15–16; Codex Tchacos 10, 4–5). Jesus presents himself as the one who comes from the unnameable 'He-Who-Is', but indicates that this is also true of James and that for both of them salvation from the powers consists in the return to their origin. In the first conversation Jesus answers some questions from James, including one about the twelve world-rulers (archons), who

91 Ed. W. R. Schoedel, NHS 11 (1979), pp. 65–103; A. Veilleux, BCNH-T 17 (1986), pp. 1–114. Codex Tchacos: Kasser and Wurst, *The Gospel of Judas ... Critical Edition*, pp. 115–61; Brankaer and Bethge, TU 161 (2007), pp. 81–254.

92 For the relationship between the two versions, see W.-P. Funk, 'The Significance of the Tchacos Codex for Understanding the First Apocalypse of James', in DeConick, *The Codex Judas Papers*, pp. 509–33, and A. Marjanen, 'The Seven Women Disciples in the Two Versions of the First Apocalypse of James', in DeConick, *The Codex Judas Papers*, pp. 535–46.

have seventy-two heavens underneath them which are inhabited by evil powers. These powers will oppose him and also James and cause them to suffer, but they will not gain the upper hand. James expresses his fear of this imminent suffering, and does so in the form of a hymn in which he indicates the differences between Jesus and himself. It is not unlikely that this hymn originally circulated separately from the present context (v, 28, 7–29, 3; Codex Tchacos 14, 21–15, 8). James wonders: 'What will they (the evil powers) do? What will I be able to say? Or what word will I be able to speak in order to escape from them?' James receives the answers to these questions in the second conversation. Jesus predicts James's suffering, but focuses not so much on his coming martyrdom as on his journey up to Him-Who-Is, past the heavenly evil powers, who try to stop him. Here the author has used an existing text which also occurs in a closely related form in Irenaeus, *AH* 1, 21, 5 and Epiphanius, *Panarion* 36, 2–3, who has preserved Irenaeus' Greek text. It concerns a ritual for the dying in use among Valentinian gnostics. Irenaeus ascribes it to the Marcosians, the followers of Mark the Magician, but Epiphanius says that it was practised among the followers of Heracleon.[93] The dying person was anointed and told the words which he should speak to the stern gatekeepers and toll-collectors of the heavenly powers during his ascent. The *First Revelation of James* not only indicates the answers of the deceased, but also the questions that he will be asked (v, 33, 11–35, 26; Codex Tchacos 20, 7–22, 23). This seems the most original version of the ritual, because such dialogues are the most usual in this genre of texts. Thus the first questions and answers read:

> If you fall into their hands, one who is their guard will say to you: 'Who are you and where do you come from?' You are to say to him: 'I am a son and I come from the Father.' He will say to you: 'What kind of son are you and to what kind of Father do you belong?' You are to say to him: 'I am from the pre-existent Father; a son in the Pre-existent One.' (v, 33, 11–24; Codex Tchacos 20, 7–18)

[93] The Coptic, Greek and Latin texts are printed alongside one another in A. Veilleux (ed.), *La Première Apocalypse de Jacques (NH V, 3). La Seconde Apocalypse de Jacques (NH V, 4)*, BCNH-T, 17 (Quebec: Presses de l'Université Laval, 1986), pp. 87–8; English translation in E. Thomassen, *The Spiritual Seed: The Church of the 'Valentinians'*, NHMS 60 (Leiden: Brill, 2006), pp. 406–8. It has been argued that this ritual for the dying was in fact the Valentinian sacrament of the *Apolytrōsis*, 'Redemption', which is mentioned in several Valentinian texts; see N. D. Lewis, 'Apolytrosis as Ritual and Sacrament: Determining a Ritual Context for Death in Second-Century Marcosian Valentinianism', *JECS* 17 (2009), 525–61. Most scholars, however, take the term 'Apolytrosis' as indicating the salvific effects of the sacraments of baptism and the Eucharist (see below p. 104). Moreover, as Thomassen, *Spiritual Seed*, p. 363, remarked, there is nothing in Irenaeus' description of the ritual which confirms that it was actually named 'the Redemption'.

In the rest of the dialogue the deceased instructs the hostile powers and the Demiurge about their origin from the fallen Sophia, who is called Achamoth, as in Valentinian texts. After the passage on the soul's return Jesus instructs James about several aspects of gnosis. Thus the twelve archons are the prototypes of the twelve apostles, who are reduced in this way to the category of the ignorant. Moreover, there is a passage about the transmission of the revelation, via Addai, Manael, Levi and his son (Codex Tchacos 23, 13–25, 14; v, 36, 20–38, 10). The conclusion provides a brief description of James's martydom, which begins when he blames the twelve apostles for not knowing the way of truth. According to the Codex Tchacos (the text of NHC v has been almost completely lost), a deliberate confusion took place with another James, an escaped prisoner, and so the innocent James was condemned to death. His final words were: 'My Father in heaven, forgive them, for they do not know what they are doing!' (Codex Tchacos 29, 18–30, 26; v, 42, 20).

The *First Revelation of James* is probably a product of Syrian Christianity, which was centred in Edessa. This is suggested by the name Addai, who is supposed to have written down Jesus' revelations to James. According to Syrian traditions preserved in Eusebius, *Ecclesiastical History* I, 13, it was Addai (Thaddeus) who established Christianity in Edessa, having been sent there from Jerusalem by the apostle Thomas. Traditions about the earliest Jewish-Christian congregation of Jerusalem and its 'bishop' James the Just were long kept alive in Syria. But the *First Revelation of James* is an evidently gnostic work, which was apparently aimed at tracing back Jesus' gnostic teachings to the earliest Jewish Christianity. The clear Valentinian influence proves that the work originated at the earliest in the second half of the second century. But a date in the first half of the third century is equally possible.

Revelation of Paul The *Revelation* (or *Apocalypse*) *of Paul* (NHC v, 2)[94] describes a heavenly journey of the apostle Paul to the tenth heaven. Paul's statement in 2 Corinthians 12:2–4 that he was once caught up into paradise in the third heaven strongly stirred the imagination of later generations of Christians. Thus we have long known another *Apocalypse of Paul*, but this one cannot be older than the fourth century and its earliest version has been preserved in a Latin translation.[95] According to Irenaeus, *AH* II, 30, 7, there were Valentinians who claimed that Paul had been

[94] Ed. W. R. Murdock and G. W. MacRae, NHS 11 (1979), pp. 47–63; J.-M. Rosenstiehl and M. Kaler, BCNH-T 31 (2005).

[95] Published by T. Silverstein and A. Hilhorst, *Apocalypse of Paul. A New Critical Edition of Three Long Latin Versions*, Cahiers d'Orientalisme 21 (Geneva: P. Cramer, 1997).

initiated into the mysteries situated above the Demiurge, but his account shows that Irenaeus was not acquainted with the *Revelation of Paul*, and the latter cannot be a reaction to his remarks either.[96] It is possible, however, that the *Revelation* embroidered on Valentinian ideas about Paul's heavenly journey, but this does not imply that the work as a whole should be regarded as Valentinian.

The work is relatively thin in substance; we are told almost nothing about most of the heavens which Paul traverses. So it is conceivable that we are actually dealing with a heavily abridged version or a summary of an originally more detailed work. The introduction reports that Paul meets a little child on his way to Jerusalem, who in reality is the Holy Spirit, who will accompany him on his journey through the heavens. He exhorts him to awaken his spirit, 'so that he will be able to understand what is hidden in the visible' (19, 13–14), and then leads him from the 'mountain of Jericho' to the third and the fourth heaven. Paul's sojourn in the fourth heaven is treated at somewhat greater length (19, 20–21, 22). The Holy Spirit points out his image to him, that is his material body, which is on the earth below, amidst the twelve apostles. This is an answer to Paul's uncertainty about the state in which he experienced his heavenly journey (2 Cor. 12:2 and 3: 'whether in the body or out of the body I do not know; God knows'): so it was out of the body! In the fourth heaven Paul also sees how a soul 'from the land of the dead' is delivered there by angels and then flogged and interrogated by the 'toll-collectors' and accused by witnesses. As punishment the soul is reincarnated in a body prepared for it. In the fifth heaven Paul sees how a large angel with an iron bar in his hand and three other angels with whips drive the souls to judgement. In the sixth heaven he sees a great light shining from the seventh heaven, after which he passes on immediately to the seventh heaven, which is again described in somewhat more detail (22, 23–23, 28). Paul sees an old man there, probably clothed in a white garment and seated on a throne which shone seven times more brightly than the sun (the text is full of lacunae), who asks where he is going. Paul answers: 'I am going to the place where I came from.' Asked where he comes from, Paul gives a surprising answer. He does not say, as one would expect, that he comes from the world of light, but talks about his future mission in the world. This would seem to point to an abridgement or revision of an earlier version. The old man then asks him how he will get out of the seventh heaven,

[96] Convincingly demonstrated by M. Kaler, in Rosenstiehl and Kaler, BCNH-T 31 (2005), pp. 129–43.

in view of all the rulers and powers present there. On the advice of the accompanying Spirit, Paul then gives him the 'sign' (*sēmeion*) which is to give him safe passage. The old man bows his head 'down to his creation and his powers', and Paul can continue his heavenly journey. The radiant old man in the seventh heaven is the gnostic Demiurge, the creator-god, who is located in the the seventh heaven in other gnostic writings as well. He cannot stop Paul, because his magic 'sign' is too powerful for him. He therefore leaves him alone, is in fact no longer interested in him, but turns once again to 'his creation'. All we are told about the rest of the heavenly journey is that Paul carries on to the tenth heaven via the eighth and the ninth heaven, where he greets those present there. The work ends abruptly: 'and we ascended to the tenth heaven and I greeted my fellow spirits'.

That the *Revelation of Paul* is a gnostic work is clearly shown by the meeting with the creator-god in the seventh heaven. But otherwise its gnostic character is too vague for it to be attributed to a particular gnostic movement. For that matter, a system of ten successive heavens never occurs in gnostic texts, and is virtually unknown elsewhere, too. Nothing can be said about its place of origin, and about its date no more than that the work must have originated in the second or third century.

Books of Jeu The *Books of Jeu* (Codex Brucianus 1)[97] is almost exclusively interested in the structure of superterrestrial realms. The views of the Barbelo myth on the world-creator, on humankind chained in ignorance and on his liberation through the gnosis brought by Christ are presupposed, but are given hardly any explicit formulation. The work cannot therefore be seen as a clear representative of the Barbelo myth. The focus is entirely on the soul's ascent through the heavenly spheres. In this framework the work offers an astonishing description of the countless heavenly powers and the places (called 'treasures', *thēsauroi*) which they inhabit, with drawings and diagrams, their magic names and the formulas one needs to know to pass them on the journey through the celestial regions. Chapters 5–28 of the first book contain a discussion of sixty 'treasures' of Jeu, who is called 'the true God', though he is not the highest God, the Father of the Saviour. Jeu himself inhabits the first 'treasure', which is described in detail, the other 'treasures' (also said to be Jeu's) spring from him 'at my Father's command'. Within these 'treasures' there are twelve 'emanations' (*probolai*) and three 'guards' (*phylakes*) who guard the gates

[97] Ed. C. Schmidt, TU 8, 1–2 (1892); V. MacDermot, NHS 9 (1978), reprint of Schmidt's 1892 edition, translation and notes by MacDermot.

of this 'treasure'. These emanations are called 'ranks', and within each there are twelve 'heads'. The accompanying drawings schematically indicate the structure of such a 'treasure'. From I, 33 on, after a lacuna of four pages, these schematic surveys are omitted and a lengthier discussion follows. It shows that the disciples will travel through all these heavenly abodes together with Jesus. Each time the work therefore depicts the 'seal' (*sphragis*) and mentions the words which must be used to pass the guards. The magic orientation of this form of gnostic religion becomes particularly clear here: knowledge of the names of the divine entities, the structure of their worlds and of the signs and formulas needed to penetrate this world are considered indispensable in order to ascend to the highest God. The first book ends with a long eulogy to the Father of the All.

In the second book Jesus instructs his male and female disciples about the great mysteries of 'the Treasure of Light', to which receiving angels lead the soul upwards, through all the worlds of the invisible God (II, 42). Before doing so, Jesus strictly commands his disciples not to reveal the mysteries to the followers of the world-creator and his henchmen, but only to people worthy of it, who have left behind the world and its gods. The disciples are first baptized by water, fire and the Holy Spirit, in an elaborately described ritual with clearly magic features, after which they are freed from their sins (II, 45–8). This is followed by a description of what the disciples will encounter during their ascent through various worlds, until they finally reach the highest 'Treasure of the Light'. Before entering there, they must pass through at least forty aeons, where each time they must submit proof of the forgiveness of their sins by mentioning the name of the aeon, using a number and a seal (a picture is included) and speaking certain words (II, 52). Curiously, the twelfth aeon is the abode of 'the Invisible God and Barbelo (the Mother) and the unbegotten God (the Son)', that is the three highest divine figures of the gnostic Barbelo myth. Above them, in the thirteenth aeon, reside 'the great invisible Spirit and the great virginal Spirit and twenty-four emanations of the invisible God'. The divine 'trinity' of the Barbelo myth is here no more than a gnostic erratic block, which has become entirely separated from its original context and been accommodated in a more comprehensive, autonomous system of divine worlds. The final part of the second book has been lost.

It is hard to give a date. Though the work deals with the structure of the divine world, there is no agreement with the descriptions in the Platonizing revelations to be discussed next. The identical theme of the heavenly journey could point to an origin in the same period, the first half of the third century. But the *Books of Jeu* does not show any Platonic influence. As regards the spiritual climate, however, there is a clear similarity to the *Pistis Sophia*, which also refers a few times to the *Books of Jeu*, as we saw in the discussion of the Bruce Codex.[98] So the *Books of Jeu* is older than the *Pistis Sophia* and also more deeply immersed in late classical Egyptian magic. The content of these texts has not been much studied. They are usually dismissed as late products of a gnosis run wild and sometimes dated to the first half of the fourth century (*c.* 330). A more common date given is the third century, on the assumption that the fourth book of the *Pistis Sophia* was written in the first half of that century and the first three books in the second half. In that case the *Books of Jeu* must have been written before the mid third century, specifically in Egypt. This may well be right; at any rate there are no arguments against it.

Zostrianus *Zostrianus* (NHC VIII, 1)[99] is one of four gnostic texts which show striking influence from second- and third-century Platonism; it is also the longest treatise of the Nag Hammadi library (132 pages). Regrettably, the manuscript is severely damaged: it is full of lacunae and parts of many pages have been lost, so that no meaningful text can be extracted, in particular from pages 32–4 and 89–108. Zostrianus is a mythical figure, whose son or grandson Armenius, according to later traditions, was the father of Zoroaster, founder of the Persian religion. But *Zostrianus* has nothing to do with Persia or Zoroaster, though the latter is mentioned at the end in a note added later in Greek code: 'Words of truth of Zostrianus. God of truth. Words of Zoroaster' (132, 6–9). Apparently a later copyist wanted to involve the famous Zoroaster in the genesis of this work, probably as the one who passed on the revelation granted to Zostrianus. In itself the discovery of *Zostrianus* and *Allogenes* was a great surprise, because before that only the titles of these works were known, from Porphyry's *Life of Plotinus*, 16. Porphyry reports there that in the mid third century certain figures in the school of Plotinus based themselves on 'revelations by Zoroaster, Zostrianus, Nicotheus, Allogenes, Messus and other people of the kind'.[100] Plotinus opposed the views put forward there and at his request his pupils did the same. The next chapter will take a closer look at their opposition to the gnostics.

[98] See p. 18.

[99] Ed. J. H. Sieber and B. Layton, NHS 39 (1991), pp. 7–225; C. Barry, W-P. Funk, P.-H. Poirier and J. D. Turner, BCNH-T 24 (2000).

[100] For Porphyry's entire report, see p. 134.

Zostrianus presupposes the Barbelo myth, particularly in the form given to it in the *Holy Book of the Great Invisible Spirit.* But whereas earlier gnostic works are strongly interested in the genesis of our world of ignorance and death and the question how one can be redeemed from it, *Zostrianus* pays scant attention to this subject matter. Gnosis does not come to mankind as a gift from above to below, but is granted to the gnostic via an enlightening ascent through the various levels of the spiritual world. The entire focus is on this process of ongoing enlightenment and deification. The actual revelation in *Zostrianus* is framed by a description of its occasion (the many questions and spiritual confusion of Zostrianus) and outcome (recording of the revelation and its proclamation). Thirteen different levels can be distinguished in his ascent from the earth to the top of the spiritual world. Above the realm of the creator of the material world there are three levels, called 'Impression' (*antitypos*), 'Exile' (*paroikēsis*) and 'Repenting' (*metanoia*), which also drew the attention, and ridicule, of Plotinus, as we shall see below.[101] The top of the spiritual world is formed by the Invisible Spirit, who is absolutely transcendent, raised above being and thought. He is called the 'Thrice Powerful', because the powers of 'Being', 'Life' and 'Thought' reside in him. These three terms are well known from similar discussions in third-century Platonism. From the Invisible Spirit flows the Barbelo aeon as his First Thought, enclosing all the archetypes of what comes after her. Within Barbelo various aeons are distinguished, Kalyptos (the Hidden One), Protophanes (the First-Appearing One), Autogenes (the Self-Begotten One) and the 'Thrice-Male Child'. Some names of the heavenly figures that Zostrianus meets also occur in the *Secret Book of the Great Invisible Spirit*, but many others are new. One of the most striking features in *Zostrianus* is that on each level the seer is baptized once or several times. The baptismal ritual, which is mentioned in a number of texts that describe or presuppose the Barbelo myth, is not an earthly affair, but is performed in the heavenly spheres during the ascent. Having arrived at the level where Sophia dwells, Zostrianus is informed about her 'fall' and the genesis of the world. Unfortunately, the passage in which this is narrated is badly damaged, so that more remains obscure than some translations suggest (9, 1–11, 2). She probably looked down and thus created the darkness of unordered matter, in which the eternal forms were reflected as a result of her appearance. The creator then creates the perishable world after the image of the reflection that he had received in his mind: 'through a reflection of a reflection he worked upon

[101] See p. 135.

the world'. The origin of the creator is not mentioned, but he is valued negatively, because he can make only perishable things and has no knowledge of the spiritual world. The view of the Barbelo myth that Sophia acted on her own authority and therefore wrongly is also presupposed here, for the text reports that she did penance and was allocated a place of rest. These elements of the myth are incorporated in a complicated system of the metaphysical world, which tries to give an answer to the question which dominated second- and third-century Platonism: how can the multiplicity of things be explained from the undivided unity of the supreme principle? The Platonistic bias of *Zostrianus* and the three works to be discussed next has been greatly emphasized in the study of these texts, particularly in the studies by John D. Turner,[102] and indeed there is no one who doubts this. Even someone who wonders whether perhaps Turner in his penetrating studies over-Platonizes *Zostrianus* and related works cannot ignore Michael Tardieu's brilliant discovery that *Zostrianus*, in 64, 13–66, 11 (and scattered in 66, 12–84, 22), used the same Platonic source as the Christian philosopher Marius Victorinus (first half of the fourth century) in his *Adversus Arium* 1, 49–50.[103] All this does not alter the fact that we are dealing here with a religious text, not a philosophical one. This is not only shown by the whole purport of the work, the mystic ascent to and contemplation of the highest divine being, but also by the eulogies and prayers which occur in it, which sometimes have a strongly magic character.[104]

The clear interwovenness with the Platonic tradition also determines the various dates proposed for *Zostrianus* in its present form. Some researchers believe that this work reflects views of Plotinus' pupil Porphyry and that it must therefore have its origins in the second half of the third century or even in the first half of the fourth century. If Plotinus knew *Zostrianus*, this must have been an older version. Others hold, and this seems most likely, that the Platonism presupposed in *Zostrianus* already existed before Plotinus and that he must have known this work in its present form. In that case it must have been written earlier, in the first half of the third century, perhaps in Egypt.

102 Turner, *Sethian Gnosticism and the Platonic Tradition*, and his long introductions in C. Barry *et al.*, *Zostrien (NH VIII, 1)*, BCNH-T 24 (2000), pp. 32–225, W.-P. Funk *et al.*, *Marsanès (NH X)*, BCNH-T 27 (2000), pp. 1–248, and W.-P. Funk *et al.*, *L'Allogène (NH XI, 3)*, BCNH-T 30 (2004), pp. 1–188.

103 M. Tardieu, *Recherches sur la formation de l'Apocalypse de Zostrien et les sources de Marius Victorinus*, Res Orientales 9 (Bures-sur-Yvette: Groupe pour l'Étude de la Civilisation du Moyen-Orient, 1996), pp. 7–114.

104 See p. 141.

Allogenes *Allogenes* (NHC XI, 3)[105] is one of the other gnostic works which, according to Porphyry, were discussed in the school of Plotinus. The word *allogenēs* literally means 'of another origin, genus, kind' or 'stranger'. Epiphanius of Salamis says that the gnostic Archontics and Sethians used books with the title *Allogeneis* and other works written in the name of Seth or his seven sons, who are themselves also called *allogeneis*, 'people of another kind, strangers' (*Panarion* 39, 5, 1 and 40, 2, 2). Though no text says this explicitly, the name Allogenes is usually assumed to be a designation of Seth, the third son of Adam and Eve, of whom Eve remarked at his birth that God had given her 'another seed' (thus, literally, the King James Version in Gen. 4:25; the Greek of the Septuagint has *sperma heteron*, the word *allogenēs* is not used there). Seth and his spiritual offspring, the gnostics, are therefore *allogeneis*, strangers amidst other people. In the nameless fourth treatise of the Codex Tchacos, Allogenes is the central figure, which has led to the modern title *The Book of Allogenes* (see further below), but there is no connection between this Allogenes and Seth. In the work *Allogenes* of NHC XI, 3 Allogenes is not identified with Seth, either; the name Seth does not even occur in it. At the end of *Allogenes* (69, 16–19) we find, before the title, the remark: 'The seal of all the books of Allogenes', which suggests that this is the conclusion to an entire series of books of Allogenes. In itself, therefore, another book *Allogenes* could have circulated in the school of Plotinus than the one preserved in Nag Hammadi. But the marked similarity to *Zostrianus* and to the views opposed by Plotinus leaves no doubt that Plotinus knew our *Allogenes*. It should therefore be dated to the first half of the third century. It may have its origins in Egypt, but clear indications as to its provenance are lacking.

Allogenes takes the form of a report of several revelations to Allogenes, which he has written down for his son Messos. It is striking that Porphyry, in his report about the gnostic writings read in the school of Plotinus, after mentioning the revelation to Allogenes, also attributes such a work to Messos (*Life of Plotinus* 16). This could be due to confusion on Porphyry's part, but of course it may also be that there did in fact exist a 'Revelation of Messos'. The text of *Allogenes* is full of lacunae and the first five to six lines of many pages have been lost (even the first 15 lines of pages 65–9), but nevertheless the course of the revelations described is easy to follow. The work consists of two parts which are clearly distinct, both temporally and spatially. In the first part (45, 1–58, 6) Allogenes is simply in his

[105] Ed. A. Clark Wire, J.D. Turner and O.S. Wintermute, NHS 28 (1990), pp. 172–267; W.-P. Funk, P.-H. Poirier, M. Scopello and J. D. Turner, BCNH-T 30 (2004).

earthly body and is instructed in five revelations about the highest levels of the divine sphere, that is, the Barbelo aeon and the Invisible Spirit, who dwells above it. The revelations are given by a heavenly figure, called Youel, who also plays a role in *Zostrianus*. In the second part (58, 7–69, 15), which takes place a hundred years later (the generations before the Flood were long-lived!), Allogenes is taken up from the earth and witnesses the glorious powers of which Youel had spoken. He is advised by 'the powers' of Barbelo's Lights (Salamex, Semen and Arme). The divine world of *Allogenes* is less complicated than that of *Zostrianus*, but here, too, the upper echelon is formed by the Invisible Spirit and the Barbelo aeon, between which 'the Thrice-Powerful One' has probably insinuated himself as an independent entity. Within Barbelo we find the same divine powers as in *Zostrianus*: Kalyptos, Protophanes, Autogenes and the 'Thrice-Male Child'. In *Allogenes* there is a clear tendency to place above the Invisible Spirit an even higher divine hypostasis, referred to as 'the Unknowable One', though these two are sometimes also identified with each other. It is striking that in the description of the Invisible Spirit in the terms of negative theology (NHC XI, 62, 27–63, 28) the same source has evidently been used as in the *Apocryphon of John* (BG 24, 9–25, 7; NHC II, 3–33).[106] In *Allogenes* (54, 6–55, 11(?)) we find the same and related eulogies known from *Zostrianus*. *Allogenes*, too, is ultimately not concerned with philosophical clarity about the source of being, but with the vision, experience and veneration of the unknowable God.

Book of Allogenes Allogenes also plays a leading role in the *Book of Allogenes*, the fourth treatise of the Codex Tchacos, or at least in its surviving part.[107] Of the eight identified pages of this work (Codex Tchacos 59–66), only the first four offer a coherent text, though the first four to nine lines of these pages have also been lost. The work bears no relation to the Platonizing *Allogenes* from Nag Hammadi discussed above. However, there can be no doubt that we are dealing with a gnostic text here.

The first event narrated is that a non-specifiable group of people climb up Mount Tabor and address a prayer there to the God 'who is above all the great aeons, who has no beginning and no end'. They beg for 'a spirit of knowledge' with regard to the divine mysteries, so that they will know

[106] A synoptic reproduction of the texts, with an English translation, in M. Waldstein and F. Wisse (eds.), *The Apocryphon of John. Synopsis of Nag Hammadi Codices II, 1; III, 1; and IV, 1 with BG 8502, 2*, NHMS 33 (Leiden: Brill, 1995), pp. 184–7 (Appendix 3).

[107] Ed. Kasser and Wurst, *The Gospel of Judas ... Critical Edition*, pp. 253–75; J. Brankaer and H.-G. Bethge, TU 161 (2007), pp. 373–442.

whence they came and whither they are going and what they must do to live. After this prayer, which is uttered by Allogenes, Satan appears and offers him all kinds of treasures. Allogenes answers: 'Get away from me, Satan, as I am not searching for you but for my Father, who surpasses all the great aeons. For I was called Allogenes, because I am of another race; I am not from your race' (60, 15–23). Another failed attempt sees the disappearance of Satan, who is designated as the World-Ruler, which probably refers to the Demiurge, the wicked creator-god. Next, Allogenes invokes 'God, who is in the great aeons' for help and salvation from all evil and for radiation with his ineffable light. God's answer is related by Allogenes himself: he is surrounded by a cloud of blinding light and a voice tells him that his prayer has been answered. After this, the manuscript is so severely damaged that no meaningful text can be reconstructed. Clearly the events described are firmly based on the biblical stories about the temptation of Jesus in the desert (Matt. 4:1–11; Mark 1:12–13; Luke 4:1–13) and the transfiguration on the mountain (Matt. 17:1–8; Mark 9:2–8; Luke 9:28–36). This indicates that Allogenes is equated here with Jesus, probably in the sense that Jesus is regarded as an incarnation of Allogenes. In that case we have here a further development of the idea in the *Holy Book of the Great Invisible Spirit* that on his third appearance Seth 'put on' Jesus. If this is right, a date after the *Holy Book* seems most likely, perhaps the late second or early third century, but again there is no way of gaining certainty here.

Marsanes *Marsanes* (NHC x, 1)[108] was probably the only work in Codex x from Nag Hammadi. This is not entirely certain, since the manuscript is badly damaged. Only the first ten pages are indubitably in the right order. Modern text editions assume a total number of sixty-eight pages, of which fourteen have been completely lost. But in reality these figures may be much higher. Moreover, only fragments have survived of many pages, so that in particular pages 13–22, 43–6, 55–68 do not offer a meaningful text. Because pages 47–54 are entirely lacking, this state of affairs means that the content of the last 26 pages is almost completely closed to us. Some caution is therefore necessary in interpreting this work.

According to the eponymous work, Marsanes is the receiver of a series of revelations, but it is unclear whether he is a mythical person from primeval times, like Zostrianus and Allogenes, or a more recent prophet and the leader of a gnostic group. In the *Untitled Gnostic Treatise* of the

[108] Ed. B. A. Pearson, NHS 15 (1981), pp. 211–352; W.-P. Funk, P.-H. Poirier and J. D. Turner, BCNH-T 27 (2000).

Codex Brucianus, which we will discuss below, we are told in chapter 7 that the powers of all the great aeons paid homage to 'the power residing in Marsanes'. In the same context Nikotheos is also mentioned as a revelatory figure, the same person under whose name a revelation circulated in the school of Plotinus (Porphyry, *Life of Plotinus* 16). But the connection between the two, if any, remains unclear. The gnostic group of the Archontics revered two prophets, Martiades and Marsianus, who made a three-day journey through the heavens (Epiphanius, *Panarion* 40, 7, 6). The name of the latter is usually interpreted as a variant of Marsanes. In this vague information Marsanes is never mentioned as the writer of a revelation.

Marsanes clearly belongs to the category of later, Platonizing texts. At the beginning of his work the author provides a list of thirteen 'seals', which denote the levels of the entire cosmos, from the material world to the top of the divine world (16–4, 24). The tenth seal relates to 'Barbelo, the male virgin, who is the aeon', the eleventh to 'the Invisible One, who possesses three powers', the twelfth to 'the Spirit, who has no Being' and the thirteenth to 'the Silent One, who is unknown'. Compared with *Zostrianus*, more differentiation has been introduced on the level above Barbelo: above the Great Invisible Spirit resides an Unknown Silent One as the highest form of the divine. A parallel of this view is offered by the systems of the Neoplatonists Iamblichus (late third and first half of the fourth century) and Theodorus of Asine (*c.* 275–360).[109] For the rest the structure of the divine world in *Marsanes* largely agrees with that of *Zostrianus* and *Allogenes*. More interesting is the second surviving part of *Marsanes*, from 18, 14 onwards, in which the 'third power' of the 'thrice-powerful Invisible Spirit' instructs Marsanes about the various fields of science, in the framework of a doctrine of the soul. Thus there are expositions on the twelve signs of the zodiac, the alphabet, numbers, names and astrology. All this is apparently incorporated in a theurgical framework, that is to say, knowledge of these matters is needed for completion of the journey upwards, in order to witness the unknowable God. Again, parallels for this can be found in the works of the Neoplatonists mentioned above. This suggests that the Greek text of *Marsanes* should probably be assigned to a fairly late date: late third or early fourth century seems the most natural assumption. It is not known where the work was

[109] For the views of these authors and a comparison with the system of Marsanes, see Turner, *Sethian Gnosticism and the Platonic Tradition*, pp. 428–46, and his 'Introduction' to the edition in BCNH-T 27, pp. 209–30.

written. Some scholars propose Syria/Palestine, but their arguments are not wholly convincing. Egypt (Alexandria) seems just as likely.

Untitled Gnostic Treatise The *Untitled Gnostic Treatise* of the Codex Brucianus shows affinity with the Platonizing gnostic texts discussed previously.[110] It offers a colourful description of the divine world, in which the numbers three, nine and twelve play an important role. For instance, nine powers emanate from the 'Father of the All' and he encompasses twelve 'depths' (chapter 2). This Father of the All is probably identical with the important figure of Setheus, who is surrounded by twelve 'Fathers'. The ninth Father is said to have three faces, one that is 'hidden' (*kalyptos*), one that is 'first visible' (*prōtophanēs*) and one that is 'self-begotten' (*autogenēs*). In *Zostrianus* and *Allogenes* these three terms refer to the three highest levels of being within the Barbelo aeon, as we saw in the discussion of these texts. Here, and also in chapter 9, they are used in a very different context, while Barbelo is not mentioned in the entire work. She is probably hidden behind the 'Mother of the All' (*pammētōr*), of whom it is said in chapter 13 that she contains the 'Forefather' (*propatōr*), who in turn receives a power which is called, among other things, 'the First-Appearing' (*prōtophanēs*) and 'the Self-Begotten' (*autogenēs*). The Mother of the All then institutes the 'Self-Father' (*autopatōr*), to whom she gives the aeon of the 'Hidden One' (*kalyptos*), 'in whom the All is'. It is clear that the *Untitled Treatise* was directly or indirectly familiar with traditions of *Zostrianus* and other Platonizing works, but treated them with great licence. The author describes in detail how numerous spiritual powers stem from the highest divine beings and from each other, served and glorified by myriads of angels and archangels. But it is hard to fathom how exactly the author visualized the structure of the spiritual universe.

We are not told how evil entered the world. The author does say that when Unity (*monas*) had brought the All to life in herself, she made a protective veil or curtain around it, and that the existent was thus separated from the non-existent (chapters 12 and 13). The non-existent is equated with the evil that has manifested itself in matter. The view of evil as the non-existent is a typically (Neo)platonic conception. The First-Born (*prōtogenētos*) Son acts as a creator, by brooding on matter like a bird, and commands his creatures to love one another and honour God and seek his essence (chapter 16). When salvation takes place, 'the Lord of Glory' (= the First-Born Son?) divides the matter into two parts, the 'land of life

[110] Ed. C. Schmidt, TU 8, 1–2 (1892); V. MacDermot, NHS 13 (1978); C. A. Baynes, *A Coptic Gnostic Treatise Contained in the Codex Brucianus* (Cambridge University Press, 1933).

and light and rest' and the 'land of death and darkness and suffering'. The first land is destined for the saved, who have worshipped him, the second for those who failed to do this (chapter 19). For the saved there is a way upwards, and once again this clearly echoes the tradition of the *Holy Book of the Great Invisible Spirit* and especially *Zostrianus*. The author mentions the 'earth in the air', and also the lands of the 'Exile' (*paroikēsis*), the 'Repenting' (*metanoia*), and the self-begotten 'Impressions' (*antitypoi*).[111] There they are also baptized, the servants Michar and Micheu(s) again being mentioned (chapter 20).

The *Untitled Treatise*, too, contains numerous hymns and hymnic prayers, which are sung by the heavenly powers and the saved people. The connection with Neoplatonism is much looser than in *Zostrianus*, *Allogenes* and *Marsanes*, the clear structure of the metaphysical world has been replaced by exuberant descriptions of the many divine powers, the language is much less philosophical, but out-and-out religious. The work aims to provide an insight into the extraordinary richness and variety of divine being, to which only one response is possible: adoration. The *Untitled Treatise* must have been written after *Zostrianus* and *Allogenes*, probably in the last decades of the third century or the beginning of the fourth. We do not know where it was written.

Three Steles of Seth The *Three Steles of Seth* (NHC VII, 5)[112] presuppose the mythological conceptions of the Platonizing works discussed above. They are hymns glorifying the divine powers which play a role in those works. The hymns are preceded by a brief report on the origin of the three steles (118, 10–23) and they conclude with some remarks about their effect and how they should be sung (127, 6–26). The introduction mentions Seth, 'the father of the living and unshakable race', as the author of the *Three Steles*. The suggestion is that Seth inscribed these texts on steles, stone slabs. This brings to mind the report that Seth wrote the *Holy Book of the Great Invisible Spirit* in 130 years and placed it on Mount Charaxio, so that at the end of time it would reveal 'the incorruptible holy race of the great Saviour' (NHC III, 68, 1–69, 4; almost completely lost in NHC IV). The *Holy Book* does not talk about steles here, but they were probably in the author's mind, since Jewish traditions about Seth, as we noted before, talk about two steles which his descendants erected before the Flood in order to safeguard the knowledge they had acquired,

[111] See also p. 82 (Zostrianus) and p. 135 (Plotinus).

[112] Ed. P. Claude, BCNH-T 8 (1983); J. M. Robinson and J. E. Goehring, NHMS 30 (1996), pp. 371–421.

even if the world were destroyed by water or fire (Flavius Josephus, *Jewish Antiquities* I, 70–1). By contrast, our gnostic text talks about three steles, apparently because a stele is dedicated to each of the three highest divine 'persons', the Self-Begotten Son, the Mother Barbelo and the Invisible Spirit. Perhaps the author of *Zostrianus* had the *Three Steles* in mind when he reported that shortly before returning to earth Zostrianus had filled three writing-tablets and left them behind as knowledge for those who would come after him, 'the living elect' (NHC VIII, 130, 1–4). His readers will certainly have made this connection. The introduction to the *Three Steles* also narrates how this legacy of Seth became known: Dositheus saw and read the steles and then wrote down the contents from memory, 'just as they were written there'. 'Dositheus' probably refers to the Samaritan sectarian and presumed teacher of Simon Magus. His name probably serves to give the text a respectable gnostic aura, for the contents have nothing to do with Samaria, Dositheus or Simon.

In the text the three steles are clearly marked by superscriptions and subscriptions, but closer examination shows that this structure cannot be original, since the first part of the first stele (118, 25–119, 15) is not addressed to the Son, the Self-Begotten One, but to the Father of Seth, Pigeradamas, that is the heavenly Adam, who according to the *Apocryphon of John* (NHC II, 8, 33–9, 4; BG 35, 5–10) resides in the first great Light. Some scholars believe that no fewer than seven original hymns can be distinguished in the *Three Steles*. However that may be, the present text has clearly been divided into three parts, as the ending will also show. In the rest of the first stele (119, 15–121, 16) the Son, 'the good Self-Begotten One', is lavishly praised. All kinds of predicates are attributed to him, and the tone is ecstatic, for instance: 'You have saved! You have saved! You have saved us!' (120, 34–5), 'You are perfect! You are perfect! You are perfect!' (121, 14–15). The second stele (119, 14–124, 12) glorifies Barbelo, the divine Mother, who sprang from the truly pre-existent God who is raised above being. She is called 'the first shadow of the holy Father, Light from Light', 'a world of knowledge' and 'a world of truth' (122, 1–4, 15; 123, 22). She is thanked for granting salvation: 'You have heard! You have heard! You have saved! You have saved! We give thanks, we praise you always! We will glorify you!' (124, 10–13). The third stele (124, 16–127, 6) also starts with such ecstatic repetitions, now addressed to the unknown Father: 'We rejoice! We rejoice! We rejoice! We have seen! We have seen! We have seen that the truly Pre-Existent One truly exists!' (124, 17–20). He is praised as 'Non-Being, Existence that precedes all existence, First Being that precedes all being, Father of divinity and life, Creator of mind,

Giver of the good, Giver of blessedness' (124, 26–30), in which the (Neo) platonic triad of Being, Life and Thought can be heard. The magic character of this text is borne out by the many magic names included in the invocation of the highest God, some of which also occur in the *Prayer of Seth*.[113]

At the end of the *Three Steles* we find some remarks about the importance of these hymns for the soul's salvation and also a statement that is best described as a liturgical rubric. The latter reads as follows: 'For they all praise these (three), individually and together, and must then be silent. And as ordained for them, they ascend or, after the silence, descend. Starting from the third, they praise the second and then the first. The way up is the way down' (127, 11–21). An indication is given here for individual and collective use of these hymns in the context of the soul's ascent via the Son and the Mother to the Father, the ground of all being. The order of the three steles must be adhered to; after the third a silence is observed, a moment of silent contemplation of the deity. Next, the hymns are sung again, but now in reverse order, from the Father via the Mother to the Son. This shows once again that the communities where Platonizing gnosis was in vogue were not concerned with philosophical precision but with religious experience, which could be undergone individually and celebrated collectively. As regards terms and conceptions, the *Three Steles* are closest to *Zostrianus* and *Allogenes* and scholars therefore usually assume that this work was written in the first half of the third century. It could have its cradle in Egypt, but there is no evidence to substantiate this.

VALENTINIAN TEXTS

Valentinian gnostic religion wanted very deliberately to be Christian and accepted in the Church. This also explains why Christian anti-gnostic authors opposed Valentinus and his pupils so fiercely. Chapter 5 of this book will look more closely at Valentinianism, here we need to discuss the authentic sources available to us for this movement. Before the discovery of the Nag Hammadi library, we possessed only a few original texts of Valentinus and his followers. In Chapter 2, when discussing the Greek tradition, it was noted that the anti-heretical authors sometimes incorporated (parts of) Valentinian texts in their works. The most famous are the *Excerpta ex Theodoto* by Clement of Alexandria, the *Letter*

[113] See pp. 15 and 141.

to Flora by Ptolemy and the anonymous *Letter of Instruction*. There are also two Greek inscriptions, whose Valentinian character used to be disputed, but is now generally accepted. The Nag Hammadi discovery has given us at least six Valentinian writings: the *Gospel of Truth* (NHC I, 3 and XII, 2), the *Treatise on Resurrection* (NHC I, 4), the *Tripartite Tractate* (NHC I, 5), the *Gospel of Philip* (NHC II, 3), the *Interpretation of Knowledge* (NHC XI, 1) and the *Valentinian Exposition* (NHC XI, 2). The brief *Prayer of the Apostle Paul* (NHC I, 1) also contains terms which could point to a Valentinian background. For this reason it will be discussed here. The *(First) Revelation of James* displays elements of an unmistakably Valentinian tradition as well, but because its central theme is the soul's heavenly journey through the hostile planetary spheres, it was dealt with in the previous section of this chapter.[114] Of the Coptic works mentioned, only the *Tripartite Tractate* and the *Valentinian Exposition* explicitly treat the main aspects of Valentinian mythology (though with very different emphases). The others merely allude to it. Of the texts preserved in Greek, the *Excerpta ex Theodoto* and the anonymous *Letter of Instruction* speak out most clearly on the myth, though to understand it properly one needs to consult the reports in the Church Fathers.

Excerpta ex Theodoto The *Excerpta ex Theodoto* (Excerpts from Theodotus)[115] is thought to have been compiled by Clement of Alexandria around 200 CE. It is unlikely that the book was ever intended for publication in this form, since it is little more than a notebook in which the author has recorded and sometimes commented on quotations from Theodotus and other gnostics for his own use. This creates a problem, because it is sometimes hard to determine where the gnostic quotation ends and Clement's commentary begins. The traditional title is rather misleading, as only five quotations are explicitly attributed to Theodotus, who is supposed to have been a contemporary of Ptolemy (*c.* 160–80). Furthermore, there are six quotations introduced by the words 'he says', which is usually taken to refer to Theodotus. But there are also quotations attributed to 'the followers of Valentinus', who are probably also meant when the formulation 'they say' is used. Literary criticism has distinguished four segments in the *Excerpta*, of which the third (excerpts 43–65) occupies a special position. This is because it contains a continuous account that corresponds so closely to what Irenaeus describes in *AH* I, 4 and 5 that there can be no doubt that Clement and Irenaeus used the same source.

114 See pp. 75–7.
115 Ed. F. Sagnard, SC 23 (1948, 1970).

Sometimes Irenaeus offers clarifying details lacking in Clement, which shows once again that Irenaeus represents his sources quite fairly, and is therefore not as biased and unreliable as many of his modern critics think. The *Excerpta* deals with almost the entire Valentinian mythology and doctrine of salvation, though not in a systematic exposition but fragmentarily. Sometimes there are contradictions, which go back to differences between the Valentinians themselves. One of the most striking features of this collection of Valentinian views is the constant appeal to texts from the Bible, particularly from the book of Genesis, the gospels and the letters of Paul. This use of the Bible is most frequent in the third segment, which most probably reflects the theology of Ptolemy. For modern readers this use of the Bible is not very convincing, because the texts, including those of the New Testament, are almost always explained allegorically. But this was common practice in that period, also in non-gnostic authors.

Letter of Instruction The anonymous *Letter of Instruction*, preserved in Epiphanius, *Panarion* 31, 5–6, talks in detail about the development and structure of the Pleroma. It is obvious that the author presupposes the Valentinian system as described in Irenaeus *AH* I, 1, 1–2 and introduces an important correction to it. This implies that the work must have been written in the late second or the third century.[116] The beginning of the *Letter* testifies to great prophetic self-consciousness on the writer's part: 'The indestructible Mind [*Nous*] greets the indestructible ones. I remind you of unnameable, ineffable and supra-celestial mysteries, which can be known neither by principalities, nor by powers, nor by those subordinate [to them], nor to any creature, but have been revealed only to the Thought [*Ennoia*] of the Unchangeable One.' The same formulation is used in *Eugnostus*, NHC III, 71, 15–18. The author then goes on to describe the origin of the Pleroma: initially all things resided ignorant in the unknown God, who is called the 'Unchangeable One', 'the Self-Father' (*Autopatōr*), the 'unageing, ever young and androgynous aeon', the 'Majesty' (*Megethos*, literally 'Greatness') and (further on in the text) 'Depth' (*Bythos*) and probably also 'Light' (*Phōs*). This eternal rest changed when his Thought (*Ennoia*), also called 'Grace' (*Charis*) and 'Silence' (*Sigē*) (according to the author, this last name is the right one), wanted to break the eternal bonds and, driven by her desire for his rest, made the Majesty susceptible to the female element. And when she had united with him, she brought to light the 'Father of Truth', 'whom the

[116] A detailed discussion in Thomassen, *Spiritual Seed*, pp. 218–30.

perfect have rightly called "Man" [*Anthrōpos*], because he is the image of the pre-existent Unbegotten One' (5, 1–2). 'Silence' then unites with Man and thus brings 'Truth' (*Alētheia*) to light. It is curious here that, unlike in other Valentinian sources, the first pair does not produce the second, but Truth springs from an incestuous union of mother (Silence) and son (Man). This gives rise to the first tetrad: Depth, Silence, Father and Truth. Driven by the same voluptuous urge that characterized her mother, Truth seduces her Father and together they produce a second tetrad, which is an image of the first: 'Man' (*Anthrōpos*), 'Church' (*Ekklēsia*), 'Word' (*Logos*) and 'Life' (*Zōē*). Next, Man and Church, 'through the will of the Depth that encompasses all things', produce a dodecad of androgynous aeons (of whom Sophia is the last), upon which World and Life bring forth a decad of such aeons (5, 6–9). In Irenaeus the decad of Word and Life is mentioned before the dodecad of Man and Church, but the names of the thirty aeons of the Pleroma are virtually the same in the two texts, though sometimes they are combined in different ways. So far the author does not depart materially from the standard Valentinian view of the Pleroma, but in what follows he proves to be a dissident. He sharply reacts against other Valentinians, whom he calls 'earthly people without understanding', thus relegating them to the position of non-gnostics. For his opponents believe that there are only the thirty aeons which he has just described, but in reality a second ogdoad has come into being that is expressed in numerical units and has also developed into thirty aeons, which in turn produce 'lights' (6, 1–5). These lights, called 'the children of unity', are brought to perfection by a union of the two ogdoads, so that they coincide with the true gnostics, 'the perfect' (6, 7–10). At this point Epiphanius breaks off his account of the letter, so that we do not know how the author conceived of the origin of evil and the realization of salvation. This original gnostic document proves that anti-gnostic authors faithfully represented the original structure of the Valentinian Pleroma, but also that later Valentinians could freely introduce radical changes.

Letter to Flora In the *Letter to Flora* Ptolemy expounds his view of the Old Testament.[117] In the second century this was a topical subject. Christianity had started as a Jewish sect in Palestine, had found its first supporters among Jews in the Graeco-Roman world, and it was therefore natural that great authority was attributed to the Jewish holy writings in

[117] Ed. G. Quispel, SC 24 *bis* (1966), with commentary. See also C. Markschies, 'New Research on Ptolemaeus Gnosticus', *ZAC* 4 (2000), 225–54; Thomassen, *Spiritual Seed*, pp. 119–29; and Dunderberg, *Beyond Gnosticism*, pp. 77–94.

Christian communities. But it was far from clear how far this authority extended and to what precisely it related, the more so because the influential apostle Paul had postulated a sharp opposition between Law and Gospel. The question of how the Jewish Law should be interpreted in the light of the Christian faith became therefore an important topic of discussion in the second century, both between Christians and Jews and among Christians themselves. Around *c.* 160 the well-known apologist Justin Martyr wrote his *Dialogue with Trypho*, a fictitious two-day debate between Justin and a Jewish rabbi on the Christian interpretation of the Jewish Law and the meaning of Christ. The debate undoubtedly reflects the discussions on these points which took place between Jews and Christians, though usually the outcome probably differed from that in Justin, where after two days Trypho is entirely convinced by the Christian arguments. Ptolemy's *Letter to Flora* fits within the Christian discourse of the mid second century on the meaning of the Old Testament. Despite differences in detail, his view shows many similarities with the position of his contemporary Justin. Ptolemy believes that Christ himself indicated that the Law consists of three parts: one part comes from God himself, another part was given by Moses and the rest is owed to 'the elders of the [Jewish] people' (4, 1–14). The first part, which God himself proclaimed, consists in turn of three parts. First there are the absolutely pure Ten Commandments, which were fulfilled by Christ. Next, there are commandments in which justice and injustice go hand in hand (e.g. 'An eye for an eye, a tooth for a tooth'), which were instituted to prevent worse, but were abolished by Christ. Finally, there are ritual precepts in God's Law with regard to sacrifices, observance of the Sabbath, circumcision and the like, which have a symbolic, spiritual meaning because they refer to a transcendental reality, and which were therefore abolished by Christ in their literal meaning (5, 1–15). The frequently heard remark that gnostic religion in its entirety rejected the Old Testament is shown to be invalid here. But Ptolemy *was* a gnostic, or at least came close to being one, as the conclusion of his letter shows.[118] He makes it clear there that the legislator is not the 'perfect' and 'good' God, 'the Father of the All', but the Demiurge, the world-creator, who 'is not good and not really evil or

[118] Markschies, 'New Research', pp. 245–6, and Dunderberg, *Beyond Gnosticism*, pp. 78–9, have argued that Ptolemy's *Letter* should not be read in the light of the doctrines that Irenaeus, *AH* 1, 1–8, ascribed to the Valentinian gnostics (as was done by Quispel); Thomassen, *Spiritual Seed*, pp. 120–1, 128–9, shows that there are indeed considerable differences with Irenaeus' report, especially with respect to the term 'the Middle' as an indication of the Creator, but also that there are distinct correspondences with other Valentinian sources.

unjust, but in himself could be called just' and who 'is an image [*eikōn*] of the supreme God' (7, 2–7).[119] This is the same view that was taught by Marcion and that embroiled him in a bitter conflict with the leaders of Rome's Christian community around 140. Ptolemy's letter has an exoteric character, he does not commit himself completely. He does promise his 'sister Flora' that later, God willing, he will show her by means of apostolic traditions how one supreme, incorruptible and good principle could bring forth the two principles that dominate the world, the destructive one, the devil, and that in the middle, the Creator (7, 8–9).

Valentinian Exposition In the codex the *Valentinian Exposition* (NHC XI, 2)[120] comprises pages 22–44, which have been preserved in such a poor state that more than half the text has been lost. The title has not survived, either, if there ever was one. The work owes its current name to modern editors, who based it on the content. The text actually consists of two parts: an exposition of the Valentinian mythology and doctrine of salvation (22–39) and five liturgical texts, which are clearly separated from the preceding text and from each other in the manuscript (40–4). Because both parts are written in the same hand and a different hand begins at the next treatise, *Allogenes*, scholars usually assume that the liturgical pieces form an appendix to the *Valentinian Exposition*. But it is uncertain whether they formed an original part of it or were added later. Despite the serious damage to the manuscript, it is clear that the author discusses several aspects of Valentinian doctrine: the unknown Father (the 'Root of the All'), the Son (the 'Only-Begotten', the *Nous*), the meaning of the 'Limit' (*Horos*) of the Pleroma, the ogdoad of highest aeons, the ten aeons brought forth by the couple Logos and Life, and the twelve aeons of the couple Man and Church, the salvation of Sophia, the creation of the upper and nether worlds, the role of the Demiurge and finally the restoration of the Pleroma's original unity. It is regrettable that so much of this work has been lost, for even in its mutilated state it is an important source for Valentinian thought. Without lapsing into polemics the author clearly occupies his own position on certain questions. Thus he expands the decad of aeons of Logos and Life to 100 and increases the 12 aeons of Man and Church to 360. Another striking departure from standard Valentinianism is the absence of the psychics

[119] On the relationship between the Demiurge and the Saviour, see Markschies, 'New Research', pp. 239–46, and H. Schmid, 'Ist der Soter in Ptolemäus' Epistula ad Floram der Demiurg? Zu einer These von Christoph Markschies', *ZAC* 15 (2011), 249–71.

[120] Ed. J. É. Ménard, BCNH-T 14 (1985); E. H. Pagels and J. D. Turner, NHS 28 (1990), pp. 89–172.

(non-gnostic Christians, who may be saved), as an intermediate group between the extremes of the hylics (material people, who will be lost) and the pneumatics (the gnostics, who are saved). These and other points will be discussed in more detail below.[121]

The five liturgical texts that follow the treatise proper are nowhere in conflict with the foregoing, but nor do they reflect the typical views of the author of the *Treatise*. They are prayers apparently used in Valentinian circles for baptism and the Eucharist: the first relates to the anointment preceding baptism, the second to the 'first baptism' (with water), the third to (the second, spiritual?) baptism, and the fourth and the fifth to the Eucharist. Though the liturgical prayers are also severely damaged, they are a welcome addition to the very little we know about Valentinian sacraments. It is not known from what time the liturgical texts date and whether they are contemporaneous with the preceding treatise. The treatise itself certainly contains old views, which are best dated to the early period of Valentinianism, but it also contains opinions which form a correction of older views, including those traditionally ascribed to Ptolemy (160–80 CE). For the work as a whole it is therefore impossible to propose anything close to an accurate date; the entire period from the second half of the second century to the beginning of the fourth is possible.

Tripartite Tractate With its eighty-eight pages, the *Tripartite Tractate* (NHC I, 5)[122] is the longest Nag Hammadi text after *Zostrianus*, and if Hans-Martin Schenke was right, we are dealing with excerpts from an even longer work.[123] The treatise has no title in the manuscript and owes its current name to the first editors, who based it on a division into three parts clearly indicated in the manuscript. The first part (NHC I, 51, 1–104, 3) treats the Pleroma and the events which took place inside and outside of it, the second part (104, 4–108, 12) is about the creation of mankind and the third about salvation (108, 13–138, 27). Given that the parts differ greatly in length, it is highly questionable whether this division is original. The work offers an extraordinarily interesting, wide-ranging and highly original exposition of Valentinian theology. The author is unknown, but must have been a powerful and independent thinker. The person speaking here is not someone instructing a small circle of kindred spirits on the fringe of institutional Christianity, but a teacher who

121 See pp. 178–84, 192–4.

122 Ed. H. W. Attridge and E. H. Pagels, NHS 22 (1985), pp. 159–337, notes in NHS 23 (1985), pp. 217–497; E. Thomassen and L. Painchaud, BCNH-T 21 (1995).

123 A summary of his views can be found in *Nag Hammadi Deutsch*, vol. 1, pp. 55–56; cf. also Attridge and Pagels, NHS 22 (1985), pp. 172–174.

addresses the Church as a whole, aware that he has something essential to contribute to the theological debate. In this regard, and also in details of content, his work can be compared with works like *De principiis* by the great non-gnostic teacher Origen (185–254). It is also one of the most difficult texts from Nag Hammadi: the Coptic is problematical and the content often hard to fathom. One of the reasons for this is that the author argues from premises only partly familiar to us. The overall pattern is clearly Valentinian, but shot through with all kinds of variations unknown from elsewhere. Conspicuous features include the 'trinity' of Father, Son and Church and the absence of the figure of Sophia as the driving force behind the developments inside and outside the Pleroma. The Father is the unknowable God, the Son is the thought, self-reflection, of the Father, and the Church is the collection of aeons, which are seen as the divine qualities of the Father expressed in the thought of the Son. Like many gnostic texts, the work starts with an elaborate description of the unknown God. Here, too, the confusion in the Pleroma and the genesis of the world is due to the actions of the youngest aeon, in this case not Sophia but the Logos. Meaning well, he tried to achieve the impossible: he wanted to penetrate the incomprehensibility of the Father and give him glory, but was stopped by the Limit (*Horos*), which protects the Father. Yet this did not happen without the will of the Father: 'The Father had brought him forth for what he knew had to happen' (NHC I, 75, 17–77, 11). The Logos ends up outside the Pleroma and this leads to the genesis of the psychical and material world. The Saviour is the product of the Pleroma: he enlightens the Logos, who in his turn produces the spiritual seeds and breathes some of these, the 'breath of life', into humans (NHC I, 104, 31–106, 25). Thorough research has shown that the author is an original representative of the Eastern branch of the Valentinian school.[124] One gets the impression that he adapted his system as far as possible to the views of non-gnostic Christianity, without giving up the essential ideas of Valentinianism. The work is usually dated to the first half of the third century, in Origen's time, and in view of the content this is in fact most likely.

Gospel of Truth The *Gospel of Truth* (NHC I, 3; XII, 2)[125] derives its title from the first words of the text: 'The Gospel of Truth is a joy for those who have received the grace from the Father of Truth to know him

[124] See pp. 193–4.

[125] NHC I, 1: ed. H. W. Attridge and G. W. MacRae, NHS 22 (1985), pp. 55–117, notes in NHS 23 (1985), pp. 39–135. Fragments of NHC XII, 2: ed. F. Wisse, NHS 22 (1985), pp. 119–22 and NHS 28 (1990), pp. 329–47.

through the power of the Word [*Logos*].' On the one hand it is a modern name, since no title is mentioned in the manuscript, on the other hand it could also be the original title, if it is correct to assume that we are dealing here with the Valentinian *Gospel of Truth* mentioned by the Church Fathers. Irenaeus, *AH* III, 11, 9, reports that the Valentinians call 'a book which they have recently produced the "Gospel of Truth", though it does not agree in any way with the gospels of the apostles'. It is probably on the basis of this report that Pseudo-Tertullian, *Adversus omnes haereses* 4, 6, says of Valentinus in the third century: 'He also has his own gospel, alongside ours.' These reports have provoked a lively debate over two questions: is NHC I, 3 identical with the *Gospel of Truth* in use among the Valentinians according to Irenaeus; and can it have been written by Valentinus himself? Neither question can be answered with certainty. Most scholars tend towards a positive answer to the first question, because they think too improbable the occurrence of two works, of which the title of one (in Irenaeus) would be identical to the powerful opening words, the *incipit*, of the other (from Nag Hammadi). As regards Valentinus' authorship, opinions are much more divided. The only positive argument adduced is the observation that the author must have been a far from mediocre figure, who cannot have remained unnoticed in his time. But obviously this is no proof that the author must have been Valentinus.

Irenaeus is perfectly right that the *Gospel of Truth* has nothing in common with the canonical gospels. It is not a 'Life of Jesus', but a profound meditation on the meaning of the salvation through gnosis brought by Christ. The author sometimes addresses his listeners or readers directly (I, 32, 31–33, 37) and at the end he talks about his own mystical experience: he was at 'the place of rest' and can now talk about nothing else (I, 42, 39–43, 2). The work does not offer a systematic exposition of a certain doctrine, but a carefully composed series of interconnecting and mutually reinforcing, constantly varying reflections on the liberating gnosis given to us and the aeons by Christ. The author prefers to express himself in striking images, in which image and interpretation almost always run together and influence each other, and he likes to use wordplay and unexpected contrasts. The somewhat shabby cloak of the Coptic translation cannot conceal that we are dealing here with a literary masterpiece. The *Gospel of Truth* is a splendid work, of great profundity and poetic power, written by a thinker and poet. Valentinus could in fact well be the author.

There is no doubt that the *Gospel of Truth* is a Valentinian work. It contains all kinds of terms from Valentinian mythology and theology, but the systematic context in which they are embedded in traditional Valentinianism is entirely lacking. God is the unknown and unthinkable Father, a Mind (*Nous*), in the Depth of which everything was initially located in an unexpressed, potential form. He encompasses the All and from him the All sprang forth. The All is the total spiritual reality, the heavenly and the earthly, that of the aeons and human beings. One of the characteristic features of this *Gospel* is that it constantly shuttles to and fro between these two worlds and that the differences between them are lost, which makes interpretation difficult. The aeons, also called 'spaces', were ignorant of God, as were human beings. This means that in actual fact they did not exist, for true existence is only achieved when knowledge is attained of the Father and oneself. Christ is the bringer of this gnosis. The pre-existent Christ, who is called the Logos or the Son, was the first to emerge from the Father. The relationship between the Father and the Son is profoundly explained in a long passage on the Name (I, 38, 6–40, 23). The Name of the Father is the Son. The Name expresses the essence and therefore the Son is the expression of, and even identical with, the unknowable essence of the Father. Jewish speculations about the Name of God seem to be in the background here. The earthly Jesus acted as a teacher and shepherd, his death had decisive significance: 'he knows that his death means life for many' (I, 20, 13–14). The meaning of Jesus' death in the *Gospel of Truth* and other gnostic texts will be dealt with at greater length in Chapter 5 below.

If we assume that Irenaeus was in fact talking about the *Gospel of Truth* found in Nag Hammadi – which after all is highly probable – it must have been written before 180. Anyone who assumes it to be a work by Valentinus himself must date it before 150, but anyone who considers it a meditation by a later author, incorporating elements of the Valentinian system, must locate the work in the second half of the second century or in the third century. The first option (before 150) seems the most probable, but no certainty can be obtained. It is certain, however, that the work in its present form must have been acceptable to many educated Christians of the second century.

Treatise on Resurrection The *Treatise on Resurrection* (NHC I, 4)[126] is sometimes also called the *Letter to Rheginus*. The usual title is mentioned at the end of the work, but is generally assumed to be a secondary

[126] Ed. J. É Ménard, BCNH-T 12 (1983); M. L. Peel, NHS 22 (1985), pp. 123–57, notes in NHS 23 (1985), pp. 137–215.

addition, based on the content, since the piece has the literary form of a letter, which at the request of a certain Rheginus addresses the question how the resurrection of the dead should be interpreted. But the beginning lacks the usual greeting to the adressee, probably because it was deliberately omitted by the person who turned it into a treatise (*logos*). At the end the author writes that the letter is also intended for the circle around Rheginus, whom he refers to as 'your brothers, my sons'. The writer is apparently an authoritative teacher, who without polemicizing sets out his views and is aware of being listened to. 'Many look forward to what I have written to you' (50, 11–13). The Valentinian character of this doctrinal epistle is disputed by some scholars, and in fact it is not explicitly expressed. But it does contain all kinds of terms that Valentinians also liked to use, so that at the very least the work can be said to have a Valentinian colouring. It is generally dated to the second half of the second century. The author and the place where he wrote are unknown.

The letter fits perfectly within the discussions on the resurrection held in the second century. The central question was whether the resurrection should be taken literally, in the sense of 'resurrection of the flesh', or more spiritually. Because gnostics attached no importance to the body, they defended a spiritual explanation of the traditional Christian doctrine of resurrection, and in fact this is found in the *Treatise on Resurrection*, too. The author makes a close connection between Christ's resurrection and the resurrection of Christians: Christ's resurrection guarantees our resurrection. This is not something that awaits us only after our death, but is an already realized fact. Rheginus must regard himself as already being resurrected (49, 22–3). This is not to say that there is no resurrection from death, only not in the sense of a bodily but of a spiritual resurrection.[127]

Gospel of Philip The *Gospel of Philip* (NHC II, 3)[128] is not a gospel in the usual sense, but a collection of individual Christian-gnostic reflections. Since the first German translation by Hans-Martin Schenke (1959) they are usually divided into 127 sections. Though closer examination has shown that separate textual units can be distinguished within these sections, this has fortunately not led to new divisions into sections. The existence of a *Gospel of Philip* was already known from a report in Epiphanius of Salamis, *Panarion* 26, 13, 2–3. According to Epiphanius, it contained

[127] See also pp. 202–5.

[128] Ed. W. W. Isenberg, NHS 20 (1989), pp. 129–215; H.-M. Schenke, TU 143 (1997); Lundberg, NHMS 73 (2010), 468–539.

the following passage on the soul's ascent through the spheres of the hostile heavenly powers:

The Lord has revealed to me what the soul must say when it ascends to heaven, and how it must answer each of the powers above:

'I got to know myself,
and collected myself from everywhere.
I did not beget children for the Ruler,
but tore out his roots
and collected the dispersed members.
And I know who you are,
for I am one of those who are from above.'

However, this passage does not occur in the Coptic *Gospel of Philip*, so that it is unclear whether Epiphanius had a different version of the same gospel or an entirely different text with the same title. This last is quite possible, as is shown by the presence of two different texts in the Nag Hammadi library, both of which are called the *Revelation of James* (NHC v, 3 and 4). According to some early Byzantine writers, the *Gospel of Philip* was also used by the Manichaeans, but again we do not know whether this was the book discussed here. It is doubtful whether the title which the work bears in NHC II, 3 is in fact original or whether it was added later by somebody, for instance a copyist. We find nothing in the text that points to a special relationship with Philip, leaving aside the question whether this name refers to the apostle (e.g. Mark 3:18) or the evangelist (e.g. Acts 6:5), since the two figures were identified in the early Christian tradition. As the only apostle, however, Philip is quoted in the work, as the source of the report that Joseph the Carpenter had made Jesus' cross from a tree which he himself had planted: 'And his child [literally 'seed'] hung on what he had planted' (73, 8–16 (section 91)). But it is hard to see that this was the reason for attributing the entire work to Philip, as some scholars have assumed.

There has been much debate on the nature of this gospel, because its literary genre is difficult to determine.[129] To the reader it seems a string of unconnected statements about God and Christ, the sacraments and

[129] Three studies, published almost simultaneously and differing strongly in their conclusions, clearly demonstrate the many problems of the *Gospel of Philip*: M. L. Turner, *The Gospel According to Philip. The Sources and Coherence of an Early Christian Collection*, NHMS 38 (Leiden: Brill, 1996); H.-M. Schenke, *Das Philippus-Evangelium (Nag Hammadi Codex II, 3). Neu herausgegeben, übersetzt und erklärt*, TU 143 (Berlin: Akademie-Verlag, 1997); and L. Painchaud, 'La composition de l'Évangile selon Philippe (NH II, 3): une analyse rhétorique', in *Society of Biblical Literature Seminar Papers* (Atlanta: Scholars Press, 1996), pp. 35–66. A new approach appears in Lundhaug, *Images of Rebirth*, pp. 153–399.

salvation, believers and non-believers, gnostic and non-gnostic Christians, words of Jesus and exegetical discussions. An important question is: are all the statements and reflections written by one author or were they gathered from various sources? If they are the work of one author, it is legitimate, where possible, to explain one textual unit by means of another; if not, great caution is required. Recent research generally concludes that the entire work is pervaded with the same spirit and that there is no reason to assume more than one author. If this is right, it no longer really matters whether we are dealing here with excerpts from a larger work or individual notes for personal use. Another point on which scholars have reached a certain consensus relates to the Valentinian character of the work. Though not all the statements are typically gnostic and certainly not all the gnostic elements display the features of Valentinianism, the work contains many views which are typically Valentinian and none completely at odds with it.

As regards content, what most complicates the interpretation of the *Gospel of Philip* is the lack of a clear structure and the strongly evocative and veiled, symbolic language, so that it is often unclear what the author is exactly trying to say. Any perusal of the work reveals the constant recurrence of certain themes, in particular discussions of the sacraments and ethical admonitions. We have no knowledge of any other gnostic text in which the sacraments play such an important role. For this reason Wesley W. Isenberg surmised in 1989 that this gospel actually contains excerpts from a Christian-gnostic sacramental catechism.[130] This line has been pursued by later research. In a recent study L. K. van Os concludes that the *Gospel of Philip* is formed from the personal notes which a leader of a Christian-gnostic community had compiled for the purpose of baptismal catechesis. In this view, the structure of the text is entirely determined by the course of the instruction of the persons to be baptized. It remains to be seen to what extent further research on the *Gospel of Philip* will endorse these conclusions. In any case this study offers a lucid interpretative framework for one of the most fascinating but also one of the most difficult texts from Nag Hammadi.[131]

[130] In his edition, p. 134.

[131] L. K. van Os, 'Baptism in the Bridal Chamber: The Gospel of Philip as a Valentinian Baptismal Instruction' (digital dissertation, State University Groningen, 2007). His conclusions were largely adopted by Painchaud in his introduction to the French translation of the *Gospel of Philip*, 'Notice', in *Écrits gnostiques*, pp. 335–9. However, in a book published at the same time, H. Schmidt, *Die Eucharistie ist Jesus: Anfänge einer Theorie der Sakramente im koptischen*

The *Gospel of Philip* has also provided clarity on the various sacraments common among the Valentinians. In 67, 27–30 (section 68) we are told: 'The Lord has fulfilled everything in a mystery: baptism, anointment, eucharist, redemption and bridal chamber.' There has been much debate on the question whether 'redemption' (*apolytrōsis*) and 'bridal chamber' (*nymphōn*) were separate sacraments, but close analysis shows that these terms, too, relate to the initiation ritual of baptism and anointment followed by the celebration of the Eucharist and actually indicate their effects.[132] The 'bridal chamber' symbolizes the union of the baptized person with the Holy Spirit resulting from baptism and anointment, but obviously also stands for the ultimate union of the gnostic with his heavenly counterpart in the celestial bridal chamber.[133] Apparently the Valentinians recognized the same sacraments as non-gnostic Christians.

As regards date, we need to take a certain development of Valentinianism into account. The second half of the second century is certainly eligible, but the first half of the third century is possible, too. The criteria for a more exact determination of the date are lacking. Given the author's preference for Syriac words and etymologies, scholars often think that he lived in Syria. But he could also have come from there and recorded his notes elsewhere.

Inscriptions Two Greek inscriptions, the 'Bridal Chamber inscription' and the epitaph for Flavia Sophe, also mention the Valentinian motifs of baptism and bridal chamber. At least, that is the opinion of most scholars, though sometimes the Christian character of the first and the Valentinian character of the second are questioned.[134] The inscriptions are so short that they can be quoted in full here. The Bridal Chamber inscription was found in the Via Latina in Rome and is dated by some to the mid

Philippusevangelium (NHC II, 3), Supplements to Vigiliae Christianae 88 (Leiden: Brill, 2007), argues that this gospel is not a baptismal catechism but a treatise on the sacraments in general.

132 Lundhaug, *Images of Rebirth*, pp. 311–16, denies a direct sacramental meaning for the passage, and takes it as referring to 'everything which Jesus did, as related in Scripture' (his baptism in the River Jordan, the Last Supper, his redemptive death). The *apolytrōsis* has also been interpreted as a sacrament for the dying; see Lewis, 'Apolytrosis', pp. 548–57, and p. 76 above.

133 A thorough discussion of the Valentinian initiation can be found in Thomassen, *Spiritual Seed*, pp. 333–414 (pp. 341–50: *Gospel of Philip*).

134 Both texts are printed, translated and briefly discussed by Thomassen, *Spiritual Seed*, pp. 350–3 (with references to earlier literature). He gives, however, only the front of Flavia Sophe's stone and was unfamiliar with the new edition by P. McKechnie, 'Flavia Sophe in Context', *ZPE* 135 (2001), 117–24. A new investigation of the Bridal Chamber inscription, now at the Capitoline Museum and catalogued as NCE (= Nuovo Catalogo Epigrafico) 156, was undertaken by H. G. Snyder, 'A Second-Century Christian Inscription from the Via Latina', *JECS* 19 (2011), 157–95 (with a good photograph of the stone on p. 160). Snyder argued for a reading of the text as a funerary epigram for a Valentinian Christian, not as a baptismal inscription. Although it may be admitted that there is a rather thin line between funerary and baptismal imagery, this new

second century and by others to the third century or later. The text reads as follows:

Fellow [brothers] celebrate for me with torches the bath of the bridal chamber.
They hunger for the banquet in our house,
singing hymns to the Father and praising the Son.
May a single fountain, namely of Truth, flow there![135]

Though the imagery derives from matrimonial customs (bath of the bride, accompaniment by torches, banquet), the inscription cannot refer to the celebration of a marriage. This is already ruled out by the mention of 'fellow brothers' and of the glorification of the 'Father' and the 'Son'. Incidentally, in the first line one can also read 'fellow brothers of the bridal chamber', which is reminiscent of the expression 'son/sons (or child[ren]) of the bridal chamber' in the *Gospel of Philip* (NHC II, 67, 4–5; 72, 20–1; 76, 5; 86, 5 (sections 66, 87, 102, 127)). This inscription probably derives from a villa in which a few rooms were furnished for the meetings of a Christian 'house congregation', which had a Valentinian orientation, as appears from the reference to the 'bath of the bridal chamber': after the baptismal bath the baptized and other persons went, with burning torches and while singing hymns, in procession to the room where the Eucharist, the banquet, was celebrated.

The Epitaph for Flavia Sophe was also found in the Via Latina in Rome. The first letters of the first six lines form an acrostichon with the name Flavia (*Flabia*); its final part has been lost. The date is uncertain, suggestions vary here, too, from the late second century into the fourth. This last date is proposed by McKechnie, whose reading of the text is followed below. On the stone a husband addresses his probably young wife Sophe as follows:

> Yearning for the light of the Father, my sister and spouse, Sophe,
> anointed in the bath of Christ with imperishable holy oil,
> you hastened to behold the divine faces of the aeons,
> the great Angel of the Great Council, the true Son,
> when you went to the bridal chamber and ascended [imperish]able
> to the [house] of the Father
> …

explanation raises so many questions that, in the view of the present writer, the baptismal interpretation remains the most probable.

[135] Lit. 'May there be at that place the flowing of a single source, namely of Truth.' The translation of this line is by no means certain, because the stone is damaged at the beginning (… *gēs*) and the end (*rhys* …) of the line. The translation above presupposes [*pē*]*gēs* ('of a source/fountain') and *rhy*[*sis eiē*] ('may there be a flowing'), respectively; moreover, the word *kai* in *kai alētheias*

The back of the stone also has a chiselled text, in a different hand, which says that the deceased person is dead only for those who are dead themselves:

> She did not find a common end to her life, when she died.
> She died and she lives and she sees in reality the imperishable Light.
> She lives for those who live and died for those who are really dead.
> Earth, why do you marvel at the nature of the deceased?
> Are you afraid?

In the inscription on the front of the stone the bridal chamber stands for the union of Sophe's soul with Christ, her heavenly partner, to which the baptism in the bath of Christ already referred. Some scholars have also connected the 'bath of Christ' and the 'holy oil' with a sacrament for the dying, as a kind of second baptism, but this seems less probable.[136] The text teems with typically Valentinian expressions, which individually are perhaps not so significant, but together make the Valentinian inspiration of the epitaph unmistakable: the 'light of the Father', the 'Angel of the Great Council' (cf. Isa. 9:5 (LXX): *Megalēs Boulēs Angelos*) and 'True Son' as designations of Christ, the 'entering of the bridal chamber', etc. What is said here about Flavia Sophe corresponds to the description in the *Excerpta ex Theodoto* 64: 'They enter the bridal chamber inside the Limit and achieve the vision of the Father, themselves become aeons who share in the Nous, to celebrate the spiritual and eternal weddings of the conjugation.'

Interpretation of Knowledge The *Interpretation of Knowledge* (NHC XI, 1)[137] has often been taken as a gnostic sermon, but most probably it is a brief treatise in the form of a letter. It is not entirely clear how the title (Coptic *thermēnia ntgnōsis* = Greek *hē hermēneia tēs gnōseōs*) should be understood. Possible translations are 'The interpretation regarding gnosis' (objective genitive) or 'The interpretation provided by gnosis', that is 'The gnostic interpretation' (subjective genitive). The latter view is most likely. Sadly, the manuscript is severely damaged, so that some two-thirds of the text has been lost. In many cases lacunae can be filled with fairly great certainty, but there are entire pages of which the content can no longer be reconstructed (esp. pp. 3–8) and countless passages in which the details of the argument elude us. Nevertheless, it is completely clear in what situation the

(lit.: 'and of truth') is taken as an epexegetical *kai* ('that is, namely'). The first word of the line has also been read as [*au*]*gēs*, 'of light', and as [*si*]*gēs*, 'of silence', and the lacuna at the end has also been filled in as *rhy*[*sis estin*], which leads to the translation 'There is the flowing of only light [or silence] and truth at that place.'

136 Lewis, '*Apolytrosis*', pp. 545–55; see pp. 76 and 104.

137 Ed. E. H. Pagels and J. D. Turner, NHS 28 (1990), pp. 21–88; W.-P. Funk, L. Painchaud and E. Thomassen, BCNH-T 34 (2010).

Interpretation of Knowledge was written and what the work is trying to say. It offers a unique insight into a Christian congregation in which gnostics and non-gnostics are still living together, but tensions are growing over the possession of spiritual gifts (*charismata*), for instance those of prophecy and speaking in the congregation. The author is clearly one of those who possess such gifts – and here evidently coincide with the gnostics – whereas the person he is addressing belongs to the group which does not share in them. In the original Greek text the addressee could have been a woman; what is certain is that through him or her the writer addresses all the members of the congregation who find themselves in the same situation. In relation to the charismatics, this group felt relegated to the position of second-rate congregation members. The author is afraid that this is endangering church unity and implores his readers not to give in to envy, but to accept the diversity in gifts gratefully. The images he uses here are well known from the Pauline letters of the New Testament: the congregation as the one body of Christ, in which each member has his own useful place, and Christ as the head of the Church (e.g. Rom. 12:4–5; 1 Cor. 12:12–27; Col. 1:18). Just as Christ humbled himself in his earthly life until his death on the cross, so humility should be the highest virtue for Christians.

Though the author prizes church unity, there is no doubt that his theology has strong Valentinian leanings. This is evinced by his views on the heavenly origin of the body of Christ (12, 29–33) and by similarities to the *Gospel of Truth*, the *Treatise on Resurrection* and Clement of Alexandria's *Excerpta ex Theodoto*. It is striking that he attributes salvatory significance to Christ's death and recognizes the authority of the current canonical gospels and the letters of Paul. A Christian congregation in which these views were held, in which spiritual gnostics and non-gnostic believers were still living together and in which leadership was vested in the charismatic offices of prophet and spiritual leader of the congregation and not yet in the institutionalized office of bishop, is still conceivable in the mid second century. The *Interpretation of Gnosis* must therefore have been written around 150 CE. Speculation on the place of origin is difficult: Rome is unlikely, Egypt (Alexandria) quite possible, but it could also be any other place where Valentinian views had caught on and the institutionalized office had not yet ousted the charismatic offices.

Prayer of the Apostle Paul The *Prayer of the Apostle Paul* (NHC I, 1)[138] is found on the two sides of the front flyleaf of Codex I. The title, at the end of the text, is followed by a short colophon: 'In peace. Christ is

138 Ed. D. Mueller, NHS 22 (1985), pp. 5–11, notes in NHS 23 (1985), pp. 1–5.

holy.' The prayer consists of three parts. The first starts with an invocation of the Saviour, who is called 'Mind' (*Nous*), 'Treasure House', 'Fullness' (*Pleroma*) and 'Rest' (*Anapausis*). Next, the author invokes He-Who-Is, who is pre-existent, in the name exalted above every name, Jesus Christ. He is asked for his unrepented gifts through the Son of Man, the Spirit (*Pneuma*), the Paraclete of Truth: for the authority to pray to him, for healing of the supplicant's body and salvation of his eternal light-soul and his spirit (*pneuma*) and for revelation of the 'First-born of the fullness [*pleroma*] of grace' to his mind (*nous*). Finally, appealing to his faith and hope, the supplicant prays for what no angel eye has seen and no archon ear has heard and no human heart has conceived (cf. 1 Cor. 2:9), that is, the appearance of Christ, who is said to have become an angel, 'after the image of the psychical god'. The author prays for the gift of 'the beloved, elect, blessed Majesty, the First-born, the First-begotten and amazing mystery of your house', after which the prayer ends with a doxology.

In this prayer, scholars have discovered parallels in hermetic literature and magic papyri, and also many similarities to Valentinian works. The phrase 'the psychical god' refers to the Demiurge, the creator-god, who according to Western Valentinianism had a psychical nature. Though the prayer is generally considered to be inspired by Valentinianism, it can also be viewed as testifying to a broader Christian-gnostic religiosity, in which Valentinian elements were incorporated, too. Nothing can be said about the place of origin, while possible dates are the second half of the second century and the third century.

POLEMICAL TEXTS

Some gnostic texts strike a decidedly polemical note, usually against certain 'orthodox' views of what was called 'the Great Church', but also against ideas of fellow gnostics. We already encountered examples of the former in discussing the *Gospel of Mary* and the *Gospel of Judas*.[139] This is also the case in the *Second Treatise of the Great Seth* (NHC VII, 2), the *Apocalypse of Peter* (NHC VII, 3) and the *True Testimony* (NHC IX, 3), but the last two writings polemize against other gnostics, too. We found this in the Valentinian *Letter of Instruction* as well.[140]

Second Treatise of the Great Seth The title of the *Second Treatise of the Great Seth* (NHC VII, 2)[141] raises quite a few questions. In Codex VII of

[139] See pp. 58 and 74–5.
[140] See p. 94.
[141] Ed. L. Painchaud, BCNH-T 6 (1982); G. Riley, NHMS 30 (1996), pp. 129–99.

Nag Hammadi it is preceded by the *Paraphrase of Seëm*, but that is an entirely different kind of work, and one in which Seth plays no role at all. There was in fact a *Paraphrase of Seth*, but its content was very different from that of Seëm.[142] Only if someone had identified the *Paraphrase of Seëm* with that of Seth, could he have called the succeeding work, NHC v, 2, the *Second Treatise of the Great Seth*. But Seth does not figure in the *Second Treatise* either and the work does not show remarkable similarities to the writings referred to as 'Sethian'. Thus it has nothing in common with the *Holy Book of the Great Invisible Spirit*, in which the 'Great Seth' does occur as a revelatory figure. The Coptic translator must have already found the present title in his Greek original, because he has left it untranslated (without article: *Deuteros logos tou megalou Sēth*). Perhaps the text once formed part of a collection of texts which were somehow associated with Seth. Via Epiphanius, *Panarion* 40, 7, 4, we know that works circulated under the name of Seth. In any case the title seems secondary, the original title, if there ever was one, having been lost.

The *Second Treatise of the Great Seth* mentions and presupposes all kinds of well-known gnostic ideas, but does not treat them systematically. Its main theme is the history of Christ, from his heavenly origin via his earthly existence to his return into the divine world – a history that repeats itself in the gnostic. The structure of the text has sometimes been seen as following the same pattern that characterizes Hellenistic works about the vicissitudes of the soul, but on closer inspection these similarities are rather superficial and obvious. The *Second Treatise* presents itself as a revelation of Christ to the 'perfect', which refers to the gnostics whom the author addresses. In general the work has a calm, discursive tone, but it also contains some strongly polemical passages.

In the Pleroma reposes the highest deity, the 'perfect Majesty', in an ineffable light, which is called 'the Truth' and 'the Mother' of all. Christ is apparently seen as the first Son of this Mother, since he says of himself that he 'alone is perfect'. Furthermore, the Pleroma contains the heavenly Church (*ekklēsia*), from which the souls of the 'perfect' also originate and to which they will return. We are not told how the souls of the gnostics ended up on earth, but the author says that Sophia was responsible for putting together the human bodies (49, 10–51, 7). When Christ descended into a human body, the world rulers, the archons, and therefore the human beings, too, became confused. A distinction is drawn between those who are with the world-creator Yaldabaoth and those with

[142] See p. 154.

his son Adonaios: the first group is doomed to destruction, the second may yet be somehow saved. Such a division is also found in the *Hypostasis of the Archons* (NHC II, 4) and the *Origin of the World* (NHC II, 5), but there the counterpart of Yaldabaoth is not *Adonaios* but Sabaoth.[143] The people who belong with Adonaios are probably identified with non-gnostic Christians here. The reference to Yaldabaoth indicates that the author knew the gnostic Barbelo myth or a variant of it; here, too, Yaldabaoth boasts that he is the only God (NHC VII, 52, 10–54, 13). The evil powers thought to crucify Jesus, but this only expressed their impotence. The author strongly emphasizes that the Saviour himself did not suffer. He has Christ say: 'I was not afflicted at all. Those there punished me, but I did not die in reality, but only in appearance' (55, 15–19). Christ stresses that it was 'another' who suffered, by which he probably means his mortal body. His true self was elsewhere: 'But I was rejoicing in the height at all the wealth of the rulers and the offspring of their error, their empty glory, and I was laughing at their ignorance' (56, 14–19). In discussing the gnostic views on Christ we will look more closely at this. But it is already clear here that Jesus' death on the cross does not have direct salvatory significance for gnostics. This is noted in one of the very first sentences of the *Second Treatise*, with an unmistakable polemic against the view of baptism prevailing among non-gnostic Christians since Paul:

> It is a form of slavery to say: 'We shall die with Christ [cf. Rom. 6:3–5] with an imperishable and undefiled spirit.' An incomprehensible wonder is the scriptural word on the ineffable water [of baptism], that is, the word used by us [cf. John 14:20; 17:21–23]: 'I am in you and you are in me, as the Father is in <me and> you, without evil.' (49, 26–50, 1)

Through the words of Christ the author also turns against the non-gnostic ecclesiastical institutions and their high regard for the Old Testament. The non-gnostics are led astray by the demonic rulers over our world. They mimic the heavenly Church 'by proclaiming a doctrine of a dead person and lies, in order to imitate the freedom and the purity of the perfect Church' (60, 21–5). In a long passage with a clearly poetic structure the author dismisses all the important persons of the Old Testament as ridiculous figures who were subservient to the archons and only increased people's ignorance. Thus he says of Moses:

> Moses was a laughingstock, a 'faithful servant' [cf. Num. 12:7; Heb. 3:5]. By calling him 'a friend' [cf. Jas. 2:23, on Abraham] they wickedly bore witness

[143] See pp. 52 and 54.

concerning him, because he never knew me, neither he nor those who preceded him. From Adam to Moses and John the Baptist, none of them knew me nor my brethren. (63, 26–64)

The *Second Treatise of the Great Seth* presupposes a situation in which the 'Perfect' are persecuted by the utterly ignorant, the non-Christians, and by the non-gnostic Christians. This emerges from a passage in which the Saviour identifies with his followers:

When we went forth from our [heavenly] house, when we descended to this world and came into bodily being in the world, we were hated and persecuted, not only by the ignorant, but also by those who think they richly possess the name of Christ, whereas they are empty of knowledge. They do not know who they are, like dumb animals! (59, 19–29)

This indicates that the *Second Treatise* was written after the rift between gnostic and non-gnostic Christians had become a fact and the two groups had started to exclude each other from the true Church. This phenomenon did not take place everywhere at the same time, in Rome earlier than in for instance Alexandria, but in any case not before the last quarter of the second century. Most scholars – though without convincing evidence – take Alexandria to be the place of origin of the *Second Treatise*. If this is correct, it is best dated to the first decades of the third century. If the work was written elsewhere, the last decades of the second century are also possible.

Revelation of Peter The *Revelation* (or *Apocalypse*) *of Peter* (NHC VII, 3)[144] has nothing to do with the early Christian work of the same name that has been best preserved in an Ethiopian translation and describes the tortures of sinful souls in hell. The aim of the work recovered in Nag Hammadi is to defend the gnostic interpretation of Christianity, and particularly of Jesus' crucifixion, as the only correct interpretation. The core of the work consists of two visionary experiences undergone by Peter, with in between a long exposition by Jesus. The text starts with an encouraging word from Jesus to Peter, in which he praises 'those who belong to the Father' and also Peter himself, because they have listened to 'the Son of Man who is exalted above the heavens'. Peter is encouraged to be strong (70, 13–72, 4). In a vision, Peter then sees how the priests and the people bear down on them to stone them. Jesus tells him not to be afraid, for they are 'blind persons without leaders'. He tells Peter to cover his eyes and asks him what he sees. Naturally the answer is that he sees nothing:

144 Ed. M. Desjardins and J. Brashler, NHMS 30 (1996), pp. 201–47.

thus it also is for those who menace them. When told to cover his eyes again, he sees a shining light that descends on the Saviour. In the same way Peter first hears the shouting of the crowd that wants to crucify Jesus and then hears him being praised: 'As you sit, they are praising you!' (72, 4–73, 10). After thus encouraging the frightened Peter, Jesus gives a long monologue in which he speaks about the apostasy which will also occur among Christians: the 'orthodox' Christians and others with different beliefs are the real heretics (73, 10–81, 3). The work contains all kinds of allusions to Christian views which the author rejects, but which are generally too vague to assign to specific groups. He is probably thinking of supporters of Paul's crucifixion and baptism theology (dying and rising up with Christ) when he says: 'And they will adhere to the name of a dead man, thinking to be purified, whereas they will be defiled even further' (74, 13–16). In another passage he seems to target the Simonians, who revered Simon Magus and the ex-prostitute Helen (to whom a series of reincarnations was attributed): 'And some, because they hold their own through a power of the archons, will name themselves after a man and a naked woman of many shapes and many sufferings' (74, 28–34). The true gnostics, who are the only people with an immortal soul, are called 'the little ones'. These certainly do not include the 'others outside our number, who call themselves "bishops" and also "deacons", as if they have received their authority from God, whereas they fall under the judgement of the places of honour [cf. Matt. 23:6]. These people are waterless canals' (79, 22–31). It is generally assumed that the 'waterless canals' are an Egyptian adaptation of the 'waterless springs' mentioned in 2 Peter 2:17, which could indicate an Egyptian origin of the *Revelation of Peter*. Scholars have pointed to the influence of 2 Peter elsewhere in this work, too, though this is not always equally convincing. At the end of his revelatory speech Jesus again encourages Peter. This is followed by a vision with the same underlying intention, narrated by Peter. In fact these are two visions narrated successively (NHC VII, 81, 3–83, 15). Peter sees how Jesus is seized, while feeling how Jesus touches him. Jesus is nailed to the cross, and at the same time he sees above the cross a Jesus who is laughing gladly. Jesus explains to him that the latter is the 'living Jesus', while the crucified Jesus is his fleshly part, which replaces him. The intention of this vision is to show that the crucified Jesus who plays such an important role in the Church's theology is not the real Jesus, but his bodily shell. Peter goes on directly to narrate another vision, which seems a variant of what he had just told. He saw someone approach who resembled the person who had appeared laughing above the cross. He was filled with a holy

Spirit. It was the Saviour, irradiated by an ineffable light and praised by a crowd of angels. The Saviour once again explains the crucifixion scene witnessed by Peter, in which the non-gnostic view is sharply rejected. This will be examined more closely in the discussion of gnostic Christology.[145] The *Revelation of Peter* ends with an order to Peter to pass on all he has seen to 'the strangers', who are not of this world, that is to the gnostics of the group for whom this work is intended. After a final encouragement, Peter then comes to himself.

As regards place and time of origin, there are more uncertainties than hard facts. We pointed out above that the expression 'waterless canals' has been viewed as an Egypt-orientated change of 'waterless springs' in 2 Peter 2:17. The tone and content of the passage in the *Revelation of Peter* show similarities to 2 Peter 2, so that this assumption is not impossible. If correct, it is natural to assume that the *Revelation of Peter* was written in Egypt. Furthermore, some scholars see so many points of agreement with the views of the Alexandrian gnostic Basilides, whom later tradition placed in the time of Emperor Hadrian (117–38), that they regard this, too, as a strong argument in favour of an Egyptian origin. Other scholars, far from convinced by the connection with Basilides, rather think that the *Revelation of Peter* may have had its roots in Syria. But although there are indications in this direction, conclusive evidence is once again lacking. An origin in Egypt seems therefore more probable, in any case there are no arguments against it. Even if the connection with Basilides were an established fact, the *Revelation of Peter* must have been written considerably later, since the situation of conflict between gnostic and non-gnostic Christians presupposed in the work was not yet conceivable in his time. The sharp tone of the polemic shows that the religious fellowship between the group responsible for the work and other, non-gnostic Christians had broken up. In Egypt and many other regions this became possible only in the last decades of the second century. The *Revelation of Peter* speaks slightingly about 'bishops' (*episkopoi*) and 'deacons'; the intermediate spiritual rank, that of priests (*presbyteroi*), is not mentioned. This could indicate that the work originated in the time that the terms *episkopoi* and *presbyteroi* were used indiscriminately for the same group of spiritual leaders and the 'monarchical' office of bishop had not yet gained general currency. This development, too, did not occur in Egypt until the late second century. If this conclusion may be drawn from the absence of *presbyteroi* and the work was in fact conceived in Egypt, it may date from the last

[145] See p. 200.

decades before the year 200 or the first decades afterwards. But a later date in the third century cannot be ruled out.

True Testimony The *True Testimony* (NHC IX, 3),[146] also called the *Testimony of Truth*, is the modern name for a treatise defending the true gnostic doctrine against non-gnostic Christians and against other gnostics. Perhaps the original title, as so often, was given underneath the text in the manuscript, but the end of the work has regrettably been lost. In fact the manuscript is in such a poor state that only about half the work has been preserved. The present title derives from a pivotal sentence in the treatise: 'This is therefore the true testimony: If someone knows himself and God, who transcends the truth, he will be saved and wreathed with the unfading wreath' (44, 30–45, 6). This point of view, in effect a brief definition of what gnosis means, pervades the entire work. This comes out at the very beginning in a sharp rejection of 'the law'. Someone under the law cannot get to the truth, since the law urges marriage, sexual intercourse and the begetting of children, and to do this is to turn away from the light and remain enthralled by the rulers of darkness (29, 6–30, 18). The author explains the biblical story about Jesus' baptism by John the Baptist in the sense that the water of the River Jordan is sexual desire and John the 'archon of the womb'. On the other hand the Son of Man, who descended on Jesus at the baptism, revealed that 'the dominion of carnal procreation had come to an end' (30, 18–31, 22). This strongly ascetic attitude is constantly expressed in the treatise. For the author, sexual abstinence is one of the main features of true Christianity; without this abstinence one cannot achieve gnosis. A second aspect much emphasized is the rejection of martyrdom as a means of direct salvation. People are wrong to think they will live if, in word only but not in reality, they confess before the authorities: 'We are Christians', for in ignorance they thus give themselves up to death, without knowing where they are going and even without knowing Christ. The author is polemizing here against the widespread early Christian view that after death the martyr of faith will be directly united with Christ in heavenly bliss. He also rejects the bodily resurrection at the end of time. Salvation and resurrection are only for those who possess the gnosis brought by Christ, the Son of Man (31, 22–41, 4). Taking his cue from the story of the Fall in paradise, the author shows that the God of the Old Testament is a limited, ignorant and jealous god: he did not know where Adam had hidden himself and

[146] Ed. B. A. Pearson and S. Giversen, NHS 15 (1981), pp. 101–203; A. and J.-P. Mahé, BCNH-T 23 (1996).

he begrudges Adam the fruit of the tree of life! This is followed by a discussion of the snake in paradise, the snakes of the Egyptian sorcerers and Moses (Exod. 7:8–12) and the serpent of bronze in the desert, which is associated with Christ in accordance with John 3:14 (48, 19–49, 10).

From page 49 onwards, large parts of the manuscript have been lost, so that the train of argument is hard to follow, if at all. This applies to pages 49–55, where the argument against non-gnostic Christians is pursued, and it also goes for pages 55–68, where the author targets what he believes to be incorrect views of other gnostics (55, 1–60, 4) and discusses the contrast between those who belong to the Son of Man and the race of Adam (60, 4–69, 7). It is particularly regrettable that precisely this section has been preserved so poorly, because it would give us a unique insight into the differences of opinion between gnostics and the resulting polemic. Valentinus and the Valentinians are opposed, like Basilides and his son Isidorus. It does not become clear what exactly the objections are, but these and similar gnostics are as sharply rejected as the Christians of the Church: they possess 'empty wisdom' and they will 'be condemned' by the archons and be punished by an 'inextinguishable fire'. The Simonians, too, are repudiated, but in their case the central objection has been preserved: they marry and beget children! This was probably also the main objection to the Valentinians, because they did not reject marriage outright.[147] One gets the impression that the author also grouped the 'heretical' gnostics with the children of Adam. It is noted of this last group that they not only produce children, but that the women even have sexual intercourse again while suckling their children. Moreover, they are avaricious and lend money at interest, and small wonder, says the author, for 'the father of Mammon is also the father of sexual intercourse' (68, 6–8). At the end of the *True Testimony* the author discusses a few themes that exercise him, including the contrast between false and true baptism. Baptism by water in the Church involves the rulers of the world, though the person being baptized thinks that he is 'sealed', that is can be certain of his salvation. But the Son of Man did not baptize any of his disciples. True baptism is only possible if one abjures the world; to fail to do so is to be condemned to destruction (69, 7–32).

Despite the poor state in which it has been passed down, the *True Testimony* is an extremely interesting work. It shows us that in their polemics the gnostics, both among themselves and against non-gnostic Christians, were no less spirited than anti-gnostic authors. The fact

[147] For the gnostic views on sexuality and ethics in general, see below p. 202, with note 108.

that the author talks about Isidorus, the son of Basilides, and about the pupils of Valentinus indicates that he belongs to the second or third generation after Basilides and Valentinus. As regards date, this brings us at the earliest to the last decades of the second century or otherwise to the first decades of the third century. This last seems most likely, since the fierceness of the polemic suggests that the break with the Christians of the Great Church was an established fact and the gnostic movement had become divided, to the point of hostility. It is difficult, if not impossible, to determine to which gnostic school the author belonged. Though he opposes the Valentinians, some scholars believe that his work betrays so much influence of Valentinianism that we are dealing here with someone who had broken away from the main movement of the Valentinians. We saw in the Valentinian *Letter of Instruction* that this could lead to heated polemics. Yet the Valentinian character of the *True Testimony* is more speculation than proven fact, since here, too, it is clear that if an author uses terms which are more or less characteristic of a certain movement, this is not in itself evidence that the author also regarded himself as a supporter of this movement. Some scholars have assumed that the author was none other than Julius Cassianus, the leader of the Alexandrian Encratites, a strongly ascetic group that advocated strict abstinence (*enkrateia*) from sex, meat and wine. Certainly the author will have felt comfortable with a number of Cassianus' views, but there are also clear differences between the two. The conclusion must therefore be that the name of the author of the *True Testimony* is unknown. It may well be that the work was written in Egypt. In a city like Alexandria all the information which the author evidently possessed was doubtless present. Yet this must also have been the case in other large cities, like Rome. At most we can say that nothing in the work argues against an origin in Alexandria.

OTHER MYTHOLOGICAL TRADITIONS

Some Nag Hammadi texts have a clearly mythological content, but show few or no similarities to the myths which formed the basis of the texts discussed in the previous sections. These works are *Eugnostus (the Blessed)* (NHC III, 3; V, 1), the *Paraphrase of Seëm* (NHC VII, 1) and the *Concept of our Great Power* (NHC VI, 4).

Eugnostus *Eugnostus* survives in two Coptic translations, which not only originated independently of each other, but go back to Greek originals which also differed from each other. In NHC III, 3 the title is

Eugnostus the Blessed, in NHC V, 1 simply *Eugnostus*.[148] The work presents itself as a letter from a gnostic teacher to the circle of his followers, as the salutation shows: 'Eugnostus the Blessed to those who are his. Greetings!' Its popularity is not only attested by the two independent translations, but also by the fact that virtually the whole work is incorporated in the *Wisdom of Jesus Christ*.[149] *Eugnostus* provides a description of the divine world which differs greatly from what the Barbelo myth and Valentinian gnosis had to say about this, though there are some resemblances. The work consists of two parts, of which the first constitutes a coherent whole (III, 70, 1–85, 9) and the second part, after a transitional passage (III, 85, 9–21), returns in a somewhat confused argument to a few aspects in the first part, but adds new elements (III, 85, 21–90, 11). This second part seems a drastic revision of the original ending of *Eugnostus*.

Eugnostus starts with an introduction in which the author argues that philosophy does not lead to knowledge of God; this requires a different source of knowledge, namely revelation. He then describes how the divine world develops out of the highest God. Here he does not follow the 'Father-Mother-Son' model, which became best known via the Barbelo myth, but the 'Man-Son of Man' model. This is known from various systems in the Church Fathers, but in authentic gnostic works it occurs only in *Eugnostus*, and even then in a variant form.[150] Before everything, according to *Eugnostus*, there is the ineffable 'He-Who-Is', who can be described only in the terms of negative theology.[151] The unknown God is called the 'Lord of the All' and 'Primeval Father' (*Propatōr*). The plurality within divine being comes about in a way also known from the *Apocryphon of John*: the Primeval Father sees himself within himself as in a mirror and his mirror image becomes independent as the second 'Person' of the deity, who is called 'Self-Father' (*Autopatōr*) and 'Self-Begetter' (*Autogenetōr*). He produces a multitude of glorious, subservient beings, who do duty as his retinue (III, 74, 20–76, 12). This 'self-grown, self-created Father' then brings forth a third divine level: the androgynous 'Immortal Man'. His male aspect is called 'Begotten, Perfect Mind', his female aspect 'All-Wise Begetting Wisdom [*Sophia*]'. Immortal Man creates for himself a great retinue, 'gods, archangels and angels, ten thousands without number, to serve him' (V, 5, 21–8, 26; III partly defective). The conception of God in *Eugnostus* is that of an

[148] Ed. D. M. Parrott, NHS 27 (1991); A. Pasquier, BCNH-T 26 (2000) and BCNH-T 33, *Commentaire* (2010).

[149] See pp. 64–5. [150] See pp. 154–6. [151] See pp. 151–2.

oriental king, who is surrounded by countless servants, as we also find in the Old Testament and later Jewish and Christian literature. Next, Immortal Man and his partner, Great Sophia, produce an androgynous son, 'First-Born Son of God', whose female aspect is 'First-Born Wisdom'. He is also called 'Son of Man', 'First Begetter-Father' and 'Light-Adam', and he, too, creates 'angels, ten thousands without number, to serve him' (v, 8, 27–10, 2; III, 81, 1–21). Finally, the Son of Man and his Wisdom beget a great androgynous light, called 'Saviour, Begetter of all things', whose female aspect is named 'Wisdom, Begettress of all things'. In turn these produce a group of six androgynous subservient beings, all of whom have the words 'Begetter' and 'Wisdom' in their names. Ultimately this leads to a system of 360 powers in 360 heavens (III, 81, 21–85, 9). Though *Eugnostus* describes exclusively an undisturbed divine Pleroma, the name 'Saviour' (who is called the 'Son of the Son of Man' in the transitional passage), shows that in this system there was also originally a rift in the Pleroma, which had to be healed by a Saviour. So the pleromatic system of *Eugnostus* consists of five levels of divinity: the Primeval Father, the Self-Begetter, Immortal Man, the Son of Man and the Son of the Son of Man, the Saviour. Because the Son of Man is called 'Light-Adam', it is natural to assume that his son, the Saviour, is identified with the heavenly Seth. This suggests a connection with the saviour figure of Seth that occurs in a number of texts of the Barbelo myth. But the question is to what extent the different names given to the same divine being in *Eugnostus* were added by later readers on the basis of conceptions familiar to them. It is not difficult to see that the Son of Man and the Son of the Son of Man with their respective Sophias are reduplications of Immortal Man and his Sophia.

The ending of *Eugnostus* must have been radically changed by a later redactor, although there are scholars who do not see any rupture here.[152] In the transitional section to the second part, Immortal Man, the Son of Man and the Son of the Son of Man are referred to as 'aeons'. They are in the aeon of the eternal God, which is located above the eighth celestial sphere and the chaos underneath it. In the second part the three aeons are designated as 'the Beginning', 'the Middle' and 'the End', but also other names lacking in the elaborate first part are ascribed to them. Thus the third aeon is now suddenly called 'Assembly' (*ekklēsia*), 'on account of the vast multitude which appeared in the multitudinous One'. But there

[152] For example Pasquier, *Commentaire*, pp. 124–57.

is also talk about the 'Assembly of the Eighth Sphere', which is apparently the abode of the saved who have received gnosis from the Saviour, though this is not said in so many words. The introduction of aeons like 'Assembly' (*Ekklēsia*) and 'Silence' (*Sigē*) (as another name of Sophia) suggests that a Valentinian gnostic was at work in this part. All this means that we can no longer determine what the ending of *Eugnostus* originally looked like.

We do not know who the teacher Eugnostus was. His work betrays more than usual knowledge of Jewish conceptions and offers clear parallels with the work of the Jewish religious philosopher Philo of Alexandria (first century CE). As the last chapter of this book will show, the originally Jewish conception of heavenly 'Man' (*Anthrōpos*) was widespread in Egypt, and all in all it is very likely that *Eugnostus* was written in Egypt. There is no doubt that Eugnostus was a gnostic, but there is debate over whether he was a Jewish or a Christian gnostic. Almost all recent researchers believe that the author of *Eugnostus* was a gnostic of Jewish origin, which is in fact most probable. As regards date, an origin in the first half of the second century seems most likely.

Paraphrase of Seem The *Paraphrase of Seëm* (NHC VII, 1)[153] is one of the best-preserved but also one of the most difficult writings of Nag Hammadi. The title in itself is curious; in Coptic *tparaphrasis nsēem*. The Greek word *paraphrasis* means the same as the English word 'paraphrase', a rendering or rewriting of a text in one's own words. It would thus involve the rendering of a revelation given to a certain Seëm. Perhaps the title originally belonged to one of the work's sources, since in 32, 27 an explanatory rendering of a liturgical passage starts with the words. 'This is the paraphrase.' It has also been assumed that these words are the concluding title of all the foregoing and that everything following was added later. The second part of the title is usually translated 'of Shem', the natural assumption being that this refers to Shem the son of Noah. But this is far from certain and indeed unlikely, since this Shem is always called *Sēm* and never *Sēem* in the Greek translation of the Old Testament. Rather he seems to be a kind of Adam, for it is said that he 'was the first being upon the earth' (1, 20–21). As regards content a better title for the work would be 'The revelation of Derdekeas to Seëm', as it offers a revelation in which Derdekeas, 'the son of the pure, boundless Light' (4, 2–4), relates how the world of chaos came into being and he, Derdekeas, acted

[153] Ed. F. Wisse, NHMS 30 (1996), pp. 15–127; M. Roberge, BCNH-T 25 (2000), a revised but abbreviated English version in NHMS 72 (2010).

as a Saviour to liberate the Spirit from matter.[154] It is doubtless a gnostic work, though the word 'gnosis' does not occur in it, being more or less replaced by the term 'faith' (*pistis*). Formally the work takes a form not unusual in such revelations: the revelation is embedded in a narrative frame, in which the seer first tells how he fell into a different state of consciousness (his body was 'asleep') and was led upwards, and which concludes with a report on the return to his normal state of consciousness and the order to make the revelation known. However, the content of the revelation is very hard to understand (and thus reproduce). There is indeed no agreement among editors and translators on how the text should be interpreted. Some believe that the Coptic translator was not equal to his task and that the Greek text he translated was itself very poorly composed, others see it as the result of a long development in which various abridged revelations were telescoped, and others hold that the author describes a complicated but essentially coherent system. Even if this last were true, which may be doubted, we can at least say that the author has not pulled it off. In his view, there are three primeval principles, which at first existed separately. 'There was Light and Darkness and in between them there was Spirit [*Pneuma*]' (1, 25–28). According to Hippolytus, *Refutatio* v, 19, 2, the same three principles also occurred in the gnostic sect of the Sethians: 'The substances of the principles are Light and Darkness, and in between them is the pure Spirit [*Pneuma*].'[155] According to the *Paraphrase*, part of the Spirit (*Pneuma*) 'falls' into the Darkness and enlightens the mind (*nous*) which dwells there. A large portion of the work describes how Derdekeas descends into the Darkness to save the pneumatic light-particles and the *nous* itself. This process of salvation implies the creation and further history of the world, in terms with a strong sexual colouring (an important role for 'the Womb'). Nature turns out to be an anti-divine power that thwarts the Saviour and the possessors of spirit in many ways. In this context we also see some familiarity with the Old Testament story of the Flood (Gen. 6–8): together with the dark water and Darkness, Nature tries to destroy Seëm and his pneumatic race by means of a flood, but the Saviour ensures that there is a tower (!) to which he can flee (24, 30–25, 22). The destruction of Sodom

[154] G. A. G. Stroumsa, *Another Seed: Studies in Gnostic Mythology*, NHS 24 (Leiden: Brill, 1984), p. 79, has suggested deriving the name Derdekeas from the Aramaic *dardeqa'*, 'male child', which is an epithet of Seth in a number of gnostic texts. Cf. M. Jastrow, *A Dictionary of the Targumim, the Talmud Babli and Yerushalmi, and the Midrashic Literature* (London: Luzac & Co.; New York: G. Putnam's Sons, 1903), p. 321b: 'tender, young, small, boy, young pupil'. See also M. Roberge, *The Paraphrase of Shem (NH* VII, *1). Introduction, Translation and Commentary*, NHMS 72 (Brill: Leiden, 2010), p. 129.

[155] See p. 154.

by fire and brimstone (Gen. 19) is also explained as an attempt by evil Nature to eradicate the followers of Seëm, the Sodomites (28, 34–29, 33). To save the light-particles of the Spirit, Derdekeas will unite with the demon Soldas, who seems to be his earthly form, and he will undergo baptism by a demon who proclaims a baptism by water. This could refer to John the Baptist, which may indicate some familiarity with the New Testament. But the Saviour vehemently opposes baptism by water and the idea that sins would thus be washed away: 'Seëm, people have been led astray by all kinds of demons: they think that through the baptism of impure water, which is dark, weak, ineffective and destructive, water will take the sins away' (37, 19–25). Some scholars believe the crucifixion of the Saviour, in the form of Soldas, is also presupposed in the text, which would point to knowledge of Christianity. As usual, however, the language in which this is reported is extremely obscure and vague. To give an impression of this and because it is an important passage, a verbatim quotation may be useful. Derdekeas says that he appeared without defect in order to end the wickedness of Nature:

> For at that time she [Nature] wanted to ensnare me. She was about to fix [Greek *pēssein*] Soldas, who is the dark flame, who will stand on the [height (?) ...] of error, so that he might ensnare me. She [Nature] took care of her faith, because she is vainglorious. And at that time the light was about to separate from the Darkness and a voice was heard in creation, saying: 'Blessed is the eye that has seen you and the mind [*nous*] which supported your greatness at my desire.' From above it will be said: 'Blessed is Rebouel among all races of men, for it is you alone, woman, who have seen.' And she will listen. And they will behead the woman who possesses the perception that you will reveal on earth. (39, 28–40, 19)

Does the beginning of the passage refer to the crucifixion? The Greek word *pēssein* (a later form of *pēgnunai*) means 'to fasten, fix'. Authors from the fourth century sometimes use *pēgnunai* in the sense of 'to erect a cross'; it probably could also have the meaning 'to affix [to the cross]'.[156] The connection with the woman Rebouel, who is perhaps the same as the one to be beheaded, is completely obscure; later she turns out to be a daughter of the demon who proclaimed baptism by water (40, 30–1).

Apart from references to the Flood (though without any mention of Noah) and the destruction of Sodom, a possible allusion to Jesus and his crucifixion, and perhaps the use of the word 'faith', there are no elements that explicitly point to Jewish or Christian influence. It is a poorly composed, barely intelligible work which propagates a mythological system entirely outside the tradition of the prevailing mythological gnosis. The

[156] See Roberge, *Paraphrase of Shem*, p. 69.

polemic against baptism by water could be aimed against the Christian ritual, but more likely the author was targeting the baptismal practice of one or more baptist sects that flourished in the Syrian hinterland in the second and third centuries. Mani (216–77), founder of the gnostic religion of Manichaeism, campaigned with similar acerbity against the baptismal practice of the Elkesaites. Indeed, there are more striking parallels between the conceptions of the *Paraphrase of Seëm* and Manichaeism: the personification of natural phenomena like winds and clouds, the battle between the ambassador of Light, the Saviour, and Darkness, and above all the view that at the end of history the forms of Nature, the main expression of Darkness, together with the winds and their demons, will be squeezed together into a dark lump (*bōlos*) of matter (45, 14–20). This is not to suggest that the *Paraphrase of Seëm* is a Manichaean work, but that it originated in the religious and cultural context which produced Manichaeism as well. If this is correct, it must have been written in the Syrian-Mesopotamian world in the third century.

Concept of Our Great Power The *Concept of Our Great Power* (NHC VI, 4)[157] is also an extremely difficult text, as regards both content and translation. The common title is found at the end of the work. Above the text we find a double title: *Mental Perception – The Concept* [*noēma*] *of the Great Power*, in which *Mental Perception* (a rendering of the Greek *aisthēsis dianoētikē*) was originally probably a paraphrase of the word *noēma* in the second title. The Coptic in this text is often so peculiar that one wonders whether the translator was up to his task. Moreover, there are strong indications that the text of his Greek original was already corrupt in many places. Various research groups have in fact reached totally different interpretations of this work. The French-speaking group at the Université Laval in Quebec sees the work as an original literary unity with a clear structure, the 'Berliner Arbeitskreis' (H.-M. Schenke) views it as a loose collection of brief oracular sayings without any meaningful coherence, whereas researchers of the American group in Claremont, in particular F. E. Williams, regard it as a work composed from different sources, but offering a reasonably coherent whole in its final redaction.[158] It seems quite certain that the *Concept of Our Great Power* is not an original literary unit. Anyone who reads the work with an open mind

[157] Ed. F. Wisse and F. E. Williams, NHS 11 (1979), pp. 291–323; P. Cherix, OBEO 47 (1982).

[158] For a rapid overview of the various points of view, compare the introduction to the work by J.-P. Mahé, M. Desjardins and M. Roberge in *Écrits gnostiques*, pp. 899–906, and by H.-M. Schenke in *Nag Hammadi Deutsch*, vol. 11, pp. 484–7, and the study by F. E. Williams, *Mental Perception. A Commentary on NHC VI, 4: The Concept of Our Great Power*, NHMS 51 (Leiden: Brill, 2001), pp. xxviii–lxiv.

encounters so many sudden transitions, changes of person and inner contradictions that he or she is forced to conclude that all kinds of originally unconnected matters have apparently been strung together. So there is certainly something to be said for the position of the Berlin group. If one follows Schenke in presenting the translation in small textual units with spaces between them, it is striking how little coherence the text displays. Nevertheless – as Schenke admits – a certain main outline can be recognized in the work. The *Concept of Our Great Power* is an apocalyptic work, a revelation by or on behalf of the Great Power, which depicts a development from the creation to the destruction of the world. Various periods are distinguished: the era of the flesh (till the Flood), the present period of the soul (till the final conflagration of the world), and finally the period of 'Beauty' or of the 'Bridal Chamber', in which the saved find rest in the repose of the Great Power. The expression 'Great Power' is a well-known term for the supreme divine principle, which was particularly common in the circle of the Simonians, the gnostics who based themselves on Simon Magus. Williams has therefore argued that a Simonian, non-Christian work forms the earliest source of the text. But this is by no means a foregone conclusion. For apart from the fact that the term 'Great Power' was also used elsewhere for the supreme God, the arguments adduced for an early Simonian source are too weak to be convincing.

The work centres on gnosis as the precondition for salvation. This comes out in the very first sentences:

> And he who will know our Great Power will become invisible and no fire will be able to consume him, but it will purify. And it will destroy every thing that has power over you. For everyone in whom my form appears will be saved, from seven days old to 120 years. (36, 3–12)

All kinds of other gnostic elements can be detected in the *Concept of Our Great Power*. Thus the creator of material reality, identified with fire and the underworld, is doomed to go down with his creation. But on the other hand the traditional gnostic myth of creation seems to have exerted little influence.

A curious feature of this work is that some parts have a clearly Christian slant, whereas others lack it entirely. There is even a lengthy passage on the death and resurrection of Christ, though his name is never mentioned (40, 24–43, 2). According to the beginning of this passage, the Saviour had also once been active in the time of Noah:

> Then, in this era of the soul, the man will appear who knows the Great Power. He will receive and know me. He will drink from the milk of the Mother of the

work. He will speak in parables. He will proclaim the era to come, just as he spoke to [or in] Noah in the first era, that of the flesh.

The death of the Saviour is more hinted at than described directly: he was delivered up to the ruler of the Underworld, who however could not detain him, so that all emphasis lies on the victory over the evil powers and the subsequent resurrection. On the other hand the text does say that the sun set during the day and the day darkened, which again suggests the crucifixion. But it remains unclear how far this implies salvation for those who will enter the era of rest. Elsewhere in the work, after a description of the evil that dominates the psychical aeon, we find a call to spiritual awakening reminiscent of similar statements in hermetic literature: 'You are still asleep and dream dreams. Wake up and turn around and taste and eat the true food! Hand out the Word and the Water of Life!' (39, 33–40, 5).

In the context of the disasters which will occur in the eschaton the text provides some information that has been seen to indicate the time in which the *Concept of Our Great Power* originated. The passage in question reads as follows:

The Ruler [*archōn*] and the rulers of the West, came to the East, the place where the Logos had first appeared. Then the earth trembled and the cities tottered. Then the birds ate and were sated with their dead. The earth mourned, together with the inhabited world; they became desolate. At that point, when the times had been fulfilled, evil rose up mightily, to the extreme limit of what is calculable. Then the Ruler of the West stood up and from the East he will be active and instruct people in his wickedness, with the aim of destroying all teaching, the words of true wisdom, because he loves false wisdom. (43, 35–44, 20)

The language is clearly apocalyptic and therefore by definition vague. The question is whether the passage refers to real historical events. The first Ruler and the rulers of the West who travel to the East have been connected with Vespasian and Titus, who in 69/70 CE in Palestine ('the place where the Logos had first appeared') suppressed the Jewish rebellion and destroyed Jerusalem (thus the French research group and Williams). This is not in itself impossible. The second Ruler, who wreaks havoc from the East, has been identified with Diocletian, who moved the imperial capital to the East and instigated the last great persecution of Christians in 304 (thus the French researchers). So in that case the work would have originated or at least received its definitive form in the first decades of the fourth century at the earliest. But scholars have also suggested Emperor Julian, the 'Apostate' (360–3), who turned against Christianity (thus

Williams, who assumes that this note reflects the final revision of the text). The only useful thing to be said about these datings is that, in view of the manuscript date, a final redaction after Emperor Julian is highly improbable, if not impossible, and that a dating of the entire work to the decades after 304 is no more than an ill-founded guess. We simply do not know where and when the *Concept of Our Great Power* came into existence. Because the text doubtless went through a protracted development, a date in the second century seems too early, but the third century is certainly a possibility.

CHAPTER 4

Anti-gnostic literature

Until the mid twentieth century, gnostic studies focused almost exclusively on the information found in anti-gnostic authors. This was understandable, because only a few direct sources were available, and some of these were quite late. After the discovery of a large number of authentic writings, scholarly interest has shifted almost completely to these new sources. This, too, is understandable, but not correct, since the reports of anti-gnostic authors form an indispensable addition to what we know from the authentic sources. Moreover, they provide a wealth of information about gnostic views for which there are no parallels in the authentic works. Needless to say, their reports should be read with a critical eye, as it was obviously in their interest to blacken the names of their opponents. They discuss gnostic views not with the aim of understanding their deeper intentions, but in order to reject them in the light of their own positions. Even when they represent gnostic conceptions fairly, which is by no means always the case, it is clear that these conceptions were not always properly understood. In Antiquity, opposition to gnostics came from two sides: from Christian theologians and non-Christian philosophers. The main representatives of both groups will be discussed here: Irenaeus, Hippolytus and Epiphanius among the theologians, and Plotinus and his direct pupils among the philosophers.

IRENAEUS

Irenaeus came from Asia Minor and was appointed bishop of Lyons and Vienne, in the Rhône valley, in 178. He was confronted there with a rapid spread of the gnostic movement, partly thanks to the mission activity of a Roman Christian with a Valentinian background. This prompted him to study gnostic views and refute them in a voluminous work in five parts ('books'), entitled *On the Detection and Overthrow of What Is Falsely Called Gnosis*. In modern literature the work is always referred to as *Adversus haereses* (*AH*), 'Against Heresies'.[1] The complete work has been preserved in an early Latin translation; the Greek text survives only in (often abridged) quotations by later authors. Book I offers a description of the gnostics and the gnostic systems which he had come to know, sometimes larded with sarcastic asides and on occasion interrupted by a brief summary of the Church's faith (in *AH* I, 10 and 22). In Book II he refutes the gnostics on rational grounds, in Book III proceeding from apostolic doctrine, in Book IV on the basis of Jesus' teachings, while Book V is largely devoted to a defence of bodily resurrection, the 'resurrection of the flesh'. In his refutation Irenaeus elaborates his own 'salvation-historical' theology, which profoundly influenced later theological developments.[2]

Irenaeus was well informed about the views of the Valentinians, in particular those of Ptolemy and his followers (I, 1–9) and Marcus Magus (I, 13–21), for which he seems to have consulted original documents. He also provides information on the many differences of opinion between the Valentinians, some of which he probably had by hearsay (I, 11–12), and on many other gnostics, for which he drew both on earlier anti-gnostic works (I, 23–8) and on original sources (I, 29–31, 2). Indeed, Irenaeus was not the first to turn against the gnostics. In the mid second century the well-known apologist Justin Martyr (d. 165) had written a *Treatise against All Heresies*, as he himself states (*Apology* I, 26, 8). This statement concludes a chapter in which he gives a brief genealogy of heresies (*haireseis*). As arch-heretic he mentions Simon Magus (cf. Acts 8:9–24), followed by his pupils Menander and Marcion, who postulated another, perfect God above the imperfect Creator. His *Treatise*, usually referred to by the Greek name *Syntagma*, probably contained a much more detailed survey of the development of Christian *haireseis*. Initially the word *hairesis* did not have the sense of 'heresy' at all; it was used to denote a philosophical school and the branches it sprouted in the course of time. The history of Greek philosophy is often described as a number of schools (*haireseis*), each of which went back to its own founder, with internally a succession of teachers who offered their own variant and elaboration of the founder's ideas and thus formed a separate *hairesis*. Justin was himself a philosopher, with his own Christian school in Rome. The philosophical historiography of the day apparently led him to see Christianity, too, as a philosophical movement, with Christ as the founder, and internally a

[1] A. Rousseau and L. Doutreleau (eds.), *Irenée de Lyon. Contre les Hérésies*, 10 vols., SC 263, 264 (Livre I), 293, 294 (Livre II), 210, 211 (Livre III), 100(1), 100(2) (Livre IV), 152, 153 (Livre V) (Paris: Éditions du CERF, 1952–82).

[2] See for example E. F. Osborn, *Irenaeus of Lyons* (Cambridge University Press, 2001).

successive series of teachers, who developed the original doctrine in their own *hairesis*. But in his usage the word *hairesis* is already moving strongly in the direction of 'heresy'.[3] Though he says that the followers of Simon, Menander and Marcion are called 'Christians', 'just as the name of philosopher is common to philosophers, even if they do not share the same doctrines' (*Apology* I, 26, 6), this is no more than an apologetic argument: if the emperor leaves those Christians alone, why not all Christians? In fact he sees dissenting opinions not as views whose tenability needs to be tested on rational grounds, but as blasphemous errors inspired by demons (I, 26, 1. 4. 5). Unfortunately, Justin's *Syntagma* has been lost, like the work against heretics by Justin's younger contemporary Hegesippus, which Eusebius tells us about in his *Ecclesiastical History* (IV, 7, 15–8, 1). But Justin's idea of a succession of Christian heretics going back to Simon Magus was adopted by Irenaeus and later anti-gnostic authors. In his *Apology* Justin probably mentioned only the first two and the last of his list in the *Syntagma*, for Irenaeus likewise mentions Simon Magus and Menander as the first heretics and Marcion as the last. He interpolated a number of others, no doubt depending at least partly on Justin: Saturninus (a pupil of Simon and Menander), Basilides, Carpocrates, Cerinthus, Ebionites (pupils of Carpocrates and Cerinthus), Nicolaites, Cerdo (pupil of Simon) and Marcion (pupil of Cerdo). To these he adds Encratites (pupils of Saturninus and Marcion), unspecified followers of Basilides and Carpocrates, who advocated promiscuity and the consumption of sacrificial meat, and finally the *Gnōstikoi* and others, who go back to Simon and on whose doctrines Valentinus and his followers built (*AH* I, 23–31).[4] No researchers still take these and similar 'genealogies of heresies' seriously: they are constructions that serve to indicate that, starting from Simon Magus, one heresy produced another and thus things went from bad to worse – this in contrast to the unity of doctrine in the one Catholic Church. Of course, this is not to say that gnostics did not form schools and did not influence each other.

Irenaeus' reliability is often questioned in modern research, but not always with justification. Of course, he is squarely opposed to the gnostics and although he tries to refute them on rational grounds in Book II, it is clear from the outset that he rejects their views for religious reasons which are based on the Bible and the tradition. For him, the primary and

[3] A. le Boulluec, *La notion d'hérésie dans la littérature grecque, IIe–IIIe siècles*, 2 vols. (Paris: Études Augustiniennes, 1985).

[4] Separate articles on the gnostic teachers mentioned here are to be found in the *Dictionary of Gnosis*.

most fundamental point (*AH* II, 1, 1: *primum et maximum capitulum*) is the gnostic view that above the biblical Creator, who is considered imperfect or evil, resides the unknown true God, who is the father of Jesus Christ. He does not hesitate to call his opponents 'people without sense, fools' (*insensati, anoētoi*; e.g. *AH* I, 9, 3) or to ridicule them. In particular Marcus Magus bears the brunt of his attack: he describes him as a religious charlatan, who tried to seduce female followers, using love magic, and he assumes that his reader will laugh heartily at Marcus' foolish number and letter speculations (*AH* I, 13). But if one disregards this quite normal polemical tone, the conclusion must be that in Book I he sincerely tried to represent the views of his opponents as accurately as possible, preferably on the basis of written sources.[5]

HIPPOLYTUS

About forty years after Irenaeus wrote his *Adversus haereses* in Lyons, another major anti-heretical work was published in Rome, called the *Refutation of All Heresies*. It is usually referred to shortly as the *Refutatio* (from the Latin title: *Refutatio omnium haeresium*) or the *Elenchos* (from the Greek title: *Kata pasōn haireseōn elenchos*).[6] Its author has long been identified with the learned Roman priest Hippolytus, who was considered a prolific writer of exegetical, chronological and dogmatic works which for the greater part have been lost, but whose *Contra Noetum*, a treatise against Noetus, an adherent of the monarchian view of the Trinity, is also still extant. According to his traditional biography, Hippolytus became so embroiled with his bishop Callistus (d. 222) over dogmatic and moral issues that he had himself appointed counter-bishop by a group of sympathizers. He died as a martyr in 235, together with the second successor of Callistus, Pontianus (230–5), with whom he had become reconciled.[7] This traditional picture has been seriously questioned in recent research, resulting in the thesis that the *Refutatio* and *Contra Noetum* cannot have been written by the same author, which implies that at least two different writers authored the works that are traditionally ascribed to Hippolytus.

[5] For examples, see pp. 76, 92–3.

[6] Editions: P. Wendland, *Hippolytus. Refutatio omnium haeresium*, Hippolytus' Werke, vol. III, GCS 26 (Leipzig: Hinrichs, 1916) and M. Marcovich, *Hippolytus. Refutatio omnium haeresium*, Patristische Texte und Studien 25 (Berlin and New York: Walter de Gruyter, 1986). Scholars mostly prefer Wendland's edition because of the hypercritical character of Marcovich's work.

[7] C. Scholten, 'Hippolytos II (von Rom)', *RAC* XV (1991), cols. 492–551; D. A. Bertrand, 'Hippolyte de Rome', in R. Goulet (ed.), *Dictionnaire des philosophes antiques*, vol. III (Paris: Éditions du CNRS, 2000), pp. 791–9.

In this view, the name of the author of the *Refutatio* is unknown, though it, too, might have been Hippolytus.[8] The discussions about the identity of the author have not yet led to a scholarly consensus, which is no wonder, given the involvement of almost all aspects of the history of Christianity and Church in Rome in the first decades of the third century. However, the question of the author's identity has no bearing on the information on gnostic teachers and sects provided by the *Refutatio*, which, moreover, also in the recent discussions, has retained its traditional date, about 220 CE. Because of the undecidedness of the discussion about the author's identity and in order to avoid constantly referring to 'the author of the *Refutatio*', the author is called Hippolytus in this book, though the reader should keep in mind that the traditonal ascription to the martyr Hippolytus might be wrong. Moreover, the assumption made here is that the work is a literary unity and that Hippolytus is the only author, though these, too, are controversial matters. An earlier *Treatise (Syntagma) against All Heresies* by Hippolytus, referred to in *Refutatio* 1, Proem 1, has not been preserved, but it is assumed quite generally that its material was incorporated in the *Refutatio* and in anti-gnostic works by later authors as well.

The structure of the *Refutatio*, which comprises ten books, is wholly determined by the polemical method that Hippolytus employs. He wants to demonstrate that the heretics derived their doctrines from pagan Greek 'wisdom'.[9] The first four books are devoted to a description of this

[8] Brief overviews of the main points of the discussion in Bertrand, 'Hippolyte de Rome', pp. 793–5, and E. Norelli's introduction to a collection of studies on the *Refutatio* and its author (with much recent literature), ed. G. Aragione and E. Norelli, *Des évêques, des écoles et des hérétiques. Actes du colloque international sur la 'Réfutation de toutes les hérésies', Genève, 13–14 juin 2008* (Prahins: Édition du Zèbre, 2011), pp. 13–15; see also G. Aragione, 'Bibliographie sur l'Elenchos et la question de l'auteur (1940–2010)', in Aragione and Norelli (eds.), *Des évêques, des écoles et des hérétiques*, pp. 325–40. There is an extensive discussion of all the problems involved in A. Brent, *Hippolytus and the Roman Church in the Third Century. Communities in Tension before the Emergence of a Monarch-Bishop*, Supplements to Vigiliae Christianae 31 (Leiden: Brill, 1995); see also his 'The Elenchos and the Identification of Christian Communities in Second–Early Third Century Rome', in Aragione and Norelli (eds.), *Des évêques, des écoles et des hérétiques*, pp. 275–314. According to Brent, Callistus was the first bishop who claimed monarchic authority over the entire Roman Church; the martyr Hippolytus is thought to have been the writer of *Contra Noetum* and, in fact, the successor of the author of the *Refutatio* as leader of the Christian group that rejected Callistus' authority. However, M. Simonetti, 'Per un profilo dell'autore dell'Elenchos', in Aragione and Norelli (eds.), *Des évêques, des écoles et des hérétiques*, pp. 257–73, argues that Brent's picture is anachronistic; in his view, monarchic episcopacy existed already in Rome before Callistus.

[9] See W. Löhr, 'The Continuing Construction of Heresy: Hippolytus' Refutatio in Context', in Aragione and Norelli (eds.), *Des évêques, des écoles et des hérétiques*, pp. 25–42, who points out that in the *Refutatio* 'the anti-heretical discourse is integrated into the apologetic discourse' (p. 37); on this apologetic aspect especially see C. Scholten, 'Autor, Anliegen und Publikum der Refutatio', in Aragione and Norelli (eds.), *Des évêques, des écoles et des hérétiques*, pp. 135–66.

wisdom: Book I offers a concise survey of Greek philosophy; Books II and III, which dealt with Greek mysteries and myths, have been lost; Book IV discusses astrology and magic. In Books V–IX over thirty heretics and heresies are passed in review, with Hippolytus indicating for each individually on which pagan, usually philosophical, views they depend. In his view, the ideas of the Greek philosophers about the divine were more sublime (*semnotera*) than those of the heretics, because these had adapted and distorted them (I, Proem 8; also VIII, 15, 3). Finally, Book X first gives a summary of the Greek philosophies, then of the heresies and ultimately an exposition of true Christian doctrine. Strikingly, Hippolytus does not merely reproduce there what he had already offered in the previous books, but once again quotes his sources. Although he mainly targets the gnostics, other 'heresies' are also discussed, including a sharp attack on Bishop Callistus, whom he calls the leader of a sect (IX, 11–12), and a long exposition on the Jews (IX, 18–30). Because he reduces all the views he dislikes to pagan, in particular philosophical, influence, his work is also an important source for our knowledge of Greek philosophy.[10]

Hippolytus knew the work of Irenaeus and used it to advantage, but he offers much material that cannot be found elsewhere. This is often called, in a German term, Hippolytus' *Sondergut*. Thus he provides a description of the ideas of the Alexandrian gnostic Basilides (VII, 14–27) which differs totally from and is in fact incompatible with what Irenaeus reports (*AH* I, 24, 3–7). Gnostic groups like the Naassenes (V, 6–11) and teachers like Justin the Gnostic (V, 23–7) and Monoimus the Arab (VIII, 12–15) would have remained totally unknown to us without Hippolytus' work. In the *Sondergut* Hippolytus gives many literal quotations. The study of his quotations of Greek philosophers has taught us that although he reproduces his sources quite faithfully, he does not hesitate to transpose passages within quotations or insert a passage which was not originally there at all or sometimes even modify the original formulations in order to tailor them to his own argument. However, long ago scholars discovered something curious about his *Sondergut*: there are striking parallels between the systems described, as regards both content and formulation. They contain many allegorical interpretations of Greek myths and offer many more biblical quotations than for instance the authentic writings of Nag Hammadi. Various explanations have been suggested for these similarities, though the problem has not yet been investigated in all its

[10] J. Mansfeld, *Heresiography in Context: Hippolytus'* Elenchos *as a Source for Greek Philosophy*, Philosophia Antiqua 56 (Leiden: Brill, 1992).

complexity. Most likely, Hippolytus made use of an existing 'gnostic dossier', which still clearly betrays the hand of its Christian-gnostic compiler, but also underwent a redaction by Hippolytus himself.[11]

The tone of Hippolytus' polemics is much harsher and more uncontrolled than that of Irenaeus, but there can be no doubt that his work is vital to our knowledge of the gnostic movement in the second and the early third century. It makes us aware that the authentic gnostic writings reflect only part of the multicoloured gnostic world of ideas.

EPIPHANIUS

For thirty years Epiphanius of Salamis (*c.* 315–403) was head of a monastery near Eleutheropolis in Palestine, before he became bishop of Constantia in Cyprus. He was famous for his erudition and is now notorious for his unreliability.[12] Between 375 and 377 he wrote a work entitled *Panarion* (from Latin *panarium*, 'breadbasket'), which he himself describes in his Preface 1, 1, 2, as 'a medicine chest against the bites of wild animals and snakes', meaning the heretics.[13] In it he describes eighty heresies – a number not based on reality, but predetermined. For, as he himself indicates, it derives from the biblical Song of Solomon 6:8: 'There are sixty queens and eighty concubines, and maidens without number. My dove, my perfect one, is the only one.' So the eighty heresies are the concubines (who should not really exist) and the only true one, the most beautiful of all, is the orthodox Church. To reach this number of eighty, he takes a very broad view of the term heretic: he starts with the Barbarians, the Scyths, the Greeks and the Jews and then discusses the main Greek philosophies and Jewish sects. Thus in the period before Christ he arrives at no fewer than twenty 'heresies'. For the Greek philosophers he has used sources of widely varying quality, but most striking is that he fails to appreciate the seriousness of the philosophical questions formulated by the Greeks: it is all wicked talk, heresy. Hippolytus' proposition that the heretics drew their 'wisdom' from the Greeks and in particular Greek philosophy is

[11] See also C. Scholten, 'Quellen regen an: Beobachtungen zum "gnostischen Sondergut" in der *Refutatio omnium haeresium*', in J. A. van den Berg, A. Kotzé, T. Nicklas and M. Scopello (eds.), *'In Search of Truth': Augustine, Manichaeism and other Gnosticism. Studies for Johannes van Oort at Sixty*, NHMS 74 (Leiden: Brill, 2011), pp. 567–91.

[12] W. Schneemelcher, 'Epiphanius von Salamis', *RAC* v (1962), pp. 909–27.

[13] K. Holl, *Epiphanius (Ancoratus und Panarion)*, vol. i, *Ancoratus und Panarion haer. 1–33*, GCS 25 (Leipzig: Hinrichs, 1915), vol. ii, *Panarion haer. 34–64*, GCS 31(2), rev. edn, ed. J. Dummer (Berlin: Akademie Verlag, 1980), vol. iii, *Panarion haer. 65–80. De fide*, GCS 37(2), rev. edn, ed. J. Dummer (Berlin: Akademie Verlag, 1985).

taken to extremes by Epiphanius. From chapter 20 onwards he discusses the Christian heresies, starting with Simon Magus and ending with the Messalians, a contemporary group of Christians who roamed about, did not work and considered the Church sacraments unnecessary, but put great emphasis on prayer, strict ascesis and possession of the prophetic Spirit. Epiphanius collected a vast amount of material, but it is very hard to assess. Often he has demonstrably misunderstood his sources, sees non-existent connections between groups, draws conclusions which are evidently wrong, uses his imagination for lack of sources and for lack of arguments resorts to gross slander to gun down his opponents. What is totally lacking is any appreciation of the deeper intentions of the opinions he disputes and the sincerity of their defenders. Nevertheless, his *Panarion* is indispensable for the history of Christian gnostic religion and of other movements which deviated from the established orthodoxy. He often quotes his sources literally, sometimes in their entirety or in large part.[14] However, owing to the nature of his work, researchers often reach contradictory conclusions. The *Panarion* is frequently unreliable and irritating to the modern reader, but it cannot be ignored.

PLOTINUS AND HIS PUPILS

Not only Christian theologians but also Platonic philosophers opposed gnostic speculations. We know this for certain about Plotinus and his pupils, who in the mid third century came up against Platonizing gnostics who frequented Plotinus' school. These based themselves on, among other works, *Zostrianus* and *Allogenes*, recovered in Nag Hammadi. Porphyry, in his *Life of Plotinus*, 16, gives an extended account of this, but its beginning is not entirely clear.[15] It says that in Plotinus' time not only many of the Christians frequented his school but also 'others' whom he calls 'sectarians, who had abandoned [or had started from] the old philosophy' and who now can be confidently identified as gnostics. The question is whether these 'others' were also Christians, distinguished from the 'many' as sectarians (*hairetikoi*), or non-Christian philosophers who in Porphyry's view had deviated from the old philosophy. The Greek wording

[14] See pp. 16 and 93–6.

[15] On the *Life of Plotinus*, with text, translation and many studies, see P. Brisson *et al.*, *Porphyre. La vie de Plotin*, 2 vols. (Paris: Vrin, 1982–92); on chapter 16 see M. Tardieu, 'Les gnostiques dans la *Vie de Plotin*. Analyse du chapitre 16', *ibid.*, vol. II, pp. 503–63, with, on pp. 547–63, a very useful appendix: 'Répertoire chronologique (1933–1990) des publications relatives aux chapitre 16 de la *Vie de Plotin*'.

suggests the former option, which is reflected in the following translation. Moreover, if the 'others', who are clearly the target of Porphyry's remarks, were not Christians but merely pagan philosophers, then Porphyry would not have had any reason to mention the Christians at all. He writes:

> There were in his time many Christians, including sectarians who had abandoned the old philosophy, Adelphius and Aquilinus and their followers,[16] who possessed a great number of writings by Alexander the Lybian and Philocomus, Demostratus and Lydus,[17] and produced revelations by Zoroaster, Zostrianus, Nicotheus, Allogenes and Messus and other people of the kind. Thus they deceived many others, as they deceived themselves, by contending that Plato had not penetrated the depth of intelligible being. For that reason he frequently refuted them in his lectures and wrote a treatise which I have entitled *Against the Gnostics*; he left it up to us to examine the rest. Amelius came to forty books in writing against the book of Zostrianus. I myself, Porphyry, wrote a great number of refutations of the book of Zoroaster. I showed that it was a spurious and recent work, made up by the founders of the sect in order to suggest that the doctrines they had chosen to honour were those of the ancient Zoroaster.

Sadly, Amelius' voluminous work has been lost, as have the arguments that Porphyry himself put forward. But Plotinus' treatise *Against the Gnostics* does survive, in his *Enneads* II, 9, which originally, as the last part, formed a unit with III, 8; V, 8; and V, 5 (in that order).[18] In II, 9 Plotinus first opposes the gnostic view that there are more levels of being (hypostases) than the three which he himself assumed, the One (*to Hen*), the Mind (*Nous*) and the World-Soul (*Psychē*). Evidence that Plotinus had read the gnostic works includes his mention of some of these new gnostic

[16] Other translations are: 'There were in his time many Christians and others, and sectarians who had abandoned the old philosophy, men of the schools of Adelphius and Aculinus' (A. H. Armstrong, *Plotinus, with an English Translation*, vol. I (London: W. Heinemann; Cambridge, MA: Harvard University Press, 1966), p. 45); 'In his time there were many Christians, including sectarians trained in the old philosophy, Adelphius and Aquilinus and their followers' (A. D. Nock, 'Gnosticism', in *Essays on Religion and the Ancient World*, vol. II (Oxford University Press, 1972), p. 943); 'In [Plotinus'] time there were among the Christians many others, members of a school of thought [*hairetikoi*], who were followers of Adelphius and Aquilinus and had started out from classical philosophy' (Layton, 'Prolegomena to the Study of Ancient Gnosticism', p. 342). Tardieu, 'Les gnostiques', pp. 509–14, has forcefully defended the view that the word *hairetikoi* should be translated as 'heretics'. He argues that Porphyry adapted himself to contemporary Christian usage, because the word is typically Christian Greek, with the meaning 'heretic', whereas it does not occur in general Greek in the sense of 'adherent of a specific philosophical school of thought'.

[17] Tardieu, 'Les gnostiques', pp. 515–20, argues that these people were 'authors of philosophical treatises, who had nothing to do with Christianity nor with Gnosticism'. Their identity cannot be established with any degree of certainty.

[18] For Plotinus' criticism of the gnostics, see Turner, *Sethian Gnosticism and the Platonic Tradition*, pp. 711–20; also Logan, *The Gnostics*, pp. 46–50.

hypostases in II, 9, 6, namely 'exiles' (*paroikēseis*), 'impressions' (*antitypoi*) and 'repentings' (*metanoiai*). For these also occur in *Zostrianus* (NHC VIII, 5, 17–29), as aeons through which Zostrianus passes on his ascent and where he is baptized in living water, and also in the *Untitled Gnostic Treatise*, 20, of the Codex Brucianus, which similarly talks about a baptism in the fountain of living water.[19] Plotinus is scathing, he calls the gnostic terms 'typically something of people who introduce new jargon to make a case for their school'. He observes that part of their doctrine is borrowed from Plato, 'but the novelties they put forward, with the aim of establishing their philosophy, have nothing to do with the truth'. The fall of Sophia and the subsequent creation of the world by the Demiurge are rejected by Plotinus on philosophical grounds; he is convinced that the beautiful cosmos cannot have been made by an evil creator (II, 9, 10–13). Plotinus criticizes the gnostics' rejection of the importance and even the possibility of character building, which can help humans to become virtuous and wise. They focus only on themselves: 'So what is left for them is pleasure and selfishness and that which does not connect them with other people and is merely satisfaction of needs, unless one of them is by nature better than these doctrines' (II, 9, 15).

Plotinus has deliberately restrained his criticism, 'for I am held back by a certain regard for some of our friends, who became acquainted with this doctrine before they became our friends and, inexplicably, still cling to it' (II, 9, 10). This shows that gnostics were among Plotinus' trusted pupils and friends. For these people the form of Platonism taught by Plotinus must have been highly attractive, because it could be adapted, though only with some difficulty, to their gnostic positions. There are in fact some clear resemblances between the views of Plotinus and the gnostics on the development and structure of the spiritual world, the most striking being the idea of emanation of the lower from the higher. Works like *Zostrianus* and *Allogenes* must have been written before these gnostics became acquainted with Plotinus, others may have come from their circle. The fundamental philosophical criticism which Plotinus and his followers levelled against the gnostic worldview did not, as far as we can ascertain, have any influence on the Christian opposition to gnostic ideas.

[19] See pp. 82 and 89.

CHAPTER 5

Gnosis: essence and expressions

THE GNOSTIC EXPERIENCE

The primary means of expressing religious experience are myths and rituals; rational reflection on this experience is always secondary. This also applies to ancient gnostic religion. However, the myths that express the gnostic experience are largely artificial and thus to a certain extent rational reflection in narrative form, which is made still more complicated by their display of confusing variety and complexity. Though by no means all gnostic writings offer an elaborated myth, it is always presupposed in some form or other. The complexity of the myths described or precisely their implicitness hampers the reading of gnostic texts, so that it is often difficult for modern readers to get to the very core of ancient gnosis. But this core can be summed up in a few words.

Above all, gnosis is a personal, existential certainty: I come from God, I partake in his essence, I will return to him. It is an enlightened insight into the origin, present situation and destiny of mankind. The myth explains the nature of the divine world and how evil and the material world came about and the divine essence of human beings became entangled in matter. This does not involve neutral, theoretical knowledge, but a religious knowing, an inner enlightenment, based on revelation from the divine world. The pluriformity of the gnostic myth suggests that myths are used more to evoke an image of reality than describe it accurately. Gnostics were not concerned with the truth of the myth but with the reality of liberation from the grasp of evil powers. What the gnostics sought was not rational truth but existential certainty. In a sense the intense interest in various myths in authentic gnostic writings and in anti-gnostic authors is therefore misleading. Someone who knows his true earthly situation and thus has knowledge of his divine essence – that person has knowledge. Someone who truly knows himself knows God, and someone who knows God knows himself, and at the same time this knowledge means liberation from matter and a return to God. Redemption is the elimination of ignorance.

Liberating gnosis is therefore self-knowledge and knowledge of God at the same time. Gnostic texts often stress the importance and connection of these two kinds of knowledge. This may be clarified by some examples. The *True Testimony* (NHC IX, 44, 30–45, 6) says:

> If someone knows himself and God, who transcends the truth, he will be saved and wreathed with the imperishable wreath.

The *Book of Thomas* (NHC II, 138, 16–18) says:

> A person who has no knowledge of himself knows nothing, but who knows himself has also gained knowledge of the depth of the All!

Clement of Alexandria, *Excerpta ex Theodoto* 78, 2, quotes gnostics who said that baptism liberates us from the coercion of fate, but added that this applies not only to the bath of baptism, but also to gnosis, which knows:

> who we were and what we have become,
> where we were and in what we have been cast,
> to where we hasten and from what we are saved,
> what birth is and what rebirth.

Finally, the *Gospel of Truth* (NHC I, 22, 13–20) says:

> A person who thus has gnosis knows whence he has come and whither he will go. He knows, like a drunk person who has left behind his drunkenness, has come to himself and has put his affairs in order again.

Not only sobering up after drunkenness, but also awaking from sleep or from a bad dream is an often-used image for the arrival of gnosis. This image was not confined to the domain of gnosis, as is shown by the Pauline Letter to the Ephesians 5:14, where an early Christian hymn is quoted: 'Sleeper, awake! Rise from the dead, and Christ will shine on you.' A well-known gnostic example is found in the *Gospel of Truth*, where ignorance about God is described as a nightmare. On waking up with a start, one finds it was fortunately just a bad dream. The text (NHC I, 29, 32–30, 16) concludes:

> Thus it is with those who have cast off ignorance like sleep, they consider it to be of no value, nor do they hold its products to be real, but leave them behind like a dream in the night and regard knowledge of the Father as the dawn. Thus each one acted while in ignorance, as if he was asleep, and thus he arrived at knowledge as if he awoke. Happy the person who comes to himself and wakes up, blessed he who has opened the eyes of the blind!

The essence of ancient gnostic religion, then, is the spiritual insight that humans are divine in their deepest core, that they have ended up in earthly reality because of a fateful development and that this insight itself already implies a return to the divine world. This insight is not something which a human being achieves by himself; the veil of ignorance which covers him needs to be removed, his mind needs to be enlightened. And this is only possible via a revelation by one or more ambassadors of the unknown God, who manifest themselves in the material world. For the gnostics, it was clear that the content of gnosis was something entirely new: the God revealed in it transcended all known gods, including the God of traditional Jews and Christians, and evil came about in a different way from what was taught in the existing philosophies and religions. Their documents did contain elements of the truth, but these required a different interpretation. Hence the great stories from the Jewish and Christian traditions, in particular Genesis and the gospels, as well as those from Greek mythology, needed to be read in a new way.

One of the most difficult questions in gnostic studies is that of the personal perception of the individual gnostic. How does one arrive at this new insight and what is the role of the gnostic teacher? How is the return to the divine origin experienced and do certain rituals play a role here? Is the received enlightenment celebrated collectively, too? The gnostic myths do describe the need for gnostic illumination, but they are usually very reticent about the gnostic's own experience. Ultimately, all gnostic systems are centred on the certainty that there is a way back to the divine origin. In fact, the role of the gnostic teacher was not so much that of a philosopher who teaches a coherent system as that of a psychotherapist or shepherd of souls. Yet little is known about the role which the leader of a gnostic group played in the individual gnostic's personal experience of enlightenment and in its possible collective celebration. But we can assume that this role was not the same everywhere. The available sources leave no doubt that there were different kinds of gnostic communities. Some had the nature of a philosophical school, others were free religious communities, in which philosophical, Jewish, Christian and 'pagan' ideas could play a more or less important role, and still others saw themselves as part of the Christian Church, in which they sometimes formed a separate faction within a local Christian community. There was by no means always a sharp demarcation between these groups. Thus one could belong to a certain school and at the same time form part of a Christian congregation. In the first centuries CE a standard education model was for a school to be formed around an authoritative teacher, in Christian circles, too. Examples among non-gnostics are Justin Martyr (*c.* 150), Clement of Alexandria (*c.* 200) and Origen (*c.* 230), among gnostics, Basilides (*c.* 130) and his son Isidorus, and Valentinus (*c.* 140) and his pupils Heracleon and Ptolemy (*c.* 160–80). The extant works of these teachers show that they not only taught a philosophical-religious system, but above all wanted to offer spiritual guidance to their pupils, so that they would become different people religiously and morally. We know that the non-gnostic teachers did not position themselves outside the church community (Origen was even a priest in the last decades of his life), we know this for certain about Valentinus, too, and there is no reason to assume that things were different with Basilides and people like Heracleon and Ptolemy. In Antiquity philosophical schools were always religious communities as well, in which tribute was paid to the founder of the philosophical movement to which the school belonged. Usually there was a statue of the founder in the school, and this also occurred among gnostics. Irenaeus reports that the Simonians revered statues of Simon Magus in the guise of Zeus and of Helen in that of Athena (*AH* 1, 23, 4). The bishop of Lyons also states that the followers of the Alexandrian gnostic Carpocrates possessed several images of Christ, some painted, others made of various kinds of material, which were supposedly based on a portrait of Christ commissioned by Pilate. Apparently they wreathed these images and placed them alongside those of secular philosophers like Pythagoras, Plato and Aristotle: 'And they shower them with all the other honours customary among the pagans' (*AH* 1, 25, 6). This last may be an insinuation of Irenaeus himself, but it could in fact well be true. Jesus was clearly regarded here as the founder of a Christian philosophy, something that would not have seemed strange to, for instance, Justin, who also liked to present Christianity as a philosophy (and always continued to wear the philosopher's mantle).

From the third century we have some surviving works – including *Zostrianus*, *Allogenes* and *Marsanes*[1] – which describe at length the ascent of a mythical seer to the top of the spiritual world, an ascent which can be considered exemplary for that of the gnostic in general. In discussing these works, we saw earlier that the focus is no longer on the origin and nature of the earthly situation and the proclamation of gnosis by a saviour, but almost exclusively on the structure of the divine world and what happens to the gnostic during his upward journey. The movement is no longer from top to bottom, as in the traditional gnostic myth, but from bottom to top. Though these are relatively late writings, it does seem certain that the soul's upward journey through unknown worlds is a fundamental gnostic experience which precedes the mythography. Because gnosis also has an esoteric aspect, sources are reticent on the question

[1] See pp. 81–8.

whether secret techniques were practised from the outset in order to lead the soul up to its divine origin. But later, in any case, this did happen. In particular the third century saw an emergence of the notion in philosophy that pure thought is insufficient for union with the divine and that this requires magic spells. Great influence was exercised here by the so-called *Chaldaean Oracles* (*Oracula Chaldaica*), which were written in the late second century.[2] The word 'theurgy' ('divine work') is mostly used to denote this magic path to contact with the deity. In an early work, entitled *The Return of the Soul* (*De regressu animae*), Porphyry distinguished between the spiritual soul and the rational soul (*nous*), the first being the astral body of the second. He argued there that the spiritual soul could be saved by theurgic rites or a life of self-restraint, but that this soul could not ascend higher than the gods of the ether. In his view, however, the rational soul, in virtue of its intellect, could ascend by itself to the Father, without requiring a theurgic purification of the spiritual soul. This is possible for only a few people, which means that for the large majority the soul's ascent could be realized only via theurgic practices.[3] But in third- and fourth-century Platonism there were also philosophers who considered theurgic rites to be necessary in all cases, so for the rational soul, too. This was for instance the opinion of Porphyry's pupil Iamblichus (first half of the fourth century).[4] Plotinus himself strongly opposed the idea, but it is characteristic that his school accommodated pupils who did occupy themselves with magic practices – and these were the gnostics. In *Against the Gnostics* II, 9, 14 he accuses them:

> But above all in yet another way they assail the purity of the supreme principles. For when they write down magic formulas as if they address them to those principles, not just to the Soul, but even to those above it, what else do they do but make the principles obey those who utter spells, charms and incantations and cause them to be led by their word – provided that one of us is more skilled than others in saying the right things in the right way: songs, cries, snorting and hissing tones, and all the rest which has been described as exercising magic power there.

Plotinus goes on to remark that, according to his opponents, diseases are demonic beings that can be exorcized by spells. Again, this was not an

[2] R. Majercik, *The Chaldaean Oracles. Text, Translation, and Commentary*, Studies in Greek and Roman Religion 5 (Leiden: Brill, 1989); also E. des Places, *Oracles Chaldaïques, avec un choix de commentaires anciens* (Paris: Les Belles Lettres, 1971).

[3] These views of Porphyry were discussed in detail, and disputed, by Augustine, *De civitate dei* x, 27–30; see van den Broek, *Studies in Gnosticism*, pp. 207–19.

[4] See below p. 144.

unusual notion among the gnostics, as is shown for instance by the long list of demons that 'rule' over the various parts of the body in the *Secret Book of John* (NHC II, 15, 29–17, 32). But no doubt the theurgic practices mentioned in the quotation involved more than the exorcism of demons for a practical earthly goal. It was a way of penetrating to the highest divine levels, above the World-Soul, though it was necessary to know the right formulas and way of uttering them. This report by Plotinus puts various elements from the gnostic writings read in his school in the correct perspective.[5] The frequent enumerations of magic names of the supreme divine level leads to knowledge of and union with this level. One example among many is a eulogy in *Allogenes*:

> Autoer, Beritheus, Erigenaor, Orimenios, Aramen, Aphleges, Elelioupheus, Lalameus, Yetheus, Noetheus! You are great! He who knows [you] knows the All! You are One, you are One, the good one, Aphredon! You are the aeon of the aeons, the one who always is.
>
> Then she praised the entire One as follows: Lalameus, No[eth]eus, Senaon, Asine[us], [O]riphanius, Mellephaneus, Elemaoni, Smoun, Optaon, He-Who-Is! You are He-Who-Is, the Aeon of the aeons, the Unbegotten One, who is higher than the unbegotten ones, Yatomenos, it is for you alone that all the unborn are begotten, the Unnameable One! (NHC XI, 54, 17–37)

Some of the names from the laudation of the One also occur in the *Prayer of Seth*, which may have a gnostic but certainly has a magic background.[6] Speculations on letters and numbers in writings like *Zostrianus* and *Marsanes* also have a theurgic function: someone who possesses the right combinations can get through to the deity. Here is just one example, from *Zostrianus*, an invocation of the aeon Protophanes:

> Phoē Zoē Zēōē Zē[oē] Zōsi Zōsi Zaō Zēōōō Zēsen Zēsen! The individuals and the four who are eightfold are alive! Ēoooo Ēa Ēō! You precede them, you are in them all! (NHC VIII, 127, 1–7)

Recent research has shown great scholarship and diligence in bringing to light the Platonist slant of *Zostrianus* and related works, but here we see that this is a somewhat one-sided approach. These works were written in

[5] This theme deserves a broader treatment. So far the scholarly discussion has focused mainly on the relation between Neoplatonic and gnostic theurgy; see B. A. Pearson, 'Gnostic Ritual and Iamblichus's Treatise On the Mysteries of Egypt', in *Gnosticism and Christianity in Roman and Coptic Egypt*, pp. 224–48; Turner, *Sethian Gnosticism and the Platonic Tradition*, pp. 603–35.

[6] See p. 15. Cf. also the eulogy to the highest God in the *Three Steles of Seth*, NHC VII, 126, 5–17: 'O hidden one, blessed Senaon, who begot himself, [Asi]neus, Mephneus, Optaon, Elemaon, the great Power! Emouniar, Nirabeus, Kandephoros, Apredon, Deiphaneus! For me you are Armedon, the Begetter of power. Thalanatheus, Antitheus. You exist in yourself, you exist before yourself, and no one became active after you.'

an environment that was permeated by magic and theurgy. Plotinus had a keener eye for this than many modern investigators.

We can no longer accurately determine how the gnostics viewed the operation of these theurgic exclamations. Conceivably, they believed that the theurgist could force the divine powers via magic actions and words to connect themselves with him, which in itself would be a typically magic view. An interesting example of this is found in the so-called 'Mithras Liturgy'. This is not a regular liturgy from the Mithraic mystery religion, but a magic text which describes how magic ritual, formulas and prayers can be used to climb up through the heavens to the highest God, Mithras.[7] The text refers to itself as an *Apathanatismos*, a ritual for obtaining immortality (741, 747, 771). Several times in the prayers the magician therefore mentions that he has become reborn and immortal in his ascent. Thus he says to the Helios (639–50):

> Hail, Lord, who is great in power, great Ruler, King, Greatest of the gods, Sun, Lord of heaven and earth, God of gods,[8] powerful is your breath, strong is your might, Lord! If it be your will, announce me to the greatest God, who begot and made you: that a human being wishes to worship you and beseeches you with all his human power – that is to say, I NN, whose mother is NN, born from the mortal womb of NN and from seminal fluid, and who, because he has been reborn today through you, has become immortal out of so many myriads in this hour, in accordance with the will of the exceedingly good God.

We should note here that the idea of a spiritual transformation described as a rebirth or deification was widespread in the first centuries CE. In connection with the 'Mithras Liturgy' scholars have often, and rightly, pointed to Corpus Hermeticum XIII (*On Rebirth*), in which a full transformation of the initiate is also described. Since the discovery of the Nag Hammadi library, we can now also add the *Discourse on the Eighth and Ninth* (NHC VI, 6).[9] In *Allogenes* the eponymous seer says during his heavenly journey:

> I saw the light that [surrou]nded me and the good that was in me. I was deified. (NHC XI, 52, 10–12)

7 H. D. Betz, *The 'Mithras Liturgy'. Text, Translation, and Commentary*, STAC 18 (Tübingen: Mohr, 2003; paperback edn 2005). The text is part of the great Parisian magic papyrus (*PGM* IV, 475–820), in English translation, by M. W. Meyer, also published in H. D. Betz (ed.), *The Greek Magical Papyri in Translation, Including the Demotic Spells* (Chicago and London: University of Chicago Press, 1986), pp. 48–54.

8 The words 'Sun, Lord of heaven and earth, God of gods' (lines 640–1) have been erroneously omitted in Betz's translation.

9 See above p. 35.

And in the *Holy Book of the Great Invisible Spirit* the gnostic exclaims in a hymn:

Now I know you, I have mixed with the unchangeable.
I have armed myself with a weapon of light.
I have become light. (NHC III, 66, 27–67, 4)

But this conception is also known in the Jewish sphere, though there it never (except for the later Cabbala) involves deification but transformation into an angel. The Cologne Mani Codex[10] contains a quotation from the *Revelation of Seth*, in which Seth (Sethel) talks (p. 51) about his transformation during his heavenly journey:

When I heard these things, my heart rejoiced and my consciousness changed and I became like one of the greatest angels. That angel laid his hand on my right arm and he pushed me out of the world from which I was created and he brought me to another place which was very large.

A similar conception occurs in the Hebrew *Sefer Hekhalot*, which is also known as *3 Enoch*. Enoch was taken up into the heavens (cf. Genesis 5:24) and changed there into the highest angel, Metatron, to whom are revealed all the mysteries and knowledge (3–20). When he was taken up into the heavens, he says, 15, 1:

At once my flesh turned to flame, my sinews to blazing fire, my bones to juniper coals, my eyelashes to lightning flashes, my eyeballs to fiery torches, the hairs of my head to hot flames, all my limbs to wings of burning fire, and the substance of my body to blazing fire.[11]

[10] Edition of the Greek text with a German translation by L. Koenen and C. Römer, *Der Kölner Mani-Kodex. Über das Werden seines Leibes. Kritische Edition aufgrund der von A. Henrichs und L. Koenen besorgten Erstedition*, Papyrologica Coloniensia 14 (Opladen: Westdeutscher Verlag, 1988). A revised German translation in L. Koenen and C. Römer, *Mani. Auf der Spur einer verschollenen Religion* (Freiburg, Basle and Vienna: Herder, 1993). Greek text and English translation of the first ninety-nine pages of the codex in R. Cameron and A. J. Dewey, *The Cologne Mani Codex (P. Colon. Inv. Nr. 4780) 'Concerning the Origin of his Body'*, Early Christian Literature Series 3: Texts and Translations 15 (Missoula, MT: Scholars Press, 1979).

[11] Translation by P. Alexander, '3 (Hebrew Apocalypse of) Enoch', in J. H. Charlesworth (ed.), *The Old Testament Pseudepigrapha*, vol. 1 (Peabody, MA: Hendrickson, 2009; = Yale University Press, 1983), p. 267. For a comparison between the heavenly journeys in the Jewish *hekhalot* and *merkavah* literature and the gnostic heavenly journeys in *Zostrianus*, *Allogenes* and *Marsanes*, see G. P. Luttikhuizen, 'Monism and Dualism in Jewish-Mystical and Gnostic Ascent Texts', in A. Hilhorst *et al.* (eds.), *Flores Florentino. Dead Sea Scrolls and Other Early Jewish Studies in Honour of Florentino García Martínez*, Supplements to the Journal for the Study of Judaism 122 (Leiden: Brill, 2007), pp. 749–75. As regards form, however, we should also point to the influence of Jewish and Christian apocalyptic visions, briefly discussed in R. van den Broek, 'Spiritual Transformation in Ancient Hermetism and Gnosticism', in R. A. Gilbert (ed.), *Knowledge of the Heart. Gnostic Movements and Secret Traditions*, Canonbury Papers 5 (London: Lewis Masonic, 2008), pp. 30–43 (esp. pp. 39–42).

As regards magic in gnostic texts, we should also note the following. Though in magic the magician can, as it were, 'force' the invoked deity to manifest himself and render his assistance, the magic power inheres not so much in the magician himself as in the magic aids, rituals and prayers which he uses, provided that they are properly performed. This was doubtless an important viewpoint among the gnostics, too, since gnosis was always experienced not as something freely available, but as a grace bestowed. It is likely that they agreed with Iamblichus in thinking not that the theurgist as a human being brings about the connection and union with the divine, but that this is granted in and through the theurgic act itself. 'The tokens [*synthēmata*] themselves perform the proper work by virtue of themselves.'[12] The theurgic act thus has much in common with the 'orthodox' view of the sacraments in the early Church: in baptism the priest does not effect forgiveness of sins and resurrection to a new life, but these are granted in and through the immersion itself in the name of God. The sacraments effect salvation *ex opere operato*, that is to say, through the fact of the performance itself.[13] Though theoretical reflections on the operation of theurgy are lacking in gnostic writings, it is therefore perfectly conceivable and indeed probable that the gnostic experience of it agreed with Iamblichus' discussions. This brings us to the nature of the theurgic acts and to the question whether these also occurred in earlier expressions of gnostic religion, that of the second century.

In light of the above it seems certain that the gnostic hymns and prayers in which all kinds of heavenly powers are invoked in strange names had a theurgic function. In that case the most famous of these hymns, the *Three Steles of Seth* (NHC VII, 5), is not just a curious liturgical document of philosophically orientated gnosis, but a theurgic instrument for the soul's ascent to, and union with, the supreme deity. The gnostic writings which, like the *Three Steles*, were current in third-century Platonist-gnostic circles, *Zostrianus* (NHC VIII, 1), *Allogenes* (NHC XI, 3) and *Marsanes* (NHC X), do not show any Christian influence, and yet they repeatedly talk about a baptism which the mystic undergoes in the supersensory world.[14] The same applies to the *Holy Book of the Great Invisible Spirit* (NHC III, 2 and IV, 2), in which Jesus is mentioned only in passing. It is virtually

[12] Iamblichus, *De mysteriis Aegyptiorum* II, 11; ed. E. des Places, *Jamblique. Les Mystères d'Égypte* (Paris: Les Belles Lettres, 1966), p. 96 (97, 5–6).

[13] The non-identity of Christian-sacramental and theurgic conceptions is largely determined by the difference in their view of God and the related doctrine of creation; see Majercik, *Chaldaean Oracles*, pp. 23–24.

[14] See pp. 60–1, 82, 89 and 187.

unthinkable that, in the rites of the communities in which these books circulated, baptism did not somehow play a role as a theurgic ritual for establishing contact with the deity.

The standard rejection of magic practices in non-gnostic Christian literature of the first centuries could suggest that these did not occur among Christians. Apart from the hard-and-fast rule that anything rejected by Church leaders is guaranteed to occur in practice, we also know from various sources that ordinary believers called in magicians and consulted astrologers for all kinds of purposes. The fact is, the ancient world was pervaded by magic.[15] Presumably, as Christian intellectuals, gnostic teachers who continued to consider themselves part of the Church will have shared its aversion to magic as an instrument for realizing all kinds of earthly matters (property, love, an opponent's destruction, etc.). But this need not mean that they rejected theurgic rites for uniting the soul with God. The sources show that in particular the Valentinians, who were after all the most Church-orientated gnostics, interpreted the ecclesiastical sacraments in this sense. But this does take us to a different world from that of the Platonizing gnostics of Plotinus' time. It was pointed out above that the sacraments in the early Church had an almost magic significance: baptism really washed away previously committed sins and the Eucharist really allowed people to share in the body of Christ and thus in his resurrection. As we found in the discussion of the *Gospel of Philip*, the Valentinians saw the mystery of the Bridal Chamber as the climax of Christian initiation: baptism and anointment bestowed 'redemption' (*apolytrōsis*), which culminated in the soul's union with her heavenly bridegroom, her 'angel', also collectively referred to as Christ.[16] We are taking too modern a view if we see these sacraments as only 'symbolic', as acts which by earthly means point to a higher spiritual reality. In the mystery of the Bridal Chamber the gnostic really returns to the Pleroma, though this will only be fully and for ever realized after death. The scholarly literature does not usually regard the Valentinian sacraments as theurgic rituals. Yet this is certainly what they are from the perspective of the study of religion in general: baptism and anointment actualize the soul's ascent to the Pleroma and the union with its heavenly partner. Whether this usually involved speculations on the nature of the ascent, comparable

[15] See Betz, *The 'Mithras-Liturgy'*, and, for example, M. Meyer and P. Mirecki (eds.), *Ancient Magic and Ritual Power*, RGRW 129 (Leiden: Brill, 1995); P. Mirecki and M. Meyer (eds.), *Magic and Ritual in the Ancient World*, RGRW 141 (Leiden: Brill, 2002); F. Graf, 'Magic II: Antiquity', in *Dictionary of Gnosis*, pp. 719–24.

[16] See pp. 104 and 106.

with those in writings like *Zostrianus*, is largely beyond our ken. But there is one testimony which makes it perfectly clear that it would be wrong to regard the Valentinian views as merely a somewhat adapted version of the Church's sacramental doctrine. This is Irenaeus' report on Marcus Magus.

In his *Adversus haereses* Irenaeus devoted a substantial part of the first book to the views and practices of a certain Marcus and his pupils (1, 13–15, perhaps also 1, 16, 1–2). No gnostic was more sharply attacked by Irenaeus than this Marcus: he accuses him of sorcery, avarice and the seduction of beautiful, preferably rich women. Since Irenaeus he has therefore been called Marcus Magus. His pupils, called 'Marcosians', are said to have successfully propagated Marcus' ideas among Christians in the Rhône valley (*AH* 1, 13, 7) – Irenaeus' own diocese – which may partly explain Irenaeus' fervour. Marcus was a Valentinian gnostic who was active in the third quarter of the second century, in Asia Minor among other places.[17] Though this charismatic figure deserves a fuller discussion, only his version of the Bridal Chamber liturgy and his letter speculations are relevant in this context. In Marcus the mystery of the Bridal Chamber was apparently connected with reception of the prophetic gift (the usual anointment after baptism implied the gift of the Holy Spirit). Irenaeus relates that the women to whom Marcus wanted to impart his Grace (*Charis*), 'preferably elegant, purple-clad, very rich ladies', were encouraged by him to prophesy. He addressed them as follows:

> I want you to participate in my Grace, because the Father of the All always sees your angel before his face. For the place of Majesty [*megethos*] is in us, we must become one [or come together in the One]. Receive first Grace from me and through me. Prepare yourself as a bride who awaits her bridegroom, so that you are what I am and I am what you are. Place the seed of light in your bridal chamber. Receive from me the bridegroom, encompass him and be encompassed by him. See, Grace has descended upon you: open your mouth and prophesy! (*AH* 1, 13, 3)

Clearly Irenaeus has not invented this, but is quoting a Marcosian source. As the climax of initiation the gnostic soul experiences here the union with her heavenly partner, her bridegroom, who in proper Valentinian fashion is identified with the angel that always beholds the countenance of the Father in heaven (Matt. 18:10). At that moment the Pleroma ('the place of Majesty') is present in him and the initiate. Marcus acts as a

[17] N. Förster, *Marcus Magus: Kult, Lehre und Gemeindeleben einer valentinianischen Gnostikergruppe. Sammlung der Quellen und Kommentar*, WUNT 114 (Tübingen: Mohr, 1999).

mystagogue, but apparently also coincides with the heavenly bridegroom: he gives the woman his Grace, so that they become one. The expression: 'so that you are what I am and I am what you are' points to a mystic identification with the divine. The formula 'You are me and I am you' is often used by the magician in magic spells to express his identity with the invoked deity (and his power over him). In the *Gospel of Thomas*, 108, Jesus says: 'Whoever drinks from my mouth shall become like me and I myself shall become he, and what is hidden will be revealed to him.' That is what happens here in the mystery of the Bridal Chamber: the soul becomes one with her heavenly bridegroom in the Pleroma.[18] Marcus' words do not rule out that a sexual union also took place. If that was the case, he will not have been the first and certainly not the last leader of a religious group in whom the spiritual and the physical merged into each other. Irenaeus does in fact attach this conclusion to his report: the woman is so grateful for the Grace received and the gift of propecy that she will reward Marcus 'not only by giving him her possessions – hence he has amassed such enormous wealth – but also by having physical intercourse with him, since she wanted to become one with him in every way, so that she may arrive with him at the One.'

Marcus' letter speculations are also important in this connection. In his detailed report on this, in *AH* I, 14, Irenaeus bases himself on one of Marcus' own works. In this work he presented himself as the only receiver of a revelation on the development of the divine world. This revelation was granted to him by *Sigē* ('Silence'; the same as 'Grace', *Charis*, mentioned above), who according to the Valentinians formed the highest divine level together with *Bythos*, 'Depth'. She speaks here on behalf of the first four aeons of the deity (Depth and Silence, Mind and Truth). Irenaeus rightly mocks *Sigē* by calling her 'blathering, verbose' (*phlyarousa*, *verbosata*), for she is indeed far from silent (I, 15, 5). The point of Marcus' argument is that God becomes conscious of himself and unfolds into his aeons by speaking letters and syllables. In this way his Name, that is his essence, is revealed. God himself utters the first part of his Name, a word of four letters: *archē*, 'beginning, origin', and adds a second syllable, so that the

[18] A different interpretation (influence of ancient views regarding the acquisition of prophetic powers via the drinking of blood and sexual union with a deity) has been proposed by N. Förster, 'Die Bedeutung des sogenannten Eucharistiesakramentes der Markosier und die Texte aus Nag Hammadi', in S. Emmel *et al.* (eds.), *Ägypten und Nubien in spätantiker und christlicher Zeit. Akten des 6. Internationalen Koptologenkongresses, Münster, 20.–26. Juli 1996*, vol. II, *Schrifttum, Sprache und Gedankenwelt*, Sprachen und Kulturen des christlichen Orients 6(2) (Wiesbaden: Reichert Verlag, 1999), pp. 465–73.

ogdoad of supreme Valentinian aeons is revealed. The same process brings forth the groups of ten and twelve aeons: 'The pronunciation of the entire Name thus led to thirty letters and four syllables'. Each of these produces its own sound: 'The restoration of all things will take place, she says, when the All returns to one single letter and produces the same sound, of which our collectively uttered "Amen" is an image, as she assumes' (*AH* I, 14, 1). In turn, the name of each letter consists of a number of letters, of which the name again consists of a number of letters. This can be continued *ad infinitum*, thus giving an idea of the dizzying depths of God's essence. There is no need to describe Marcus' letter speculations at length here. A more important question is: what was his aim? Irenaeus could only mock: 'I am sure, my dear friend, that when you read all this, you will laugh heartily at such conceited wisdom of these people' (*AH* I, 16, 3). Modern readers will probably agree, but this is too easy. Marcus and his followers were not just concerned with a game of letters and words, but with the operation of the hidden, magic or theurgic power concealed in the letters and words. By pronouncing these in a certain way, meditating on them and opening up to their hidden powers, the spirit could raise itself into the divine world. As of old, and especially in the first centuries CE, letter and number speculations (letters also have a numerical value in Greek) played an important role in magic and religious philosophy.[19] For Marcus, the deeper meaning of letters and letter combinations was apparently a route by which the soul could rise to the divine Pleroma to be united there in a Valentinian sense with its partner, its 'angel'.

In the scholarly literature Marcus is commonly regarded as a Valentinian maverick, a religious charlatan who exploited the ideas of the basically respectable Valentinians.[20] There does in fact seem to be something fishy about some of his practices, if at least there is truth in what Irenaeus says about his Eucharist celebrations (*AH* I, 13, 2). To the astonishment of his followers he supposedly poured consecrated wine from a small cup into a much larger one until the larger cup overflowed – which seems a cheap magic trick. But Irenaeus may have the story by hearsay or perhaps he misunderstood his source. Irenaeus' entire report shows that

[19] Still relevant is F. Dornseiff, *Das Alphabet in Mystik und Magie*, 2nd edn, Stoicheia 7 (Leipzig and Berlin: B. G. Teubner, 1925; reprinted Leipzig: Zentralantiquariaat der DDR, 1975). See also J.-P. Brach, 'Number Symbolism', in *Dictionary of Gnosis*, pp. 874–83.

[20] It is noteworthy that Dunderberg, in his *Beyond Gnosticism*, leaves Marcus almost completely out of the picture. He confines himself to a reference to 'Irenaeus' allegation that Marcus sought followers from the upper class' (p. 116) and the suggestion that Irenaeus' report on 'sexual misconduct' among the Marcosians is mere slander (pp. 137–8).

Marcus was a charismatic religious personality who held great attraction for non-gnostic Christians, too. As we said, Irenaeus' fierce opposition to the Marcosians is certainly connected with their active presence in his diocese and their influence on his flock. This influence went to the very heart of the Christian congregations, as emerges from Irenaeus' story about a deacon in Asia Minor whom Marcus had invited into his house – with disastrous consequences. The deacon's beautiful wife 'was corrupted in spirit and body by this magician and was long his follower. After she had been converted by the brothers with great difficulty, she spent the rest of her life in penance, weeping over and lamenting the corruption which she had suffered through the magician' (*AH* I, 13, 5). There is no guarantee that Marcus was an exception: if Irenaeus had not been so annoyed at his followers and had not laid hands on original writings of Marcus, we would hardly have known of his existence, since Irenaeus is our only significant source for his views. The nature of Christianity in the second century and the structure of the Christian congregations form a jigsaw puzzle of which many pieces are missing. Though there were profound thinkers among the Valentinians, like the author of the *Tripartite Tractate* (NHC I, 5), their principal interest was not in a dogmatic faith, but in the religious experience of the ascent to the Pleroma and the union with their 'angel'. This was practised in the circles of the Marcosians, with sacramental, theurgic rites and mystic submersion in the revealing power of letters and words.

The gnostics kept their cards close to their chest, and so were possibly much more esoterically and theurgically orientated than the Church Fathers knew. Both opponents and authentic sources confirm that initiates were pledged to secrecy. This was not simply motivated by the educational principle that instruction has to be accommodated to the student's level of perception, as has been argued with respect to the Valentinians.[21] We pointed out above in discussing *Melchizedek* that the seer is commanded twice there not to disclose the revelations granted to him to the unworthy.[22] At the end of the *Secret Book of John* John is ordered to 'keep secure' the revelation given to him, which means: to keep it secret and pass it on unimpaired to kindred spirits. The order is followed by a curse

[21] Dunderberg, *Beyond Gnosticism*, pp. 191–5, who also introduces the term 'scholastic esotericism', as relating to topics that were discussed by scholars of the same level of learning only. The modern usage to speak of the gnostics as adherents of 'Schools of Thought', with teachers and pupils, tends to obscure the fact that they were primarily religious people, who through revelatory myths and rituals sought to find their way back to their original unity with the divine.

[22] See p. 64.

on anyone who exchanges the book for a gift or food. A similar command is found in the *Second Book of Jeu*, 43: the revelation of Jesus may only be given to those who are worthy. The hermetic *Discourse on the Eighth and Ninth*, 59, also ends with the requirement that the reader 'guard what Hermes has said' (NHC VI, 63, 23–4). The second-century gnostic Justin, whose doctrine will be discussed below, made his followers swear the following oath before initiation:

> I swear by him who is above all things, the Good One, that I will keep these mysteries and betray them to no one, and also that I will not return from the Good One to the created world. (Hippolytus, *Refutatio* V, 27, 2)

The same oath was sworn by Elohim, the Creator, when he had ascended to the supreme, unknown God, the Good One, and had not returned thence to his creation. After the oath these gnostics also ascended to the Good One and saw 'what no eye has seen, nor ear heard, nor the human heart conceived' (cf. 1 Cor. 2:9). And they drank 'the living water', which they interpret as a bath in the water above the firmament, 'in which spiritual, living people are washed' (Hippolytus, *Refutatio* V, 27, 3). Here we find that the gnostic experience of an ascent to the highest God and a baptism in the heavenly spheres is not something typical of the Platonizing gnostics from the first half of the third century, but that this already occurred in the second century.

GOD AND HIS WORLD

If the core of the gnostic experience is: I come from God, I partake of his essence, I return to him, then it is important to know who God is and what his world looks like. The gnostics gave widely varying answers to these questions. Another important consideration here was the need to explain why a human's essential core had left this divine world and become entangled in matter. This last was not something new – since Plato the soul's fall into matter was a well-known theme in the ancient world[23] – but with the gnostics it was not just a philosophical image that helped to explain reality, but a painful experience of being alienated from the divine and menaced by evil powers. What went wrong up there? It was therefore inevitable that this occasioned speculations about God and the nature of the divine world. The starting point here could be either a monistic or a dualistic conception of God. Nearly all the great gnostic

[23] See p. 208 below.

systems which we know from the Graeco-Roman world were monistic, that is to say, they started from one supreme divine principle, the source of all being. This principle could involve a certain duality, as we shall see, but as a whole it was perfect and good. Dualistic systems were much less common, and are found in pure form only outside the direct sphere of influence of the Greek world.

The Unknown God

Various gnostic texts start with an elaborate description of the Unknown God, or rather, with a description of his indescribability. *Eugnostus* presents a good example:

He-Who-Is is ineffable.
No Principality knew him, no Power, no Subordination, nor any creature from the foundation of the world, except he alone.
For he is immortal and eternal, without birth, for everyone who is born will perish. He is not born.
He has no beginning, for everyone who has a beginning has an end. <He is without beginning.>[24]
He has no name, for whoever has a name is the product of another. He is unnameable.
He has no human form, for whoever has a human form is the product of another. He has his own form of being ...
He is infinite,
he is incomprehensible,
he is ever incorruptible,
he is someone whom nothing resembles,
he is unchangeably good,
he is without deficiency,
he is everlasting,
he is blessed,
he is unknowable, but knows himself,
he is immeasurable,
he is untraceable,
he is perfect, since he lacks nothing,
he is imperishably blessed.
He is called the Father of the All. (NHC III, 71, 13–73, 3)

The passage has many parallels, both in gnostic and in non-gnostic texts, and forms a reflection of Greek philosophical thought on God, particularly

[24] Literally in Coptic: 'nobody rules over him', which is a mistranslation of Greek *anarchos estin*; cf. inter alios Tatian, *Oratio ad Graecos* 4, 1: God alone 'is without beginning [*anarchos*] and himself is the beginning [*archē*] of all things.'

as found in second-century Middle Platonism. This way of talking about God is characterized by use of the *via negativa*, talking about God in negative terms to express his absolute transcendence: he is incomprehensible, unutterable, invisible, unnameable, immeasurable, unlimited, etc. An additional method used was the *via eminentiae*, in which denied contradictions are transcended: he is not large and not small, but more than that; without quality and quantity, but more than that. A Greek philosophical example of this mode of argumentation is provided by the following passage from the tenth chapter of the *Didaskalikos*, a work by the Middle Platonist Alcinous:

> The first God is eternal, ineffable,
> complete in himself, that is, without need,
> ever complete, that is, perfect at all times,
> wholly complete, that is, perfect in all respects …
> And he is the Good, because he brings about the good for all things according to their capacity to receive it, since he is the cause of all good …
> He is ineffable and comprehensible by the mind alone … because he is neither genus, nor species, nor variety, but has not a single property: neither anything evil … nor anything good … nor anything neutral … nor quality … nor the lack of quality … And he is neither part of anything, nor a whole that consists of parts …
> He does not move, nor is he moved.[25]

A difference between the Platonist and gnostic views is that, according to Alcinous, God can only be comprehended by the human mind, on the basis of the rule that only like (the divine Mind, *Nous*) can be known by like (the human mind, *nous*). This was rejected by the gnostics: we know God through revelation, not through our thought. Non-gnostic Christians held different opinions on this in the second century. The apologist Athenagoras called God 'comprehensible only by mind [*nous*] and reason [*logos*]' (*Legatio* 10, 1), but the apologist Justin says that though he used this expression in his pagan period, he understood later that illumination by the Holy Spirit is indispensable (*Dialogue with Trypho* 3, 7–4, 1). The gnostics gratefully employed Platonic terminology to formulate God's absolute transcendence.

[25] Alcinous, *Didaskalikos* 10 (164, 31–3; 165, 5–16); ed. J. Whittaker, *Alcinoos. Enseignement des doctrines de Platon* (Paris: Les Belles Lettres, 1990), pp. 23–4, with many parallels in the notes on pp. 100–6. Much information on the conceptions of God in Antiquity in R. van den Broek, T. Baarda and J. Mansfeld (eds.), *Knowledge of God in the Graeco-Roman World*, EPRO 112 (Leiden: Brill, 1988), including J. Mansfeld, 'Compatible Alternatives: Middle Platonist Theology and the Xenophanes Reception', pp. 92–117; also Z. Pleše, *Poetics of the Gnostic Universe. Narrative and Cosmology in the* Apocryphon of John, NHMS 52 (Leiden: Brill, 2006), pp. 74–91.

Dualism

A dualistic religious system starts from two primeval principles or rather two worlds (of Good and Evil, Light and Darkness), which from eternity existed independently, but clashed at a certain moment, with disastrous consequences. The most famous example of such a system is Manichaeism.[26] An example contemporary with the movements discussed here is Mandaeism. According to the Mandaeans, the World of Light consists of many light-realms and light-beings that were generated via emanation from the 'First Life'. The World of Darkness came out of the 'Dark Water', the primeval chaos, and is led by a male and a female being, 'Ur' and 'Rucha' (Spirit), who produced for example the demonic powers of the zodiac and the planets.[27] The same dualistic scheme is mentioned by Basilides (*c.* 125), in a verbatim quotation preserved in the *Acta Archelai* by Hegemonius (first half of the fourth century), 67, 4–12.[28] For a long time Light and Darkness existed as self-contained entities alongside each other, until they noticed each other and looked at each other. Darkness then wanted to participate in the Light, but Light did not share this need. However, because he did look at the Darkness, a reflection of the Light was projected into the Darkness, the result being that the visible creation shows a mixture of Light and Darkness, with all the problems this entails. We do not know to what extent this reflects Basilides' own views. It does not fit in well with the other reports on his doctrine, though these are so contradictory that his real views can no longer be reconstructed.[29] The Audians, the followers of a certain Audius (Syria, first half of the fourth century), also started from a strict dualism of Light and Darkness, in which the realm of Light was ruled by the Father and

[26] See p. 5 above.

[27] Discussed in detail by K. Rudolph, *Theogonie, Kosmogonie und Anthropogonie in den mandäischen Schriften. Eine literarkritische und traditionsgeschichtliche Untersuchung*, FRLANT 88 (Göttingen: Vandenhoeck & Ruprecht, 1965), pp. 17–96; K. Rudolph, 'Mandaeans', in *Dictionary of Gnosis*, p. 753.

[28] C. H. Beeson (ed.), *Hegemonius. Acta Archelai*, GCS 16 (Leipzig: Hinrichs, 1906), pp. 96–7; the passage has also been included as Fragment 1 of Basilides in W. Völker, *Quellen zur Geschichte der christlichen Gnosis*, Sammlung ausgewählter kirchen- und dogmengeschichtlicher Quellenschriften, Neue Folge, 5 (Tübingen: J. C. B. Mohr [Paul Siebeck]), 1932, pp. 38–40. English translation in *Hegemonius. Acta Archelai (The Acts of Archelaus)*, trans. M. Vermes, with Introduction and Commentary by S. N. C. Lieu, Manichaean Studies 4 (Turnhout: Brepols, 2001), pp. 149–50.

[29] It is in fact disputed whether Basilides was actually a gnostic, see W. A. Löhr, 'Basilides', in *Dictionary of Gnosis*, pp. 164–8 (not a gnostic), and B. A. Pearson, 'Basilides the Gnostic', in A. Marjanen and P. Luomanen (eds.), *A Companion to Second-Century 'Heretics'*, Supplements to Vigiliae Christianae 76 (Leiden: Brill, 2005), pp. 1–31 (gnostic).

Mother of Life, who beget a large number of angels.[30] The Audians belong to the tradition of the *Secret Book of John*, but apparently took the path of dualism, which was popular in Syria and Mesopotamia.

A variation on the dualist view is offered by the *Paraphrase of Seëm*, in which three primeval principles are assumed: 'There was Light and Darkness and in between them there was Spirit [*Pneuma*]' (NHC VII, 1, 25–8). The Light was 'Thought, full of hearing and speaking', a unity, and the Darkness 'wind in waters, in possession of Mind [*nous*], which was wrapped in a restless fire'. The Spirit in between them was a 'quiet, humble light' (NHC VII, 1, 32–2, 6). These worlds clash when the Darkness notices the existence of Mind and seizes part of it.

In discussing the *Paraphrase of Seëm* it was already pointed out that, according to Hippolytus, *Refutatio* V, 19, 2, the same three primeval principles were also known to the Sethians: 'The substances of the principles are Light and Darkness, and in between them is pure Spirit [*Pneuma*].' For a full survey of their doctrine, Hippolytus refers to a book that, curiously enough, is called the *Paraphrase of Seth* (V, 22). Though there are major differences between the *Paraphrase of Seëm* and what Hippolytus reports on the Sethians, the description of the three primeval principles also displays similarities.[31] In the Sethians *Pneuma* (literally 'breath, wind, spirit') is not a 'friendly, humble light', nor is it a powerful wind or soft current of air, which one would rather expect, given the meaning of *pneuma*. It is best compared with the powerful scent of ointment or perfume. The light of the Light and the scent of *Pneuma* penetrate the lower Darkness, which, as we said, is not without Mind and wants to hold on to the Light and the Spirit.

Man and Son of Man

Some systems feature the divine figures 'Man' and 'Son of Man'. Monoimus the Arab, known to us only via Hippolytus (*Refutatio* VIII, 12–15; X, 17, 5), assumed a twofold principle of the All: Man, who is unborn and immortal, and the Son of Man, who is born, though independently of time and of a willed plan. They are indivisible, like a fire and the light it diffuses. Monoimus also employs letter speculations: the Roman letter

30 H.-C. Puech, 'Audianer', in *RAC* I (1950), cols. 910–15, and G. Bee, 'Audians', in *Dictionary of Gnosis*, pp. 141–2.

31 See Roberge, *Paraphrase of Shem*, pp. 84–93, who concludes that the few connections between the two texts can be explained by a common cultural milieu: 'Neither text could have served as the basis for the other. It is equally futile to appeal to a common source or to a shared school.'

I (= the number 1) expresses the unity of the All. Moreover, he was familiar with the Christian notion that the I (as iota) denotes Jesus. The Son of Man possesses everything that is in his Father and he is therefore the ultimate source of the creation. It is unclear whether Monoimus assumed a lower, imperfect creator-god, though he judges the human situation negatively.[32]

The Naassenes, 'Snake Worshippers' (from Hebrew *nāḥāš*, snake; Hippolytus, *Refutatio* v, 6–11), also distinguished between the principles Man and Son of Man, who together form a unity, but above whom they placed the highest God. On the other hand the three principles are also referred to, more philosophically, as the Pre-existent One, the Self-Begotten One, and Outpoured Chaos; the relationship with the above-mentioned three is not entirely clear. All that exists, including the divine element and the heavenly Man, has a threefold structure: noetic, psychic and material. In the famous Psalm of the Naassenes the three basic principles of the All are referred to as First-Born Mind (*Nous*), Outpoured Chaos and Soul (*Psychē*); the last apparently stands between the two others and is the principle of creation.[33] *Eugnostus the Blessed* presents a structure of the divine world that is much more complicated than that of the Naassenes. He distinguishes between Immortal Man, the Son of Man and the Son of the Son of Man, above whom reside the highest, unknowable God and the Self-Begetter.[34]

Finally, in this context we need to call attention to the first divine entities of a group of gnostics reported on by Irenaeus (*AH* 1, 30). They were later identified with the Ophites, 'Snake Worshippers' (from Greek *ophis*, snake), who do not, however, show any affinity with the Naassenes. To some extent their views agree with those of the *Secret Book of John*, but this does not apply to the doctrine of God. As the highest principles they assumed: first the Father of all things, who is called First Man, then his Son, who proceeds from him as his Thought and is referred to as Son of Man or as Second Man, and in the third place the Holy Spirit, who is also called the First Woman and Mother of the living. Beneath these three was unformed matter, referred to as water, darkness, abyss and chaos. Father and Son impregnate the Spirit, who then produces a son, Christ, who

[32] See M. Marcovich, 'Monoimus' Letter to Theophrastus', in *Studies in Graeco-Roman Religions and Gnosticism*, Studies in Greek and Roman Religion 4 (Leiden: Brill, 1988), pp. 134–43, and R. van den Broek, 'Monoimus', in *Dictionary of Gnosis*, pp. 800–1.

[33] For more information on the Naassenes, see R. van den Broek, 'Naassenes', in *Dictionary of Gnosis*, pp. 820–2; for the Psalm, see below p. 190.

[34] See above pp. 117–18.

with his mother is taken up in the 'imperishable aeon', and a daughter, Sophia, who plunges into the waters of the primeval chaos. We will look at this more closely further on in the chapter. The structure of the deity supported by the gnostics of Irenaeus *AH* 1, 30 – two fathers, a mother and two children – is a rather curious variant of the Father-Mother-Son model that will be dealt with below. Perhaps the text of Irenaeus' source was corrupt or he misunderstood his source. It is conceivable that originally the First Man and the First Woman (the Holy Spirit) produced the Son of Man (Christ).[35] In that case the apex of the divine world would here, too, consist of Father, Mother and Son. This is reminiscent of the even simpler model of the Archontics, on which Epiphanius, *Panarion* 40, reports. They taught that the eighth heaven was the abode of the supreme, good God, who was called the Father of the All, and of the Mother on High, who was also designated as the Luminous Mother. The soul, too, comes from the eighth heaven; the seven heavens beneath it are ruled by the evil archons, of whom Sabaoth is the leader in the seventh heaven. The doctrine of the Archontics also shows great similarity to conceptions in the *Secret Book of John* and the *Nature of the Rulers*, but apparently they started from a much simpler structure of the divine world than that assumed in these writings.[36] It is striking, though, that in the views discussed so far the highest divine 'persons' are not surrounded by a large number of divine entities, aeons, as is the case in the great gnostic systems to be dealt with below. This observation is not without significance, because it makes us aware that the gnostic movement in Antiquity was much more diverse, also with regard to the image of God, than is suggested by the usual fixation on the tradition of the *Secret Book of John* and that of the Valentinians.

Three principles

In the gnostic systems of the second and third centuries the top of the divine world consists more often of three than of two hypostases (divine forms of being, comparable with the 'persons' of the Christian Trinity). Gnostic studies have been greatly exercised by the question how far the gnostics were influenced here by the philosophical conceptions of God

[35] Thus J. Holzhausen, *Der 'Mythos vom Menschen' im hellenistischen Ägypten. Eine Studie zum 'Poimandres' (= CH 1), zu Valentin und dem gnostischen Mythos*, Theophaneia 33 (Bodenheim: Athenäum-Hain-Hanstein, 1994), p. 191n. 101.

[36] On the Archontics, see R. van den Broek, 'Archontics', in *Dictionary of Gnosis*, pp. 89–91.

current in second- and third-century Platonism particularly. According to some scholars, philosophy has priority here and should hence form the basis for approaching the gnostic myths; others believe that although the gnostics were certainly influenced by philosophical views in the design of their myths, priority here belongs to myth and the religious experience it expresses.

A central problem of Hellenistic philosophy was how the unity of the One (the Monad, *monas*) could give birth to the infinite plurality of Duality (the Dyad, *dyas*). The One was always identified with the Good, while evil was somehow derived from the principle of duality and multiplicity, which was usually associated with matter. So-called Middle Platonism, in vogue in the first two and half centuries CE, usually started from three basic principles of all reality.[37] The highest principle was often referred to as *Nous*, 'Mind', but sometimes it was described as 'elevated above Mind and Being'.[38] The second principle was designated as (Second) Nous or as Logos. Plato's Ideas, the primeval images of visible reality, were now seen as thoughts in the Mind of God. The third principle was mostly identified with the formless primeval matter from which the world was made as the forms of the Ideas were expressed in it. The view that a divine triad is the starting point of all existing reality was widespread in the first centuries. In Neoplatonism these were the One (*to Hen*), Mind (*Nous*) and the World-Soul (*Psychē*), in Christianity the Father, Son and Holy Spirit. Small wonder, therefore, that a triad of supreme divine principles was also popular in gnostic speculations.

Hippolytus reports at length on a certain Justin the Gnostic, so named to distinguish him from the apologist Justin Martyr, his probable contemporary (*Refutatio* v, 23–7 and x, 15, 1–7). Justin was almost certainly a Jewish Christian, who developed an entirely distinctive gnostic system.[39] His three highest principles were: the Good One, Elohim and Edem. The Good One was raised above the other two, as he alone possessed foreknowledge. Elohim is called 'the father of all created things', and resembles the biblical Creator-God, as his name already indicates. Edem owes her name to the Garden of Eden, Paradise (Gen. 2:8–14). She has an ambivalent

[37] J. Dillon, *The Middle Platonists. A Study of Platonism 80 B.C. to A.D. 220* (London: Duckworth, 1977).

[38] Plato, *Republic* vi, 509b, already elevated the Good above Being. For the history of this expression, see J. Whittaker, 'Epekeina nou kai ousias', in *Studies in Platonism and Patristic Thought*, Collected Studies Series 201 (London: Variorum Reprints, 1984), no. xiii.

[39] On this figure, see R. van den Broek, *Studies in Gnosticism*, pp. 131–41 and 'Gospel Tradition and Salvation in Justin the Gnostic', *VC* 57 (2003), 363–88; summary: 'Justin the Gnostic', in *Dictionary of Gnosis*, pp. 656–8.

character, which may tend towards both good and evil. Elohim and Edem have no idea of the existence of the Good One. According to Justin, sexuality and procreation are good, and in fact Elohim and Edem unite, which results in twenty-four angels, twelve belonging with the father and twelve with the mother. They are allegorically called 'trees', and together form Paradise: the third angel of the Father is called Baruch ('Blessed One') and is identified with the Tree of Life, the third angel of the Mother is called Naas ('Snake') and is identical with the Tree of Knowledge. Once the visible cosmos and human beings (who get their spirit from Elohim and their soul from Edem) have come into being in this way, 'as fruit of their joyful union' (*Refutatio* v, 26, 14), Elohim ascends to the highest heavens to see whether there is any deficiency in the perfection of creation. There he discovers a light that far surpasses the light which he himself had made and he hears a voice saying: 'Sit at my right hand!' (Ps. 110:1). He thus gets to know the unknown, supreme God, and he stays with him. When Edem notices that Elohim has abandoned her, she is angered and causes moral and spiritual corruption among humans, which leads Elohim to instigate the process to save his spirit in mankind. So in Justin the supreme principle is the unknown God, who does not interfere in cosmic matters; Elohim is the independent creative principle, and is not presented as the son of the God; to some extent the ambivalent Edem plays the role of matter in some forms of Middle Platonism.

Hippolytus also discussed various other systems figuring three primeval principles. They are all part of his *Sondergut*,[40] but because they diverge so widely we cannot assume out of hand that he manipulated his sources. He probably used a source in which comparable systems were brought together. The three principles of the Sethians (*Refutatio* v, 19–21) were mentioned above in the discussion of the *Paraphrase of Seëm*. The gnostic sect of the Perates (*Refutatio* v, 12–17) taught that there is one origin of all things, which like a river divides into infinitely many parts. The first branch is formed by the 'Triad' (*trias*), of which the first part is called the 'fatherly Majesty', the second part consists of an infinite number of powers and the third part is the realized particular nature of things. The first is 'unbegotten', the second 'self-begotten' and the third 'begotten' (v, 12, 2–3). They also called these three parts Father, Son and Matter, where the Son, also termed Logos, occupies an intermediate position between the two others (v, 17, 1–2).[41]

[40] See p. 131.

[41] W. Ä. Löhr, 'Perates', in *Dictionary of Gnosis*, pp. 939–40.

The doctrine of God in the Barbelo myth: the Secret Book of John

As we saw above in the discussion of gnostic literature, the tradition of the Barbelo myth has left traces in a large number of writings. Because the *Secret Book of John* is the best known of these, we will look more closely here at the structure of the divine world described there, though the subject has already been discussed above.[42] Irenaeus, *AH* 1, 29, knew a version of the first part of the *Secret Book*, which differed from it on a few points only. The *Holy Book of the Great Invisible Spirit* provides the same outline as the *Secret Book* and Irenaeus, with a number of additions. It is typical of the Barbelo myth that, on the one hand, the top of the divine world has a trinitarian structure, formed by Father, Mother and Son, and, on the other, that these three produce a large number of lower entities. All these divine powers together form what many texts call the Pleroma (*plērōma*), the 'Fullness', the perfect whole of the divine world. All the inhabitants of the Pleroma, including the three highest, are called 'aeons' (*aiōnes*). This word calls for some clarification.

The Greek word *aiōn* means 'a (long) period of time', 'epoch', 'age', and in the plural 'eternity' (e.g. in Rom. 16:27: 'for ever', literally 'into the ages', *eis tous aiōnas*).[43] In the Hellenistic world, particularly in Alexandria, Eternal Time was worshipped as Aion. From the meaning 'time/age' the word *aiōn* developed into another word for 'world' (e.g. Matt. 12:32: 'whoever speaks against the Holy Spirit will not be forgiven, either in this aeon [*aiōn*; NRSV: 'age'], nor in the aeon to come'). The word *aiōn* in gnostic texts is often rendered in modern translations as 'aeon', where the word 'world' or 'realm' would be more apposite. The earliest Christian literature often talks about 'aeons' in connection with God, though it is not entirely clear what this means. Thus 1 Timothy 1:17 calls God the 'King of the aeons [*tōn aiōnōn*; NRSV: 'ages']', Hebrews 1:2 says that God 'created the aeons [*tous aiōnas*; NRSV: 'worlds']' through his Son, and Clement of Rome (*c.* 95) talks about God as the 'Creator and Father of the aeons [*tōn aiōnōn*]' in his *Letter to the Corinthians* 35, 3. Given such usage, it is not surprising that the gnostics referred to the divine powers in the Pleroma as 'aeons'. But we need to be aware here that the word 'aeon' in gnostic texts always has a spatial aspect, too. This explains why the *Gospel of*

[42] See pp. 45–6.

[43] Liddell and Scott, *Lexicon*, p. 45 s.v.; Lampe, *Patristic Lexicon*, pp. 55–6; H. Sasse, 'Aiōn', in Kittel *et al.* (eds.), *Theological Dictionary of the New Testament*, vol. 1, pp. 197–209. H. M. Keizer, *Life, Time, Entirety. A Study of Aion in Greek Literature and Philosophy, the Septuagint and Philo* (digital dissertation, University of Amsterdam, 1999).

Truth often speaks about the aeons as 'spaces', and why the *Secret Book of John* (BG 35, 5–36, 15; NHC II, 8, 33–9, 24) places the heavenly Adam, True Man, Seth and others in certain aeons, while at the same time this indicates a historical periodization. Perhaps influence was exercised here by Greek interpretations of the Persian primeval god Zervan Akarana, Unborn Time, who produced the opposite gods Ahura Mazda (Ormuzd) and Ahriman: according to Eudemus of Rhodes (fourth century BCE), this primeval principle was called both 'Place' (*Topos*) and 'Time' (*Chronos*).[44] As we shall see, the aeons are hypostasized aspects of the highest, unknowable God, with a temporal-spatial dimension.

Though, through their complexity, the Pleroma of the *Secret Book of John* and related writings and that of the Valentinians have become the best known, there were in circulation other conceptions of the Pleroma which seemed to have developed independently. Thus Irenaeus, *AH* I, 24, 3, ascribes to Basilides a Pleroma in which a number of divine figures issue from each other: thus the Unborn Father begets Mind (*Nous*), Understanding (*Logos*), Insight (*Phronesis*) and Wisdom (*Sophia*). The last two produce powers, rulers and angels, who create the first heaven and produce another group of angels, who make the second heaven, a process which repeats itself until 365 heavens have been realized.

In the *Secret Book* the top of the Pleroma is formed by the Unnameable Father (the great Invisible or Virginal Spirit) and his first Thought (*Ennoia*), who is called Barbelo.[45] After a lengthy description of the Unknown God, we are told how Barbelo comes into being: the Father sees himself reflected in the light-water that surrounds him, he becomes aware of himself and this thought becomes an independent entity. At her request, three aeons as servants are added to Barbelo: Foreknowledge, Imperishability and Eternal Life.[46] Together the Father and Barbelo then produce a Son, a Light that is an image of the light of the Father. The Father anoints him with his goodness and he is therefore called the Good One (*Chrēstos*) or the Anointed One/Christ (*Christos*). To him are also added three aeons as servants: Mind, Will and Word. The upper echelon of the Pleroma thus looks as follows (with the Greek names in parentheses):

[44] F. Wehrli (ed.), *Die Schule des Aristoteles. Texte und Kommentare: Eudemos von Rhodos* (Basle: B. Schwabe & Co., 1955), p. 70 (fragment 150).

[45] The following description is mainly based on the short recension in BG 22, 16–36, 15.

[46] The Long Recension adds here a fifth aeon: Truth (*Alētheia*; NHC II, 5, 32–4), but this cannot be the original version, as appears from the Ogdoad mentioned below, which also occurs in the *Holy Book of the Great Invisible Spirit* (NHC III, 42, 5–11; IV, 51, 22–52, 2).

Father x Barbelo, [First] Thought ([*Prot*]*ennoia*), Providence (*Pronoia*)
Aeons: Foreknowledge (*Prognōsis*)
Imperishability (*Aphtharsia*)
Eternal Life (*Aiōnia Zōē*)

Light (Christ)
Aeons: Mind (*Nous*)
Will (*Thelēma*)
Word (*Logos*).

The unity of Barbelo and Christ with their aeons makes for two groups of four aeons each, who subsequently unite and thus form an androgynous group of eight (ogdoad), with this result:

Thought	x	Word
Christ	x	Incorruption
Eternal Life	x	Will
Mind	x	Foreknowledge.

These four androgynous pairs produce a large group of lower aeons. Here the descriptions of the *Secret Book* and of Irenaeus start to display differences, one reason being that the *Secret Book* has deliberately removed the children of Thought and Word (Autogenes and True Man), because the author identified the first child, Autogenes, with the Son, Christ. Moreover, the *Secret Book*'s passage on the third pair, Eternal Life and Will, has become very confused, though its original meaning can be reconstructed from Irenaeus. The details need not be discussed here,[47] but another aspect does merit attention: like the aeons connected with the Mother and the Son, almost all the aeons produced by the four pairs have a Greek abstract word as their name. The only exceptions are True (or Perfect) Man and the four servants of Christ, the great Lights (*phōstēres*), who are produced by the pair Christ and Imperishability. The Lights bear strange, Semitic-sounding names (with variable spellings), strongly reminiscent of names in magic texts: Armozel (Irenaeus: Harmogenes), Oroiael (Irenaeus: Raguhel), Daveithe and Eleleth. Next, each of these four aeons is given three attendant aeons, all of which, again, have Greek abstract words as their name: Grace (*Charis*), Truth (*Alētheia*), Form (*Morphē*); Providence (*Pronoia* (long recension: Conception, *Epinoia*)), Perception (*Aisthēsis*), Memory (*Mnēmē*); Understanding (*Synesis*), Love (*Agapē*), Idea (*Idea*); Perfection (*tmnttelios* = *Teleiotēs*), Peace (*Eirēnē*), Wisdom

[47] See van den Broek, *Studies in Gnosticism*, pp. 56–66.

(*Sophia*).[48] There can be only one conclusion here: the Pleroma of the Barbelo myth, as best known from the *Secret Book* and Irenaeus, was carefully constructed and must be the work of one person. So the myth did not develop slowly, but was devised integrally by someone who wanted to accommodate almost all the important concepts from Greek philosophy and psychology in the Fullness, the Pleroma, of the divine Spirit. As such there is nothing Christian about this, and it is therefore probable that the identification of the Son with Christ is secondary (induced by the fact the Father anoints his Son, the Light, with his Goodness).

If the above is correct, where do the strange names come from? The names of Barbelo and the four Lights, Armozel, Oroiael, Daveithe and Eleleth, occur in many other gnostic and magic texts, but no relation to the other, Greek, aeons of the *Secret Book* is visible there. Indeed, none of these Greek abstract names of aeons recurs in later gnostic texts. The only exception is the *Holy Book of the Great Invisible Spirit*, in which the Greek names for the female aspects of the Ogdoad and the four Lights do occur, if in a somewhat different arrangement. But the work does talk again about servants of the four great Lights, who also have 'magic' names: Gamaliel, Gabriel, Samblo and Abrasax (NHC III, 52, 16–53, 12; IV, 64, 10–65, 5). These, too, are found in other gnostic and magic texts, but without the female counterparts attributed to them in the *Holy Book*. Though the *Secret Book of John* was a popular text, there seems to have been hardly any imitation of its elaborate pleromatic system. It cannot be strictly proved, but the most plausible explanation for the presence of the strange names in the Pleroma of the *Secret Book* is that they stem from an older and much simpler magic view of the cosmos.

Valentinus and the Valentinians

The Valentinians are the best known to us of all gnostic groups, both via authentic writings and from the reports of their opponents.[49] Their name derives from Valentinus, a prominent spiritual teacher in Rome around 136–60, but the relation between his views and those of the various groups named after him is very unclear, and therefore controversial. This also

[48] The *Holy Book of the Great Invisible Spirit* shows a further development of this tradition: each of the four Great Lights has a consort, respectively Grace (*Charis*), Perception (*Aisthēsis*), Understanding (*Synesis*) and Prudence (*Phronēsis*), and they each have a minister who also has a consort, respectively Gamaliel + Memory (*Mnēmē*), Gabriel + Love (*Agapē*), Samblo + Peace (*Eirēnē*) and Abrasax + Eternal Life (*pōnh nsha eneh* = *Aiōnia Zoē*).

[49] See pp. 91–108 and 146–9.

goes for the conception of God. The lack of clarity is caused in particular by the fact that we know next to nothing about Valentinus himself. It is uncertain where he came from, though Epiphanius says more than two centuries later that he has heard rumours that Valentinus came from Egypt and was schooled in Alexandria (*Panarion* 31, 2, 2–3). This is perfectly possible and indeed not unlikely, but we have no evidence. Around 200 Tertullian claims that Valentinus and Marcion, who was in Rome at the same time, were initially orthodox, but later were 'more than once thrown out of the Church' (*De praescriptione haereticorum* 30, 2). On the one hand he praises Valentinus' great intellectual and oratorical gifts, but on the other states that he lapsed into heresy out of rancour, when his pursuit of an episcopate was thwarted (*Adversus valentinianos* 4, 1). But this is generally regarded as a legend designed to discredit Valentinus. Tertullian is apparently embarrassed by the absence of reports that Valentinus and his group were ever cast out of the Church. In fact, this also applies to the Marcionites, but they separated themselves from the other Christians in Rome, after serious conflicts. It seems certain that Tertullian projects the situation in the Church of his own time (one bishop who guards the unity of his congregation) back to the mid second century, when no such situation existed in Rome. We know that at this time the Roman Christians were divided into a number of rather loosely connected groups, of which the Valentinians were one. Of course, this did not mean that there were no disagreements. Justin says that there are groups who call themselves Christians, but are actually not, and he mentions as examples the Marcionites, Valentinians, Basilidians and Saturnilians (*Dialogue with Trypho* 35, 6). This means that mid-second-century Rome already had Christians who were referred to (probably by others) as 'Valentinians', followers of Valentinus.

The information about Valentinus' doctrine is sparse, too. Clement of Alexandria has preserved six short fragments from his letters and sermons and Hippolytus one of his 'psalms'.[50] It is impossible to reconstruct Valentinus' doctrine from these paltry remains, whose context is unknown. A question also arises whether it is legitimate to use the authentic Valentinian writings and the later reports on Valentinian views in explaining these fragments. The German scholar Christoph Markschies

[50] For the biographical data on Valentinus and the authentic fragments, see Thomassen, *Spiritual Seed*, pp. 418–90; Holzhausen, *Der 'Mythos vom Menschen'*, pp. 80–163; Holzhausen, 'Valentinus and Valentinians', in *Dictionary of Gnosis*, pp. 1144–57; C. Markschies, *Valentinus Gnosticus? Untersuchungen zur valentinianischen Gnosis mit einem Kommentar zu den Fragmenten Valentins*, WUNT 65 (Tübingen: J. C. B. Mohr [Paul Siebeck], 1992).

believes it is not. Starting from the authentic fragments, he has come to the conclusion that Valentinus was a Platonic theologian, whose doctrine formed an intermediate stage between the Jewish philosopher of religion Philo (*c.* 50 CE) and the Christian theologian Clement of Alexandria (*c.* 200): his theology was philosophically, not gnostically, inspired, and certainly did not contain any 'Valentinian' elements. The barely concealed agenda here is to relieve Valentinus of the stigma 'gnostic'; Valentinian gnostic speculation was the work of semi-educated followers, just as the gnostic interpretation of Christianity in general was devised by and for Christians of small learning.[51] Few have endorsed these views, which have a strong theological thrust. Einar Thomassen, at present the greatest expert on Valentinianism, believes that it is most certainly possible to indicate in the various authentic texts and the reports on the Valentinians a number of common features which must go back to Valentinus himself.[52] But we can no longer reassemble the detailed shape of his doctrine. Indeed, it is questionable whether he ever expounded his ideas in a systematic manner. Remarkably, no Valentinian source ever appeals to Valentinus' authority. Everything we know shows him to be the charismatic leader of a Christian community with spiritual leanings (the concept of church, *ekklēsia*, plays an important role in his thought), not the head of a philosophical school. On the basis of what they learned from Valentinus, his pupils drew up the various Valentinian systems that we now know. A key role may have been played here by Ptolemy (*c.* 160–80), the author of the *Letter to Flora*, because he is often thought to have designed the best-known structure of the Valentinian Pleroma.

The Valentinian Pleroma

Two different views of the Pleroma can be distinguished in the Valentinian sources. According to the first type (type A), the aeons are initially inside the Father in an unconscious state and come to be independently and

[51] See also C. Markschies, 'Valentinian Gnosticism: Towards the Anatomy of a School', in J. D. Turner and A. McGuire (eds.), *The Nag Hammadi Library after Fifty Years. Proceedings of the 1995 Society of Biblical Literature Commemoration*, NHMS 44 (Leiden: Brill, 1997), pp. 401–38, and *Gnosis. An Introduction*, trans. J. Bowden (London and New York: T&T Clark, 2003), p. 83: '"Gnosis" evidently came into being … in the metropolitan centres of education in antiquity, as an attempt by semi-educated people to explain their Christianity at the level of the time'; 'Gnosis' was 'an attempt to make Christianity and its specific world-view understandable to semi-educated contemporaries and thus competitive in a religious market of possibilities', p. 119 (= *Die Gnosis*, 2nd edn (Munich: C. H. Beck, 2006), pp. 84 and 116).

[52] Thomassen, *Spiritual Seed*, pp. 426–9 (fifteen subjects).

consciously in a process best described as the self-unfolding of the essence of the Father. They have neither names nor a fixed number. According to the second view (type B), the Pleroma consists of thirty aeons which originate from each other in a hierarchical order and have Greek abstract concepts as their name. The type A conception is the oldest and agrees most with what is reported to be Valentinus' own opinion; it occurs in the *Gospel of Truth* and the *Tripartite Tractate*. The second view, type B, is much better known: it occurs in the *Letter of Instruction* and the *Valentinian Exposition*[53] and in the descriptions of the Church Fathers. A detailed discussion of these views and the more or less important variations on them would go far beyond the scope of this book, but we should note the following.[54]

According to type A, the Pleroma was initially inside the Father in an unconscious state or, which is the same, inside his Mind or Logos or Son. The aeons are also compared to words, which only arrive at conscious existence when they are uttered by the Word, the Logos. A few quotations may clarify this:

> When they were in the Father's thought, that is, in the hidden Depth [*Bathos*], the Depth knew them, but they were unable to know the Depth in which they were, nor could they know themselves, nor anything else. (*Tripartite Tractate*, NHC I, 60, 16–26)
>
> When they were the Depths [*bathos*] of his thought, the Word [*Logos*], which was the first to come forth, caused them to appear, together with the Mind [*Nous*], which speaks the one Word in silent Grace [*charis*]. (*Gospel of Truth*, NHC I, 37, 7–12)

One of the most striking features of this view of the Pleroma is that the process in which the aeons become conscious through the Logos is presented as a salvation which is actually the same as the reception of gnosis by human beings. This is why the *Gospel of Truth* displays a constantly shifting perspective from aeons to human beings and vice versa: they go through the same process of liberation. This will be dealt with in more depth at the end of this chapter. The *Tripartite Tractate*, which has a much more systematic structure than the meditative *Gospel of Truth*, contains a lengthy discussion of the three inseparable, eternal principles: (1) the unknowable Father; (2) his Son, who reposes eternally in the Father and in whom the Father thinks himself; and (3) the heavenly Church,

[53] See pp. 93–4 and 96–7.

[54] For a detailed discussion, see Thomassen, *Spiritual Seed*, pp. 193–244, to whom the following is partly indebted.

the whole of aeons and human beings who thanks to the goodness of the Father are brought to gnosis by the Son. At first the aeons were enclosed in the thought of the Father, but out of love he wanted to make them into independent, conscious beings, who possess free will: in the emergence of the aeons God unfolds his being and becomes conscious of himself (NHC I, 60, 1–75, 17).

The hierarchically structured type B Pleroma, with thirty aeons that all have a name, was probably devised by Ptolemy. This is also what Tertullian claims in his discussion of the various views of the Valentinians. He writes in his *Adversus valentinianos* 4, 2:

> Ptolemy ... distinguished the aeons by names and numbers, so that they became personal beings, though located outside of God, whereas Valentinus had included them in the totality of the deity himself, as thoughts, affects and emotions.

Ptolemy's view, or in any case that of his pupils,[55] is described at length by Irenaeus (*AH* I, 1–2). The fact that the Ptolemaean pleromatic system presupposes type A is shown by the use of terms which also occur in the quotations given above, but have not yet been accommodated in a systematic framework there: 'Depth' (*Bathos*), 'silent' (cf. Silence, *Sigē*), 'Grace' (*Charis*), 'Mind' (*Nous*), 'Word' (*Logos*). According to the Ptolemaean system, there is a perfect aeon who is incomprehensible, invisible and eternal and existed before everything in deep repose. He is called Primeval Beginning (*Proarchē*), Primeval Father (*Propatōr*) and Depth (*Bythos*). Together with him there was his Thought (*Ennoia*), also referred to as Grace (*Charis*) and Silence (*Sigē*). At a certain moment it occurred to Depth to pour a seed into Silence, so that she became pregnant and produced Mind (*Nous*), who is also called Only-Begotten (*Monogenēs*), Father (*Patēr*) and Beginning (*Archē*). Together with Nous, who is the only one capable of containing the greatness of the Primeval Father, Truth (*Alētheia*) was produced. This is the first Tetrad, the 'root of all things', consisting of two androgynous couples: Depth and Silence, Mind and Truth. Mind and Truth produce two other successive pairs, resulting in the following ogdoad:

[55] The views expounded in Irenaeus, *AH* I, 1–8 (the 'Great Account'), are usually ascribed to Ptolemy, but it seems more probable that Irenaeus based himself on various sources (or an existing account) in order to give a picture of Valentinianism in general, including the ideas of Ptolemy and his followers; cf. C. Markschies, 'New Research on Ptolemaeus Gnosticus', *ZAC* 4 (2000), 249–52, and Dunderberg, *Beyond Gnosticism*, pp. 197–9.

Depth (*Bythos*) x Silence (*Sigē*)
↓
Mind (*Nous*) x Truth (*Alētheia*)
↓
Word (*Logos*) x Life (*Zōē*)
↓
Man (*Anthrōpos*) x Church (*Ekklēsia*).

The rest of the Pleroma results from Word and Life producing ten aeons (five androgynous pairs) and Man and Church twelve aeons (six androgynous pairs). The names of these twenty-two aeons are Greek words: adjectives for the male partners and nouns for the female ones. The name of the last female aeon is Wisdom (*Sophia*). There is no doubt that the Valentinian views on the Pleroma are closely connected with philosophical, in particular Pythagorean, reflections on the question of how the One can generate infinite duality and multiplicity.[56] Furthermore, it seems certain that the second pair of this Pleroma goes back to Plato, who had argued in his *Republic*, 517b, that in the spiritual world the Good produces Truth (*Alētheia*) and Mind (*Nous*), just as the philosopher produces mind (*nous*) and truth (*alētheia*), when he has intercourse with true Being (490b).

Though later Valentinians introduced variations on this system, the basic structure remained curiously constant. Yet controversy did arise. Thus Hippolytus, *Refutatio* VI, 29, 3, reports that there was passionate disagreement among the Valentinians on the question whether the Primeval Father did or did not have Silence (*Sigē*) as female partner. There were those who denied this vehemently and assumed that the first pair was that of Mind and Truth. This left them with only twenty-eight aeons, but the number thirty was apparently so unassailable that they felt compelled to add a new pair, Christ and the Holy Spirit (VI, 31, 3). We saw above in discussing the Valentinian *Letter of Instruction* how heated the differences of opinion could be: its author assumed a second group of thirty aeons and calls the Valentinians who thought otherwise 'earthly people without understanding', that is, without gnosis.[57] When imaginative language becomes dogma, accusations of heresy are liable to fly about, and this is no different for gnostics.

[56] See Thomassen, *Spiritual Seed*, pp. 269–314.
[57] See p. 94.

MANKIND AND ITS WORLD

If the source of all that exists is perfect and good, how come our world and human beings are not? This is a central problem in every philosophical or religious system which assumes that the supreme Being or God is also the Good (One). Evil is then a reality that should not actually exist, and it has therefore often been characterized in philosophy and theology as non-Being and the absence of the Good (*privatio boni*). Gnostic thinkers also struggled with this problem. The author of the *Gospel of Truth* remarks several times that the imperfection, that is the ignorance, of the aeons and human beings is not the fault of the perfect Father. For from the beginning the aeons were in an unconscious state inside the Father, whose wish in fact it was that they would achieve knowledge. The author knows that this involves a major problem and he therefore expresses himself subtly: 'Oblivion did not come about *through* the Father, though it did come about *because* of him' (NHC I, 18, 1–3). Whichever way you look at it, in a religious system that assumes one perfect supreme principle, evil must have been at least potentially present in the divine world. Only by starting from two primeval principles, two eternal worlds of Light and Darkness, can one maintain that evil does not somehow originate in the Good. But even then there is no escaping the fact that good and evil are mixed in human beings and their world, which requires an explanation.

Dualistic systems

In gnostic mythologies that presuppose a dualistic conception of God it is sometimes assumed that the material world and humans are the result of collaboration between the realm of Light and that of Darkness. In Mandaeism it is Ptahil, the fourth and last emanation of Life, who works together with the evil planetary powers in creating the earth and the human being. The first man, Adam, contains a light-substance, called 'the inner Adam', which comes from the world of Light and coincides with his soul or spirit.[58] A similar conception seems to have circulated among the Audians: the angel who created the other angels of the realm of Light creates the world and human beings in collaboration with the seven planetary powers, who descend from the power of Darkness. Because the Audians saw every part of the human body as being ruled by the seven

[58] For a detailed survey of the complicated Mandaean ideas, see Rudolph, *Theogonie, Kosmogonie und Anthropogonie*, pp. 138–96, 248–338; a brief summary in Rudolph, 'Mandaeans', p. 753.

evil powers, they rejected procreation and denied the resurrection of the body. In their view, there are two kinds of human beings: one is carnal and doomed to destruction, because he stems from the children begotten with Eve by the evil powers, the other is spiritual and is saved, because he has a divine origin.[59] We earlier found a more subtle explanation for the mixture of Light and Darkness in our world in a literal quotation from Basilides: not the Light itself but a reflection of the Light falls upon the Darkness, which takes possession of it. In that context attention has also been drawn to the views of the *Paraphrase of Seëm* and of the Sethians in the *Paraphrase of Seth* according to Hippolytus, where it is the Spirit, the third principle between Light and Darkness, which (whether or not with a ray of Light) gets entangled in the material world.[60]

Some monistic systems

In gnostic systems with a strictly monistic conception of God the origin of evil lies within the divine world itself. Because the idea of a *creatio ex nihilo* still lay completely outside the scope of the gnostic mythmakers, their myths always naturally assume the existence of an unformed, in a certain sense 'neutral', matter, the primeval chaos. The best-known mythological system is that of the *Secret Book of John*, because it offers an overall picture: the origin of the divine world (theogony), of the material world (cosmogony) and of the human being (anthropology), and all this in order to explain how evil entered the world and humans can be saved from it. Also, a number of its elements constantly return in other texts, suggesting that it wielded a powerful influence. Yet this is largely an illusion, since the existence of many other traditions besides that of the *Secret Book* makes it clear that this work is little more than a variation on a theme developed very differently by others. In the *Secret Book* it is the last and lowest aeon, Sophia, who will give rise to problems. The complicated Pleroma of this text, with a cascade of successive, increasingly lower aeons, was doubtless partly devised to keep the origin of evil as far as possible from the Unknowable Father. But there were other systems in which this entire intermediate level was lacking and it was the female counterpart of the Father who was herself responsible for the creation. According to Irenaeus, *AH* 1, 23, 2, Simon Magus (or in any case the Simonians) taught that the First Thought (= Helen)

59 Puech, 'Audianer', cols. 913–14; Bee, 'Audians', p. 142.
60 See pp. 153–4.

of the highest God (= Simon) had produced the angels and archangels in the lower parts of the cosmos. These had taken her prisoner, because they did not want to be mistaken for the children of someone else: they confined her in a female body and forced her in the course of time to change from one woman into another, including Helen of Troy. She ended up in a brothel in Tyre, where Simon found and saved her. She is clearly a symbol of the soul, who prostitutes herself in the world of the senses – an image that also occurs in the *Treatise on the Soul* (NHC II, 127, 22–128, 17) and *Authoritative Teaching* (NHC VI, 23, 12–16; 23, 24–24, 22).[61] A similar view, but one relating to the heavenly Man, was taught by the Naassenes: Man and the Son of Man form a unity, the androgynous Adamas, who on the one hand is the creator and on the other the 'inner human', who suffers in the earthly Adam and his offspring. (Hippolytus, *Refutatio* V, 7–8, in a complicated description of their doctrine.) In these systems the female or male creator has become imprisoned in her or his creation and undergoes there the suffering caused by the evil powers. That these powers are evil is assumed as a matter of course, not explained.

Particularly interesting in this context is the creation myth of 'other gnostics' on which Irenaeus, *AH* I, 30 reports – interesting, because it offers a combination of the 'Man/Son of Man/First Woman' conception of God with a cosmogony and anthropogony that correspond to those of the *Secret Book of John*. According to this report, the First Man and the Son of Man (or the Second Man) begot with the First Woman (or the Holy Spirit) a third male being, Christ, by shining their light on her.[62] But this light was so strong and abundant that she could not wholly contain it, so that she 'overflowed' on the left side and the power of that light plunged into the dark waters of the chaos. This power, that is Christ's weak sister, is called 'the Left One', 'the Lewd One', Sophia, and the 'Androgynous One'. From her mother this Sophia carried a 'light-dew' (*humectatio luminis*) with her, and when she sank to the bottom of the chaos, the material substances were drawn to this light-dew and clung to it, so that Sophia received a material body. Through the light-dew she is then able to free herself from the chaos: she leaps up and unfolds there into the visible heavens. She still has a watery body, but is also able to free herself from this through her desire for the Light above her. She is called 'the woman issued from a woman'. Her abandoned body is her son, who

[61] See also pp. 32–3.
[62] See pp. 155–6.

via his mother possesses an immortal element. He is called Yaldabaoth and becomes the creator of the world (Irenaeus, *AH* 1, 30, 1–4). From this point the description of the genesis of the world and the human race largely agrees with that in the *Secret Book of John*. But there is no reason to assume that Irenaeus' 'other gnostics' suddenly started to follow the *Secret Book* here; it is more natural to assume joint dependence on an earlier source.

Saturnilus

The fact that the *Secret Book of John* is based on an earlier and simpler model is shown by the report on the gnostic Saturnilus (Greek: Satorneilos; Latin: Saturninus) in Irenaeus, *AH* 1, 24, 1–2, for which he probably depended on Justin's *Syntagma*.[63] Saturnilus worked around 120 in Antioch on the Orontes, in Syria. He was supposedly a pupil of Menander, who in turn is said to have been a pupil of Simon Magus, but this report seems to be more inspired by the wish to construct a succession of heretics than that it represents a historical reality.[64] In any case there was already a group of Saturnilians in Rome before 150 (Justin Martyr, *Dialogue with Trypho* 35, 6). Saturnilus taught that the entirely unknown Father had made 'angels, archangels, forces and powers' and that seven of these angels had created the world and all that is in it. They made the first human being after the radiant image of the highest Power that had appeared to them, but which they could not hold on to because it had immediately withdrawn again to the highest regions. That is why they said: 'Let us make a human being after the image and likeness' (cf. Gen. 1:26). But after doing this, they could not make him stand upright: he crawled over the ground like a worm. Then the Power on high took pity on his imitation and sent a spark of life into him, thus causing him to stand up and live. After death, according to Saturnilus, this spark returns to its origin, and the body reverts to dust (1, 24, 1). In itself this story is not yet gnostic. The creation of the human being by God and (or via) the angels could be easily inferred from Genesis 1:26: 'Let us make humankind' – an interpretation which already occurs in Philo in the first century (*De opificio mundi* 72–5).[65] This report is followed in Irenaeus by an elaboration which does not entirely tally with

[63] See p. 128. [64] See pp. 127–8.

[65] A great deal of material on this theme can be found in Markschies, *Valentinus Gnosticus?*, pp. 18–24 ('Exkurs I: Schöpfung unter Mithilfe von Engeln oder durch Engel').

the foregoing (1, 24, 2). Perhaps his source was unclear or he reproduced it too concisely, but it is also conceivable that we are dealing here with a later gnostic interpretation of Saturnilus' doctrine. The angels are now described as the evil world-rulers and Irenaeus reports that according to Saturnilus 'the God of the Jews was one of the angels' and that Christ had come 'to destroy the God of the Jews and to save those who believed in him, that is to say, those who have the spark of life within them'. For the angels created two kinds of human beings, good and evil. The identification of the evil Creator with the God of the Bible, the radiant image from the divine world after which the angels make the first human being, who crawls over the earth and who can stand upright only after divine intervention, all these are themes which return in the *Secret Book of John* and other gnostic creation myths. It is not unlikely that this basic pattern of the gnostic exegesis of Genesis, whoever was responsible for it, developed from a non-gnostic Jewish commentary, a midrash, on Genesis 1 and 2. A Jewish background could also explain why in Mandaeism, too, primeval man cannot stand and crawls over the earth after his creation.[66]

The Secret Book of John and related texts

In the *Secret Book of John* the breach in the Pleroma starts with the last aeon, Wisdom (*Sophia*). She wants to produce something by herself, without the approval of the Father and her partner. The curious thing is that in the *Secret Book* Sophia is one of the three handmaidens of Eleleth, the fourth Great Light, not his partner. According to the *Holy Book of the Great Invisible Spirit* (NHC III, 52, 13–14), Wisdom (*Phronēsis*) was the partner (*syzygos*) of Eleleth, but the gnostics of Irenaeus, *AH* 1, 29, 2 called her his servant (*ad subministrationem*). There is another and probably older tradition in which Sophia did not have a partner at all and went searching outside of the Pleroma. A trace of this can also be found in the *Secret Book*, when it says that she undertook her rash action after 'she had not found her partner' (NHC II, 9, 33; BG 37, 6–7). This older tradition has been preserved in the closely related system in Irenaeus, *AH* 1, 29. It is said there that 'the first angel', who acts as a servant of the 'Only-Begotten' (*Monogenēs*), produces the Holy Spirit, 'whom they also call Wisdom [*Sophia*] and the Lewd One [*Prounikos*]'. Because this aeon had no partner, she went in search of one, into the regions of the primeval

[66] Rudolph, *Theogonie, Kosmogonie und Anthropogonie*, for example pp. 252, 271.

chaos. But she regretted giving in to this impulse without the Father's approval, and then, 'actuated by simplicity and goodness', brought into the world something that was full of ignorance and recklessness. He was the First Ruler (*Prōtarchōn*), the creator of our world (Irenaeus, *AH* I, 29, 4). But it is doubtful whether Irenaeus' source is thinking of Armozel when talking about 'the first angel' of the First-Begotten. It seems more likely that the author was thinking of the fourth angel, Eleleth, who, if counted from below, is the first. For in the *Holy Book of the Great Invisible Spirit* (NHC III, 56, 22–57, 19), the *Three Forms of First Thought* (NHC XIII, 39, 13–32) and the *Gospel of Judas* (Codex Tchacos 50, 23–51, 17) it is Eleleth who produces a cloud (Sophia), from which the creators of the world are born. But the fact that Sophia did not have a partner is ignored here.

Apparently there were various traditions about the way Sophia became the mother of the Ruler of chaos. In the *Secret Book* it was her wish to produce something by herself, without agreement from the Father and her partner. Because in the divine world any thought or word immediately becomes an entity by itself, she immediately produces a being that is, of course, imperfect. It is a snake or a dragon with a lion's head and fiery eyes.[67] She casts him out of the Pleroma, conceals him in a cloud of light and sets him on a throne, which later turns out to be the dome of heaven. She calls him Yaldabaoth (in part of the tradition also Yaltabaoth). He is clearly identified with the God of the Bible, whose majesty appears in a cloud (e.g. Exod. 16:10) and whose throne is heaven (Isa. 66:1: 'Heaven is my throne and the earth is my footstool'). Yaldabaoth goes on to create a large number of servants, evil powers, of whom the twelve signs of the zodiac and the seven planets are the most important. All these powers have strange, Semitic-sounding names, which leave little doubt that they came from a magic context and also had a magic function in the *Secret Book*. It would go too far in this context to discuss the many aspects involved in these lists.[68] Pertinent, however, is that the planets also have a female aspect here, which like the attendants of Barbelo, Christ and the four great Lights have a Greek abstract word as a name:

[67] It is quite possible that the iconography of Yaldabaoth reflects the representations of the Egyptian lion-faced snake Chnoubis, but there is no proof for the 'almost inevitable conclusion' that Jewish priests of the temple in Leontopolis created the benign lion-headed creator-god Yaldabaoth in order to accommodate their own God to the Egyptian Chnoubis, and that Yaldabaoth only became demonized under Christian influence, as is argued by Mastrocinque, *From Jewish Magic to Gnosticism*, pp. 77–85.

[68] See Pleše, *Poetics of the Gnostic Universe*, pp. 181–200; Rasimus, *Paradise Reconsidered*, pp. 103–28.

Athoth	Goodness (Moon)
Eloaios	Providence (Mercury)
Astaphaios	Divinity (Venus)
Yao	Dominion (Sun)
Sabaoth	Kingship (Mars)
Adonin	Jealousy (Jupiter)
Sabbataios	Wisdom (Saturn).

The author of the *Secret Book*, who gave Greek abstract terms as names to so many aeons, is likely to have devised the Greek names in this case, too. The magic names of the planets were not invented by the author of the *Secret Book*, for they occur in many texts, with variable spellings. Four derive from the names of God in the Hebrew Bible: Yao (*YHWH*), Eloaios (*Elohim*, 'God'), Sabaoth (*Sabaoth*, '[Lord of] Powers'), Adonin (*Adonai*, 'Lord'). The magic character of the planet names is shown not only by the fact that they often occur in magic papyri and on a magic amulet, but also by the diagram of the Ophites discussed by the anti-Christian philosopher Celsus (*c.* 170) and by Origen (*c.* 248).[69] Origen tells us that, according to the gnostics, the soul ascending through the spheres of the planetary powers was obliged to recite certain sayings and show magic signs to be able to pass. Thus she was supposed to say to Astaphaios:

Ruler of the third gate, Astaphaios, surveyor of the primeval source of water, behold this one initiate and let me pass, who was purified by a virginal Spirit, since you contemplate the essence of the world. Let grace be with me, Father, let it be with me. (*Contra Celsum* VI, 31)

In the system of the 'other gnostics' in Irenaeus, who are often identified with the Ophites (*AH* I, 30, 4–5), and in the *Origin of the World* (NHC II, 101, 23–102, 2 (section 16)), the same names occur as in the diagram of the Ophites.[70]

The pleromatic and cosmological systems of the *Secret Book of John* are apparently based on a magic worldview, populated by countless powers

69 See Rasimus, *Paradise Reconsidered*, pp. 242–55, and the reconstructions of the diagram by nine different scholars in Plates 1–9 there; a photograph of the amulet, published by Bonner (see above p. 13 and next note), is also found in Rasimus's Plate 16. The discussion of the diagram and its background in Mastrocinque, *From Jewish Magic to Gnosticism*, pp. 94–121 (photograph of Bonner's amulet on p. 71), should be treated with much reserve, because it is too speculative.

70 That is, Yaldabaoth, Yao, Sabaoth, Adonaios, Eloaios, Horaios and Astaphaios (the last three in Origen as Astaphaios, Ailoaios, Horaios). It is of interest to note that on the obverse of the magic gem the name Ariel (*Aariēl*) appears alongside that of Yaldabaoth (*Ialdabaōth*), which is strongly reminiscent of *On the Origin of the World*, NHC II, 100, 23–6 (section 12), where it is said of Yaldabaoth that 'the Perfect call him Ariael, because he resembled a lion' (Ariel = Hebrew *'ari*, lion and *'ēl*, God).

with strange magic names. It would be somewhat naïve to think that these names have lost their magic significance in gnostic myths. All indications point in the opposite direction! We referred above to the importance of magic and theurgic practices in the individual and collective gnostic experience. We should conclude, therefore, that this apparently already played a role in the initial development of gnostic mythology. The magic worldview is an essential part, the magic names are indispensable in it. Only someone who knows these names and the accompanying sayings and actions can influence the powers. They govern not only the signs of the zodiac and the spheres of the planets (BG 39, 4–44, 9; NHC II, 10, 26–13, 1) but also all the parts of the body and the soul (NHC II, 15, 29–19, 10). Above there is found the divine world, with in ascending order the four great Lights (Armozel, Oroiael, Daveithe and Eleleth), the Son, the Mother (Barbelo) and the Father, the great invisible Spirit (BG 22, 16–36, 15; NHC II, 2, 25–9, 24).[71] Knowledge of the magic names gives access to the upward path, back to the origin.

The creation of the cosmos is followed by the creation of the first human beings and their experiences inside and outside of Paradise. For this narrative the author of the *Secret Book* used an existing gnostic exegesis, the basic features of which we already encountered in Saturnilus. Another indication that this exegesis is not an invention by the author himself is that it presupposes an entirely different view of the Pleroma from that described in the *Secret Book*: not the 'Father-Mother-Son' model but that of 'Man-Son of Man'. The same gnostic revision of the story of Genesis is known from the 'other' gnostics of Irenaeus, *AH* I, 30, 6–9; it also occurs in the *Nature of the Rulers* and *On the Origin of the World*. The brief contents are as follows: Yaldabaoth (the biblical Creator-God) thinks that he is the only God and he therefore exclaims after creating the celestial bodies: 'I am a jealous God and there is no other God besides me!' (cf. Exod. 20:5 and Isa. 45:5). Immediately a voice is heard from the world above him: 'Man exists and the Son of Man!' In the water of the primeval chaos appears the image of the heavenly Man, upon which Yaldabaoth says to his powers: 'Come, let us make a human being after the image of God and after our likeness.' The powers first create a psychic body, but they cannot make it stand up; it lies motionless. A ruse by the 'Mother-Father of the All' leads Yaldabaoth to breathe some of the power of his mother Sophia into Adam. As a result, he himself is weakened and Adam receives the breath of life (Gen. 2:7). Because Adam has greater insight than the

[71] See also p. 218.

powers that created him, these become jealous and cast him down into matter. There they mould a material body for him and place him in Paradise, with the aim of subjecting him in ignorance.

The rest of the first chapters of Genesis are explained in the same gnostic sense in the *Secret Book*, though there are interpretations which deviate from what other texts show to be the prevalent view. Thus the snake in Paradise was often interpreted in a positive sense, as the one who was the first to bring gnosis to Adam and Eve, so that they perceived the true nature of Yaldabaoth and his henchmen. This is for instance the case in Irenaeus, *AH* I, 30, 7, the *Nature of the Rulers*, NHC II, 89, 30–90, 1 (section 9) and *On the Origin of the World*, NHC II, 118, 25–119, 19. But in the *Secret Book of John* the snake is the one who taught Adam and Eve sexual activity and the undoing this brings. The 'enlightenment' of Adam and Eve is effectuated by a female saviour figure, Enlightening Insight (luminous Epinoia), who was already present in Adam and is a manifestation of Sophia. In actual fact the creation of Eve was a failed attempt of the Demiurge to bring out this divine power in Adam.[72]

According to the *Secret Book*, Cain and Abel were begotten by Yaldabaoth with Eve (BG 62, 3–20; NHC II 24, 8–25), and Seth, 'the image of the Son of Man', is the son of Adam himself, albeit that he was begotten asexually, 'in the manner of birth in the aeons' (NHC II, 24, 35–25, 2). He is the spiritual ancestor of the gnostics. Cain and Abel are demonic powers who have been placed over the four elements. They have animal heads and magic names which derive from the divine names of the Hebrew Bible: Eloim and Yave. The *Secret Book* follows its own path here, since related texts give a different impression of things. In Irenaeus, *AH* I, 30, 7, the evil powers beget children with Eve who are called 'angels', but according to I, 30, 9 Cain and Abel were born outside of Paradise as children of Adam and Eve, and the same applies to Seth and his sister and wife Norea (not mentioned in the Bible), 'from whom all the rest of mankind issued'. The *Nature of the Rulers* is not entirely clear with regard to Cain, but he was probably begotten by the evil powers. Abel and Seth are the children of Adam and Eve, but Norea 'came from above' (NHC II, 91, 11–92, 4; 92, 26). In *On the Origin of the World*, Cain is not mentioned by name (perhaps NHC II, 116, 33–117, 4 refers to his generation by the archons); Abel is the son of the first ruler, the other children were begotten by 'the seven powers and their angels' (NHC II, 117, 17–18).

[72] See above pp. 47–8.

According to the gnostic exegesis of Genesis, the Flood was an attempt by Yaldabaoth to exterminate both the human beings and the divine element in them, but it failed because Sophia (under different names) intervened by having Noah build the Ark. Here, too, the *Secret Book* (BG 73, 4–11; NHC II, 29, 6–12) goes its own way by having Christ emphatically declare that 'not only Noah, but many other people of the unshakable race' hid not in the Ark but in a cloud of light. In order to gain control over the human race, Yaldabaoth then ordered his 'angels' to beget children 'after the image of their spirit' with human women (cf. Gen. 6:1–4).

As is evident from the surviving texts, the gnostics were mainly interested in biblical primeval history, because they not only found a description there of how the human race had ended up in its situation of ignorance, but also how the light of gnosis had already dawned in the primeval age. The gnostic exegesis of Genesis 1–8 follows a fixed pattern, but one on which considerable variation was apparently possible. No authentic text or summary reporting on it seems to have preserved the original gnostic interpretation. Though it may be doubted whether such an original version ever existed, this does seem to be probable. Around 120 Saturnilus appears already to have been familiar with the basic pattern of this exegesis, indeed, it may be that he was the first to advance it and that he or his pupils committed this explanation to writing. But here we enter an area, that of the origin of the gnostic traditions, where speculations are rife but hard facts rare. We will return to this in the last chapter.

Biblical history after the Flood received scant attention in gnostic exegesis. Only the 'other gnostics' of Irenaeus, *AH* I, 30, appear to have extended the line of what could be called the 'reverse history of salvation' after the Flood. It is uncertain, but not impossible, that they depended here on the same source which also contained the primeval history. According to this report, Yaldabaoth entered into an agreement with a certain Abraham, in which he gave the earth to Abraham's offspring, on condition that they would continue to serve him. It was Yaldabaoth who, under the direction of Moses, led the offspring of Abraham from Egypt, gave them the Law and thus made them Jews. Each of the seven planetary gods, with Yaldabaoth as their leader, chose heralds who were to glorify them and proclaim them as gods, the idea being that others would also worship these gods (I, 30, 10).[73] These heralds are the prophets of the

[73] For the text, see also the '*note justificative*' in the edition by Rousseau and Doutreleau, *Irénée de Lyon. Contre les Hérésies, Livre I*, vol. 1, pp. 308–9.

Old Testament, who were divided among the planetary gods as follows (I, 30, 11):

Yaldabaoth: Moses, Joshua, Amos and Habakkuk
Yao: Samuel, Nathan, Jonah and Micah
Sabaoth: Elijah, Joel, Zechariah
Adonai: Isaiah, Ezekiel, Jeremiah, Daniel
Elohim (= Eloaios): Tobias and Haggai
Horaios: Micah and Nahum
Astaphaios: Ezra and Zephaniah.

But Sophia also used these prophets, so that they often talked about, and thus reminded people of, the First Man, the imperishable Aeon, and Christ on high. This gave rise to two kinds of people, who were symbolically designated as, on the one hand, sprung from the infertile Elizabeth (cf. Luke 1:7) and, on the other, from the Virgin Mary. Obviously the last group are the gnostics.

Valentinians

Valentinianism focuses on the central theme of salvation by Christ. Here, too, salvation is the removal of ignorance, the fulfilment of a passionate desire for knowledge of God, in short, the reception of gnosis. The Valentinians assumed that all reality was threefold, divided into a spiritual, *pneumatic* world (the Pleroma), a *psychic* world (the sphere of the Demiurge) and a *material* world (visible, physical reality). For a proper understanding of Valentinian Christianity we need to realize that Christ has performed his work of salvation in all these three worlds. Hence in a description of Valentinian views it is virtually impossible to discuss the fall of Sophia and the origin of the Demiurge and the world without immediately involving Christ's salvific work as well. As far as possible we will now first talk mainly about the fall and its consequences; in the next section, the meaning of Christ will be dealt with at greater length.

In Valentinian theology, too, it is the last and youngest aeon, Sophia, who is responsible for the breach in the Pleroma. But in the *Tripartite Tractate* Sophia has been replaced by a male aeon, the Logos. This breach can be philosophically interpreted as the moment in which the tension between unity and plurality (in mythical terms: between the unity of God and the plurality of the Pleroma) can no longer be maintained. It is certain that Valentinus and the Valentinians made use of philosophical discussions about unity and plurality to shape their ideas.[74] However, they were motivated not by a philosophical question but by a religious one: how did I end up in this world and how can I be delivered from it? Because Irenaeus in *AH* 1, 2, 1–5, 6 offers the most coherent description of the breach in the Pleroma and the genesis of the world and the human race this will be discussed here first. They are usually thought to be the views of Ptolemy and his followers, but that has been questioned, and with good reason,[75] and they certainly do not represent the original view of Valentinus and that of all other Valentinians. These will be discussed afterwards. But because of its comprehensiveness Irenaeus' description offers the best access to Valentinian thought.

The breach in the Pleroma comes about because the last aeon, Sophia, passionately wants something that is impossible: to understand the greatness of God. For only the highest aeon but one, Mind (*Nous*), is capable of knowing the unknown supreme God. All the aeons below him are increasingly deprived of this knowledge and increasingly also feel the desire to know God. Hence it is said that Sophia was gripped by a passion which had started with the aeons directly below Mind and Truth. This led to a great conflict in her 'on account of the majesty of the Depth [*Bathos*], the unsearchability of the Father and on account of her love for him'. She would have been swallowed up by 'the sweetness of the Father' if she had not been stopped by the Limit (*Horos*), which separates the aeons from the 'ineffable Majesty'. She came to herself with difficulty and cast off her former thought (*Enthymēsis*) and the passion connected with it (*AH* 1, 2, 2). Through the activity of the Limit, which is also referred to by names such as the Cross and the Saviour, Sophia was saved and the calm and unity of the Pleroma were restored. To prevent something similar from ever happening again, the Only-Begotten, the Nous, produces a new pair of aeons: Christ and the Holy Spirit. Christ provides the aeons with knowledge, which entails that nobody can know the Father other than through the Only-Begotten Son. The Holy Spirit teaches the aeons to sing the praises of the Unknowable One and thus makes all of them equal to the First Ogdoad. Together the aeons then produce 'the perfect Fruit' of the Pleroma, Jesus, who is also called Saviour, Christ, Logos and the All, along with his retinue, angels of the same descent as he (*AH* 1, 2, 5–6).

According to the Valentinians, therefore, Christ also brought gnosis into the world of the aeons, the heavenly Church. But restoration of the

[74] See p. 167.

[75] See above p. 166.

original situation was not yet complete, for Sophia's errant impulse, her passionate *Enthymēsis*, had been expelled from the Pleroma and became there a weak and female being with a pneumatic core. She is often called the 'lower Sophia' in contrast to the 'higher Sophia' in the Pleroma; she is sometimes also referred to as Achamoth (derived from the Hebrew *ḥoḳmāh*, wisdom). Christ descends to her and gives her a substantial form, but no knowledge. As a result, she feels an aspiration to the higher world, the world of the aeons, but she cannot get through to it on account of the Limit, which also separates the Pleroma from the underlying world. She is overcome by conflicting emotions: on the one hand the tendency towards higher things (*epistrophē*), on the other by grief (*lypē*) and fear (*phobos*).

The creation of the world is subsequently instigated when Christ, who had returned to the Pleroma, sends Jesus the Saviour and his angels to her. He gives her gnosis, thus freeing her from her emotions. This gives rise to two substances: a partially good one, resulting from her upwards aspiration (the psychic element), and a bad one, resulting from her emotions of grief and fear (the material element). This last is elaborated in a poetic manner: Achamoth's tears produced the moisture, her laughter the light. Irenaeus thinks all this is silly and pokes fun at it (*AH* 1, 4, 1–4). Achamoth herself is impregnated by the light of the angels and brings forth 'fruits' after the image of the angels (the pneumatic element). She then constructs from the psychic element the Demiurge, 'the God, Father and King of all things', the creator of everything outside of the Pleroma, both the psychic and the material. The Demiurge creates the seven heavens, which in reality are spiritual beings, angels. Paradise, where Adam was, is located above the third heaven. Essentially the creation is a reproduction of the higher reality of the Pleroma, at the instigation of Achamoth. But the Demiurge did not know this, he did not even know about his mother's existence. Thus he created heaven without knowing Heaven and man without knowing Man. He thought he was alone and had made everything on his own initiative, and therefore proudly cried out: 'I am God, and besides me there is no one!' He also created the evil spirits, the demons led by the devil, the 'Lord of the world' (*Kosmokratōr*), and finally the four elements of which all earthly things are made (*AH* 1, 4, 5–5, 4). It is important to observe that, according to the Valentinians, the Demiurge is not entirely evil, but occupies an intermediate position between Achamoth and the devil, in a spatial sense, too: until her final salvation Achamoth dwells in the eighth heaven, the Demiurge in the seventh heaven (as head of the lower celestial spheres) and the devil in the earthly sphere. The Demiurge's position is strongly reminiscent of that of

Sabaoth in the *Nature of the Rulers* and *On the Origin of the World* and of that of Adonaios in the *Second Treatise of the Great Seth*.[76]

As his last act of creation the Demiurge makes 'the earthly human' (*ton anthrōpon ton choïkon*), but not from the dust of the earth (cf. Gen. 2:7), as the term earthly suggests, but from an invisible substance, the unstable substrate of matter. Into this being he breathes the psychic element, 'the psychic human'. That is the material and psychic human being, who was finally clothed with the carnal body, 'the garment of skin' (cf. Gen. 3:21). But this being also contains a spiritual, pneumatic element, introduced in him unintentionally by the Demiurge. For Achamoth had unobtrusively placed in the Demiurge the pneumatic element that she had produced after contemplating the light of the angels of Jesus the Saviour. When the Demiurge inspires the soul into the human being, this pneumatic element is placed in him, as a seed that can develop until he is prepared to receive the Logos. All these pneumatic seeds together form the Church (*Ekklēsia*), which is an image of the Church of the aeons in the Pleroma (*AH* 1, 5, 5–6).

The above views of the Valentinians show some overall similarities to the myth of the *Secret Book of John* and related texts: the last aeon, Sophia, starts off the development which leads to the human's earthly situation; she is the mother of the Demiurge, who is the head of the planetary gods created by him; she finds a provisional resting-place in the eighth heaven. But in elaborating on this information the Valentinians follow a path all of their own. To mention but a few elements: the reason for Sophia's fall is not her wish to make something by herself, but the passionate desire for knowledge of God; Sophia's role outside the Pleroma and the creation of the Demiurge and man differ markedly from what other gnostic myths say about this; the strongly magic character of the gnostic worldview has completely disappeared. There can be no doubt that the Valentinian view is secondary, based on an older mythological model, the Barbelo myth, that is in the vein of the *Secret Book of John*. The opposite view is defended only by scholars who hold that gnosis was an intra-Christian movement that increasingly expressed itself in mythological terms. It is, however, certain that Valentinus himself was familiar with the older myth of the creation of Adam by the ignorant angels. He says in one of his fragments that Adam frightened the angels who created him because he knew more than could be expected of a creature. The reason for this, says Valentinus, was that Adam had been invisibly given a seed of divine being. He struck

[76] See pp. 52, 54 and 110.

terror into the angels for the pre-existent Man that was in him, which is why they quickly concealed their work (the idea probably being that they cast him down into matter).[77]

As we noted earlier, there were also other Valentinian views on the breach in the Pleroma and its consequences. Thus, to mention only one example, there were Valentinians who said that Christ was not produced by Mind (and Truth), but by Sophia herself when she was already outside of the Pleroma. However, he shook off the shadow and ascended to the Pleroma. Sophia remained behind without her spiritual element and then gave birth to two other children: the Demiurge and the devil. Irenaeus, *AH* I, 11, 1, ascribes this view to Valentinus himself, but there is good reason to doubt the correctness of this.[78] In this view there is no separation between a higher Sophia in the Pleroma and her personified bad thought (*Enthymēsis*) that resides in the eighth heaven as the lower Sophia: Sophia herself ends up outside the Pleroma. This view, which is probably the oldest, was also taught by Theodotus, witness Clement of Alexandria, *Excerpta ex Theodoto* 32 (cf. also 23, 2), and it also occurs in the *Valentinian Treatise* (NHC XI, 33, 35–7) and in the *Tripartite Tractate*, if with an important difference there.

In the *Tripartite Tractate* the breach in the Pleroma is caused by the youngest and smallest aeon, the Logos. He wanted to 'grasp the incomprehensibility' and glorify 'the ineffability of the Father'. He acted in good faith and 'from an abundant love', but what he wanted exceeded his power and authority. He was therefore excluded by the Limit from the world of the Father and the other aeons. But the author remarks emphatically that all this was subject to the will of the Father: 'the Father had brought him forth with a view to what he knew had to happen' (NHC I, 75, 17–77, 11). Once outside the Pleroma, the Logos produces shadows and imitations of what he had wanted to achieve in the higher world with his arrogant thought. These become negative powers that will ultimately generate matter. The Logos repents and begs for help, and his prayer and the memory of the Pleroma produce a new group of powers, which have a psychic structure and clash with the material powers. In answer to his prayer for help the Pleroma then brings forth the Son, who manifests himself to the Logos and his two groups of descendants, the material and psychic powers. As a reaction to this appearance from the world of

[77] Fragment 1, in Clement of Alexandria, *Stromateis* II, 36,1–4. Discussions containing an opposite view can be found in Markschies, *Valentinus Gnosticus?*, pp. 11–53, and Holzhausen, *Der 'Mythos vom Menschen'*, pp. 80–101.

[78] See Thomassen, *Spiritual Seed*, pp. 23–7.

the Pleroma the Logos then begets a third group, now with a pneumatic structure, the spiritual seed, also called 'the Church' (NHC I, 78, 28–95, 38). He appoints a Ruler as head of all the powers, who as Demiurge creates everything by his word. Humans, too, are created by him and his servants, from the material and psychic elements, but the Logos breathes into them the spiritual element, which is called 'the Breath of Life' and 'the Breath of the exalted aeon' and 'the Invisible'. This is the 'living soul' that gives life to what was dead, the power by which one arrives at knowledge: 'for what is dead is ignorance'. The human being must first experience death, 'that is to say, complete ignorance of the All, and all the resulting misery', in order to 'acquire the greatest good, namely eternal life, which is a complete knowledge of the All and the reception of all good things' (NHC I, 104, 4–108, 12). Ignorance is death, gnosis is life. Just as the world outside the Pleroma was made from the material, psychic and spiritual elements produced by the Logos, so mankind as a whole is divided into three kinds: material people (the 'hylics', from *hylē*, matter), psychic people (the 'psychics', from *psychē*, soul) and spiritual people (the 'pneumatics', from *pneuma*, Spirit). The true nature of human beings only comes to light when the Saviour has come (NHC I, 118, 14–122, 12).

Though the *Tripartite Tractate* swarms with aeons, there is no trace of the strict division of the Pleroma into thirty aeons. Did the author suppress this deliberately or does his work testify to a stage of Valentinianism in which the Pleroma ascribed to Ptolemy and his pupils was still unknown? Most scholars tend towards the latter view, though it is generally assumed that the work should be dated to the late second or early third century. As in the texts with just one Sophia, the Logos, too, is saved only at the end of time, which reflects an earlier stage than the system with two Sophias. The big problem is that we know so little about Valentinus' own views. According to Tertullian, Valentinus held that the aeons were initially in an unconscious state within the Unknowable Father, and we find this, too, in the *Tripartite Tractate*, which also seems to suggest that this work reflects early Valentinian notions.[79] Though the *Tractate* spiritualizes almost everything, the text does presuppose the mythical motif that the Demiurge's servants helped to create Adam – a motif we also found in Valentinus.[80] The ideas of the *Tractate* show many similarities to those of the *Gospel of Truth*. But this gospel formulates the creation myth poetically. The ignorance of the aeons brings about fear

[79] See p. 166. [80] See p. 181.

and uncertainty, which ultimately gives rise to the illusion of the material world:

> When the All went in search of him from whom it had come forth – and the All was inside of him, the Incomprehensible and Unthinkable One who is superior to any thought – the ignorance regarding the Father brought about anguish and fear. The anguish became dense like a fog, so that no one was able to see. As a result, Error grew powerful, it moulded its matter in folly, without knowing the Truth. It started to create and fabricated in power and beauty the substitute for the Truth. (NHC I, 17, 4–21)

It is not immediately clear who or what is meant by 'Error'. The word could refer to Sophia or to the Demiurge, but also to ignorant mankind in its earthly situation. In the *Gospel of Truth* the situation of the aeons runs constantly parallel with that of human beings, both in their ignorance and in their salvation. The language was probably kept deliberately vague to leave room for different interpretations.

SALVATION

The gnostic who has knowledge of his divine origin and understands the true nature of his sojourn on earth also knows that he is liberated from the powers of evil and is reconnected with the divine world. But this is not something that a human finds out by himself. Gnosis is not the result of rational deliberation, but of inner enlightenment through a divine Saviour. Often more than one Saviour is involved, though of course in Christian gnosis Christ is the Saviour par excellence. However, this salvation is never salvation from sin, but a liberation from ignorance. The content of the gnostic experience was already discussed in the first section of this chapter. Some aspects of this will be dealt with here, too, but now in connection with the removal of ignorance effected by the Saviour.

Salvation without Christ

That the gnostic movement of Antiquity was not a typically Christian phenomenon is shown by the fact that there were systems in which Christ played no role at all. According to the Mandaeans, light-beings are sent to the earth to free the divine light-substance in the human being, the 'inner Adam', from the grip of the material and evil body. They do this by conveying to human beings knowledge of their origin. The most important of these ambassadors from the light-world is 'Knowledge of Life' (*Manda dHiia*), but the three heavenly descendants of Adam, Abel, Seth and Enosh (the son of Seth), also play a significant role. It is remarkable that there are only mythical, no historical saviour figures in Mandaeism.[81] It is important to establish this, because the same applies to almost all the gnostic systems in the Graeco-Roman world which are not typically Christian: only Christian gnostic religion has a historical Saviour, Jesus Christ.

In the *Paraphrase of Seëm* the Saviour is Derdekeas.[82] He descends into the world of Darkness to save the part of the Spirit (*Pneuma*) that had fallen into the chaos and had thus enlightened the Mind (*Nous*) of the chaos. In this process of enlightenment the creation and the further history of the world takes place. The work contains allusions to the flood, the destruction of Sodom and, perhaps, a vague reminiscence of Jesus' crucifixion. But Derdekeas is certainly not a veiled designation of Christ; the *Paraphrase* is not a Christian work.[83]

In the *Holy Book of the Great Invisible Spirit* Seth is pre-eminently the saviour, but he is by no means the only one. Immediately after the creation of Adam appears Metanoia, 'Repentance', by virtue of the Father's will, so that through her 'the deficiency' might be filled up. She prays for the salvation of both the archons and the descendants of Adam and Seth (NHC III, 59, 9–60, 2; IV, 71, 1–10). Seth then places his 'seed' in the generation of Sodom and Gomorrah. His descendants suffer three terrible disasters: a flood, a conflagration and the catastrophes of the final days: famines and pestilences, temptations and the activity of false prophets. At the request of the heavenly Seth, 400 'guards' arrive to protect his offspring (NHC III, 60, 9–62, 24; IV, 71, 18–74, 9). Finally, Seth himself is sent to save his errant race. He manifests himself in the flood, the conflagration and in the final days. The description of the entire salvific process contains three references to Jesus. The first does not mention him by name, but says only that Seth instituted baptism 'through a body begotten by the Logos, which the great Seth had secretly prepared for himself through the Virgin, so that the saints might be begotten by the Holy Spirit' (NHC III, 63, 10–14; IV, 74, 24–75, 1). This alludes to the baptism of Jesus by John the Baptist. So the baptism of the (apparently nonmaterial) body of Jesus was the institution of baptism, which played such an important part in the group of the *Holy Book*. The second reference does mention Jesus, again in connection with baptism, but also with his

[81] Rudolph, 'Mandaeans', pp. 753–4.
[82] On this text, see pp. 119–22.
[83] For another view, see p. 222 below.

crucifixion. Through his Providence the Father instituted holy baptism, 'through the Incorruptible One begotten by the Logos, namely the living Jesus, whom the great Seth put on. And he crucified the powers of the thirteen aeons.' In the shape of Jesus, Seth himself is therefore the first to undergo the 'Sethian' baptism and crucify the powers of evil in his crucifixion. Thus Seth/Jesus is not just the Saviour, but also the prototype of the saved gnostic. But Jesus is never identified in the *Holy Book* with Christ, the Anointed One. The latter does get mentioned, but only as a highly placed aeon, when the text talks about 'the thrice-male child of the great Christ, whom the great invisible Spirit had anointed' (NHC III, 44, 22–4; cf. 54, 18–20). Though there are some clear Christian elements in Seth's mission, this does not mean that we are therefore dealing with a Christian text. To make this plain, it is useful to quote the relevant passage in full and also to look at what follows it:

> Then the great Seth was sent by the four lights, by the will of the Self-Begotten One and the whole Pleroma, through the gift and the good pleasure of the great Invisible Spirit and the five seals and the whole pleroma.
> He passed through the three advents which I mentioned before, the flood, the fire and the judgment of the rulers, the powers and the authorities, to save the race that had gone astray:
> through destruction of the world and baptism through a body begotten by the Logos, which the great Seth had secretly prepared for himself through the Virgin, so that the saints might be begotten by the Holy Spirit,
> through invisible, secret symbols,
> through a destruction of the world against the world,
> through the renunciation of the world and the god of the thirteen aeons
> and [through] the invocation of the saints and the ineffable ones <in the> womb <of> the great light of the Father,
> who pre-existed with his Providence
> and instituted through her the holy baptism that surpasses heaven,
> through the Incorruptible One, who was begotten by the Logos,
> namely the living Jesus, whom the great Seth put on.
> And he nailed down the powers of the thirteen aeons.
> And he thus established those who are brought and taken away.
> He armed them with the armour of the knowledge of his truth,
> with an unconquerable power of incorruptibility. (NHC III, 62, 24–64, 9; IV, 74, 9–75, 24 (with minor deviations))

In all likelihood the last three lines are talking about those who undergo baptism. In the group of gnostics in which the *Holy Book* originated there was undoubtedly a certain baptismal practice, but not in the sense of the common Christian baptism as forgiveness of sins, but as a participation in the mystic baptism which the gnostic underwent in his ascent through the heavenly spheres. The passage quoted above is in fact followed by a long enumeration of the spiritual powers that present themselves to the ascending recipient of baptism. Here, too, Jesus is mentioned, now for the third time, as the one who dwells with Seth in the great Light Oroiael. The text reads:

> There appeared to them the great servant Yesseus Mazareus Yessedekeus, the living water,
> and the great army leaders, James the Great and Theopemptos and Isaouel,
> and they who preside over the spring of truth, Micheus and Michar and Mnesinous, and he who presides over the baptism of the living, the purifier Sesengenpharanges [thus the superior text of NHC IV],
> and they who preside over the gates of the waters, Micheus and Michar,
> and they who preside over the resurrection, Seldao and Elainos,
> and the receivers of the great incorruptible race, the strong people of the great Seth,
> and the servants of the four Lights: the great Gamaliel, the great Gabriel, the great Samblo, and the great Abrasax,
> and they who preside over the rising of the sun, Olses and Hypneus and Heurumaious,
> and they who preside over the entrance into the rest of eternal life, the governors Mixanther and Michanor,
> and they who guard the souls of the elect, Akramas and Strempsouchos,
> and the great power Heli Heli Machar Machar Seth,
> and the great invisible ineffable and unnameable virginal Spirit,
> and Silence,
> and the great Light Harmozel, the dwelling-place of the living Autogenes, the God of truth, and [of] him who is with him, the incorruptible man Adamas,
> [and] the second, Oroiael, the dwelling-place of the great Seth and [of] Jesus, who belongs to Life and came and crucified what is under the law,
> [and] the third, Daveithe, the dwelling-place of the sons of the great Seth,
> [and] the fourth, Eleleth, the dwelling-place where the souls of the sons are at rest,
> [and] the fifth, Yoel, who presides over the name of him to whom it will be granted to baptize with the holy incorruptible baptism that surpasses heaven. (NHC III, 64, 9–65, 25; IV, 75, 24–77, 19)

This enumeration takes us completely back to the world of the Pleroma described in the first part of the *Holy Book*. Again we see here the magic, theurgic aspect of the gnostic experience discussed at length in the first section of this chapter. Knowing the magic names of the heavenly powers is indispensable to any ascent to the highest regions of the divine world. Conceivably, this knowledge was mediated in baptism. In the 'ascension' texts that circulated in the school of Plotinus – *Zostrianus*, *Allogenes*, *Marsanes*, etc. – the same heavenly figures occur, with frequent baptisms in the heavenly regions. Christ remains entirely unmentioned in these texts, too.[84]

In discussing the *Revelation of Adam* we found a close relationship between this work and the *Holy Book of the Great Invisible Spirit*.[85] Adam predicts that the race of the earthly Seth will be saved from the flood by unspecified angels 'in high clouds, who will bring those people into the place where the Spirit of Life dwells' (NHC v, 69, 19–25). In the conflagration 'great clouds of light will descend and other clouds of light will come down on them from the great aeons. Abrasax, Sablo and Gamaliel will descend and rescue those people from the fire and the wrath and bring them above the aeons and the rulers and the powers' (NHC v, 75, 17–27). In the eschaton the race of Seth will be saved by the 'Enlightener with gnosis', who is an incarnation of the heavenly Seth. All kinds of views on him are proclaimed, but only the 'race-without-king' know who the Saviour really is:

> God chose him from all the aeons. He made knowledge of the Undefiled One of truth come to be [in] him. He said: 'The [great] Enlightener has come [from] foreign air, [from] a great aeon. And he enlightened the race of those people whom he had chosen for himself, so that they might enlighten the entire world.' (NHC v, 82, 21–83, 4)

In the group of gnostics which produced this work, baptism also played an important role, in which the celestial figures of Micheus, Michar and Mnesinous and Yesseus Mazareus are cited as well. Christ is not mentioned and in general no Christian influence can be detected in this text.

Christ as the last Saviour

In many gnostic texts Christ does occur as Saviour, in the sense that he brings gnosis, but only as one who confirms what more mythical saviour figures had already revealed. A moot question in some cases is whether this addition of Christ is due to later Christianization of an originally non-Christian text. This applies for instance to the *Nature of the Rulers* (NHC II, 4).[86] A number of mythical Enlighteners play a role here: Pistis Sophia (NHC II, 87, 7–8; 94, 28–33; 95, 31–4 (sections 3, 24, 29)),

[84] See pp. 81–8.
[85] See p. 60.
[86] For the conceptions of salvation in the related *Origin of the World*, see p. 55.

Incorruptibility (II, 87, 11–20 (section 4)), the Spirit (II, 88, 11–16 (section 6)), the spiritual Eve (II, 89, 3–90, 12 (sections 8, 9)), Norea (II, 91, 34–92, 3; 92, 18–26 (sections 12, 15)), Eleleth (II, 93, 2–97, 21 (sections 20–39), via Norea) and Zoe (II, 95, 5–13; 95, 31–4 (sections 26, 29)).[87] Strikingly, with the exception of the Spirit and Eleleth, all these figures are female. Christ is not explicitly mentioned anywhere. But towards the end the text probably alludes to him when it says that the final judgement will take place 'when the True Man in a human body will reveal [the Spirit of?] Truth, which the Father has sent'. The True Man 'will instruct them about everything and anoint them with the ointment of eternal life' (II, 96, 32–97, 4 (sections 36–7)). The author seems to be using Christian language here: that the Spirit of Truth is sent by the Father recalls John 14:17, while the words 'anoint' and 'ointment' (*chrisma*) suggest Christ the Anointed. A careful analysis of this passage provides much evidence that NHC II, 96, 17–97, 21 (sections 32–9) are a later revision of an earlier text. The same holds for the conclusion of *On the Origin of the World*.[88] The only unmistakably Christian remark in the *Nature of Rulers* is found at the beginning: a reference to the apostle Paul, with a free quotation of Ephesians 6:12. However, according to most scholars, this too is an introductory remark by the text's last redactor.

In the *Secret Book of John* Christ plays a clear role as a bringer of gnosis, but he is not the only one. In the prologue and the epilogue the book presents itself as a revelation of the glorified Christ to a wavering John. During this revelation John asks a number of questions about problems which evidently concerned the author, to which Christ responds at length. But in the creation of Adam and during the events in paradise the enlightening gnosis is already brought by the spiritual Eve and Enlightening Insight (the luminous *Epinoia*), who are both manifestations of Sophia.[89] Only in the long recension do we see a progressive Christianization, when in the revelation of gnosis at the Tree of Knowledge the figure of Enlightening Insight is supplanted by Christ. It is also Enlightening Insight who informs Noah of the impending flood, and in the Song of Pronoia it is another manifestation of Sophia, Perfect Providence, who rouses the human being from his sleep of ignorance and permanently frees him from death via baptism with the five seals. Again the saviour figures who proclaim gnosis are female here. In the *Secret Book* Christ is

[87] A detailed discussion of these figures can be found in Ingvild S. Gilhus, *The Nature of the Archons. A Study in the Soteriology of a Gnostic Treatise from Nag Hammadi (CG II, 4)*, Studies in Oriental Religions 12 (Wiesbaden: Harrassowitz, 1985), pp. 37–109.

[88] See p. 55. [89] See pp. 47–8.

the one who clarifies the nature of salvation, but he is certainly not the first and only one to bring about gnostic enlightenment. One gets the impression that the author of the *Secret Book*, who was undoubtedly a Christian, added him to older conceptions in which he originally played no role.

Christ as the only Saviour

A poetic summary of the work of the gnostic Saviour is offered by the well-known Naassene Psalm, preserved in Hippolytus, *Refutatio* v, 10, 2. This psalm talks about the fate of the Soul, which as the third original principle is located between God and Chaos. Her earthly state is described in oppressive images: she is pursued by the powers of Chaos, like a deer by hunters, she wanders in a labyrinth without exit. Then help arrives from above:

> Jesus, however, said: 'Look, Father,
> this prey of evil powers,
> strays away from your Spirit to the earth.
> She is trying to flee bitter Chaos,
> but does not know how to escape from it.
> Therefore, send me, Father!
> With the seals I will descend,
> I will pass through all the aeons,
> I will disclose all the mysteries,
> and show the forms of the gods:
> I will pass on the secrets of the Holy Way,
> under the name of Gnosis.'[90]

According to the Naassenes, heavenly Man had a pneumatic, a psychic and a material aspect and these three aspects had descended upon 'one man, Jesus, the son of Mary'. Through the three forms of being he had spoken to the three communities which exist in the All: that of the angels, that of the psychics and that of the hylics. He revealed the truth to those worthy of it, the gnostics, or, more precisely, the Naassenes themselves. They said according to Hippolytus, *Refutatio* v, 9, 21–2:

> We are the pneumatics … who pass through the true gate, which is Jesus the blessed. And of all people only we are Christians, who perform the mystery at the third gate and are anointed there with indescribable oil from the horn, like

[90] See M. Marcovich, 'The Naassene Psalm in Hippolytus (*Haer.* 5.10.2)', in *Studies in Graeco-Roman Religions and Gnosticism*, pp. 80–8.

David [cf. 1 Sam. 16:13], not from the earthen vessel, like Saul, who cohabited with the evil demon of carnal desire [cf. 1 Sam. 10:1].

So the Naassenes distinguished between the person of Jesus, the son of Mary, and the threefold divine power of the heavenly Man that had descended upon him. Such a distinction was common among Christian gnostics, albeit the divine component of the historical Jesus was usually referred to as the Christ. This view should not be regarded as a 'heretical' distortion of the Church's pure doctrine of Christ, but as one of the many answers to a complex of questions that was fiercely debated in second-century Christianity: the relation of the divine and the human in the historical Jesus and the significance of his death and resurrection. After discussing some other gnostic views on the salvation by Christ, we will look at this more closely.

According to Justin the Gnostic, after getting to know the Good One and abandoning Edem,[91] Elohim did everything he could to save his spirit (*pneuma*) in mankind. He sent his third angel, Baruch, to Moses and the prophets to spread knowledge of the Good One, but the first angel of Edem, Naas, enticed them so that they did not listen to Baruch. The uncircumcised 'prophet' Hercules was also sent by Elohim to defeat the twelve angels of Edem (his twelve labours), but he failed as well. Finally, Baruch is sent to Nazareth and finds Jesus there, the twelve-year-old son of Joseph and Mary, who is tending sheep. He is sent out to explain to the people what had happened in the beginning and to bring knowledge of Elohim and the Good One. When Naas failed to entice Jesus, too, he had him crucified, upon which Jesus gave back his body and soul to Edem, dedicated his spirit to Elohim and ascended to the Good One (Hippolytus, *Refutatio* v, 26, 24–32). According to Justin the Gnostic, therefore, Jesus was the first who had listened to Baruch's exhortation to leave Edem and ascend to the Father, Elohim, and the Good One. As explained above, his followers underwent the same in this life: they had to swear an oath and then ascended to the Good One, which was accompanied by a drinking ritual, seen as a baptism in the heavenly regions.[92]

According to the 'other gnostics' of Irenaeus, *AH* 1, 30, Christ was the only Saviour from the outset. As we described above, he was taken up in the Pleroma with his mother, while his sister Sophia ended up in matter.[93] Sophia fails to find rest and calls in the help of her mother, the First

[91] See p. 158. [92] See p. 150. [93] See p. 170.

Woman. The First Man Christ is then sent to his sister and to the light-dew in the netherworld. Sophia announces his arrival via John the Baptist and prepares Jesus as the earthly vessel of the coming Christ. Christ 'clothes' himself in Sophia, they rest in each other and become bride and bridegroom. Because Jesus was begotten through the operation of God himself, he exceeded all people in wisdom, purity and righteousness. Christ, united with Sophia, descended into him, and thus Jesus Christ came into being. When he started to perform miracles and openly proclaimed that he was the Son of the First Man, the archons and the 'Father of Jesus', that is the Demiurge, were angered and tried to kill him. But before Jesus was crucified, Christ and Sophia withdrew from him to the Incorruptible Aeon. However, Christ did not forget Jesus, but sent a power below that resurrected him from the dead. His resurrectional body was psychic and pneumatic, his material body remained in the grave. After his resurrection Jesus stayed on earth for eighteen months and taught the true state of affairs to a few chosen disciples. But most of his disciples misinterpreted his resurrection: they thought that his material body had risen from the dead – this obviously in reference to the view of non-gnostic Christians. After his ascension Jesus sits at the right hand of his Father, Yaldabaoth, and receives there the souls that have cast off their earthly bodies and have 'known' him, that is, have accepted the gnosis about his true nature and that of the heavenly Christ. But Yaldabaoth fails to see that the risen Jesus is seated next to him, and the more souls Jesus receives, the more Yaldabaoth is diminished. For he cannot send back those souls to the earth; only the souls into which he has breathed life can be reincarnated. Apparently the tacit assumption is that Jesus and the saved souls ultimately return to the divine world, for the 'coming consummation will take place when all the dew of the Spirit of Light will be gathered and carried off to the Aeon of Incorruptibility' (Irenaeus, *AH* 1, 30, 12–14).

For the Valentinians, too, Christ is the only Saviour.[94] Characteristic of Valentinianism is that Christ appears under various names as Saviour in all three levels into which total reality is divided: the pneumatic, the psychic and the material world. We explained above how Christ restores peace in the spiritual world once and for all by bringing the knowledge of the Father, that is gnosis, to the aeons. He sends Jesus the Saviour, who is also called Christ and Logos, to the psychic world of Sophia to save her from her emotions and give her gnosis. As a result, she produces

[94] An extensive discussion on the various forms of the Valentinian doctrine of salvation can be found in Thomassen, *Spiritual Seed*, pp. 46–118. Only the main aspects can be treated here.

pneumatic seeds which are breathed into humans by the Demiurge.[95] The Saviour in the material sphere is obviously the Jesus Christ of the gospels, but the Valentinians disagreed on the nature of his earthly appearance. According to their opponents, there were two schools of thought: the Eastern school and the Italian or Western school.[96] For a proper understanding of the Valentinian doctrine of salvation, we need to explore this in more detail.

According to Hippolytus, *Refutatio* VI, 35, 6–7, the Western school, of which Ptolemy and Heracleon were the best-known representatives, taught that Christ had a psychic body, whereas the Eastern school, to which Theodotus and a certain Axionicus belonged, ascribed to him a purely spiritual, pneumatic body. This last view seems to be the oldest, if at least Tertullian is right to remark that Valentinus himself taught that 'Christ's flesh was spiritual' (*De carne Christi* 15, 1). In any case we know that this was Theodotus' opinion: when descending through the spheres the Saviour put on, in the psychic world, the spiritual seed of Sophia as flesh for the Logos. Therefore Theodotus talked about the spiritual body of Jesus as 'Sophia'. The spiritual seed needed salvation, because it came from the psychic world, and so Jesus' spiritual body also had to be saved. This was only possible if he took on the same material body as all other people and participated in human suffering. When he commends his Spirit to God at his crucifixion, he gives back Sophia, that is, the entire pneumatic 'Church', to the Father (Clement of Alexandria, *Excerpta ex Theodoto* 1, 1–2 and 26, 1). In this view, the salvation relates only to the 'pneumatic seed', that is the pneumatics (in whom this seed sprouts); the category of the psychics is completely absent and does not even seem to exist. The *Tripartite Tractate* (NHC I, 5) also clearly belongs to the Eastern school of Valentinianism, though Sophia has been replaced here by the Logos and a modest space has been reserved for the psychics. Though the information they supply is scanty, we can attribute to the same school: the *Treatise on Resurrection* (NHC I, 4), the *Gospel of Philip* (NHC II, 3), the *Interpretation of Knowledge* (NHC XI, 1) and the *Valentinian Exposition* (NHC XI, 2).

What we know about the conceptions of Christ in the Western school of the Valentinians comes mainly from Irenaeus' report in *AH* I, 6, 1–2. This school came closer to non-gnostic Christianity in the sense that it

[95] See pp. 180–1.

[96] See Thomassen, *Spiritual Seed*, pp. 39–45, J.-D. Kaestli, 'Valentinisme italien et valentinisme oriental: leur divergences à propos de la nature du corps de Jésus', in Layton (ed.), *The Rediscovery of Gnosticism*, vol. I, pp. 391–403, and J. Kalvesmaki, 'Italian versus Eastern Valentinianism?', *VC* 62 (2008), 79–89.

paid a great deal of attention to the psychics, that is, the non-gnostic Christians. That is why the supporters of this school taught that Jesus had had a psychic body. It was effectively composed of three elements: Achamoth, the lower Sophia, gave the pneumatic element to the descending Saviour and the Demiurge clothed him in the 'psychic Christ', while out of the cosmos he received a body that is psychic, but was incomprehensibly made in such a way that it was visible and tangible and could suffer. According to these Valentinians, the arrival of Christ was primarily intended for the psychics, the non-gnostic Christians, for due to their psychic nature they can choose good or evil. Though they do not possess 'perfect gnosis', they can be 'confirmed', that is, achieve a certain form of salvation, by means of 'good works and simple faith'. According to the Western Valentinians, the Saviour had a psychic body, because he was of significance for the psychics in particular; in a certain sense the pneumatics were saved by nature, but for material people, the hylics, no salvation was possible. Irenaeus, *AH* 1, 7, 2, states that there were also Valentinians for whom the Saviour did not descend on Jesus until he was baptized in the Jordan and who therefore taught that the composition of his body started with Achamoth's pneumatic element. They said that the psychic Christ who had clothed the pneumatic part was a son of the Demiurge, that he had spoken through the prophets, that he had passed through Mary 'like water through a tube'[97] and that at the baptism in the Jordan the Saviour had descended from the Pleroma in the form of a dove. Only the psychic Christ and the also psychic but visible and palpable body that had been incomprehensibly made for him out of the cosmos had suffered on the cross. But this suffering had taken place 'in a mysterious way [*mystēriōdōs*]', that is to say, 'with a hidden spiritual meaning'.[98] For thus the heavenly Christ could be made symbolically visible, that is the Christ who, in order to save Sophia, had extended himself on the Limit (*Horos*) of the Pleroma, which was also called Cross (*Stauros*).

Gnostic and non-gnostic Christology

Because the Valentinians placed Christ at the centre of their doctrine of salvation and thus professed to be fully Christian, their Christology was a

[97] For this image, see M. Tardieu, '"Comme à travers un tuyau". Quelques remarques sur le mythe valentinien de la chair céleste du Christ', in Barc (ed.), *Colloque international sur les textes de Nag Hammadi*, pp. 151–77.

[98] Thus the interpretation by Rousseau and Doutreleau in their edition, *Irénée de Lyon. Contre les Hérésies, Livre I*, vol. 1, pp. 208–9.

focal point for their opponents. But it would be an error to think that all gnostics entertained such complicated theories about the person of Jesus Christ. Like non-gnostic Christians, most gnostics believed that Jesus had really suffered on the cross. The gnostic views, including those of the Valentinians, can only be properly understood in the context of the early Christian debate on the relation between God and Christ and between the divine Christ and the historical Jesus.[99]

With respect to theology, the second century has been characterized as a laboratory in which all kinds of Christian possibilities were tested that could be competitive on the religious market (and, it may be added, could be directional for the future of Christianity as well). The Christian gnostic thinkers also worked in this spiritual laboratory.[100] For a correct understanding of their position we should be aware that in the second century Christian thought was still in a state of flux, that there were not yet dogmas accepted by the majority and that the monocratic, authoritative episcopacy did not start to develop until the second half of that century, and mainly only in the big cities. From the middle of the second century certain ecclesiastical circles can be seen to champion the theory that Christianity was originally undivided: Jesus supposedly taught the pure doctrine to his apostles and they in turn passed it on to their followers, the leaders of the early Church; only later were there people who in their conceitedness believed that they knew better and thus introduced heresy into the Church.[101] But nothing could be further from the truth: the person and the meaning of Jesus was judged differently by Christians from the very beginning, and it was only in the second half of the second century that, in this regard, too, the large Christian communities started to define their limits and thus their identity – again first in the big cities and in Rome earlier than, for instance, in Alexandria. However, virtually all Christians did agree that God had manifested himself in Christ, that his teachings and life, his death and resurrection had salvific

[99] What follows is an adaptation of R. van den Broek, 'The Gnostic Christ', in O. Hammer (ed.), *Alternative Christs* (Cambridge University Press, 2009), pp. 16–32. R. Roukema, *Jesus, Gnosis and Dogma* (London and New York: T&TClark, 2010), compares the gnostic conceptions of Jesus mainly with the information in the New Testament, so that the real historical context is for the greater part neglected. On the gnostic conceptions, see also: D. Voorgang, *Die Passion Jesu und Christi in der Gnosis*, Europäische Hochschulschriften, Reihe XXIII: Theologie 432 (Frankfurt am Main: Peter Lang, 1991), and Majella Franzmann, *Jesus in the Nag Hammadi Writings* (Edinburgh: T&T Clark, 1996).

[100] Markschies, *Gnosis. An Introduction*, p. 120 (= *Gnosis und Christentum*, p. 112).

[101] According to Hegesippus, who in the mid second century travelled through the Roman Empire, the Church was undivided until the time of the Emperor Trajan (98–117). See Eusebius, *Ecclesiastical History* III, 32, 7–8 and IV, 22, 4–7.

significance, and that he had then returned to his heavenly origin. But widely different answers were given to the question how exactly all this should be interpreted.

For all the theological discussions which flared up in the second century, we should consider that these will have had little effect on ordinary, often illiterate believers. The great majority of Christians were not intellectuals who wanted to understand and to know, but simple believers who experienced their salvation through participation in the mysteries of the Church: the baptismal rite and the Eucharist. Christianity was primarily a mystery religion that guaranteed its adherents remission of sins and eternal life after death. Most Christians will not have seen any virtual difference between God and Christ, as is testified in particular by literature of a more 'popular' character, such as the apocryphal Acts of the Apostles. Among church leaders this was also the standard view for a long time, because it guaranteed both the unity of God and the divinity of Christ. In Antiquity this view was called 'monarchianism', but modern historians usually talk about 'modalism', because in a more elaborated form Father, Son and Spirit were seen as 'modes', manifestations, of the one God. In connection with the crucifixion Ignatius of Antioch, who is usually dated before 117, does not hesitate to speak about 'the suffering of my God' (*Letter to the Romans* 6, 3) or 'the blood of God' (*Letter to the Ephesians* 1, 1). And Zephyrinus, who was bishop of Rome from 198 to 217, taught: 'I know but one God, Jesus Christ, and except him no one else who was born and suffered' (Hippolytus, *Refutatio* IX, 11, 3). But more intellectual Christians thought this was too simple and made use of philosophy to arrive at a more satisfactory view. People who wanted to defend Christianity and make it acceptable to non-Christians, the so-called Apologists, distinguished between the unknowable God the Father and his Son, the pre-existent Christ, whom they identified with the Logos of Greek philosophy. The concept of Logos played an important part in the Stoa as the rational aspect of God which pervades the entire cosmos as a creative power. In Middle Platonism it became the term for the cosmos-orientated manifestation, the creative force, of the Unknowable God. In this form it became a central concept in the religious philosophy of Philo of Alexandria, but the Logos in the prologue to the Gospel of John can also be interpreted in the same sense: 'In the beginning was the Logos, the Logos was with God and the Logos was God. He was in the beginning with God. All things came into being through him, and without him not one thing came into being' (John 1:1–3). Much more can be said about this, but here it is enough to observe that in the second century the Logos became the key concept among intellectual Christians in determining the relationship between God and the divine element that had appeared in Jesus Christ. This gave rise to a divine duality, which was a unity at the same time (the Holy Spirit was still largely out of the picture). Despite the many problems which this caused, Christian thought had thus taken a path which in the fourth century led to the trinitarian dogma: one divine being, three persons.

We saw above that the gnostic Christians took an entirely different path. Christ, the Logos and the Son do occur in the divine Pleroma, but they always form part of a much larger number of divine powers, while their position within this group varies from system to system. Like Plotinus and his followers, the non-gnostic theologians opposed the cascade of aeons which developed from the highest God according to the gnostics. The non-gnostic doctrine of God had much more in common with that of Greek philosophy than with the gnostic view of the Pleroma. This raises the question: what exactly is the background of the gnostic view of God? Is it entirely different from that of non-gnostic theology and non-Christian philosophy? This question will be addressed in the last chapter.

In the second century the more intellectual Christians also became aware of another problem: how was the union of the divine and the human in the historical Jesus to be conceived? Greek thought traditionally drew a sharp distinction between the unchanging divine world of Being and the changeable world of Becoming. These two could not go together, could not unite, and this made the unity of God and a human being in the historical Jesus inconceivable. One of the earliest solutions to this problem was the view that Jesus did not have a real human body of flesh and blood, but an illusory body. Around the year 100 we already encounter this view in the letters of John: 'Every spirit that confesses that Jesus Christ has come in the flesh is from God, and every spirit that does not confess Jesus is not from God. And this is the spirit of the antichrist' (1 John 4:2–3; cf. 2 John 7). Such a Christology is called 'docetic', derived from Greek *dokein*, 'to seem'. In itself this view is not gnostic, for it is easily reached from the antithesis between the eternally divine and the transiently temporal. Initially people hardly saw any difficulty in the union of God and the human being in Jesus, certainly not ordinary believers, but not leading figures either. It was simply assumed that Jesus was at the same time truly God and truly human, who had suffered and died, while docetism was strongly opposed. This led to deliberately antithetical statements, in virtually liturgical forms, as in Ignatius of Antioch, in his *Letter to the Ephesians* 7, 1:

There is only one physician,
carnal and spiritual,
begotten and not begotten,
God who appeared in the flesh,
true life in death,
both from Mary and from God,
first passible, then impassible,
Jesus Christ, our Lord!

Later ecclesiastical thought developed along the lines of this unity of God and the human being in Jesus Christ, people being prepared to put up with the internal contradiction. The first to find formulations for this that cleared the way for the great Christological decisions of the fifth century was Tertullian of Carthage (*c.* 200). In his *Adversus Praxean* 27 he wrote: 'We observe a double status, not confused but conjoined [*non confusum sed coniunctum*] in one person God and human, Jesus.' But for some orthodox Christians this initially went too far. Origen, the great Alexandrian theologian, who was vehemently anti-gnostic and would have nothing to do with docetism, believed that there had to be a connecting element between the divine and the human in Jesus that had not been corrupted by sin. Like the gnostics, he held that originally there was only a pre-cosmic, spiritual world; in this world the souls lapsed from God the Logos through a decision of their own free will. Only one soul remained pure by adhering wholly to the Logos, and in a perfect unity with this pure soul the Son of God was born out of Mary. For, as Origen concluded: 'Without a mediator the union of the divine nature with a material body was impossible' (*De principiis* II, 6, 3).

In view of the above, it is clear that the Valentinian speculations on Christ's pneumatic or psychic body are strongly docetic in nature, even though his body is sometimes said to be capable of suffering. In any case they extended the line of docetism, in the sense that the Saviour did not have a material body. Other gnostic texts sometimes clearly state that Jesus only seemed to have suffered. In the *Second Treatise of the Great Seth* the Saviour says about his apparent suffering:

I, then, was in the mouths of lions. As to the plan they had conceived against me – to the destruction of their error and their foolishness – I did not give in to them, as they had planned. I was not afflicted at all. Those there punished me, but I did not die in reality but only in appearance … For my death, which they think happened, <happened> to themselves in their error and blindness. They nailed their [own] man to the cross, to their [own] death. For their thoughts did not perceive me, because they were deaf and blind. But by doing this they pronounced judgement upon themselves. As for me: they did see me and they punished me, but it was someone else, their Father, who drank the gall and the vinegar. It was not I, <when> they struck me with the reed. It was someone else who took the cross on his shoulder, namely Simon. It was someone else on whom they placed the crown of thorns. But I was rejoicing in the height at all the wealth of the rulers and the offspring of their error, their empty glory, and I was laughing at their ignorance. (NHC VII, 55, 9–56, 20)

According to this text, it seems as if Christ was crucified, but in reality it was another, though we cannot simply assume that it was Simon of Cyrene (cf. Mark 15:21 and parallels). In effect the archons crucify themselves! The view of the *Second Treatise* shows similarity to that of Basilides, at least according to Irenaeus, *AH* I, 24, 4: Christus was sent to the world as a human being, performed miracles there, but he did not suffer. He had changed Simon of Cyrene so far that people thought he was Jesus, after which Jesus had assumed the appearance of Simon and standing at the cross had laughed at the archons.

However, most gnostics believed with all other Christians that Jesus had really suffered on the cross. A distinctly non-docetic view of Jesus' body and his suffering is taught in the treatise *Melchizedek*, though this work at the same time glorifies the divine Triad of the Barbelo myth and its aeons.[102] But because, like Origen, they held that the divine and the human could not possibly enter into a union, they regarded the historical Jesus only as the material shell which the divine Christ had put on, either at his birth or at the baptism in the Jordan. Moreover, the body was judged very negatively by most gnostics, created as it was by the Demiurge to keep the divine element imprisoned. Gnostic and non-gnostic Christians also agreed that the divine aspect of Jesus did not suffer in the crucifixion, because the divine element is unchanging and cannot suffer or die. Non-gnostic Christians believed that the divine element, the Logos, had remained untouched with Jesus in his suffering and had then resurrected his body from the dead. Irenaeus, *AH* III, 19, 3, wrote:

Just as he was a human being to be tempted, so he was also the Logos to be glorified. The Logos was at rest during the temptation, dishonouring, crucifixion and death, but the human being was 'swallowed up' [by the Logos] [cf. 1 Cor. 15:54; 2 Cor. 5:4] in his victory, his abiding mercifulness, his resurrection and his ascension.[103]

[102] See p. 63.

[103] For the text, see the remarks by Rousseau and Doutreleau in their edition, *Irénée de Lyon. Contre les Hérésies, Livre III*, vol. 1, pp. 343–5. The words 'abiding mercifulness' (*hypomenein kai chrēsteuesthai*) most probably refer to Christ's descent to the underworld and his preaching to the spirits that were imprisoned there (cf. 1 Pet. 3:19).

The gnostics, however, generally held that the divine Christ had abandoned Jesus before his death on the cross. In the *Revelation of Peter* this is an important theme.[104] Peter receives a vision:

When he had said this, it seemed to me as if he was seized by them. And I said: 'What do I see, Lord, is it really you whom they are seizing and are you holding on to me? Who is it that is joyful and laughing above the cross? And is it another whose feet and hands they are nailing down?' The Saviour said to me: 'The one you see above the cross, joyful and laughing, that is the living Jesus, but he into whose hands and feet they are driving the nails, that is his fleshly part, his substitute. They are putting to shame the one who came into being in his likeness. Look at him and look at me!' When I had looked, I said: 'Lord, no one sees you. Let us flee from here.' But he said to me: 'I told you: they are blind. Let them be! And look how much they do not know what they are saying. For instead of my servant they have put to shame the son of their own glory.' (NHC VII, 81, 3–82, 3)

Then Peter sees the Saviour again, in a glorified state, but still resembling the Living Jesus he had seen above the cross. He is encouraged and given the following explanation of what he had previously seen:

Be strong, for it is you to whom it is given to know these mysteries through a revelation, namely that the one who was crucified is the first-born, the house of the demons, the clay vessel in which they live, the one of Elohim, the one of the cross that is under the law. But the one who stands near him is the living Saviour, *who was first in him* whom they seized, *but was set free*. He stands there joyfully, observing that those who did evil to him are divided amongst themselves. Therefore he laughs at their lack of perception, because he knows that they were born blind. Therefore the one who suffers must remain behind, for the body is the substitute, but *that which has been set free is my incorporeal body*. (NHC VII, 82, 18–83, 8)

The author clearly states here, in the italicized sentences, that the Saviour was in the historical Jesus, from whom he detached himself on the cross. In the *Gospel of Judas* Jesus talks about his body as 'that which bears me': 'Tomorrow they will torture the one who bears me', and to Judas he says: 'You will sacrifice the man who bears me' (Codex Tchacos 56, 6–8[105] and 19–21). It is far from certain that this last is intended as a compliment, in the sense that Judas is praised because his action will allow release of the divine element in Jesus. But the quotations from the *Revelation of Peter* also make it clear that the one who is crucified is not actually Jesus, 'my

[104] See also p. 192, on the views of the 'other' gnostics of Irenaeus, *AH* I, 30.
[105] For the text of this passage, see Wurst and Meyer, in Krosney, Meyer and Wurst, 'Preliminary Report on New Fragments of Codex Tchacos', p. 292.

servant', but 'the son of their own glory', 'the clay vessel', the material body that the archons had made to imprison the divine spark. Thus the liberation of the Saviour from his earthly vessel also symbolizes the liberation of the gnostic's divine core from his earthly body. We find the same view expressed in the *First Revelation of James*.[106] Talking about his suffering, the glorified Christ says to James:

For I am the one who was *in myself from the beginning*. For I did not suffer in any way, nor did I die. And this very people did me no harm. Rather that was done to the image of the rulers and for that it was in fact prepared. The archons prepared him, then he came to his end. (Codex Tchacos 18, 6–9 (NHC v, 31, 17–20 with some differences))

The crucifixion is a sign of the defeat of the powers of evil: they are incapable of killing the Saviour and destroy their own artefact. In this sense the crucifixion and the death of Jesus have salvific meaning for the gnostic, too. The same idea is formulated in the *Gospel of Truth*, when the author remarks that Christ enlightened the people who dwelled in the darkness of oblivion:

Therefore Error was angry with him and pursued him. It was pressed hard by him and stripped of its power. He was nailed to a tree and became a fruit of the knowledge of the Father. But this fruit did not destroy when it was eaten, on the contrary, it granted real existence to those who ate of it. They rejoiced in the discovery, for he found them in himself and they found him in themselves. (NHC I, 18, 21–31)

So Jesus' death on the cross means the destruction of Error, who is personified ignorance here, and the gift of gnosis. In Valentinian theology, the salvific meaning of Jesus' death could even be interpreted as the remission of sins. The author of the *Interpretation of Knowledge* takes the typically Valentinian view of the heavenly body of Christ for granted,[107] but he also says that 'through him who was scorned we receive the re[missio]n of sins and through him who was scorned and who was redeemed we receive grace' (NHC XI, 12, 25–9). The Valentinians could speak about Jesus and the meaning of his death with a warmth that is quite rare in early Christian literature. The author of the *Gospel of Truth* says in amazement:

Therefore the merciful, faithful Jesus took on his sufferings patiently … for he knew that his death would mean life for many … He was nailed to a tree,

[106] See pp. 75–7. The *Second Revelation of James* also has a docetic Christology, see p. 67.
[107] See above, p. 107.

he made known the edict of the Father on the cross. Oh, what great teaching: he humiliates himself unto death, though clothed in eternal life! He took off the perishable rags and put on imperishability, which no one can take from him. (NHC I, 20, 10–34)

At first sight this seems a view of Jesus' death which must have appealed to many non-gnostic Christians as well, and most likely did, but on a careful reading it is striking that the passage contains no reference to the resurrection of Jesus' body. This need not mean that the author denied Jesus' resurrection; he may have taken it in a spiritual sense.

The resurrection of Jesus and of Christians

In second-century theological discussions the resurrection of Christ played an important role, because it was broadly seen as the condition and guarantee for the resurrection of the individual believer. This was already how Paul explained it in the mid first century in 1 Corinthians 15, where he remarks: 'Christ was truly raised from the dead, as the first of the dead' (verse 20). Because of their devaluation of the body, as the product of the Demiurge and his evil powers, the gnostics rejected the physical resurrection of Jesus and of Christians. In an ethical respect this negative view of the body almost always led to an ascetic way of life in general and the rejection of sexuality and procreation in particular.[108] But some gnostics did allow for a spiritual resurrection. We pointed out earlier that the 'other' gnostics of Irenaeus *AH* I, 30, 13 taught that Christ, glorified from the cross, sent a power to the dead Jesus to resurrect him in what they called a 'psychic and spiritual body'.[109] He left his material

[108] For the authentic texts, see above pp. 32–3, 41–2, 66, 114. Anti-gnostic authors often accused the gnostics of unbridled promiscuity, but this was a well-known way of discrediting opponents, cf. R. M. Grant, 'Charges of "Immorality" against Various Religious Groups in Antiquity', in van den Broek and Vermaseren (eds.), *Studies in Gnosticism and Hellenistic Religions*, pp. 161–70. Gnostic groups in which sexuality and procreation were judged positively, in a religious-sacramental sense, included the Valentinians in any case; on their views, see the study by April D. DeConick, 'Conceiving Spirits: The Mystery of Valentinian Sex', in W. J. Hanegraaff and J. J. Kripal (eds.), *Hidden Intercourse. Eros and Sexuality in the History of Western Esotericism*, Aries Book Series. Texts and Studies in Western Esotericism 7 (Leiden: Brill, 2008; paperback edn New York: Fordham University Press, 2011), pp. 23–48. On Valentinian ethics in general: Dunderberg, *Beyond Gnosticism*, and P. L. Tite, *Valentinian Ethics and Paraenetic Discourse. Determining the Social Function of Moral Exhortation in Valentinian Christianity*, NHMS 67 (Leiden: Brill, 2009). The Borborites, with their notorious, eucharistically interpreted, sexual practices should also be mentioned here, though they did reject procreation; cf. R. van den Broek, 'Sexuality and Sexual Symbolism in Hermetic and Gnostic Thought and Practice (Second to Fourth Centuries)', in Hanegraaf and Kripal (eds.), *Hidden Intercourse*, pp. 1–21.

[109] See p. 192.

body behind, but this was not understood by his disciples. They did not know that 'flesh and blood cannot inherit the kingdom of God' (1 Cor. 15:50). They therefore lapsed into the grievous error of believing that Jesus had risen from the dead in his material body. This is obviously a polemic against the non-gnostic view that the resurrection of Jesus and of the believer should be interpreted not spiritually but materially.

The same spiritual view is propagated by the *Treatise on Resurrection*, one of the many second-century writings on this subject.[110] The author is convinced that Christ has risen: 'We have come to believe that he rose from the dead, we say of him: "He became the destroyer of death"' (NHC I, 46, 15–19). The saved person has also effectively been resurrected, because he died and rose with Christ:

> The Saviour swallowed death. You should know this! For he left behind the perishable world and exchanged it for an imperishable world. He arose by swallowing the visible by the invisible, he opened the way for our immortality. Then, as the Apostle said, we suffered with him and we arose with him and we went to heaven with him [cf. Rom. 8:17; Eph. 2:4–6]. (NHC I, 45, 14–28)

This recalls what is said of two otherwise unknown teachers in the early second century: 'Among them [i.e. people who spread profane chatter] Hymenaeus and Philetus, who have swerved from the truth by claiming that the resurrection has already taken place. They are upsetting the faith of some' (2 Tim. 2:17–18). But according to the *Treatise on Resurrection* death certainly does involve a resurrection. The author compares Christ to the sun and Christians to sunbeams:

> Now if we manifest ourselves in the world as people who wear him, we are his beams, and we are embraced by him until our setting, that is to say, our death in this life. We are then drawn up by him to heaven, like beams by the sun, without being held by anything. This is the spiritual [*pneumatikē*] resurrection, which swallows the psychic [*psychikē*] in the same way as the fleshly [*sarkikē*]. (NHC I, 45, 23–46, 2)

Paul's influence is abundantly clear here. He, too, had expounded a spiritual view of resurrection in his first letter to the Corinthians. He, too, closely connected the resurrection of Christ and that of the believer: the latter is unthinkable without the former (1 Cor. 15:12–22). But the resurrected body is not a replica of the earthly body, though there is a form of continuity, as between a seed and a fruit: 'It is sown a psychic body [*sōma psychikon*, i.e. a body moved by the soul; cf. Gen. 2:7; NRSV: 'a physical

[110] See pp. 100–1.

body'], it is raised a spiritual body [*sōma pneumatikon*]' (1 Cor. 15:44). As the above quotation shows, the author of the *Treatise on Resurrection* is familiar with the tripartition of the human being into spirit (*pneuma*), soul (*psychē*) and body or flesh (*sōma* or *sarx* (Paul's term)). But there is resurrection only for the spiritual part, or as he says elsewhere:

> The thought of those that are saved will not perish, the mind of those who know him will not perish. Therefore we are elected to salvation and redemption: for we are predestined from the beginning not to lapse into the foolishness of the ignorant, but to attain to the wisdom of those who know the truth. (NHC I, 46, 21–32)

Like (Pseudo-)Paul in Ephesians 1:4, this gnostic also voices his firm conviction of being elected and predestined for salvation by God from eternity. But doubtless he interpreted the substance of this salvation differently, as the gift of gnosis and not as the forgiveness of his sins through the blood of Christ. There has been much debate on whether the *Treatise on Resurrection* teaches not only a spiritual resurrection but also a form of physical resurrection. The author raises this question in a passage that is hard to translate (NHC I, 47, 38–48, 3). His answer is that after death only the inner human will arise, whom he describes as the 'living members' who are within the 'visible members'. Resurrection means the 'disclosure' of this inner human, but it is certainly not an illusion, witness the appearance of Moses and Elijah at Jesus' glorification on the mountain (Matt. 17:3; Mark 9:4; Luke 9:30–31). This reference implies that the pneumatic resurrection body can be seen in a recognizable manner, which seems to point to a certain continuity between the earthly shell and the resurrection body after all. Clearly the author of the *Treatise on Resurrection* is closer to Paul than many of his contemporaries, who increasingly argued the literal meaning against the gnostics. Hence they preferred to talk about 'resurrection of the flesh' rather than use the formerly more common but vaguer expression 'resurrection of the dead'. Irenaeus seems to have been thinking of the *Treatise on Resurrection* when he wrote: 'And some believe that neither their soul nor their body can receive eternal life, but only their "inner human". They believe that this is their mind in them, of which they decree that it alone can ascend to perfection' (*AH* V, 19, 2). Not Paul's spiritual view but a solid faith in the resurrection of the material body came to prevail in the Church. Around 200 this faith found its expression in the Roman baptismal creed: 'I believe in the resurrection of the flesh.'[111]

[111] On this creed, see J. N. D. Kelly, *Early Christian Creeds*, 3rd edn (London: Longman, 1972), pp. 100–66.

Though the gnostics sometimes assigned salvific meaning to the death and resurrection of Jesus, they generally set less store by it than their non-gnostic fellow believers. As explained above, they primarily saw evil in human beings as ignorance to be removed, not as sin to be atoned. Christ is the Enlightener, who lifts the veil of ignorance. This is forcefully expressed in the *Gospel of Truth*:

> This is the gospel of him who is sought, that was revealed to the perfect through the mercy of the Father: the hidden mystery, Jesus Christ. Through him he enlightened those who were in darkness because of oblivion. He enlightened them and showed them a way, and this way is the truth he taught them [cf. John 14:6]. (NHC I, 18, 11–21)

There is no gnostic text which discusses gnosis more profoundly and comprehensively than the *Gospel of Truth*. According to this text, it is only through gnosis that aeons and human beings attain independent, conscious existence in God. This is described in terms of 'being called', 'being pronounced', 'becoming visible', 'taking form' and 'receiving a name'. The Depth of the divine Spirit initially contained 'the All', that is, total reality, in an unconscious state. When the All itself tried to know its origin, its ignorance produced terror and fear like a dense fog, in which Error created its own world.[112] This means that the events in our world actually take place in the unconscious, ignorant part of the Father. Because ignorance is the same as non-existence, our world with its terrors and horrors does not really exist. What we think we see in our ignorance are illusions and fearful dreams, whose true nature we only recognize when we receive gnosis, that is: when we get to know God and come to ourselves, become ourselves. The pre-existent Christ was the first to emerge from the Father. He received and *is* the Name, that of the Father, and brings the knowledge of the Father to the All, to aeons and humans. So, in the view of the *Gospel of Truth*, everything that happens in the world of the aeons and humans is one great process of becoming conscious, which comes about within the deity.[113]

[112] See p. 184.

[113] Thomassen, *Spiritual Seed*, p. 314: 'As long as the world continues to exist, we remain within the womb of the Father, waiting to be born, and to receive form and Name when he wills.'

CHAPTER 6

Backgrounds

THE QUEST FOR THE SOURCE

Much has been written about the origin of the gnostic movement, but no consensus has been reached. No one doubts that gnostic texts contain various elements deriving from Greek philosophy (mainly Platonism), Judaism and Christianity, and it is on these three possible sources that modern scholarship has particularly focused. However, nobody has been able to demonstrate convincingly that the origin of the gnostic current is to be located in one of these movements. Nor is this surprising, since major religious and cultural movements can never be explained from one single source, as a whole complex of factors is always involved. Moreover, the search for the origin of gnosis has almost always started from its expressions. This has yielded a wealth of new knowledge and insights, so that the influence of these movements on the forms of gnosis is easier to judge. But it has not led us to the source of the gnostic current.

Perhaps it is illuminating to approach the question of origin from a different angle, not from the manifestations of gnostic religion, but from its essence. As we explained in the previous chapter, the forms of expression may differ enormously, but *what* they express is always the same: the essential core of human beings hails from the divine world, it is imprisoned in the material world and must be liberated from that world to return to its origin. This is not just a theoretical, philosophical conclusion, but an existential question of life and death: *I* come from God, I share in his essence, I must return to him, but I am trapped in material reality, I have become alienated from my origin, I need salvation. Someone who experiences his existence in this way, who thinks in this way, is not a Platonist (anymore), for it is not his rationality (*nous* and *logos*) that leads him to his destination, but an external intervention. Nor is he a Jew (anymore), for he does not see God as the good Creator of this world and denies that there is a sharp distinction between God and the human being. Nor is he a Christian of the type that subscribes to these Jewish views. Whether he could nevertheless be a Christian is a moot question. We will now look more closely at the philosophical, Jewish, Christian and generally religious components of the gnostic modes of expression.

GREEK PHILOSOPHY (PLATONISM)

It is beyond dispute that gnostic myths incorporate a substantial component of Greek philosophy. This is already shown by the descriptions of the supreme, Unknown God in various texts like the *Secret Book of John*, *Eugnostus*, *The Tripartite Tractate* and *Zostrianus*, which form a sampling of Middle Platonist negative theology. The discovery that the author of *Zostrianus* and the Christian philosopher Marius Victorinus used the same Platonist source speaks volumes in that regard.[1] The gnostic texts which circulated in the school of Plotinus around 250 (works like *Zostrianus* and *Allogenes*) can be read against the background of Middle Platonist and Neoplatonist views on the structure of the spiritual world and the highest levels of Being. But a number of liturgical and magical passages in these texts and especially the hymns of the related *Three Steles of Seth* remind us that we are dealing here not with philosophical but with religious texts in which the ascent to God is the central theme. If it had been the aim of the authors of these gnostic writings to disseminate philosophical ideas about God and the cosmos in a veiled manner, they should have chosen a different form. For only modern scholars with detailed knowledge of late classical philosophy are able to indicate the philosophical structure in the confusing accumulation of constantly new levels of aeons. Contemporary authentic philosophers, like Plotinus, Porphyry and Amelius, were roundly dismissive.[2]

When gnostic authors reflected on God and the world, they could obviously only do so within the context of the major themes of Hellenistic philosophy. We mentioned earlier a central theme: the question how a closed Unity (*monas*) could give birth to the unlimited plurality of the Duality (*dyas*); another question was the nature of the soul and its relation to the body. As early as the second century CE the answers of philosophers to these questions were incorporated by gnostic authors in

[1] See p. 83. [2] See pp. 134–5.

their myths. In modern research this insight led to a veritable quest for philosophical, above all Platonist, elements in the gnostic myths. These were almost exclusively seen as camouflaged descriptions of philosophical ideas, the conclusion often being that the origin of gnosis should be sought in Platonism.[3] But again we are dealing here with forms of expression, not with what was identified above as the essence of the gnostic experience.

But it cannot be denied that from the outset Platonism contained elements which could lead to the gnostic view of reality. The image of the human soul drawn by Plato in his *Phaedrus*, as a charioteer with a team of winged horses that had lost their feathers and had consequently 'fallen' into a body, made an indelible impression. The wings are the part of a human being that 'has the greatest share in the divine', and because the divine is 'beautiful, wise, good, etc.', 'the feathers of the soul [are] nourished and developed' by the beautiful, the wise and the good (246d–e). The soul originally witnessed divine reality and is desirous of returning to it, but this is possible only if it has preserved a memory of this reality and is guided by its rational part. Hence it is above all the philosopher's soul which has wings (249c). Plato is not confident about the number of people who have preserved a memory of divine reality:

> For, as has been said, every human soul has by nature beheld reality, because otherwise it would not have entered into a human being, but it is not easy for all souls to remember the other world from the things here, either for the souls which at the time had seen the things there only briefly, or for those which had fallen to earth and were so unfortunate through certain contacts to go the wrong way and to forget the holy things which they once had seen. (249e–250a)

Of course, we are still far removed here from gnostic views. To mention just one thing: the return to contemplation of divine reality is only possible through a proper use of the soul's rational element. The idea of the need for a saviour who reveals the true nature of things through gnosis is completely beyond Plato's ken. But developments in later Platonism, particularly in the second century CE, come much closer to gnostic views, and in this light the gnostic current has been characterized as 'Platonism

[3] This trend in research mainly emerged after publication of the book by H. J. Krämer, *Der Ursprung der Geistmetaphysik. Untersuchungen zur Geschichte des Platonismus zwischen Platon und Plotin* (Amsterdam: P. Schippers, 1964; 2nd edn 1967), in which the gnostic current was situated in the history of Platonism (pp. 223–64). A good example of this approach, connected with the assumption of major Jewish influence, is found in M. Waldstein, 'The Primal Triad in the *Apocryphon of John*', in Turner and McGuire (eds.), *The Nag Hammadi Library after Fifty Years*, pp. 154–87.

run wild' or as a part of 'the Platonic underworld'.[4] To make this clear we should briefly look at the ideas of Numenius of Apamea.[5]

Numenius (*c.* 150 CE) was a Platonist philosopher with a strongly Neopythagorean bent, which was far from unusual in his time. Although most of his work has been lost, he was highly influential: the Christian theologian Origen quotes him repeatedly and Plotinus was later accused of having appropriated his ideas.[6] Numenius started from three supreme principles. The First God, who is called the Father, the (First) *Nous*, the One and the Good, is absolute Being, perfectly transcendent and self-orientated. He is the father of the Second God, the Demiurge, who is also called *Nous*. He, too, is good, because he participates in the Goodness of the First God, but he also has an inclination towards matter. In this capacity he is the third God who gives form to unordered nature in his creative activity. At the same time this threefold 'stratification' of the divine forms a Unity, which consists in participation in the Good (One). No wonder that Christian trinitarian theologians like Origen were rather taken with Numenius' doctrine of God. Opposite the eternal Unity of God is the equally eternal Duality of matter, which in its unordered form is a negative force, the source of all evil and chaos. Our material world is fundamentally good, because it is ordered, but evil does have presence in it, nothing is entirely free from evil, and this also applies to the planetary spheres. This dualistic view of good and evil led Numenius to posit two world-souls, one good and one evil, of which the first coincides with the third God and the second is an independent negative force, roughly identical with unordered matter, though this force does owe obedience to the Demiurge. Numenius also distinguished two souls in the earthly sphere, the rational soul of humans and the irrational soul of animals. The purely rational soul derives from the divine world, but in its descent through the spheres of the planets it has clothed itself in all human psychic capacities, so that it can function in the body. On account of the evil of matter

[4] Respectively A. D. Nock, *Early Gentile Christianity and its Hellenistic Background*, Harper Torchbook edn (New York, Evanston, IL and London: Harper and Row, 1964), p. xvi (the important Introduction to the Torchbook edn (pp. vii–xvii) is lacking in the reprint of *Early Gentile Christianity* (1928) in Nock's *Essays on Religion*, vol. I, pp. 49–133; but Nock repeated his characterization in 'Gnosticism', in *Essays on Religion*, vol. II, p. 949), and Dillon, *The Middle Platonists*, pp. 385–9, who discusses Valentinianism, the Hermetic *Poimandres* (Corpus Hermeticum I) and the *Oracula Chaldaica* as examples of the 'Platonic underworld'.

[5] Good surveys of his philosophy can be found in Dillon, *Middle Platonists*, pp. 361–79, and G. Karamanolis, 'Numenius', *Stanford Encyclopedia of Philosophy*, internet edition: http://plato.stanford.edu/entries/numenius (dated 4 May 2009); the fragments have been published by E. des Places, *Numénius: Fragments* (Paris: Les Belles Lettres, 1973).

[6] Witness Porphyry, *Life of Plotinus*, 17.

present in the planets, these capacities are sources of evil in mankind. Numenius did not talk in Platonist fashion about two or three parts of the human soul, but about two opposite souls: a rational and an irrational one. He probably identified the latter with the planetary 'excrescences' of the rational soul which it casts off again on its return to the divine world. According to Numenius, it is only with our rational soul that we human beings can gain sight of the Good One and associate with him by abandoning everything that binds our senses. The best method for this (in a proper Pythagorean vein) is study of the mathematical sciences and contemplation of the numbers: 'in this way one can train oneself in the science which deals with the question: "What is Being"' (fragment 2, des Places 44).

Though it is tempting to see gnostic religion as a radicalization of ideas like those of Numenius, he, too, is miles away from gnostic views. He does in fact teach a dualistic opposition between mind and (unordered) matter, but his Demiurge is good because he participates in the goodness of the Good One, the First God, and his creation is also fundamentally good.[7] Numenius did share with many of his contemporaries a lack of confidence in reason's ability to get through to the truth of Being or God. In his view, this was particularly true of philosophy after Plato. He and many colleagues believed that the truth had been revealed in the ancient wisdom of the great religions of India, Persia, Israel and Egypt and understood and passed on by great inspired figures (the Brahmans, Zoroaster, Moses). He famously remarked: 'For what is Plato but an Attic-speaking Moses?' (fragment 8, des Places 51). He held that in Greece this wisdom had been understood by Pythagoras, whose ideas were elaborated by Plato. In this way Numenius had returned to the great two figures in whose footsteps he developed his thought, and thus he had also returned to rational thought. He speaks with mystic fervour about contemplation of the Good (fragment 2, des Places 43–4), but he stays within the frame of the rationally thinking soul. He does not assume a general ignorance about the divine world, which a saviour sent from above was supposed to remove. The idea of a divine saviour is as alien to him as to Plato or any Greek philosopher. The gnostic experience of God and of the self cannot be traced back to Platonism, but in shaping this experience gnostics did make ample use of (sometimes radicalized) Platonist views. However,

[7] This last was the fundamental proposition of all Greek philosophy (with the exception of the Epicureans, but they did not recognize a Demiurge); see J. Mansfeld, 'Bad World and Demiurge: A "Gnostic" Motif from Parmenides and Empedocles to Lucretius and Philo', in van den Broek and Vermaseren (eds.), *Studies in Gnosticism and Hellenistic Religions*, pp. 261–314.

we should note that there were also gnostic systems which contain no mark of Platonist influence, for instance those of Mandaeism, Justin the Gnostic, the *Paraphrase of Seëm* (NHC VII, 1) and the *Concept of Our Great Power* (NHC VI, 4).

JUDAISM

Because of the many striking Jewish elements in some gnostic systems, various scholars have understandably located the starting point of gnostic religion in Judaism. In doing so they base themselves almost entirely on the so-called 'Sethian' texts, and specifically on those in which the Barbelo myth is combined with the gnostic exegesis of biblical primeval history. They think that the gnostic separation between the unknown supreme God and the biblical Creator-God may have been made within or on the fringe of Judaism, in deliberate resistance to strict monotheism.[8] But there are also scholars who believe that the unmistakably Jewish elements entered the gnostic myths via Christianity so that there is no question of direct Jewish influence.[9] This last might be possible for the gnostic exegesis of Genesis, but is extremely unlikely for the Barbelo myth as a whole. Everything indicates that the structure of the cosmos and the Pleroma located above it, as we find it in the *Secret Book of John*, was devised by someone so conversant with Jewish conceptions that a Jewish background is virtually assured. At least, this conclusion seems

[8] See, for instance, B. A. Pearson, 'Jewish Elements in Gnosticism and the Development of Gnostic Self-Definition', in *Gnosticism, Judaism, and Egyptian Christianity*, pp. 124–35; N. Dahl, 'The Arrogant Archon and the Lewd Sophia: Jewish Traditions in Gnostic Revolt', in Layton (ed.), *The Rediscovery of Gnosticism*, vol. II, pp. 689–712. Turner, *Sethian Gnosticism and the Platonic Tradition*, pp. 257–8, sees the first stage of 'Sethian Gnosticism' in two movements within early Judaism: (1) the group of the 'Barbeloites' of Irenaeus, *AH* I, 29, 'of perhaps Jewish priestly lineage', who were engaged in 'meditative and lustrational practices associated with service in the heavenly temple' and 'conceived baptismal immersion … as enabling an act of transcendental vision'; they already saw the deity as 'a primal divine triad of Father, Mother and Child'; and (2) the group of the 'Sethites' consisting of 'certain morally earnest biblical exegetes who styled themselves as the worthy "seed of Seth"'. The Jewish origin of gnostic religion was always defended, though not always with the same arguments, by G. Quispel, for example in his controversial contribution 'Gnosticism and the New Testament' (1965), included in *Gnostic Studies*, vol. I, Uitgaven van het Nederlands Historisch-Archeologisch Instituut 34(1) (Istanbul: Nederlands Historisch-Archeologisch Instituut, 1974), pp. 196–212, and in many of his articles in J. van Oort (ed.), *Gnostica, Judaica, Catholica. Collected Essays of Gilles Quispel*, NHMS 55 (Leiden: Brill, 2008). According to Mastrocinque, *From Jewish Magic to Gnosticism*, the gnostic movement originated among Jewish magicians and astrologers who wanted to accommodate their traditional monotheistic beliefs to the polytheistic environment they were living in, primarily Egypt but also in Asia Minor (see below p. 213).

[9] Thus for example Luttikhuizen, *Gnostic Revisions*, pp. 6–12.

unavoidable on an unprejudiced reading and study of the gnostic mythological texts deriving from this tradition. This is not to say that the basic gnostic ideas themselves should therefore be explained from Judaism, since the gnostic views on God and the world are at odds with the fundamental principles of the Jewish religion. After all, it is characteristic of the Jewish religion as it developed in and after the Exile that God is the creator of heaven and earth and everything on it, including the human race (Gen. 1:31: 'God saw everything that he had made, and indeed, it was very good'), but also that there is a strict separation between the human being and God, absolutely ruling out any idea that humans participate in God's being. Only one conclusion is possible. For all the many Jewish elements included in certain gnostic myths – possibly even incorporated into them by ethnic Jews – the underlying view is certainly un-Jewish and any attempt to explain the fundamental gnostic experience from the Jewish religion is therefore pointless.[10] But there can be no denying that the Barbelo myth was shaped using typically Jewish ideas. This can be clarified by a few examples.

In many gnostic texts the figures of Wisdom (*Sophia*) and heavenly Man (*Anthrōpos*) play an important role, including texts not belonging to the group of the Barbelo myth. They already occur in the Old Testament as the forms in which God manifests himself in the world. The fact that a certain independence is increasingly attributed to the Wisdom of God is shown very clearly in Jewish wisdom literature. Proverbs 8:22–31 already depicts Wisdom as God's first-created being, 'daily his delight' (30). Because she was created 'as the *beginning* of his works' (22), there were rabbis who read the words 'in the beginning' in Genesis 1:1 in the sense of 'through Wisdom'.[11] The Wisdom of Solomon 7:26 says of her: 'She is the radiance that streams from everlasting light, the flawless mirror of the active power of God, and the image of his goodness.' Gnostic texts that contain the Barbelo myth draw a different picture of Sophia: she is the last aeon, whose wilfulness causes the breach in the divine world and the birth of the Demiurge. The first emanation of God himself is not called Sophia, but Barbelo, (First) Thought (*Protennoia*, *Ennoia*) and Providence

[10] This was also clearly seen by Pearson, 'Jewish Elements in Gnosticism', p. 130: 'The Gnostic attitude to Judaism, in short, is one of alienation and revolt … the attitude exemplified in the Gnostic texts, taken together with the massive utilization of Jewish traditions, can in my view only be interpreted historically as expressing a movement of Jews away from their own traditions as part of a process of religious self-redefinition. The Gnostics, at least in the earliest stages of the history of the Gnostic movement were people who can aptly be designated as "no longer Jews".'

[11] See J. E. Fossum, *The Name of God and the Angel of the Lord. Samaritan and Jewish Concepts of Intermediation and the Origin of Gnosticism*, WUNT 36 (Tübingen: Mohr, 1985), pp. 316–17.

(*Pronoia*). Remarkably, however, she bears various traits of Wisdom,[12] and scholars have therefore often conjectured that in the earliest version of the myth the top of the divine world was formed by God and his Wisdom. The insertion of so many aeons between the highest God and Sophia in gnostic systems is doubtless linked to the wish to create maximum distance between God and the entity ultimately responsible for the genesis of this evil world. In any case it is clear that the gnostic Sophia both in her positive and negative forms is none other than the hypostasized Wisdom of God, a subject of lively speculation in Jewish-Hellenistic Wisdom schools. In Christian thought Wisdom played virtually no role; she was replaced there by the Logos or the Holy Spirit, and it is therefore unlikely that Sophia entered gnostic mythology via Christianity. Her negative valuation in gnostic texts has to do with the gnostics' negative judgement of the creation, in which Jewish traditions assign to her an active and positive role. It has been suggested that the gnostic Sophia mythically expresses the religious fiasco of the moralistically orientated Jewish Wisdom traditions, but this cannot be proved. So in gnostic texts we see a division of Wisdom into a positive force (Barbelo, etc.) and a negative one (Sophia). Valentinianism brings this out in the conception of the higher Sophia, who resides in the Pleroma, and the lower Sophia (Achamoth), who is outside the Pleroma. However, even the fallen Sophia does not receive an entirely bad press: she plays an active role in the protection and preservation of the divine spark in the human race. The fact that Sophia plays such a prominent part in gnostic myths indicates that these must have been conceived in an environment closely familiar with Jewish ideas.[13]

The gnostic heavenly Man, or, to use the Greek term, *Anthrōpos*, also goes back to Jewish speculations about the manifestation of God. Scholars have often focused their search for the origin on the Platonically orientated exegesis which Hellenistic Jews applied to Genesis 1:26 (the human being created after God's image and likeness): this supposedly resulted

[12] See for instance the threefold descent of Pronoia/Wisdom in the 'Song of Pronoia' on p. 49.

[13] According to Mastrocinque, *From Jewish Magic to Gnosticism*, p. 131, the divine Anthropos, Sophia and Seth already played a role in pre-Christian gnostic ideas in Asia Minor, which were developed by Jewish Magi and astrologers who had originally come from Babylonia: 'The doctrinal system developed by these Jews no doubt included an Anthropos Son of God and (in Asia minor) an emanation of God in the form of a snake. The system must have had numerous similarities with those of the Jews of Leontopolis' (on the alleged influence of the Jewish temple in Leontopolis on the origin of gnostic conceptions, see p. 173). These ideas would have been Christianized by Nicolaus, whose followers, the Nicolaitans, are already opposed in Revelation 2:6 and 15 (*ibid.*, pp. 125–7, 130).

in the mythical figure of the divine *Anthrōpos*.[14] It is certain that the Hellenistic exegesis of Genesis played a part, but the proponents of this view take too little or no account of other and earlier Jewish speculations on which the conception of heavenly Man was initially based. A detailed survey goes beyond our scope here, and so we will confine ourselves to a few indications.[15] The first suggestion that God could manifest himself as a human being is found in the prophet Ezekiel's vision in Ezekiel 1 (593 BCE), on which Jewish mysticism speculated endlessly. In this vision he saw God's chariot with the four animals and above it, on 'something like a throne, in appearance like sapphire', he saw 'something that seemed like a human form', surrounded by a shining light: 'This was the appearance of the likeness of the glory of the Lord.' The prophet does not see God himself, but his radiant manifestation, the 'Glory of the Lord' (*kavōd YHWH*), in the form of a human being (Ezek. 1:26–28).[16] In rabbinical Judaism this led to discussions whether there were 'two powers' in heaven, as some rabbis claimed. The second power was seen as God's substitute, referred to in the mystical tradition by names such as the Angel of the Lord, the Prince of the divine Presence (literally 'of the Countenance', *Sar Happanim*), the Name, the Lesser YHWH and Metatron (= Greek: 'he who sits beside someone on a throne').[17] Because creative activity is also attributed to the second power alongside God, the gnostic Demiurge has sometimes been traced back to this Jewish conception, but in Jewish speculations the second power is always closely connected with God, is his representative and is never adversarial. These reflections were already known in Alexandria in the second century BCE, as emerges from the play *The Exodus* by the Jewish dramatist Ezekiel, in which Moses describes a

[14] Thus H.-M. Schenke, *Der Gott 'Mensch' in der Gnosis. Ein religionsgeschichtlicher Beitrag zur Diskussion über die paulinische Anschauung von der Kirche als Leib Christi* (Göttingen: Vandenhoeck & Ruprecht, 1962), and Holzhausen, *Der 'Mythos vom Menschen'*.

[15] See Fossum, *The Name of God*, pp. 266–91, and J. E. Fossum, *The Image of the Invisible God. Essays on the Influence of Jewish Mysticism on Early Christology*, NTOA 30 (Freiburg Universitätsverlag; Göttingen: Vandenhoeck & Ruprecht, 1995), esp. pp. 13–39.

[16] The importance of this text for the conception of the heavenly Man in gnostic thought was first discussed by G. Quispel, 'Ezekiel 1, 26 in Jewish Mysticism and Gnosis' (1980), in van Oort (ed.), *Gnostica, Judaica, Catholica*, pp. 461–74.

[17] On this, see A. F. Segal, *Two Powers in Heaven. Early Rabbinic Reports about Christianity and Gnosticism*, Studies in Judaism in Late Antiquity 25 (Leiden: Brill, 1977), and A. A. Orlov, *The Enoch-Metatron Tradition*, Texts and Studies in Ancient Judaism 107 (Tübingen: Mohr Siebeck, 2005), especially pp. 86–147. However, P. Schäfer, *Die Geburt des Judentums aus dem Geist des Christentums. Fünf Vorlesungen zur Entstehung des rabbinischen Judentums*, Tria Corda. Jenäer Vorlesungen zu Judentum, Antike und Christentum 6 (Tübingen: Mohr Siebeck, 2010), argues that there is a distinct Christian influence on the Jewish speculations on Metatron and related figures.

dream. On Mount Sinai he saw a throne with a 'noble Man' on it, wearing a diadem on his head and holding a sceptre in his left hand. He beckons Moses to approach, then presents him with the sceptre and the diadem and orders him to take his place on the throne. Moses sees the whole of existence, from above the heavens to beneath the earth, and all the stars kneel down before him. Philo and the rabbis were also familiar with this conception.[18] In the Hebrew *Sefer Hekhalot*, also called *3 Enoch*, such an enthronement is granted to Enoch, who is identified with Metatron.[19] In early Christianity this conception was applied to Jesus. The heavenly Man appears in apocalyptic books like Daniel (7:13–14) and *1 Enoch* (45–50) as the 'Son of Man' (i.e. 'Man'), a title which is transferred to Jesus in the New Testament, with all the attendant associations.[20] It seems most probable that the figure of the heavenly Man in gnostic texts should be understood on the basis of these Jewish speculations, which also applies for that matter to the *Anthrōpos* in the Hermetic *Poimandres* (Corpus Hermeticum 1), 12–14. Since Ezekiel 1:26–28 the heavenly Man has always been associated with light. It is therefore natural that Ezekiel the Dramatist refers to the figure whom Moses sees seated on the throne by the word *phōs*, which has a double meaning: *ho phōs* (masculine, with acute accent) means 'human being, man' and *to phōs* (neuter, with circumflex) means 'light'. Gnostic texts often play on this double meaning, and also bring in the name Adam, because in Hebrew *'ādām* means 'human being'. Some examples may clarify this. *Eugnostus the Blessed* talks as follows about the origin of the heavenly *Anthrōpos*:

The first who manifested himself in infinity before the All is a self-grown, self-created Father, full of radiant, ineffable light. In the beginning he decided that his likeness should become a great power. Immediately the beginning of that light appeared as an immortal, androgynous Man. (NHC III, 76, 14–24)

So the heavenly Man is the radiant likeness of the Father's indescribable light. And in this image the first human is then created. The *Secret Book of John* relates that when the Demiurge boasts that he is the only God he

[18] Ezekiel the Dramatist, *Exagōgē*, 68–82; ed. B. Snell, *Tragicorum graecorum fragmenta*, vol. 1 (Göttingen: Vandenhoeck & Ruprecht, 1971), p. 292. On this passage, see P. W. van der Horst, 'Moses' Throne Vision in Ezekiel the Dramatist', in *Essays on the Jewish World of Early Christianity*, NTOA 14 (Freiburg Universitätsverlag; Göttingen: Vandenhoeck & Ruprecht, 1990), pp. 63–71.

[19] See P. Alexander, '3 (Hebrew Apocalypse of) Enoch', especially pp. 257–67 (sections 2–14); van der Horst, 'Moses' Throne Vision', pp. 66–7.

[20] A brief introduction to this widely discussed theme is found in G. W. E. Nickelsburg, 'Son of Man', in K. van der Toorn, B. Becking and P. W. van der Horst (eds.), *Dictionary of Deities and Demons in the Bible*, 2nd extensively rev. edn (Leiden: Brill, 1999), pp. 800–4.

is reproved from above by a voice that calls: 'Man exists and the Son of Man', after which Man's shining form is mirrored in the waters of chaos (NHC II, 14, 13–34; BG 47, 14–48, 9). The Demiurge then says to his henchmen, according to the long recension:

> Come, let us make a human after the image of God and after our likeness, so that his image may become a light for us … Let us call him Adam, so that his name may become a radiant power for us [literally a power of light] [the short recension has, BG 49, 7–9: so that his name and his power may become a light for us]. (NHC II, 15, 2–13)

The pun on the double meaning of *phōs* is evident here: the man (*phōs*) Adam is a light (*phōs*) for the archons. These speculations about Adam also found their way to the alchemist Zosimus of Panopolis (*c.* 300), who in his *Treatise on Instruments and Furnaces*, the Letter Omega, 13, states that the first human, whom the Egyptians called Thōytos (or Thōyt = Thot/Hermes Trismegistus) and the Jews Adam, contained the spiritual human, called *Phōs*, whose descendants are called *phōtes*, 'light-people'. He strikingly remarks in this context that the traditions which he passes on can only be found among the Jews and in the holy books of Hermes (section 15). Finally, we should mention an interesting passage in *On the Origin of the World*, where the author talks about the creation of three Adams that feature in the creation story of Genesis 1 and 2. Without any introduction or transition the text says in NHC II, 117, 28–118, 2 (section 98):

> The first Adam, of the light, is spiritual [*pneumatikos*]; he appeared on the first day. The second Adam is psychic [*psychikos*]; he appeared on the sixth day, which is called [the day of] Aphrodite [= Friday]. The third Adam is earthly [*choïkos*], that is, the man of the law who appeared on the eighth day, which is called Sunday, [after the] [day of] poor rest.

The first Adam is the Light-Adam, the heavenly Man, who according to this text had manifested himself to Yaldabaoth and Pronoia (NHC II, 108, 5–14 (section 44)). He appeared on the first day and thus corresponds to the first word of creation: 'Let there be Light!' (Gen. 1:3). The creation of the other two Adams is connected with Genesis 1:26–27 and 2:7.[21] So the heavenly Man is identical to the divine Light by which God manifested himself on the first day of creation. He is the Majesty, the Glory, the Splendour of the Unknowable God. The pun on the two forms and meanings of *phōs* obviously has its origin in a Greek context, but the strong

[21] The eighth day is inferred from Gen. 2: 2 (the seventh day).

association between the heavenly Man and the Light that shines from God, his *kavōd*, is typically Jewish and ultimately goes back to Ezekiel 1:26–28. The passage quoted from *On the Origin of the World* also shows that the conception of the heavenly Man, the Light-Adam, was exegetically founded on Genesis 1:3 and not on Genesis 1:26–27. Given the background of this conception, it is highly improbable that the heavenly Man first entered gnostic thought and gnostic mythology via Christianity.[22] The gnostic variant of the Jewish *Anthrōpos* myth, like the hermetic variant of the *Poimandres*, must have originated in an environment pervaded with Jewish mystic speculations. But, as we noted above, the people who developed this variant, as part of the gnostic creation myth, were no longer Jews in a religious sense, even if they may have been so ethnically. The gnostic view of the creation cannot be traced back to Jewish beliefs.

The strength of the Jewish element in some gnostic texts is also borne out by the cosmology they assume, and particularly by the names of the planets and the signs of the zodiac. But certainly in the case of the planets this does not involve direct derivation from Jewish sources. Of course, names like Yao, Sabaoth, Adonaios and Eloaios are partly Hellenized forms of the Hebrew names of the Jewish God.[23] But the Jewish influence is only indirect and proceeds via magic practices, in which these names were often used for the planets. Thus the sequence 'Yao – Sabaoth – Adonaios' occurs in many magic formulas[24] and the other names are also often invoked for magic purposes. In the *Secret Book of John* and some related texts the planets and the signs of the zodiac form part of a well-known astrological system based on the correlation between the planets and their day and night houses in the zodiac. This explains why the name of a planet is sometimes given to the corresponding sign of the zodiac.[25] Some of these zodiacal names have an unmistakable Jewish background. Thus the name of the sign Aries is Yobel, the Hebrew/Aramaic word for 'ram' (*yōbēl*). Another example is the name of the sign Gemini, Adonin, a plural form of Aramaic *Adōn* ('lord, master') and apparently a rendering of Greek *Anakes* or *Anaktes* (from *anax*, 'lord, master'), which was a name for the two Dioscuri identified with the sign Gemini. The person who

[22] According to Holzhausen, *Der 'Mythos vom Menschen'*, the *Anthrōpos* myth was authored by Hellenistic Jewish exegetes strongly inspired by Platonism like Philo of Alexandria. Rabbinical sources and Greek-writing authors like Ezekiel the Dramatist do not play any significant role in his argument. In his view, the introduction of this myth into gnostic speculations took place via Christian gnostics like Valentinus (see below pp. 220–1).

[23] See p. 174.

[24] See van den Broek, *Studies in Gnosticism*, p. 71n. 15.

[25] See Pleše, *Poetics of the Gnostic Universe*, pp. 182–190.

originally devised this system must have been someone with knowledge of Hebrew/Aramaic. As a whole it is characterized by a large number of Semitic-sounding or real Hebrew names, as frequently found in magic texts. It is therefore most likely that the cosmological system of the *Secret Book of John* originally functioned in a magic context, as a kind of cosmic ladder by which the magus could reach the top of the divine world. This required knowledge of the magic names of the divine powers. In the short recension of the *Secret Book of John* this ascent to the divine world takes place via the planets:

Yaoth (Moon), Eloaios (Mercury), Astaphaios (Venus), Yao (Sun), Sabaoth (Mars), Adoni (Jupiter), Sabbataios (Saturn)

and the zodiac:

Yaoth (Leo), Hermas (Virgo), Galila (Libra), Yobel (Scorpio), Adonaios (Sagittarius), Sabaoth (Capricorn), Kainan (Aquarius), Abiressine (Pisces), Yobel (Aries), Harmoupiael (Taurus), (Melcheir-)Adonin (Gemini), Belias (Cancer).

Above the eighth heavenly sphere, in which the fixed signs of the zodiac move, is the divine world, which starts at the bottom with the four great Lights, the servants of the Son:

Eleleth, Daveithe, Oroiael and Armozel

followed by the Son himself:

the Light that was anointed with the goodness of the father and is therefore called the Anointed One or Christ

above which there are:

Barbelo, the Mother

and finally:

the Great Invisible/Virginal Spirit, the unknowable God.

There is nothing gnostic about the system per se, which must have been incorporated in the Barbelo myth via the world of magic. The probable reason for this was that it offered a structure of the cosmos and divine world which allowed the gnostic to gain access to the deity by theurgic-magic means.[26] For the author of the *Secret Book of John* this does not seem to be

[26] Unfortunately, Mastrocinque's *From Jewish Magic to Gnosticism* is of little help for a better understanding of the relationship between magic and gnostic religion. The author is an expert in ancient magical gems, and provides the reader with a mass of evidence concerning ancient magic and religious traditions, but his knowledge of authentic gnostic and early Christian literature

an important theme (anymore), but for the gnostics that frequented the school of Plotinus the ascent of the soul was the sole point of interest. The author of the *Secret Book* used the structure of the divine world provided by the system to weave his artfully constructed Pleroma around it, and then connected this with the gnostic exegesis of Genesis taken from a different source. This seems a later development, since there is no sign of it in the writings of Plotinian gnostics. Although these are later than the *Secret Book* and related texts, their use of the astrological-magic system is more an extension of the original magic application. The familiarity of the author of the *Secret Book* (or a later redactor) with magic is also shown by the long list of demons and angels that rule over the parts of the human body and the psychic affects (NHC II, 15, 29–19, 10). His familiarity with Jewish conceptions also emerges from a statement about the magic names of Cain and Abel, Yave and Eloim, who govern the elements which make up the body (NHC II, 24, 15–34; BG 62, 8–63, 12). The author shows here that he knows the Jewish interpretation of the two divine names: as the righteous one and the merciful one, though the latter has now been changed into the unrighteous one. The short recension follows the rabbinical explanation ('Elohim is the righteous one'; BG 62, 14–15) and the long recension that of Philo ('Yave is righteous'; NHC IV, 38, 4–6).[27] The same interpretation of the divine names was known to the author of *Eugnostus* (NHC III, 77, 23–78, 1; V, 6, 29–31), whose work generally bears such a distinct Hellenistic-Jewish stamp that he is best seen as a Jewish gnostic.[28] Much more could be said here about the Jewish elements in gnostic texts. Only Justin the Gnostic may be mentioned here, whose entirely individual system suggests strongly that he was a gnostic with Jewish-Christian antecedents.[29]

(e.g. the *Pastor* of Hermas is thought to be a writing called the *Shepherd Hermas* or *Hermas the Shepherd*, pp. 16–18), and of modern studies on gnostic texts and ideas as well, is too limited. His main sources about magic practices among gnostics are reports by anti-gnostic authors, Hippolytus in particular (his 'Sethians' are those of Hippolytus, *Refutatio* V, 19–22; modern studies on 'Sethianism', such as the important contributions by John D. Turner, are completely neglected). In the worst tradition of the History of Religions school, the data on gnostic magic are connected with 'related' religious conceptions from various regions (Mesopotamia, Egypt, Greece, Asia Minor) and times (from ancient Babylonia and Pharaonic Egypt to the fifth century CE). Because of this unrestrained blending of all kinds of traditions, the book comes to some ill-grounded hypotheses on the origin of important gnostic conceptions (see above p. 173n. 67, on the origin of Yaldabaoth, and p. 213n. 13, on the origin of gnostic ideas in Asia Minor and the role of Nicolaus in their Christianization).

[27] See N. A. Dahl and A. F. Segal, 'Philo and the Rabbis on the Names of God', *Journal for the Study of Judaism* 9 (1978), 1–28.

[28] See p. 119.

[29] See pp. 157–8.

There are gnostic systems in which Jewish influence is minimal or absent, and others in which the Jewish element is so marked that they must have developed in an environment diffused with Jewish conceptions, sometimes to the extent that we should seriously consider whether the authors themselves were not ethnic Jews. This does not prove that gnostic religion evolved from the Jewish religion, as so many have claimed. But it does prove that the mythological formulation of the gnostic outlook on reality often gratefully used religious conceptions available in its milieu of origin. This must have been a milieu in which Platonist, magic, Jewish and Christian ideas were common and easily connected.

CHRISTIANITY

As pointed out in Chapter 1, one of the recent trends in gnostic studies is to consider gnostic religion a typically Christian phenomenon.[30] Most scholars who subscribe to this view acknowledge at the same time a more or less strong philosophical or Jewish influence, the latter sometimes being thought to have been transmitted through Christian channels. From this perspective, the gnostic worldview has been described as 'probably the most vigorous attempt to make Christianity understandable to a (half-) educated elite through rigorous Platonization and mythologization … Gnosis is closely bound up with the theology that experimented with Platonism in the second century.'[31] In this view gnostic religion is no more than a Platonizing Christian philosophy of religion in mythical language.

The origin of the gnostic current has also been found in a radicalization of certain views that were present in Christianity from the outset. As an example of this approach a brief discussion of the views of Jens Holzhausen may be instructive. He sees the essence of gnosis in the opposition between the good God, the Father of Jesus Christ, on the one hand, and the Demiurge or evil angelic powers responsible for the material world, on the other. The starting point of this gnostic dualism is said to lie in an outlook on the death of Jesus which already occurs in the apostle Paul in the mid first century, that he was crucified by the

[30] See pp. 8–10.

[31] Markschies, *Gnosis und Christentum*, p. 37. Barbara Aland, too, in her collected essays, *Was ist Gnosis. Studien zum frühen Christentum, zu Marcion und zur kaiserzeitlichen Philosophie*, WUNT 239 (Tübingen: Mohr, 2009), starts consistently from a Christian origin. Like Markschies, she approaches gnosis from a theological viewpoint: the fact that gnosis belongs within Christianity does not mean 'that gnostic-Christian statements would be correct interpretations of Christian notions. The question of the dogmatic correctness or at least the *particula veri* of gnostic texts has to be raised' (p. 2).

world-rulers. Talking about the hidden Wisdom of God, Paul says: 'None of the rulers of this age understood this, for if they had, they would not have crucified the Lord of glory' (1 Cor. 2:8). By the 'rulers of this age' (or 'world') (*archontes tou aiōnos toutou*) Paul does not mean the political rulers, but the demonic powers which hold our world in thrall. According to Holzhausen, the crucifixion of the Son of God by these negative cosmic powers cast new light on the question of the nature and origin of our world, which led to the distinction between the liberating God and the creator of this world.[32] But this is a modern argument that has no support in the sources themselves. That human beings were beleaguered by 'the rulers, the authorities, the cosmic powers of this present darkness and the spiritual forces of evil in the heavenly places' (Eph. 6:12), was a widespread idea, which in Jewish and Christian circles was mainly associated with fallen angels, headed by Satan. Jesus' death on the cross was seen as the final victory over these powers. According to the author of the Letter to the Colossians – whether Paul or not is no matter here – God, through Christ on the cross, 'disarmed the rulers and authorities and made a public example of them, triumphing over them in it' (Col. 2:15). In the previous chapter we saw that this view of Jesus' death was also expressed in gnostic texts.[33] So, from a generally early Christian and also gnostic perspective, there is no reason to assume that precisely Jesus' death led to gnostic dualism.

For some scholars, the identification of the ignorant or simply evil Demiurge with the God of the Old Testament sprang from a strong anti-Jewish sentiment among the gnostics, which was particularly expressed in the gnostic exegesis of Genesis.[34] If this were true, one would also expect anti-Jewish polemics in the authentic gnostic texts, but this is not at all the case. If there is polemics, it is always aimed at non-gnostic Christians or against other gnostics, the Jews not being targeted at all.[35] Perhaps the Christian gnostic Saturnilus is an exception here, because according to

[32] Holzhausen, *Der 'Mythos vom Menschen'*, p. 147: 'From this perspective, it does not seem surprising that Christians were the first to separate the creator of the world from the saving God.'

[33] See p. 201.

[34] Voiced most strongly by Hans Jonas in his famous response to Quispel's thesis of Jewish origin, 'Response to G. Quispel's "Gnosticism and the New Testament"', in J. P. Hyatt (ed.), *The Bible in Modern Scholarship* (Nashville: Abingdon Press, 1965), pp. 279–93. The gnostic exegesis shows a 'spirit of vilification, of parody and caricature, of conscious perversion of meaning, wholesale reversal of value-signs, savage degrading of the sacred – of gleefully shocking blasphemy' (p. 287), and 'the nature of the relation of Gnosticism to Judaism – in itself an undeniable fact – is defined by *the anti-Jewish animus* with which it is saturated' (p. 288, Jonas's italics).

[35] See pp. 108–116.

Irenaeus he adopted a rather scathing tone in talking about the Jewish God. He already knew the gnostic exegesis of Genesis, if indeed he did not develop it himself.[36] According to Irenaeus, *AH* 1, 24, 2, Saturnilus taught that the God of the Jews was one of the angels who had created the world: 'And because the Father wanted to destroy all the archons, Christ came to destroy the God of the Jews and to save those who believed in him.' Clearly the gnostic who developed the gnostic exegesis of Genesis thought that biblical primeval history was important for explaining the current human situation. He could have been a gnostic of Jewish origin, but also a Christian gnostic. This last is certainly just as probable; as suggested above, it may have been developed by Saturnilus in the early second century. The explanation of what Christians soon started to call the Old Testament became a burning issue in the second century, as the works of the contemporaries Justin Martyr and Ptolemy show.[37] But the Holy Scripture of the Jews was also read and appreciated as a source of ancient Wisdom outside the circle of Jews and Christians, and the earliest form of the gnostic exegesis of Genesis could well have been devised by someone who did not have a Jewish or Christian background, because he could demonstrate his view of the human being and the world via the first chapters of Genesis. In any case nothing shows that the original author and the gnostics who adopted his explanation were actuated by anti-Jewish sentiment.

Those who seek the origin of gnostic religion in Christianity obviously have a problem with texts and systems in which the Christian element is (all but) absent. The usual way of coping with this is to state that a text need not be explicitly Christian to have a Christian origin. In that case scholars often find all kinds of hidden references to Christian conceptions. Countless examples could be advanced here, but it may suffice to mention just two. In the *Paraphrase of Seëm*, the Saviour Derdekeas, is identified with Christ: the figure of Soldas, who is crucified, is 'the earthly Jesus', whose body contains 'the celestial Christ'. The obscure passage which follows the 'crucifixion' is addressed to those who want to be baptized and the woman Rebouel mentioned here 'doubtless symbolizes the Great Church'.[38] A second example is the opinion that *Eugnostus the Blessed*,

[36] See pp. 171–2. According to Holzhausen, *Der 'Mythos vom Menschen'*, pp. 211–16, who sees all Christian gnostic speculations as dependent on Valentinus, the report on Saturnilus shows strong Valentinian influence; at most it could derive from a follower of Saturnilus influenced by Valentinianism: 'What Saturnilus really taught can no more be gathered from it' (p. 216).

[37] See pp. 94–6.

[38] Thus Roberge, *The Paraphrase of Shem*, p. 70; for the translation of the passage in question, see p. 121 above. The arbitrariness of such interpretations appears also in the explanation of the tower to which Seëm escaped from the Flood (see above p. 120): from the simple fact that in a

though it does not contain any explicit Christian elements (except for a few possibly Valentinian terms at the end),[39] was written by a Christian who wanted to make clear the meaning of his faith with the help of Jewish views and Greek philosophical concepts. By means of his myth he wanted to explain the meaning of Christian baptism, and the work should in fact be read against this background.[40] The first question which naturally arises here is why someone who believes he has something important to say would disguise his message so unrecognizably. This leads us to an important question which has not been sufficiently asked in gnostic scholarship: when can we say that a gnostic system or a gnostic text is Christian?

The presence of a Christian motif or the mention of the name Jesus or Christ is not in itself enough to identify a gnostic text or a gnostic system as Christian. If Jesus is only the earthly form of the Saviour Seth and is mentioned as only one among many other heavenly beings, as is the case in the *Holy Book of the Great Invisible Spirit*, or if he is only vaguely alluded to as 'True Man', who was the last in a series of almost exclusively female Enlighteners, as is the case in the *Nature of the Rulers*,[41] are we then concerned with Christian texts? We should not forget that with the spread of Christianity Christian names, stories and ideas became known to a wider public and were used by non-Christian authors in contexts that were not Christian in themselves. To declare any text with Christian terms to be Christian is to underestimate how far and how easily elements from various religions were connected with each other in the general religiosity of the first centuries. The spells of the magic papyri often contain biblical names, including those of Jesus and Christ, and Christian concepts, but this does not necessarily make them Christian. An interesting example that should be briefly mentioned here is the alchemist Zosimus, whose view of the 'light-people' (*phōtes*), the descendants of the spiritual Adam, was reported above.[42] In his *Authentic Treatises on Instruments and Furnaces*, the Letter Omega, 13, he describes how the *phōtes* are saved by Christ and kill their carnal Adam:

> He also appeared to the entirely powerless human beings, having become a man who was exposed to suffering and was whipped. And in secret he carries off as

completely different context, in the *Pastor* of Hermas, *Visiones* 3, 3, 5, a tower is said to be a symbol of the Church, the conclusion is drawn: 'Shem's presence in the tower thus symbolizes the situation of the pneumatics within the Great Church' (*ibid.*, p. 16n. 36).

39 See pp. 118–19 above.

40 Thus Pasquier, *Eugnoste. Lettre sur le Dieu transcendant*, pp. 195–205 (cf. also *ibid.*, pp. 182–7, for the possible use of New Testament texts).

41 See pp. 186–7 and 188–9.

42 See p. 216.

booty the light-people who are his own, because he did not suffer at all, but showed how death was trampled and pushed back. And up till now and till the end of the world he comes to carry off secretly and openly his own people and he advises them secretly, by stripping their spirit of the Adam that is with them, who … blinds them and is jealous of the spiritual and luminous human. They kill their own Adam.[43]

Zosimus was not an exception in his time. He is a convinced alchemist, is familiar with gnostic and in particular hermetic views, sees Christ as the Saviour of the light-people, in an apparently gnostic fashion, and has no problem connecting all this with Egyptian, Jewish and Greek mythological traditions. Although he allows Christ an important place in his religious system, it is highly uncertain whether he also saw himself as a Christian. In any case he certainly would not have been a Christian in the opinion of his contemporary Bishop Alexander of Alexandria. And, more important in this connection, notwithstanding Zosimus' obvious gnostic interpretation of Christ, no modern scholar has ever called him a Christian gnostic.[44]

It seems better to speak of Christian gnostic religion only when the figure of Jesus Christ plays a central role in it and is therefore essential. Because gnosis is about liberation from ignorance and a return to God, Christian gnosis is only involved if it is Christ the Saviour who brings this about. That is as far as the historian can go, he cannot determine whether the gnostic view of the meaning of Christ is correct or entirely wrong. He can only state that non-gnostic Christians believed that the gnostics were people 'who have strayed from the faith', as it is put in 1 Timothy 6:21. But also that great gnostic theologians like Ptolemy, Heracleon and the authors of the *Tripartite Tractate* and the *Gospel of Truth* were convinced that their interpretation of Christ and salvation was thoroughly Christian. But we saw above that in many non-Valentinian texts, too, Christ is pre-eminently the Saviour.[45] Whoever refuses to be led by a normative view of what is true Christianity cannot regard these Christian gnostics as half, errant or pseudo-Christians, even though that was how

[43] Translated after the edition by M. Mertens, *Les alchimistes grecs*, vol. IV, i, *Zosime de Panopolis, Mémoires authentiques* (Paris: Les Belles Lettres, 1995), pp. 6–7 (using the critical apparatus, the text has been poorly transmitted).

[44] Cf. A. [F.] de Jong, 'Zosimus of Panopolis', in *Dictionary of Gnosis*, p. 1185: 'In *The Letter Omega*, Zosimus chiefly uses Greek, Jewish, and Christian "proof-texts" to make his point, up to the point of introducing Jesus Christ as the person who will guide mankind back to its ultimate origins, but he invokes these texts mainly to establish connections with local Egyptian ideas, including Hermetic texts.'

[45] See pp. 190–2.

other Christians saw them. At the beginning of this book we noted that heresy is not a historical but a religious category: the historian does not recognize heresies, he merely observes religious differences of opinion, and he does not judge the correctness of these.

The idea, too, that the God and Father of Jesus Christ was not the same as the God of the Old Testament was acceptable for many Christians. This also struck an interested outsider like the anti-Christian philosopher Celsus (*c.* 180, Origen, *Contra Celsum* v, 54 and 61). For Marcion, a contemporary of Valentinus and Justin Martyr, this distinction was the essence of Christianity. He can only be called a gnostic to a certain degree; rather he was a follower of Paul who took the latter's doctrine of Law and Gospel to its ultimate conclusion. In his view, Jesus' message about the good, compassionate God was something entirely new, which took away the universal salvific meaning of everything that had gone before. Marcion was not the only Christian for whom the relationship with Judaism and therefore the authority of the Jewish Bible was not taken for granted. For him it was probably something that was no longer taken for granted, but there were also Christians who were (all but) unaware of the Jewish roots of Christianity. In fact, this was almost inevitable as Christianity became more widely disseminated throughout the ancient world. In the initial proclamation of the Christian faith, attention focused on the circle of Jews and interested heathens formed around the synagogues in the large cities. For these people, as for the preachers themselves, the authority of the Jewish Bible went without saying: there was no doubt that the God proclaimed by Jesus was the same as the biblical Creator of heaven and earth. As time progressed, exegesis of what was starting to be called the Old Testament did become a problem, but its authority remained intact. From this background the main movement of non-gnostic Christianity developed, with a theology that took its starting point more in the creation than in the revelation of Christ. The fact that Christianity remained a monotheistic religion despite its later trinitarian doctrine is due to this line of approach. However, in its proclaimed form Christianity was not a theological system but a religion of salvation with strong mystic overtones, centring on the figure of the dead and risen Christ. In the rites of baptism and Eucharist the believer participated in Christ's death and resurrection and thus experienced the certainty of union with God and an eternal life. In this way Christ could become the central divine figure in a religion of salvation in which Jewish roots no longer played any role. This is particularly seen in the apocryphal Acts of the Apostles, in which the Old Testament has completely disappeared from view and Christ is the God proclaimed by the apostles. Some of these Acts have been clearly influenced by gnostic ideas, others do not show this influence at all, but what all these texts have in common is that Christ preaches ascesis, in particular sexual abstinence. Such a central position for Christ gives rise to an autonomous type of Christianity, in which thought has a strictly Christological orientation and the Jewish background no longer plays any part. Where the Old Testament does stay in the picture it is no longer authoritative and its explanation is free. This is the case in Marcion among others and in many Christian gnostics. For them, Christ was the Saviour par excellence and they therefore saw themselves as true Christians. Under the influence of ecclesiastical historiography, from Antiquity to the present day, there is an almost ineradicable tendency to measure Christianity in a certain period by the great theologians who were directional for the future at that time. But we should be aware that the opinions of these great figures were not representative for what ordinary people believed and thought. This was the case in the first centuries and is still so today.

In conclusion it may be said that the occurrence of gnostic mythologies in which no Christian influence can be detected and of quite a few texts in which Christ does not figure or is named only in addition makes it impossible to find the origin of gnostic religion in Christianity. But the fact remains that gnostic views exerted a strong pull on second-century Christians in particular and that gnostic teachers and Marcion decisively influenced the development of non-gnostic Christian thought.

THE SPIRIT OF THE AGE

Research into the origin of the gnostic current has led to a much greater visibility of the philosophical, Jewish and Christian elements in gnostic writings. But this relates more to the form of gnostic religion than to the gnostic experience itself. The foregoing discussions of alleged origins lead to an answer that has been given before, but that has been pushed into the background amidst all the scholarly discussions. To put it simply: the gnostic mood was in the air. In the second and third centuries the cultural and religious attitude of people was imbued with a gnostic tendency, the signs of which can already be clearly seen in the first century. Virtually all aspects of gnosis and gnostic religion are present in the religious experience of these centuries; the gnostic vision is merely their most radical summation.[46] This is not to say, of course, that the traditional religious institutions did not function anymore or that gnostic religion found its primary impetus in the political, social and personal instability of the time. After all, the gnostics developed their systems and wrote their most important works in the prosperous and relatively peaceful age of the emperors Hadrian and Antoninus Pius.[47] A detailed discussion of the widespread mentality that forms the background of gnostic religion would go beyond the scope of this book, and therefore only a few general remarks will be made.

The greatest discovery of the Greek mind, that by arguing rationally we can understand and organize the world and our own lives, starts to lose its lustre in this period. The primacy of reason is supplanted, or at least driven back, by a need for legitimation based on ancient Wisdom held to be best preserved among non-Greek peoples. The conquests of Alexander the Great had put the Greeks in touch with the highly developed cultures of Persia, India and Egypt, whose influence was perpetuated by the founding of the great Greek-Hellenistic empires, in particular of the Seleucids (Syria-Mesopotamia) and the Ptolemies (Egypt). Works by Hellenized authors like the Babylonian priest Berossus (*Babyloniaca*) and the Egyptian priest Manetho (*Egyptiaca*), both in the first half of the third century BCE, familiarized the Greeks with the history and culture of their nations. People widely became convinced that the ancient 'Wisdom of the barbarians' offered a purer form of truth than Greek philosophy after Plato. Like the Brahmans in India, great figures like Zoroaster among the Persians, Moses among the Jews and Hermes Trismegistus among the Egyptians were regarded as sages who thanks to divine inspiration had received and passed on true philosophy. Only what was old could lay claim to truth. The well-known English saying 'What is new is not true and what is true is not new' characterizes the mentality of many philosophers and religious thinkers in the first centuries. Christians were therefore regularly confronted with the reproach that their religion was new, and so could not be true. They

[46] A work that remains an important overview of religious developments in the Graeco-Roman world since Alexander the Great (d. 323 BCE) is M. P. Nilsson, *Geschichte der griechischen Religion*, vol. II, *Die hellenistische und römische Zeit*, Handbuch der Altertumswissenschaft, section V, 2.2, 4th edn (Munich: C. H. Beck'sche Verlagsbuchhandlung, 1988), especially pp. 310–73. Also highly instructive, especially for the third century, is E. R. Dodds, *Pagan and Christian in an Age of Anxiety. Some Aspects of Religious Experience from Marcus Aurelius to Constantine* (Cambridge University Press, 1965).

[47] As was already pointed out by Dodds, *Pagan and Christian*, p. 4.

defended themselves by arguing that they were going back to Moses. This was actually a Jewish apologetic motif: Pythagoras and Plato had been influenced by Moses. Even Greek philosophers like Numenius assumed the truth of this, hence his statement 'For what is Plato but an Attic-speaking Moses?'[48] Following the same mind-set Plutarch (*c.* 100 CE) saw his Greek philosophy confirmed in the Egyptian myth of Isis and Osiris (*De Iside et Osiride*), and for the later Neoplatonists a work like the *Oracula Chaldaica*, by the theurgist Julian (*c.* 180), could become a kind of Bible in which they found authentication of their thought.[49] This makes it understandable that the gnostics preferred to cloak their views in myths and that they found their thought corroborated in biblical primeval history, which was considered to go back to Moses. In this regard they were doing the same as the Greek Numenius, the Jew Philo and the Christian Origen. The gnostic exegesis of Genesis should therefore not be seen as originating from an anti-Jewish outlook, but rather as expressing the conviction that the books of Moses secretly contained ancient Wisdom. As we remarked earlier, the author of the first gnostic exegesis need not necessarily have been a Jew or a Christian, though he must have been familiar with Jewish traditions.

As a result of the disappearance of the fixed structures of the Greek city-state and a globalizing worldview, the Hellenistic era sees an increasing conjunction of individualization and feelings of uncertainty. There is a growing sense that evil powers rule the world and threaten individual lives. The belief in demons, good and evil, starts to dominate religion. They were thought to wield their influence in the region under the moon and thus formed an intermediate layer between the world of the gods and that of mankind. In his book about the decline of the oracles Plutarch does not specify whether the doctrine of demons goes back to Zoroaster, Orpheus, the Egyptians or the Phrygians, but it seems clear to him that there is a foreign influence (*De defectu oraculorum* 415a). We can in fact assume that the extraordinary rise in demonic belief involved oriental influences. In early Judaism the demons, malevolent angels, started to play an increasing role. When Paul in Ephesians 6:12 talks about 'heavenly princes, rulers and powers of darkness and evil spirits from the heavenly spheres', Greeks and Jews knew exactly what

48 See p. 210.

49 Editions by Majercik, *The Chaldaean Oracles*, and des Places, *Oracles Chaldaïques*. See H. Lewy, *Chaldaean Oracles and Theurgy. Mysticism, Magic and Platonism in the Later Roman Empire* (Cairo: Institut Français d'Archéologie Orientale, 1956; new edn with important additions by M. Tardieu, Paris: Études Augustiniennes, 1978).

he meant. According to the *Rule of the Community*, one of the Dead Sea scrolls, God appointed two spirits: the Prince or Angel of Light and that of Darkness (3, 17–4, 1), of whom the first rules over the righteous and the second over the unrighteous. In the final days, according to the *War Scroll*, a fierce conflict will break out between the Children of Light and the Children of Darkness.[50] This is strongly reminiscent of Saturnilus' view that the creating angels made two kinds of people, good and evil. The evil people are supported by the demons, but they will be destroyed by the Saviour.[51] However, similar views were also developed in Greek philosophy. We pointed above to Numenius' opinion that there are two world-souls, a positive and a negative one, and that the human being also contains two souls, a rational and an irrational soul.[52] Similar ideas are found in Plutarch, who says in his book about Isis and Osiris that there is an ancient view, of unknown origin, that life and the cosmos are dominated by two powers, of which one leads directly to the good and the other bends away towards evil. He adds that the view of most and the wisest people is the following: there are two opposing gods, one the creator of the good and the other the creator of evil; others do not call the evil creator a god but a demon. He attributes this last position to Zoroaster, after which he expounds on the Persian gods Ahura Mazda and Ahriman, the representatives of Light and Darkness (*De Iside et Osiride* 45–7 (369a–370c)).[53] Starting from the myth of Isis and Osiris, Plutarch puts forward Osiris as the highest, good God and his opponent Typhon as the anti-divine principle of evil. Isis is the female, creative principle, which partly coincides with matter; she is not perfect, but has an inherent striving for the good. Clearly the step from such a view of Isis to the Sophia of gnostic mythology is not a very large one.[54] But for all the negative views of earthly reality and the pernicious influence of the powers of evil on it, the creation as such is not evil in Plutarch (nor in Numenius): it remains a cosmos, a beautifully ordered whole, because the unordered matter was ordered by the Logos. There is no Greek philosopher who says that the world was created by an evil god, but it is not surprising that there were people who did reach this conclusion. The

[50] F. García Martínez, *The Dead Sea Scrolls Translated. The Qumran Texts in English* (Leiden: Brill, 1994), pp. 6 and 95–125.

[51] See p. 172.

[52] See pp. 209–10.

[53] A detailed discussion of this report on Zoroastrian religion can be found in A. [F.] de Jong, *Traditions of the Magi. Zoroastrianism in Greek and Latin Literature*, RGRW 133 (Leiden: Brill, 1997), pp. 155–204.

[54] On Plutarch's philosophy: Dillon, *Middle Platonists*, pp. 184–230.

widening gap between the unchanging world of the highest, good God and the changeable and dangerous world in which we humans have to live made such a conclusion almost unavoidable.

The demonization of the worldview led to the position that the supralunary heavenly spheres were also governed by evil powers. This became an important point in connection with the view, widespread since Plato, that the soul originated from the divine world and had ended up in the earthly sphere because it had lost its feathers. As pointed out above, Numenius taught that the soul, in its descent through the planetary spheres, puts on the psychic capabilities by which it can function in the body, but which can also be a source of evil.[55] In the Hermetic *Poimandres* (Corpus Hermeticum I, 25) all these psychic properties are bad (cunning, desire, greed, mendacity, etc.), and they must therefore be cast off again when the soul ascends to its divine origin. The planetary spirits become malevolent gatekeepers, who refuse passage to the soul if it cannot correctly answer their questions or show magic signs. The magician is able to pacify these powers and thus clear the way upwards. The most famous example of such an ascent to the supreme God is the so-called 'Mithras Liturgy'.[56] The gnostic heavenly journey of the soul features the same magic aspects and describes the same transformation into a superhuman nature. The fact that it also found in Jewish texts points to the wide dissemination of such views and endeavours.[57]

The certainty that there is a pure, divine world from which the core of our being comes, the awareness that we have become alienated from our origin and trapped in material reality, which is governed by evil powers, the yearning for the world of God and the insight that we cannot return to it without divine help, the religious interpretation of the philosophical conviction that knowledge leads to truth – all these components of the gnostic sense of life were widespread in the second century. Gnostic religion arose from an intuitively grasped cohesion of diverse elements of Hellenistic religious syncretism.

The gnostic vision cannot be traced back to Platonism, Judaism or Christianity, but Platonists, Jews and Christians with a gnostic attitude, a gnostic frame of mind, did formulate this vision in terms deriving from their traditions. Its most radical form believed that the world had been produced by an ignorant, limited or even evil god. It is likely that this radical view was first given a detailed mythical form in Alexandria, on

[55] See p. 209. [56] See p. 142. [57] See p. 143.

which many variations were developed. And as often with radical solutions, their simplicity attracted many, and they therefore provoked the greatest resistance. But there were also less drastic views. Whatever the formulation, all forms of gnostic religion centred – and still centre – on liberation from the powers which rule us and on the return to our origin, God and his world, thanks to a spiritual insight (gnosis) revealed by a saviour or, less mythically, by inner enlightenment.

Bibliography

SOURCES

GREEK AND LATIN AUTHORS

Foerster, W., *Gnosis: A Selection of Gnostic Texts*, trans. and ed. R. McL. Wilson, vol. I, *Patristic Evidence* (Oxford: Clarendon Press, 1972; = *Die Gnosis*, vol. I, *Zeugnisse der Kirchenväter* (Zurich: Artemis Verlag, 1969, rev. edn 1995)).

Holl, K. (ed.), *Epiphanius (Ancoratus und Panarion)*, vol. I, *Ancoratus und Panarion haer. 1–33*, GCS 25 (Leipzig: Hinrichs, 1915), vol. II, *Panarion haer. 34–64*, GCS 31, 2nd rev. edn, ed. J. Dummer (Berlin: Akademie Verlag, 1980), vol. III, *Panarion haer. 65–80. De fide*, GCS 37, 2 bearbeitete Aufl., herausgegeben vom J. Dummer (Berlin: Akademie Verlag, 1985).

Marcovich, M. (ed.), *Hippolytus. Refutatio omnium haeresium*, Patristische Texte und Studien 25 (Berlin and New York: Walter de Gruyter, 1986).

Quispel, G. (ed.), *Ptolémée: Lettre à Flora*, SC 24 bis (Paris: Les Éditions du Cerf, 1966).

Rousseau, A. and L. Doutreleau (eds.), *Irenée de Lyon. Contre les Hérésies*, 10 vols., SC 263, 264 (Livre I), 293, 294 (Livre II), 210, 211 (Livre III), 100(1), 100(2) (Livre IV), 152, 153 (Livre V) (Paris: Les Éditions du Cerf, 1952–82).

Sagnard, F. (ed), *Clément d'Alexandrie: Extraits de Théodote*, SC 23 (Paris: Les Éditions du Cerf, 1948, 1970).

Völker, W. (ed.), *Quellen zur Geschichte der christlichen Gnosis*, Sammlung ausgewählter kirchen- und dogmengeschichtlicher Quellenschriften, Neue Folge, 5 (Tübingen: J. C. B. Mohr [Paul Siebeck]), 1932).

Wendland, P. (ed.), *Hippolytus. Refutatio omnium haeresium*, Hippolytus' Werke, vol. III, GCS 26 (Leipzig: Hinrichs, 1916).

COPTIC GNOSTIC TEXTS

The Codex Askewianus and the Codex Brucianus

Baynes, C. A. (ed.), *A Coptic Gnostic Treatise Contained in the Codex Brucianus* (Cambridge University Press, 1933).

Foerster, W., *Gnosis: A Selection of Gnostic Texts*, trans. and ed. R. McL. Wilson, vol. II, *Coptic and Mandaean Sources* (Oxford: Clarendon Press, 1974; = *Die*

Gnosis, vol. II, *Koptische und mandäische Quellen* (Zurich: Artemis Verlag, 1971, rev. edn 1995)).

MacDermot, V. (ed.), *The Books of Jeu and the Untitled Text in the Bruce Codex*, NHS 13 (Leiden: Brill, 1978), reprint of Schmidt's 1892 edn, trans. and notes by MacDermot.

Pistis Sophia, NHS 9 (Leiden: Brill, 1978), reprint of Schmidt's 1925 edn, trans. and notes by MacDermot.

Schmidt, C. (ed.), *Gnostische Schriften in koptischer Sprache aus dem Codex Brucianus*, TU 8, 1–2 (Leipzig: Hinrichs, 1892).

Koptisch-gnostischen Schriften, vol. 1, Die Pistis Sophia, Die beiden Bücher des Jeû, Unbekanntes altgnostisches Werk, GCS 13 (Leipzig: Hinrichs, 1905, rev. edns in 1925, 1954 (by W. C. Till) and 1981 (by H.-M. Schenke)).

Pistis Sophia, neu herausgegeben mit Einleitung nebst griechischem Wort- und Namenregister, Coptica 2 (Copenhagen: Gyldendalske Boghandel-Nordisk Forlag, 1925).

Berlin Gnostic Papyrus 8502 (BG)

Parrot, D. M. (ed.), *Nag Hammadi Codices III, 3–4 and V, 1 with Papyrus Berolinensis 8502, 3 and Oxyrhynchus Papyrus 1081: Eugostus and The Sophia of Jesus Christ* (NHS 27 (Leiden: Brill, 1991).

Pasquier, A. (ed.), *L'Évangile selon Marie (BG 1)*, BCNH-T. 10 (Quebec: Presses de l'Université Laval, 1983, with the Greek fragment.

Till, W. C. (ed.), *Die gnostischen Schriften des koptischen Papyrus Berolinensis 8502*, TU 60 (Berlin: Akademie-Verlag, 1955; 2nd rev. edn H.-M. Schenke, 1972).

Waldstein, M. and F. Wisse (eds.), *The Apocryphon of John. Synopsis of Nag Hammadi Codices II, 1; III, 1; and IV, 1 with BG 8502, 2*, NHMS 33 (Leiden: Brill, 1995).

Wilson, R. McL. and G. W. MacRae (eds.), *The Gospel According to Mary, BG, 1: 7,1–19,5*, in D. M. Parrott (ed.), *Nag Hammadi Codices V,2–5 and VI with Papyrus Berolinensis 8502, 1 and 4*, NHS 11 (Leiden: Brill, 1979), pp. 453–71, with the Greek fragment.

The Nag Hammadi library

Bibel der Häretiker. Die Gnostische Schriften aus Nag Hammadi, Introduction, trans. and commentary G. Lüdemann and M. Janssen (Stuttgart: Radius-Verlag, 1997).

Bibliothèque Copte de Nag Hammadi, Section 'Textes' (Quebec: Presses de l'Université de Laval; Louvain and Paris: Éditions Peeters, 1977–2010), more than 30 vols. published, with French translations and extensive commentaries.

Concordance des textes de Nag Hammadi, BCNH, Section 'Concordances', 8 vols. (Quebec: Presses de l'Université Laval; Louvain and Paris: Éditions Peeters, 1992–2006).

The Coptic Gnostic Library, General Editor J. M. Robinson, NHS 4, 15, 11, 20, 21, 22, 23, 26, 28, 31 and NHMS 30, 33 (Leiden: Brill, 1975–96; paperback edn 2000), complete edition of the Nag Hammadi codices, with English translations and (mostly brief) commentaries.

Écrits gnostiques. La Bibliothèque de Nag Hammadi, General Editors J.-P. Mahé and P.-H. Poirier (Paris: Gallimard, 2007), annotated French translation.

The Facsimile Edition of the Nag Hammadi Codices, ed. J. M. Robinson, 13 vols. (Leiden: Brill, 1972–84).

The Nag Hammadi Library in English, trans. and introduced Members of the Coptic Library Project of the Institute for Antiquity and Christianity, Claremont, CA, General Editor J. M. Robinson, 4th rev. edn (Leiden: Brill, 1996).

The Nag Hammadi Scriptures. The International Edition, ed. M. Meyer (San Francisco: HarperOne, 2007).

Nag Hammadi Deutsch, ed. H.-M. Schenke, H-G. Bethge and U. U. Kaiser, 2 vols., GCS, Neue Folge, 8 and 12 (Berlin and New York: Walter de Gruyter, 2001, 2003).

Codex Tchacos

The Gospel of Judas together with The Letter of Peter to Philip, James, and a Book of Allogenes from Codex Tchacos. Critical Edition, Coptic text ed. R. Kasser and G. Wurst, introductions, translations and notes R. Kasser, M. Meyer, G. Wurst and F. Gaudard (Washington, DC: National Geographic, 2007).

Brankaer, J. and H.-G. Bethge (eds.), *Codex Tchacos. Texte und Analysen*, TU 161 (Berlin: Walter de Gruyter, 2007).

Krosney, H., M. Meyer and G. Wurst, 'Preliminary Report on New Fragments of Codex Tchacos', *Early Christianity* 1 (2010), 282–94.

Wurst, G., 'Addenda et corrigenda to the Critical Edition of the Gospel of Judas', in DeConick (ed.), *The Codex Judas Papers*, pp. 503–7.

LITERATURE

Aland, B., *Was ist Gnosis. Studien zum frühen Christentum, zu Marcion und zur kaiserzeitlichen Philosophie*, WUNT 239 (Tübingen: Mohr, 2009).

Alexander, P., '3 (Hebrew Apocalypse of) Enoch', in J. H. Charlesworth (ed.), *The Old Testament Pseudepigrapha*, vol. 1 (Peabody, MA: Hendrickson, 2009; = Yale University Press, 1983), pp. 223–315.

Aragione, G. and E. Norelli (eds.), *Des évêques, des écoles et des hérétiques. Actes du colloque international sur la 'Réfutation de toutes les hérésies', Genève, 13–14 juin 2008* (Prahins: Édition du Zèbre, 2011).

Armstrong, A. H., *Plotinus, with an English Translation*, 6 vols., Loeb Classical Library 440–5 (London: W. Heinemann; Cambridge, MA: Harvard University Press, 1966–88).

Asgeirsson, J. M., A. D. DeConick and R. Uro (eds.), *Thomasine Traditions in Antiquity: The Social and Cultural World of Thomas*, NHMS 59 (Leiden: Brill, 2006).

Barc, B. (ed.), *Colloque international sur les textes de Nag Hammadi (Québec, 22–25 août 1978)*, BCNH-É 1 (Quebec: Presses de l'Université Laval; Louvain: Éditions Peeters, 1981).

Barnstone, W. and M. Meyer (eds.), *The Gnostic Bible*, rev. edn (Boston and London: Shambhala, 2009).

Bee, G., 'Audians', in *Dictionary of Gnosis*, 141–2.

Beeson, C. H. (ed.), *Hegemonius. Acta Archelai*, GCS 16 (Leipzig: Hinrichs, 1906).

Bertrand, D. A., 'Hippolyte de Rome', in R. Goulet (ed.), *Dictionnnaire des philosophes antiques*, vol. III (Paris: Éditions du CNRS, 2000), pp. 791–9.

Betz, H. D., *The 'Mithras Liturgy'. Text, Translation and Commentary*, STAC 18 (Tübingen: Mohr, 2003; paperback edn 2005).

Betz, H. D. (ed.), *The Greek Magical Papyri in Translation, including the Demotic Spells* (Chicago and London: University of Chicago Press, 1986).

Bianchi, U. (ed.), *Le origini dello gnosticismo / The Origins of Gnosticism. Colloquium of Messina 13–18 April 1966*, SHR 12 (Leiden: Brill, 1967).

Bible, The Holy, containing The Old and New Testaments. New Revised Standard Version, Anglicized Edition (Cambridge University Press, 2007, reprinted 2011).

Bonner, C., 'An Amulet of the Ophite Gnostics', in *Commemorative Studies in Honor of Theodore Leslie Shear*, Hesperia Supplements 8 (Princeton: American School of Classical Studies at Athens, 1949), pp. 43–6, Plate 8, no. 1.

Studies in Magical Amulets, Chiefly Graeco-Egyptian (Ann Arbor: University of Michigan Press; London: Oxford University Press, 1950).

Boulluec, A. le, *La notion d'hérésie dans la littérature grecque, IIe–IIIe siècles*, 2 vols. (Paris: Études Augustiniennes, 1985).

Brach, J.-P., 'Number Symbolism', *Dictionary of Gnosis*, pp. 874–83.

Brakke, D., *The Gnostics. Myth, Ritual, and Diversity in Early Christianity* (Cambridge, MA and London: Harvard University Press, 2010).

Brashear, W., 'Seth-Gebet', *Archiv für Papyrusforschung und verwandte Gebiete* 42 (1996), 26–34.

Brent, A., *Hippolytus and the Roman Church in the Third Century: Communities in Tension before the Emergence of a Monarch-Bishop*, Supplements to Vigiliae Christianae 31 (Leiden: Brill, 1995).

'The Elenchos and the Identification of Christian Communities in Second-early Third century Rome', in Aragione and Norelli (eds.), *Des évêques, des écoles et des hérétiques*, pp. 275–314.

Brisson, P. *et al.*, *Porphyre. La Vie de Plotin*, 2 vols. (Paris: Vrin, 1982–92).

Broek, R. van den, 'Archontics', in *Dictionary of Gnosis*, pp. 89–91.

'The Gnostic Christ', in O. Hammer (ed.), *Alternative Christs* (Cambridge University Press, 2009), pp. 16–32.

'Gnosticism I: Gnostic Religion', in *Dictionary of Gnosis*, pp. 403–16.
'Gnosticism II: Gnostic Literature, in *Dictionary of Gnosis*, pp. 417–32.
'Gospel Tradition and Salvation in Justin the Gnostic', *VC* 57 (2003), 363–388.
'Hermes Trismegistus I: Antiquity', in *Dictionary of Gnosis*, pp. 474–8.
'The Hermetic Apocalypse and other Greek Predictions of the End of Religion', in van den Broek and van Heertum (eds.), *From Poimandres to Jacob Böhme*, pp. 97–113.
'Hermetic Literature I: Antiquity', in *Dictionary of Gnosis*, pp. 487–99.
'Hermetism', in *Dictionary of Gnosis*, pp. 558–70.
'Justin the Gnostic', in *Dictionary of Gnosis*, pp. 656–8.
'Manichaean Elements in an Early Version of the Virgin Mary's Assumption', in A. Houtman, A. de Jong and M. Misset-van de Weg (eds.), *Empsychoi Logoi. Religious Innovations in Antiquity. Studies in Honour of Pieter Willem van der Horst*, Ancient Judaism and Early Christianity 73 (Leiden: Brill, 2008), pp. 293–316.
'Monoimus', in *Dictionary of Gnosis*, pp. 800–1.
'Naassenes', in *Dictionary of Gnosis*, pp. 820–2.
'Religious Practices in the Hermetic 'Lodge': New Light from Nag Hammadi', in van den Broek and van Heertum (eds.), *From Poimandres to Jacob Böhme*, pp. 77–95.
'Sexuality and Sexual Symbolism in Hermetic and Gnostic Thought and Practice (Second to Fourth Centuries)', in Hanegraaff and Kripal (eds.), *Hidden Intercourse*, pp. 1–21.
'Spiritual Transformation in Ancient Hermetism and Gnosticism', in R. A. Gilbert (ed.), *Knowledge of the Heart. Gnostic Movements and Secret Traditions*, Canonbury Papers 5 (London: Lewis Masonic, 2008), pp. 30–43.
Studies in Gnosticism and Alexandrian Christianity, NHMS 39 (Leiden: Brill, 1996).
Broek, R. van den, T. Baarda and J. Mansfeld (eds.), *Knowledge of God in the Graeco-Roman World*, EPRO 112 (Leiden: Brill, 1988).
Broek, R. van den and C. van Heertum (eds.), *From Poimandres to Jacob Böhme: Gnosis, Hermetism and the Christian Tradition* (Amsterdam: In de Pelikaan, 2000).
Broek, R. van den and M. J. Vermaseren (eds.), *Studies in Gnosticism and Hellenistic Religions Presented to Gilles Quispel on the Occasion of his 65th Birthday*, EPRO 91 (Leiden: Brill, 1981).
Bultmann, R., '*ginōskō*, *gnōsis*, etc.', in G. Kittel *et al.* (eds.), *Theological Dictionary of the New Testament*, vol. 1, trans. G. W. Bromiley (Grand Rapids, MI: W. B. Eerdmans, 1964), pp. 688–719 (= *Theologisches Wörterbuch zum Neuen Testament*, I (Stuttgart: W. Kohlhammer, 1933), pp. 688–719).
Cameron, R. and A. J. Dewey, *The Cologne Mani Codex (P. Colon. Inv. Nr. 4780) 'Concerning the Origin of his Body'*, Early Christian Literature Series 3: Text and Translations 15 (Missoula, MT: Scholars Press, 1979).

Carcopino, J., *De Pythagore aux Apôtres. Études sur la conversion du monde romain* (Paris: Flammarion, 1956).

Chadwick, H., *The Sentences of Sextus. A Contribution to the History of Early Christian Ethics* (Cambridge University Press, 1959).

Colpe, C., *Die religionsgeschichtliche Schule: Darstellung und Kritik ihres Bildes vom gnostischen Erlösermythus*, FRLANT 78 (Göttingen: Vandenhoeck & Ruprecht, 1961).

Conner, M., *Voices of Gnosticism* (Dublin: Bardic Press, 2011).

Copenhaver, B., *Hermetica. The Greek* Corpus Hermeticum *and the Latin* Asclepius *in a New English Translation with Notes and Introduction* (Cambridge University Press, 1992).

Crum, W. E., *A Coptic Dictionary* (Oxford: Clarendon Press, 1939).

Dahl, N. A., 'The Arrogant Archon and the Lewd Sophia: Jewish Traditions in Gnostic Revolt', in Layton (ed.), *The Rediscovery of Gnosticism*, vol. II, pp. 689–712.

Dahl, N. A. and A. F. Segal, 'Philo and the Rabbis on the Names of God', *Journal for the Study of Judaism* 9 (1978), 1–28.

DeConick, A. D., 'Conceiving Spirits: The Mystery of Valentinian Sex', in Hanegraaff and Kripal (eds.), *Hidden Intercourse*, pp. 23–48.

Recovering the Original Gospel of Thomas: A History of the Gospel and its Growth, Library of New Testament Studies 286 (London and New York: T&T Clark, 2005).

The Thirteenth Apostle. What the Gospel of Judas Really Says, rev. edn (London and New York: Continuum, 2009).

DeConick A. D. (ed.), *The Codex Judas Papers. Proceedings of the International Congress on the Tchacos Codex held at Rice University, Houston, Texas, March 13–16, 2008*, NHMS 71 (Leiden: Brill, 2009).

Denzey, N., 'Genesis Traditions in Conflict? The Use of some Exegetical Traditions in the Trimorphic Protennoia and the Johannine Prologue', *VC* 55 (2001), 20–44

Dictionary of Gnosis and Western Esotericism, ed. W. J. Hanegraaff, in collaboration with A. Faivre, R. van den Broek and J.-P. Brach, 2 vols. (Leiden: Brill, 2005; reprint in one volume 2006, same pagination).

Dillon, J., *The Middle Platonists. A Study of Platonism 80 B.C. to A.D. 220* (London: Duckworth, 1977).

Dodds, E. R., *Pagan and Christian in an Age of Anxiety. Some Aspects of Religious Experience from Marcus Aurelius to Constantine* (Cambridge University Press, 1965).

Dornseiff, F., *Das Alphabet in Mystik und Magie*, 2nd edn, Stoicheia 7 (Leipzig and Berlin: B. G. Teubner, 1925, reprinted Leipzig: Zentralantiquariat der Deutschen Demokratischen Republik, 1975).

Dunderberg, I., *Beyond Gnosticism: Myth, Lifestyle, and Society in the School of Valentinus* (New York: Columbia University Press, 2008).

Förster, N., 'Die Bedeutung des sogenannten Eucharistiesakramentes der Markosier und die Texte aus Nag Hammadi', in S. Emmel *et al.* (eds.),

Ägypten und Nubien in spätantiker und christlicher Zeit. Akten des 6. Internationalen Koptologenkongresses, Münster, 20.–26. Juli 1996, vol. II, *Schrifttum, Sprache und Gedankenwelt*, Sprachen und Kulturen des christlichen Orients 6(2) (Wiesbaden: Reichert Verlag 1999), pp. 465–73.

Marcus Magus: Kult, Lehre und Gemeindeleben einer valentinianischen Gnostikergruppe. Sammlung der Quellen und Kommentar, WUNT 114 (Tübingen: Mohr, 1999).

Fossum J. E., *The Image of the Invisible God. Essays on the Influence of Jewish Mysticism on Early Christology*, NTOA 30 (Freiburg Universitätsverlag; Göttingen: Vandenhoeck & Ruprecht, 1995).

The Name of God and the Angel of the Lord. Samaritan and Jewish Concepts of Intermediation and the Origin of Gnosticism, WUNT 36 (Tübingen: Mohr, 1985).

Fowden, G., *The Egyptian Hermes. A Historical Approach to the Late Pagan Mind*, rev. paperback edn (Princeton University Press, 1993).

Franzmann, M., *Jesus in the Nag Hammadi Writings* (Edinburgh: T&T Clark, 1996).

Funk, W.-P., 'The Significance of the Tchacos Codex for Understanding the First Apocalypse of James', in DeConick (ed.), *The Codex Judas Papers*, pp. 509–33.

García Martínez, F., *The Dead Sea Scrolls Translated. The Qumran Texts in English* (Leiden: Brill, 1994).

Gardner, I. and S. N. C. Lieu (eds.), *Manichaean Texts from the Roman Empire* (Cambridge University Press, 2004).

Gilhus, I. S., *The Nature of the Archons. A Study in the Soteriology of a Gnostic Treatise from Nag Hammadi (CG II, 4)*, Studies in Oriental Religions 12 (Wiesbaden: Harrassowitz, 1985).

Graf, F., 'Magic II: Antiquity', in *Dictionary of Gnosis*, pp. 719–24.

Grant, R. M., 'Charges of "Immorality" against Various Religious Groups in Antiquity', in van den Broek and Vermaseren (eds.), *Studies in Gnosticism and Hellenistic Religions*, pp. 61–170.

Griffith, M., *Sophocles: Antigone* (Cambridge University Press, 1999).

Hanegraaff, W. J., *Esotericism and the Academy. Rejected Knowledge in Western Culture* (Cambridge University Press, 2012).

Hanegraaff, W. J. and J. J. Kripal (eds.), *Hidden Intercourse. Eros and Sexuality in the History of Western Esotericism*, Aries Book Series. Texts and Studies in Western Esotericism 7 (Leiden: Brill, 2008; paperback edn New York: Fordham University Press, 2011).

Himmelmann, H., *Das Hypogäum der Aurelii am Viale Manzoni: Ikonographische Beobachtungen*, Akademie der Wissenschaften und der Literatur. Mainz, Abhandlungen der geistes- und sozialwissenschaftlichen Klasse 7 (Wiesbaden: Steiner, 1975).

Holzhausen, J., *Der 'Mythos vom Menschen' im hellenistischen Ägypten. Eine Studie zum 'Poimandres' (= CH I), zu Valentin und dem gnostischen Mythos*, Theophaneia 33 (Bodenheim: Athenäum-Hain-Hanstein, 1994).

'Valentinus and Valentinians', in *Dictionary of Gnosis*, pp. 1144–57.

Horst, P. W. van der, 'Moses' Throne Vision in Ezekiel the Dramatist', in *Essays on the Jewish World of Early Christianity*, NTOA 14 (Freiburg: Universitätsverlag; Göttingen: Vandenhoeck & Ruprecht, 1990), pp. 63–71.

Jackson, H. M., 'The Origin in Ancient Incantory *Voces Magicae* of some Names in the Sethian Gnostic System', *VC* 43 (1989), 69–79.

Jastrow, M., *A Dictionary of the Targumim, the Talmud Babli and Yerushalmi, and the Midrashic Literature* (London: Luzac & Co.; New York: G. Putnam's Sons, 1903).

Jonas, H., 'Response to G. Quispel's "Gnosticism and the New Testament"', in J. P. Hyatt (ed.), *The Bible in Modern Scholarship* (Nashville: Abingdon Press, 1965), pp. 279–93.

Jong, A. [F.] de, *Traditions of the Magi. Zoroastrianism in Greek and Latin Literature*, RGRW 133 (Leiden: Brill, 1997).

'Zosimus of Panopolis', in *Dictionary of Gnosis*, pp. 1183–6.

Kaestli, J.-D., 'Valentinisme italien et valentinisme oriental: leur divergences à propos de la nature du corps de Jésus', in Layton (ed.), *The Rediscovery of Gnosticism*, vol. 1, pp. 391–403.

Kaler, M., 'The Letter of Peter to Philip and its Messages of Gnostic Revelation and Christian Unity', *VC* 63 (2009), 264–95.

Kalvesmaki, J., 'Italian versus Eastern Valentinianism?', *VC* 62 (2008), 79–89.

Karamanolis, K., 'Numenius', *Stanford Encyclopedia of Philosophy*, internet editon: http://plato.stanford.edu/entries/numenius (4 May 2009).

Keizer, H. M., 'Life, Time, Entirety. A Study of Aion in Greek Literature and Philosophy, the Septuagint and Philo' (digital dissertation, University of Amsterdam, 1999).

Kelly, J. N. D., *Early Christian Creeds*, 3rd edn (London: Longman, 1972).

Kerchove, A. van den, *La voie d'Hermès. Pratiques rituelles et traités hermétiques*, NHMS 77 (Leiden: Brill, 2012).

King, K. L., *The Secret Revelation of John* (Cambridge, MA and London: Harvard University Press, 2006).

What is Gnosticism? (Cambridge, MA and London: The Belknap Press of Harvard University Press, 2003; paperback edn 2005).

Koenen, L. and C. Römer, *Der Kölner Mani-Kodex. Über das Werden seines Leibes. Kritische Edition aufgrund der von A. Henrichs und L. Koenen besorgten Erstedition*, Papyrologica Coloniensia 14 (Opladen: Westdeutscher Verlag, 1988).

Mani. Auf der Spur einer verschollenen Religion (Freiburg, Basle and Vienna: Herder, 1993).

Koester, H., *Ancient Christian Gospels: Their History and Development* (London: SCM Press; Philadelphia: Trinity Press International, 1990).

Krämer, H. J., *Der Ursprung der Geistmetaphysik. Untersuchungen zur Geschichte des Platonismus zwischen Platon und Plotin* (Amsterdam: P. Schippers, 1964, 2nd edn 1967).

Krosney, H., *The Lost Gospel: The Quest for the Gospel of Judas Iscariot* (Washington, DC: National Geographic, 2006).

'The Tchacos Fragments in Court', in Krosney, Meyer and Wurst, 'Preliminary Report', pp. 282–5.

Krosney, H., M. Meyer and G. Wurst, 'Preliminary Report on New Fragments of Codex Tchacos', *Early Christianity* 1 (2010), 282–94.

Lampe, G. W. H., *A Patristic Greek Lexicon* (Oxford: Clarendon Press, 1961).

Layton, B., *A Coptic Grammar, with Chrestomathy and Glossary. Sahidic Dialect*, Porta Linguarum Orientalium 20 (Wiesbaden: Harrassowitz, 2000).

The Gnostic Scriptures. A New Translation with Annotations and Introductions (Garden City, NY: Doubleday, 1987).

'Prolegomena to the Study of Ancient Gnosticism', in L. M. White and O. L. Yarbrough (eds.), *The Social World of the First Christians. Essays in Honor of Wayne A. Meeks* (Minneapolis: Fortress Press, 1995), pp. 334–50.

Layton, B. (ed.), *The Rediscovery of Gnosticism, Proceedings of the International Conference on Gnosticism at Yale, New Haven, Connecticut, March 28–31, 1978*, 2 vols., SHR 41 (Leiden: Brill, 1981).

Leask, N., 'Bruce, James, of Kinnaird', in *Oxford Dictionary of National Biography*, vol. VIII (Oxford University Press, 2004), pp. 303–6.

Létourneau, P., *Le Dialogue du Sauveur (NH III, 5)*, BCNH-T 28 (Quebec: Presses de l'Université Laval; Louvain: Peeters, 2003).

Lewis, N. D., '*Apolytrosis* as Ritual and Sacrament: Determining a Ritual Context for Death in Second-Century Marcosian Valentinianism', *JECS* 17 (2009), 525–61.

Lewy, H. *Chaldaean Oracles and Theurgy. Mysticism, Magic and Platonism in the Later Roman Empire* (Cairo: Institut Français d'Archéologie Orientale, 1956; new edn with important additions by M. Tardieu, Paris: Études Augustiniennes, 1978).

Liddell, H. G. and R. Scott, *A Greek–English Lexicon*, new edn rev. and augmented throughout by H. Stuart Jones and R. McKenzie (Oxford: Clarendon Press, 1940).

Lilla, S. R. C., *Clement of Alexandria. A Study in Christian Platonism and Gnosticism* (Oxford University Press, 1971).

Logan, A. H. B., *Gnostic Truth and Christian Heresy. A Study in the History of Gnosticism* (Edinburgh: T&T Clarke, 1996).

The Gnostics. Identifying an Early Christian Cult (London and New York: T&T Clark, 2006).

Löhr, W.A., 'Basilides', in *Dictionary of Gnosis*, pp. 164–8.

'The Continuing Construction of Heresy: Hippolytus' Refutatio in Context', in Aragione and Norelli (eds.), *Des évêques, des écoles et des hérésies*, pp. 25–42.

'Perates', in *Dictionary of Gnosis*, pp. 939–40.

'Sethians', in *Dictionary of Gnosis*, pp. 1066–8.

Loisy, A., *L'Évangile et l'Église* (Paris: Picard, 1902).

Lundhaug, H., *Images of Rebirth. Cognitive Poetics and Transformational Soteriology in the* Gospel of Philip *and the* Exegesis on the Soul, NHMS 73 (Brill: Leiden, 2010).

Luttikhuizen, G. P., *Gnostic Revisions of Genesis Stories and Early Jesus Traditions*, NHMS 58 (Brill: Leiden, 2006).

'Monism and Dualism in Jewish-Mystical and Gnostic Ascent Texts', in A. Hilhorst *et al.* (eds.), *Flores Florentino. Dead Sea Scrolls and Other Early Jewish Studies in Honour of Florentino García Martínez*, Supplements to the Journal for the Study of Judaism 122 (Leiden: Brill, 2007), pp. 749–75.

'Sethianer?', *ZAC* 13 (2009), 76–86.

McKechnie, P., 'Flavia Sophe in Context', *ZPE* 135 (2001), 117–24.

Mahé, J.-P., 'L'Hymne hermétique: une propédeutique du silence', in Y. Lehman (ed.), *L'Hymne antique et son public* (Turnhout: Brepols, 2007), pp. 275–89.

Majercik, R., *The Chaldaean Oracles. Text, Translation, and Commentary*, Studies in Greek and Roman Religion 5 (Leiden: Brill, 1989).

Mansfeld, J., 'Bad World and Demiurge: A "Gnostic" Motif from Parmenides and Empedocles to Lucretius and Philo', in van den Broek and Vermaseren (eds.), *Studies in Gnosticism and Hellenistic Religions*, pp. 261–314.

'Compatible Alternatives: Middle Platonist Theology and the Xenophanes Reception', in van den Broek *et al.* (eds.), *Knowledge of God*, pp. 92–117.

Heresiography in Context: Hippolytus' Elenchos *as a Source for Greek Philosophy*, Philosophia Antiqua 56 (Leiden: Brill, 1992).

Marcovich, M., 'Monoimus' Letter to Theophrastus', in *Studies in Graeco-Roman Religions and Gnosticism*, pp. 134–43.

'The Naassene Psalm in Hippolytus (*Haer.* 5.10.2)', in *Studies in Graeco-Roman Religions and Gnosticism*, pp. 80–88.

Studies in Graeco-Roman Religions and Gnosticism, Studies in Greek and Roman Religions 4 (Leiden: Brill, 1988).

Marjanen, A., '"Gnosticism"', in S. Ashbrook Harvey and D. G. Hunter (eds.), *The Oxford Handbook of Early Christian Studies* (Oxford University Press, 2008), pp. 203–20.

'The Seven Women Disciples in the Two Versions of the First Apocalypse of James', in DeConick (ed.), *The Codex Judas Papers*, pp. 535–46.

Markschies, C., *Gnosis. An Introduction*, trans. J. Bowden (London and New York: T&T Clark, 2003; = *Die Gnosis* (Munich: C. H. Beck, 2001; 2nd edn 2006)).

Gnosis und Christentum (Berlin University Press, 2009).

'New Research on Ptolemaeus Gnosticus', *ZAC* 4 (2000), 225–54.

'Valentinian Gnosticism: Towards the Anatomy of a School', in Turner and McGuire (eds.), *The Nag Hammadi Library*, pp. 401–38.

Valentinus Gnosticus? Untersuchungen zur valentinianischen Gnosis mit einem Kommentar zu den Fragmenten Valentins, WUNT 65 (Tübingen: J. C. B. Mohr [Paul Siebeck], 1992).

Mastrocinque, A., *From Jewish Magic to Gnosticism*, STAC 24 (Tübingen: Mohr Siebeck, 2005).

Mastrocinque, A. (ed.), *Sylloge Gemmarum Gnosticarum*, vols. I and II (Rome: Istituto poligrafico e Zecca dello Stato, 2004, 2008).

Mercer, M. J., 'Askew, Anthony', in *Oxford Dictionary of National Biography*, vol. II (Oxford University Press, 2004), p. 712.

Mertens, M., *Les alchimistes grecs*, vol. IV, i, *Zosime de Panopolis, Mémoires authentiques* (Paris: Les Belles Lettres, 1995).

Meyer, M., *The Gnostic Discoveries. The Impact of the Hag Hammadi Library* (San Francisco: HarperSanFrancisco, 2005).

Meyer, M. and P. Mirecki (eds.), *Ancient Magic and Ritual Power*, RGRW 129 (Leiden: Brill, 1995).

Mirecki, P. and M. Meyer (eds.), *Magic and Ritual in the Ancient World*, RGRW 141 (Leiden: Brill, 2002).

More, H., *An Exposition of the Seven Epistles to the Seven Churches; Together with a Brief Discourse of Idolatry; with Application to the Church of Rome* (London: James Flesher, 1669).

Nickelsburg, G. W. E, 'Son of Man', in K. van der Toorn, B. Becking and P. W. van der Horst (eds.), *Dictionary of Deities and Demons in the Bible*, 2nd extensively rev. edn (Leiden: Brill, 1999), pp. 800–4.

Nilsson, M. P., *Geschichte der griechischen Religion*, vol. II, *Die hellenistische und römische Zeit*, Handbuch der Altertumswissenschaft, section V, 2.2, 4th edn (Munich: C. H. Beck'sche Verlagsbuchhandlung, 1988; = 3rd edn 1974).

Nock, A. D., *Early Gentile Christianity and its Hellenistic Background*, Harper Torchbook edn (New York, Evanston, IL and London: Harper & Row, 1964); also in *Essays on Religion*, vol. I, pp. 49–133 (without the important Introduction to the Torchbook edn).

Essays on Religion and the Ancient World, selected and ed., with an Introduction, Bibliography of Nock's writings and Indexes, Z. Stewart, 2 vols. (Oxford University Press, 1972).

'Gnosticism', in *Essays on Religion*, vol. II, pp. 940–59.

Norelli, E. 'Des évèques, des écoles et des hérétiques: un colloque international', in Aragione and Norelli (eds.), *Des évéques, des écoles et des hérétiques*, pp. 3–23.

Oort, J. van, 'Mani', in *Dictionary of Gnosis*, pp. 756–7.

'Manichaeism', in *Dictionary of Gnosis*, pp. 757–65.

Orlov, A. A., *The Enoch-Metatron Tradition*, Texts and Studies in Ancient Judaism 107 (Tübingen: Mohr Siebeck, 2005).

Os, L. K. van, 'Baptism in the Bridal Chamber: The Gospel of Philip as a Valentinian Baptismal Instruction' (digital dissertation, State University Groningen, 2007).

Osborn, E. F., *Irenaeus of Lyons* (Cambridge University Press, 2001).

Pagels, E. H., *The Gnostic Paul. Gnostic Exegesis of the Pauline Letters* (Philadelphia: Fortress Press, 1975).

Pagels, E. [H.] and K. L. King, *Reading Judas. The Gospel of Judas and the Shaping of Christianity* (New York: Viking Penguin, 2007).
Painchaud, L., 'La composition de l'Évangile selon Philippe (NH II, 3): une analyse rhétorique', in *Society of Biblical Literature Seminar Papers* (Atlanta: Scholars Press, 1996), pp. 35–66.
'Notice' (on the Gospel of Philip), in *Écrits gnostiques*, pp. 335–41.
Painchaud, L. and P.-H. Poirier (eds.), *Coptica – Gnostica – Manichaica. Mélanges offerts à Wolf-Peter Funk*, BCNH-É 7 (Quebec: Presses de l'Université Laval; Louvain: Éditions Peters, 2006).
Pasquier, A., *Eugnoste. Lettre sur le Dieu transcendant (NH III, 3 et V, 1). Commentaire*, BCNH-T 33 (Quebec: Presses de l'Université Laval; Louvain, Paris and Walpole, MA: Éditions Peeters, 2010).
Pearson, B. A., *Ancient Gnosticism. Traditions and Literature* (Minneapolis: Fortress Press, 2007).
'Basilides the Gnostic', in A. Marjanen and P. Luomanen (eds.), *A Companion to Second-Century 'Heretics'*, Supplements to Vigiliae Christianae 76 (Leiden: Brill, 2005), pp. 1–31.
'The Figure of Melchizedek in Gnostic Literature', in *Gnosticism, Judaism, and Egyptian Christianity*, pp. 108–23.
'The Figure of Norea in Gnostic Literature', in *Gnosticism, Judaism, and Egyptian Christianity*, pp. 84–94.
'Gnostic Ritual and Iamblichus's Treatise *On the Mysteries of Egypt*', in *Gnosticism and Christianity in Roman and Coptic Egypt*, pp. 224–48.
Gnosticism and Christianity in Roman and Coptic Egypt (New York and London: T&T Clark, 2004).
Gnosticism, Judaism, and Egyptian Christianity (Minneapolis: Fortress Press, 1990).
'Jewish Elements in Gnosticism and the Development of Gnostic Self-Definition', in *Gnosticism, Judaism, and Egyptian Christianity*, pp. 124–35.
Places, E. des (ed.), *Jamblique. Les Mystères d'Égypte* (Paris: Les Belles Lettres, 1966).
Numénius: Fragments (Paris: Les Belles Lettres, 1973).
Pleše, Z., *Poetics of the Gnostic Universe. Narrative and Cosmology in the* Apocryphon of John, NHMS 52 (Leiden: Brill, 2006).
Puech, H.-C., 'Audianer', *RAC* I (1950), cols. 910–15.
'Un logion de Jésus sur bandelette funéraire', in *En quête de la Gnose*, vol. II, *Sur l'Évangile selon Thomas. Esquisse d'une interprétation systématique* (Paris: Gallimard, 1978), pp. 59–62.
Quack, J. F., 'Dekane und Gliedervergöttung. Altägyptische Traditionen im Apokryphon des Johannes', *Jahrbuch für Antike und Christentum* 38 (1995), 97–124.
Quispel, G., 'Ezekiel 1, 26 in Jewish Mysticism and Gnosis' (1980), in *Gnostica, Judaica, Catholica*, pp. 461–74.

Gnostic Studies, 2 vols., Uitgaven van het Nederlands Historisch-Archeologisch Instituut 34(1/2) (Istanbul: Nederlands Historisch-Archeologisch Instituut, 1974/5).

Gnostica, Judaica, Catholica. Collected Essays of Gilles Quispel, ed. J. van Oort, NHMS 55 (Leiden: Brill, 2008).

'Gnosticism and the New Testament' (1965), in *Gnostic Studies*, vol. 1, pp. 196–212.

Rasimus, T., *Paradise Reconsidered in Gnostic Mythmaking: Rethinking Sethianism in Light of the Ophitc Evidence*, NHMS 68 (Leiden: Brill, 2009).

Richter, S. G., *Die Aufstiegpsalmen des Herakleides. Untersuchungen zum Seelenaufstieg und zur Seelenmesse bei den Manichäern*, Sprachen und Kulturen des christlichen Orients 1 (Wiesbaden: Harrassowitz, 1997).

Roberge, M., *The Paraphrase of Shem (NH VII, 1). Introduction, Translation and Commentary*, NHMS 72 (Leiden: Brill, 2010).

Robinson, J. M., 'From the Cliff to Cairo. The Story of the Discoverers and the Middlemen of the Nag Hammadi Codices', in Barc (ed.), *Colloque international*, pp. 21–58.

'Nag Hammadi: The First Fifty Years', in Turner and McGuire (eds.), *The Nag Hammadi Library after Fifty Years*, pp. 3–33.

Roukema, R., *Jesus, Gnosis and Dogma* (London and New York: T&T Clark, 2010).

Rudolph, K., 'Mandaeans', in *Dictionary of Gnosis*, pp. 751–6.

Theogonie, Kosmogonie und Anthropologie in den mandäischen Schriften Eine literarkritische und traditionsgeschichtliche Untersuchung, FRLANT 88 (Göttingen: Vandenhoeck & Ruprecht, 1965).

Sammelbuch griechischer Urkunden aus Ägypten, vol. XII (Wiesbaden: Harrassowitz, 1976–7).

Sasse, H., 'Aiōn', in G. Kittel *et al.* (eds.), *Theological Dictionary of the New Testament*, vol. 1, trans. G. W. Bromiley (Grand Rapids, MI: W. B. Eerdmans, 1964), pp. 197–209.

Schäfer, P., *Die Geburt des Judentums aus dem Geist des Christentums. Fünf Vorlesungen zur Entstehung des rabbinischen Judentums*, Tria Corda. Jenäer Vorlesungen zu Judentum, Antike und Christentum 6 (Tübingen: Mohr Siebeck, 2010).

Schenke, H.-M., *Der Gott 'Mensch' in der Gnosis: Ein religionsgeschichtlicher Beitrag zur Diskussion über die paulinische Anschauung von der Kirche als Leib Christi* (Göttingen: Vandenhoeck & Ruprecht, 1962).

'The Phenomenon and Significance of Gnostic Sethianism', in Layton (ed.), *The Rediscovery of Gnosticism*, vol. II, pp. 588–616.

Das Philippus-Evangelium (Nag Hammadi Codex II, 3). Neu herausgegeben, übersetzt und erklärt, TU 143 (Berlin: Akademie-Verlag, 1997).

Schmidt, H., *Die Eucharistie ist Jesus: Anfänge einer Theorie der Sakramente im koptischen Philippusevangelium (NHC II, 3)*, Supplements to Vigiliae Christianae 88 (Leiden: Brill, 2007).

'Ist der Soter in Ptolemäus' Epistula ad Floram der Demiurg? Zu einer These von Christoph Markschies', *ZAC* 15 (2011), 249–71.

Schneemelcher, W., 'Epiphanius von Salamis', *RAC* v (1962), pp. 909–27.

Scholer, D. M., *Nag Hammadi Bibliography, 1948–1969*, NHS 1 (Leiden: Brill, 1971).

Nag Hammadi Bibliography, 1970–1994, NHMS 32 (Leiden: Brill, 1997).

Nag Hammadi Bibliography, 1995–2006, NHMS 65 (Leiden: Brill, 2009).

Scholten, C., 'Autor, Anliegen und Publikum der Refutatio', in Aragione and Norelli (eds.), *Des évêques, des écoles et des hérétiques*, pp. 135–66.

'Hippolytos II (von Rom)', *RAC* xv (1991), cols. 492–551.

'Quellen regen an: Beobachtungen zum "gnostischen Sondergut" in der *Refutatio omnium haeresium*', in J. A. van den Berg, A. Kotzé, T. Nicklas and M. Scopello (eds.), *'In Search of Truth': Augustine, Manichaeism and other Gnosticism. Studies for Johannes van Oort at Sixty*, NHMS 74 (Leiden: Brill, 2011), pp. 567–91.

Scopello, M. (ed.), *The Gospel of Judas in Context. Proceedings of the First International Conference on the Gospel of Judas, Paris, Sorbonne, October 27th–28th, 2006*, NHMS 62 (Leiden: Brill, 2008).

Segal, A. F., *Two Powers in Heaven. Early Rabbinic Reports about Christianity and Gnosticism*, Studies in Judaism in Late Antiquity 25 (Leiden: Brill, 1977).

Sevrin, J.-M., *Le dossier baptismal séthien. Études sur le sacramentaire gnostique*, BCNH-É 2 (Quebec: Presses de l'Université Laval, 1986).

Silverstein, T. and A. Hilhorst, *Apocalypse of Paul. A New Critical Edition of Three Long Latin Versions*, Cahiers d'Orientalisme 21 (Geneva: P. Cramer, 1997).

Simonetti, M., 'Per un profilo dell'autore dell'Elenchos', in Aragione and Norelli (eds.), *Des évêques, des écoles et des hérétiques*, pp. 257–73.

Snell, B., *Tragicorum graecorum fragmenta*, vol. 1 (Göttingen: Vandenhoeck & Ruprecht, 1971).

Snyder, H. G., 'A Second-Century Christian Inscription from the Via Latina', *JECS* 19 (2011), 157–95.

Stroumsa, G. A. G., *Another Seed: Studies in Gnostic Mythology*, NHS 24 (Leiden: Brill, 1984).

Tardieu, M., 'Aberamenthō', in van den Broek and Vermaseren (eds.), *Studies in Gnosticism and Hellenistic Religions*, pp. 412–18.

'"Comme à travers un tuyau". Quelques remarques sur le mythe valentinien de la chair céleste du Christ', in Barc (ed.), *Colloque international*, pp. 151–77.

Écrits gnostiques. Codex de Berlin (Paris: Éditions du Cerf, 1984).

'Les gnostiques dans la *Vie de Plotin*. Analyse du chapitre 16', in Brisson *et al.*, *Porphyre*, vol. II, pp. 503–46.

Manichaeism, trans. M. B. DeBevoise, introduction by P. Mirecki (Champaign, IL: University of Illinois Press, 2009).

Recherches sur la formation de l'Apocalypse de Zostrien et les sources de Marius Victorinus, Res Orientales 9 (Bures-sur-Yvette: Groupe pour l'études de la civilisation de Moyen-Orient, 1996), pp. 7–114.

Tardieu, M. and J.-D. Dubois, *Introduction à la littérature gnostique*, vol. I, *Histoire du mot 'gnostique'; Instruments de travail; Collections retrouvées avant 1945* (Paris: Éditions du CERF/Éditions du CNRS, 1986).

Thomassen, E., *The Spiritual Seed: The Church of the 'Valentinians'*, NHMS 60 (Leiden: Brill, 2006).

Tite, P. L., *Valentinian Ethics and Paraenetic Discourse: Determining the Social Function of Moral Exhortation in Valentinian Christianity*, NHMS 67 (Leiden: Brill, 2009).

Turner, J. D., 'Introduction', in C. Barry, W.-P. Funk, P.-H. Poirier and J. D. Turner (eds.), *Zostrien (NH VIII, 1)*, BCNH-T 24 (Quebec: Presses de l'Université Laval; Louvain and Paris: Éditions Peeters, 2000), pp. 32–225 (in English).

'Introduction', in W.-P. Funk, P.-H. Hubert and J.D. Turner (eds.), *Marsanès (NH X)*, BCNH-T 27 (Quebec: Presses de l'Université Laval; Louvain and Paris: Éditions Peeters, 2000), pp. 1–248 (in English).

'Introduction', in W.-P. Funk, P.-H. Poirier, M. Scopello and J. D. Turner (eds.), *L'Allogène (NH XI, 3)*, BCNH-T 30 (Quebec: Presses de l'Université Laval; Louvain and Paris: Éditions Peeters, 2004), pp. 1–188 (in English).

'The Place of the Gospel of Judas in Sethian Tradition', in Scopello (ed.), *The Gospel of Judas in Context*, pp. 187–237.

'Sethian Gnosticism: A Literary History', in C. W. Hedrick and R. Hodgson, Jr (eds.), *Nag Hammadi, Gnosticism, and Early Christianity* (Peabody, MA: Hendrickson, 1986), pp. 55–86.

'Sethian Gnosticism: A Revised Literary History', in N. Bousson and A. Boud'hors (eds.), *Actes du huitième congrès international d'études coptes. Paris, 28 juin–3 juillet 2004*, vol. II, Orientalia Lovaniensia Analecta 163 (Louvain: Éditions Peeters, 2007), pp. 899–908.

Sethian Gnosticism and the Platonic Tradition, BCNH-É 6 (Quebec: Presses de l'Université Laval; Louvain and Paris: Éditions Peeters, 2001).

Turner, J. D. and A. McGuire (eds.), *The Nag Hammadi Library after Fifty Years. Proceedings of the 1995 Society of Biblical Literature Commemoration*, NHMS 44 (Leiden: Brill, 1997).

Turner, M. L., *The Gospel According to Philip. The Sources and Coherence of an Early Christian Collection*, NHMS 38 (Leiden: Brill, 1996).

Veilleux A. (ed.), *La Première Apocalypse de Jacques (NH V, 3). La Seconde Apocalypse de Jacques (NH V, 4)*, BCNH-T, 17 (Quebec: Presses de l'Université Laval, 1986).

Vermes, M. and S. N. C. Lieu (eds.), *Acta Archelai (The Acts of Archelaus)*, trans. M. Vermes, with Introduction and Commentary by S. N. C. Lieu, Manichaean Studies 4 (Turnhout: Brepols, 2001).

Vliet, J. van der, 'Spirit and Prophecy in the Epistula Iacobi Apocrypha (NHC I, 2)', *VC* 44 (1990), 25–53.

Voorgang, D., *Die Passion Jesu und Christi in der Gnosis*, Europäische Hochschulschriften, Reihe XXIII: Theologie 432 (Frankfurt am Main: Peter Lang, 1991).

Waldstein, M., 'The Primal Triad in the *Apocryphon of John*', in Turner and McGuire (eds.), *The Nag Hammadi Library*, pp. 154–87.

'The *Providence Monologue* in the Apocryphon of John and the *Johannine Prologue*', *JECS* 3 (1995), 369–402.

The Way of Hermes: The Corpus Hermeticum, trans. C. Salaman, D. van Oyen and W. D. Wharton; The Definitions of Hermes Trismegistus to Asclepius, trans. J.-P. Mahé (London: Duckworth, 1999).

Wehrli, F. (ed.), *Die Schule des Aristoteles. Texte und Kommentare: Eudemos von Rhodos* (Basle: B. Schwabe & Co., 1955).

Whittaker, J., 'Epekeina nou kai ousias', in *Studies in Platonism and Patristic Thought*, Collected Studies Series 201 (London: Variorum Reprints, 1984), no. XIII.

Whittaker, J. (ed.), *Alcinoos. Enseignement des doctrines de Platon* (Paris: Les Belles Lettres, 1990).

Williams, F. E., *Mental Perception. A Commentary on NHC VI, 4: The Concept of our Great Power*, NHMS 51 (Leiden: Brill, 2001).

Williams, M. A., *Rethinking "Gnosticism". An Argument for Dismantling a Dubious Category* (Princeton University Press, 1996).

Wisse, F., 'Stalking Those Elusive Sethians', in Layton (ed.), *The Rediscovery of Gnosticism*, vol. II, pp. 563–78.

Wurst, G., 'Preliminary Codicological Analysis of Codex Tchacos', in *The Gospel of Judas ... Critical Edition*, pp. 27–33.

Youtie, L. C., D. Hagedorn and H. C. Youtie, 'Urkunden aus Panopolis I', *ZPE* 7 (1971), 1–40.

Zöckler, T., *Jesu Lehren im Thomasevangelium*, NHMS 47 (Leiden: Brill, 1999).

Index of ancient sources

Index of names and subjects

Lightning Source UK Ltd.
Milton Keynes UK
UKOW06f1807220216

268893UK00007B/264/P

9 781107 514799